Islamic Wealth Taxation and Financing Public Health

An Interdisciplinary Analysis of Human Rights, Islamic Law, and the Constitution of Kenya

By

Lyla A. Latif

Islamic Wealth Taxation and Financing Public Health: An Interdisciplinary Analysis of Human Rights, Islamic Law, and the Constitution of Kenya

By Lyla A. Latif

This book first published 2023

Ethics International Press Ltd, UK

British Library Cataloguing in Publication Data

A catalogue record for this book is available from the British Library

Print Book ISBN: 978-1-80441-330-2

eBook ISBN: 978-1-80441-331-9

Table of Contents

Abbreviations

AU	Africa Union
CESCR	Committee on Economic, Social and Cultural Rights
CHSSP	County Health Sector Strategic and Investment Plan
CMS	Central Medical Store
CMS/MIS	Central Medical Store Management Information System
DFRDP	District Focus Rural Development Plan
ECOSOC	Economic and Social Council
FBO	Faith Based Organisation
GC	General Comment
GDP	Gross Domestic Product
ICCPR	International Covenant on Civil and Political Rights
ICESCR	International Covenant on Economic, Social and Cultural Rights
IPK	Islamic Party of Kenya
KANU	Kenya African National Union
KEMSA	Kenya Medical Supplies Agency
KHP	Kenya Health Policy
KNH	Kenyatta National Hospital
KHSSP	Kenya Health Sector Strategic and Investment Plan

LNC	Local Natives Council
MAR	Maximum Available Resources
MSCU	Medical Supplies Coordinating Unit
MOH	Ministry of Health
MP	Member of Parliament
MUF	Mwambao United Front
NACOSTI	National Commission for Science, Technology and Innovation
NFD	Northern Frontier District
NHIF	National Hospital Insurance Fund
NHSSP	National Health Sector Strategic Plans
NSSF	National Social Security Fund
OAU	Organisation of African Unity
OPP	Out of Pocket Payment
PBO	Parliamentary Budget Office
PR	Progressive Realisation
SDGs	Sustainable Development Goals
UHC	Universal Health Coverage
UN	United Nations
WHO	World Health Organisation

Arabic Definitions

Alim	A Muslim male who is knowledgeable in Islamic matters
Bait al Maal	Treasury
Daruriyat	Necessities
Dua	Supplication
Fiqh	Islamic jurisprudence
Fuqaha	Islamic jurists
Hajiyat	Needs
Halal	Permissible
Halaqa	Islamic method of debating doctrinal issues to arrive at a consensus. Also: a religious study circle
Haram	Prohibited
Ijma	Consensus
Ijtihad	Independent reasoning
Imam	Muslim male who leads congregational prayer
Isnaad	Chain of narration
Kadhi	Muslim male judge
Madhab	School of thought
Makrooh	Disliked or offensive
Maqasid	Objectives
Usul al Fiqh	Principles of Islamic jurisprudence
Qiyas	Deductive analogy
Qur'an	Muslim scripture

Ramadhan	Ninth month of the Islamic calendar observed as the month of fasting
Ra'y	Personal judgement
Sadaqa	Charity
Sahaba	Companion of the Prophet Muhammed (صلى الله عليه وسلم)
Sheikh	An elderly scholar
Shura	Consultation
Surah	A chapter in the Muslim scripture
Sunnah	Habitual practice of the Prophet Muhammed (صلى الله عليه وسلم)
Sunni	Follower of the sunnah
Tahsiniyat	Luxuries
Taqlid	Precedent
Ulama	Muslim scholars
Ummah	Muslim community
Ustadha	Female Muslim who teaches Islamic education
Usul	Principles
Zakat	Islamic tax on wealth

Swahili Definitions

Duka	Convenience store, or kiosk
Harambee	Self help
Mheshimiwa	Member of Parliament
Mwambao	The coast or coastline
Pwani Si Kenya	'The Coast is not part of Kenya'

Table of Figures

Preface

This book presents an interdisciplinary analysis of the legal relationship between *zakat,* commonly described as obligatory almsgiving, and financing public health in Kenya. It offers significant contributions to the fields of human rights law, Islamic law, and constitutional law. These three fields representing distinct legal frameworks with different conceptual foundations converge in the debate surrounding *zakat's* potential contribution to financing public health. Through the doctrinal and theoretical examination of this convergence, the book offers important insights into socio-legal scholarship. It highlights three theoretical takeaways concerning the legal permissibility of recognising and including *zakat* as part of the maximum available resources' obligation under human rights law which requires states to use all available resources to provide essential health services, the Islamic doctrinal perspectives around the use of *zakat* for financing health, and the constitutional concerns around the Kenyan state accepting to use *zakat* with its Islamic conditions to finance public health.

Firstly, it highlights the complexity and fluidity of legal systems, especially in situations where different legal frameworks interact, which necessitates an interdisciplinary approach. Secondly, it demonstrates that legal frameworks can influence each other, and their convergence may provide innovative solutions to complex legal problems. The application of the Islamic law on *zakat* to finance public health in Kenya provides new interpretations and understandings of human rights law's obligations to ensure maximum available resources for health. Thirdly, it shows the consideration of politics in the conceptualisation and use of law as having significant implications for the fields of human rights law, Islamic law, and constitutional law.

The doctrinal and theoretical examinations presented in the book are challenged by the phenomenological accounts collected during fieldwork, shedding light on the ways that politics becomes embedded in how people conceptualise and use the law. This highlights the importance of understanding as part of socio legal scholarship how power dynamics, cultural and religious beliefs, and political structures influence the application and interpretation of legal principles, emphasising the need for scholars to incorporate a nuanced understanding of political realities when examining constitutional and religious legal frameworks.

Dr. Lyla A. Latif, 2023

Acknowledgements

All praise and gratitude are due to Allah for the blessing of knowledge. I am deeply thankful for the encouragement and support I have received from numerous individuals and institutions throughout the process of writing this book, which examines the potential of *zakat* to finance health programs in Kenya.

I would like to express my profound appreciation to Professors John Harrington, Mark Fathi Massoud and Russell Sandberg for their invaluable guidance in navigating the complexities of this interdisciplinary work. I am also grateful for the insightful feedback provided on some of the chapters by Professors Ambreena Manji and Abdullahi An'Naim, as well as Dr Stephen Smith, Dr Sara Dezalay, Dr Paul McDonough, Dr Gitte Heij, and Dr Gedion Onyango.

I extend my heartfelt gratitude to the participants of my research interviews and to all those who facilitated these interviews and assisted me during my fieldwork. Their invaluable contributions and insights have been central to the success of my research, for which I am deeply grateful to them.

My warmest thanks go to my loving mum and dad for believing in me and being my unwavering pillars of support, providing me with endless *dua* and encouragement to see this work through to completion. I would also like to extend my appreciation to my family and close friends who continuously rooted for me throughout this journey. I want to thank Attiya Waris, a visionary, and a wonderful friend for introducing me to the research world.

This work is dedicated to my parents, and all my teachers.

Chapter 1
Introduction

This book focuses on the legal relationship between *zakat* and financing public health in Kenya. Specifically, it examines whether *zakat* can legally be recognised as a source of revenue for financing public health and if human rights and Islamic law permit such a possibility. The book aims to provide an understanding of whether these legal frameworks can offer solutions to the problem of revenue limitations in financing public healthcare, with the focus on the challenges faced by the Kenyan state in accepting *zakat* as part of the health budget. The choice of *zakat* as a financing form is significant, considering that there are other financing forms such as taxation, donor aid, and health insurance. However, these are not always reliable sources of revenue.[1] Many African states face challenges in generating sufficient tax revenues due to informal economies, corruption, and tax evasion.[2] Similarly, donor aid is often subject to changing priorities and can be unreliable. Health insurance, on the other hand, can be expensive and difficult to access for many individuals, particularly in low-income settings.

The book, therefore, focuses on *zakat* because it is a continuous mandatory obligation for Muslims to annually pay 2.5 per cent taken off the total net value of their gold, silver and cash savings that have reached a specific threshold set by the Muslim clerics.[3] *Zakat* is to be given to specific beneficiaries, especially the poor. It is a longstanding and established

---

[1] J Vageesh, 'Harnessing the Power of Health Taxes' (2020) *BMJ* 369.

[2] C Lumina and N Tamale, 'Sovereign Debt and Human Rights: A Focus on Sub-Saharan Africa' (2021) *African Sovereign Debt Justice Paper Series.*

[3] Y Al Qaradawi, *Fiqh Al Zakah, Vol II: A Comparative Study of Zakah, Regulations and Philosophy in the Light of Qur'an and Sunna,* trans. Monzer Kahf (Scientific Publishing Centre, Jeddah, 2001).

religious obligation that many Muslims feel a moral duty to fulfil.[4] It is therefore, a reliable and potentially sustainable source of revenue that can be collected locally and used to support public health initiatives. Additionally, *zakat* is specifically intended to support those in need, including the poor and vulnerable, making it a particularly appropriate source of funding for health care expenses.

The book recognises that in proposing *zakat,* it brings to the fore questions around why a minority group in Kenya should be giving some of its funds to the Kenyan state to access the services it needs and for which they are already paying state-imposed taxes. The contribution of the book lies in exploring the boundaries of this claim. The book does not propose the imposition of taxes on any religious group. The proposal to use *zakat* as the potential source of revenue for financing public health in Kenya is not necessarily an argument for burdens of healthcare expenses to be borne at the local level. Rather, it is an exploration of how religious communities can contribute to public health financing, specifically through the voluntary payment of *zakat,* which is an obligation in Islam. In this way, the proposal is not imposing a new burden on these communities, but rather leveraging an existing religious obligation to support the poor and those in need.

The proposal on the use of *zakat* to finance public health is not intended to absolve the state of its responsibility to fund public health programmes. Instead, it is seen as a supplement to existing state efforts. The book examines the extent to which the legal frameworks of human rights, Islamic law, and Kenyan constitutional law permit the use of *zakat* for financing public health. It does not make any policy prescriptions or recommendations but rather seeks to contribute to scholarship on the interaction between legal frameworks and social and political realities.

The research design that supports the book to conduct its investigation combines the use of doctrine, legal theory, and the methods of inquiry

---

[4] M Kahf, '*Zakat*: Unresolved Issues in the Contemporary Fiqh', (1989) *Journal of Islamic Economics*, Vol 2, No 1, 1-22; R Powell, *Zakat*: Drawing Insights for Legal Theory and Economic Policy from Islamic Jurisprudence', (2010) 7 *PITT. Tax Review*. 43.

available under socio-legal research with Islamic doctrine and methodology. This is necessary to guarantee the validity and reliability of conducting doctrinal analysis and norm considerations, based on the recognised and robust methodologies used under human rights and Islamic law to derive legal rulings.

The book postulates that the convergence of human rights law, Islamic law, and constitutional law in the context of using *zakat* to finance public health in Kenya provides new interpretations and understandings of legal obligations to ensure maximum available resources for health. In formulating this proposition, I was aware that legal frameworks cannot be examined in isolation from the social, cultural, and political realities that shape their implementation and interpretation. Therefore, part of this proposition was investigated through fieldwork. The fieldwork findings challenged the premise by revealing the complex relationship between law and politics and the disassociation of normative claims from the lived reality of individuals. The framing of the proposition and the findings from fieldwork discussed in Chapter 7 demonstrate that socio legal scholarship must be complemented by an understanding of the political and social dynamics that influence the application and interpretation of legal principles. The importance of phenomenological accounts as part of socio legal scholarship allows for a more comprehensive understanding of the realities of legal frameworks in practice and how they are influenced by broader social and political dynamics.

The aforementioned premise provides an understanding that while doctrinal analysis and legal theory provide a solid framework for understanding the permissibility of using *zakat* to finance public health, the reality on the ground may not always match up to these ideals. This premise alongside the findings discussed in Chapter 7 shed light on how the practise of human rights and Islamic law is embedded in the social and political realities of Kenya.

There are five objectives of this book. Firstly, to examine whether the *maximum available resources* obligation under human rights law can be construed to place an obligation on states to achieve the right to health using *zakat*. Secondly, to consider how the Kenyan Government interprets its *maximum available resources* obligation under human rights law to finance health. Thirdly, to identify the existence of any criteria under Islamic law that provide legal permissibility for the use of *zakat* by a non-Islamic state. Fourthly, to understand whether the Constitution of Kenya and its legal system can recognise and lawfully implement the Islamic law conditions on *zakat*. And finally, to give voice to duty bearers and rights holders to speak about their views on the use of *zakat* to finance health.

A study based on an examination of *zakat* to finance health in Kenya – a non-Islamic Muslim-minority state – offers an exciting opportunity to explore these five objectives, particularly because of the country's historical connection with Islam. To date, studies on *zakat* have largely focused on Muslim-majority states;[5] none have considered *zakat* from the perspective of a non-Islamic Muslim-minority state with a constitution that potentially could recognise Islamic norms on *zakat*.

Currently, governments are facing austerity measures, rising debt, low taxable population, rising cost of living, amidst their obligation to implement measures needed for the enjoyment of human rights and achievement of Sustainable Development Goals (SDGs). The United Nations SDGs Agenda, the Africa Union Agenda 2063, various National Development Plans (NDP) of countries require governments to strengthen their domestic revenue mobilisation strategies and identify new revenue streams. This is crucial given that Official Development Aid is reclining. The proposal that this book makes is to offer a fiscal solution. Its relevance lies in its answer to the imperative under UN SDGs, AU Agenda 2063 and NDPs for states to source additional local funds. The book proposes a revenue stream which does not impose any additional burden on taxpayers. Further, it puts to rest the academic squabbles that deny

---

[5] S Al Sayyid, *Fiqh Al Sunnah: Az Zakah and As Siyam*, trans. Muhammad Saeed Dabas and Jamal al Din Zarabozo (Islamic Printing & Publishing Co, Egypt, 2000); Y Al Qaradawi, *Fiqh Al Zakah, Vol II: A Comparative Study of Zakah, Regulations and Philosophy in the Light of Qur'an and Sunna*, trans. Monzer Kahf (Scientific Publishing Centre, Jeddah, 2001); M Kahf, '*Zakat*: Unresolved Issues in the Contemporary Fiqh', (1989) *Journal of Islamic Economics*, Vol 2, No 1, 1-22; R Powell, *Zakat*: Drawing Insights for Legal Theory and Economic Policy from Islamic Jurisprudence', (2010) 7 *PITT. Tax Review*. 43.

compatibility of Islamic law with human rights by demonstrating the intersecting points at which Islamic law and human rights doctrine intertwine. The book provides raw data on Kenyan stakeholder perceptions on the proposal to offer *zakat* to finance public health revealing the intricate and complex law, political, cultural, and societal considerations at play.

Following from this, the next sections explain the background and scope of the study, highlights the research problems that are tackled, and sets out the structure of the book, pointing towards its research questions and methodology.

Background: Health Budget Constraints and *Zakat*

Health budget

The Kenyan health sector, as in many other countries, is dependent on the percentage of the national budget allocated to meet its development and recurrent expenses. As a result of this dependency, the health sector faces considerable challenges in meeting its expenses. It is unable to ensure equitable access to public health facilities throughout the country, especially within rural and remote areas.[6] It is incapable of posting an adequate number of healthcare workers in those areas. Further, essential medicines are unavailable, infrastructure and equipment are outdated and inadequately available throughout the country, and access to public health facilities is restricted because of distance, lack of tarmac roads, and readily available transport in rural and remote areas in the various counties.[7]

The Kenyan Government has not developed a comprehensive fiscal plan that identifies sources of revenue and matches those sources to meet the

[6] Republic of Kenya, Kenya Health Sector Strategic Plan 2018-2023: Mid Term Review Synthesis Report (2021) 55.

[7] L Latif, F Simiyu, and A Waris, 'A Case Study on the Application of Human Rights Principles in Health Policy Making and Programming in Cherangany Sub County in Kenya', (2017) *Integrative Journal of Global Health* 1, No 1.

health needs of its citizens. Instead, several health policies have been prepared by the Ministry of Health that specify the different health programmes which sum up the entire health needs of the local population. These health programmes were set out in the Kenya Health Policy Framework 1994-2010,[8] and revised later through the Kenya Health Policy 2014-2030.[9] They relate to improving maternal health, reducing infant and child mortality, and combating HIV/AIDS, tuberculosis, and other communicable and non-communicable diseases. These health programmes were implemented through the National Health Sector Strategic Plans I and II and were later improved under the Kenya Health Sector Strategic and Investment Plans of 2014-2018 and 2018-2023.[10] These policies and strategic plans were prepared without reference to a financial strategy to implement them. This means that achieving the targets under the health programmes may have been impeded by the lack of adequate funds, since the health sector is incapable of generating its own sources of revenue.

In fact, the health sector budget allocation has been consistently reducing over the years. For example, the health sector budget for the 2016/2017 fiscal year was set at 3.8 per cent – well below the recommended 15 per cent of the national budget the Kenyan Government agreed to allocate to the health sector under the Abuja Declaration 2001, which was signed by all Member States of the Africa Union to improve health finance.[11] In 2019, the health budget was increased to 5.5 per cent, and following the COVID-19 health crisis in 2020-2021, the Government increased this to 6.5 per cent. Yet, the Kenyan health budget remains below the recommended target of 15 per cent agreed under the Abuja Declaration. The suboptimal allocation

---

[8] Government of Kenya, Ministry of Health, 'Kenya's Health Policy Framework' (Nairobi: Government Printer, 1994).

[9] Government of Kenya, Ministry of Health, 'Kenya Health Policy 2014-2030: Towards Attaining the Highest Standards of Health' (Nairobi: Government Printer, 2014).

[10] Government of Kenya, Ministry of Health, 'Kenya Health Sector Strategic Plan 2014-2018' (Nairobi: Government Printer, 2014) and Government of Kenya, Ministry of Health, 'Kenya Health Sector Strategic Plan 2018-2023' (Nairobi: Government Printer, 2018).

[11] Organisation of African Unity. 'Abuja Declaration On HIV/Aids, Tuberculosis and Other Related Infectious Diseases, Abuja, Nigeria, 26-27 April 2001 OAU/SPS/ABUJA/3. Declaration.PDF (safaids.net)

of health expenditure in Kenya, with spending constituting less than 15% of GDP results in the multitude of challenges described in the paragraphs above, adversely affecting the population, including Muslim Kenyans. In this context, *zakat* emerges as a vital instrument to mitigate these challenges.

The health budget reports between 2010 and 2020 show that in addition to relying on the national budget for funds, the health sector is dependent on out-of-pocket payments (OPPs), donor aid, and international assistance to finance most of its health programmes related to maternal and child health, combating HIV/AIDS, tuberculosis, malaria, and sexually transmitted diseases, as well as providing essential medicines.[12] The sector also faced the additional financial burden of treating COVID-19 and its related long term health complications.[13] The absence of a fiscal plan through which a health financing strategy ought to have been prepared for the health sector has thus restricted the realisation of the right to health in Kenya. Its absence has also limited the health sector in identifying and promoting the use of innovative or alternative health financing sources to reduce OPPs and increase the total health spending per capita by the Government.

This is not to say that the Government has not considered innovative and alternative health financing schemes to make healthcare accessible for the poor. An example of an innovative health financing scheme is the Output-Based Aid voucher programme, funded by the German Development

---

[12] Republic of Kenya, 'Kenya Health System Assessment 2010' (Nairobi: Government Printers, 2010); Republic of Kenya, 'Kenya Health Sector Strategic Plan 2018-2023: Mid Term Review Synthesis Report' (Nairobi: Government Printers, 2021); Republic of Kenya, Ministry of Health, 'Kenya National Health Accounts 2015/2016' (Nairobi, Government Printers, 2019). Also see: E Kabia, R Mbau, R Oyando et al, 'We are called the et cetera: experiences of the poor with health financing reforms that target them in Kenya', (2019) *International Journal for Equity in Health* 18, No: 98; S Illinca, L Di Giorgio, P Salari et al., 'Socio-economic inequality and inequity in use of health care services in Kenya: evidence from the fourth Kenya household health expenditure and utilisation survey', (2019) *International Journal for Equity in Health* 18, No: 196.

[13] P N Ouma, A N Masai and I N Nyadera, 'Health coverage and what Kenya can learn from the COVID-19 pandemic' (2020) *J Glob Health* 10(2):020362.

Bank.[14] This voucher allows rural women living in poverty to access maternal health care and family planning in participating health facilities. However, the voucher must be purchased at a nominal fee.

Further, this type of health financing requires donor support and minimal OPP by users of the voucher. Placing reliance on donor aid is not consistent with article 2(1) of the International Covenant on Economic, Social and Cultural Rights (ICESCR)[15] to which Kenya is a party, and which requires states to utilise to the maximum their domestically available resources to achieve the rights recognised under the Covenant. Neither is it consistent with article 43 (1) (a) of the Constitution of Kenya that places the obligation on the Government to guarantee the highest enjoyment of the right to health. The ICESCR and the Constitution of Kenya are the basis for the book to inquire into the normative and doctrinal permissibility on the use of *zakat* for financing health. This inquiry further extends into questioning whether Islamic law permits *zakat* to be given to the Kenyan state to finance health and considers through fieldwork the acceptability of this proposition.

The obligation is first upon the domestic state to generate resources to progressively realise health rights, and then consider and place reliance on international assistance, to provide support where the government is incapable. *Zakat* is available in Kenya. It could be offered to finance public health. Chapters 4, 5 and 7 expound on this. However, in making *zakat* available to the Kenyan state as a domestic source of revenue, it will be subject to greater control, accountability, and legitimacy than donor aid. *Zakat* is a more sustainable source of revenue for Kenya than donor aid. Thus, while it may be possible and even legally permissible under Islamic

---

[14] S Lee and A Adam, 'Designing a Logic Model for Mobile Maternal Health e-Voucher Programmes in Low- and Middle-Income Countries: An Interpretive Review', (2022) *Int. J. Environ Res. Public Health,* 19:295; OECD, *OECD Development Co-operation Peer Reviews: Germany* (OECD Publishing, 2015); N Bellows, 'Vouchers for reproductive health care services in Kenya and Uganda', (2012) KFW Discussion Paper.

[15] United Nations, Committee on Economic and Social Council. 'International Covenant on Economic, Social and Cultural Rights.' United Nations, Treaty Series, 16/12/1966.

law and human rights law for *zakat* to be used in this way, it does not necessarily mean that it 'should' be mandatory or a preferred policy option.

To determine whether *zakat* should become an obligation for the financing of public health, a range of factors need to be considered, including the impact on the Muslim community, the effectiveness of *zakat* in generating revenue, and the potential implications for the broader health financing system. Additionally, the political and social dynamics that shape the implementation of *zakat* and its acceptance by the state and society will need to be considered. The 'should' question also raises broader normative issues, such as the principles of distributive justice and the role of the state in providing for the welfare of its citizens. These issues go beyond the legal frameworks of human rights, Islamic law, and constitutional law and require a multidisciplinary approach to arrive at a well informed and balanced policy decision.

The focus and contribution of this book are to examine the legal relationship between *zakat* and financing public health in Kenya from an interdisciplinary perspective. The book underscores the complexity and fluidity of legal systems, particularly in situations where different legal frameworks interact, necessitating an interdisciplinary approach. The application of Islamic law on *zakat* to finance public health in Kenya yields new interpretations and understandings of human rights laws obligations to ensure maximum available resources for health. This demonstrates that legal frameworks can influence each other, and their convergence may provide innovative solutions to complex legal problems. However, the book does not directly tackle the issue of 'could' verses 'should'. While it acknowledges that just because something is possible or permitted does not necessarily mean it should occur, the book does not provide a definitive answer to this question. Instead, it offers insights into how legal frameworks can converge and influence each other, and how this may provide innovative solutions to complex legal problems.

Zakat

Zakat is an Arabic word which means *'to purify'*– a symbolic metaphor intended to make virtuous the act of including the poor and needy members of society as part of the beneficiaries of one's wealth, without which they would be unable to afford and pay for their basic needs. *Zakat* is a fundamental pillar of the Muslim faith. It has been described by Al Qaradawi: the late contemporary Muslim authority on *zakat,* as *'financial worship'*.[16] A Nairobi-based Islamic law scholar, whom I interviewed in my fieldwork for the book, describes *zakat* as:

> A right due to the poor from the rich; by right, I mean a specific percentage of a rich person's wealth. This wealth can take many forms; money, produce from land, abundance in domestic animals which the rich must set aside for the benefit of the poor.[17]

The interviewee considered, *zakat* as a 'conscientious financial obligation towards the poor and others mentioned in the *Qur'an* arising from the decree of Allah (God).'[18] Another Islamic law expert, whom I interviewed, defines *zakat* 'as a system for the management of paupers so that they are not left out of the structures society has put in place for their wellbeing and development.'[19] A Muslim woman preacher in Nairobi, whom I also interviewed, explains that:

> Zakat is the right specific people have on our wealth. It is the moral and legal duty to set aside what Allah has ordered out of our wealth for the poor, needy, debtors, travellers and so on. Zakat purifies the giver's wealth. Zakat contributes to our society and improves it by reducing poverty. It ensures the giver plays a role in society instead

---

[16] Al Qaradawi, (n 3).
[17] Interviewee No 144. Interview date 20.02.2020 Nairobi
[18] Interviewee No 144. Interview date 20.02.2020 Nairobi
[19] Interviewee No 139. Interview date 15.02.2020 Nairobi

of being a miser and confining his wealth to himself which serves no purpose.[20]

Zakat, therefore, is the Islamic equivalent of tax on wealth. It is paid once annually by adult Muslims to specific beneficiaries. There are eight categories of beneficiaries listed in the *Qur'an*.[21] The poor and needy are considered as priority beneficiaries. Literature on *zakat* has referred to it as charity, alms, obligatory charity, and as wealth tax.[22] This book accepts the reference to *zakat* as a tax on wealth. This is because *zakat* is an obligatory payment of 2.5 per cent on the value of specified forms of wealth, made by eligible Muslims annually, to prescribed beneficiaries.[23] Seeing it as a tax on wealth allows for a discussion on whether the Kenyan state can access it.

In this regard, the issue of whether *zakat* can be considered a form of tax when collected by the state is then a valid concern. From an Islamic legal perspective, *zakat* is not considered a tax, but rather an act of worship and a religious obligation for Muslims to give a portion of their wealth to support the poor and needy in society. Conversely, conventional taxes are obligatory payments to the government, levied to fund public goods and services, without a direct religious or spiritual aspect.[24] However, when the state collects *zakat* on behalf of the Muslim community, it can be argued that it takes on a role similar to that of a tax collector. In the context of financing public health, the collection of *zakat* by the state could be seen as

---

[20] Interviewee No 133. Interview date 15.02.2020 Nairobi

[21] The following eight recipients are listed in Surah Al Tawbah, Chapter 9, verse 60; (1) the poor, (2) the needy, (3) those employed to collect *zakat*, (4) those whose hearts are to be inclined towards Islam/bringing them towards Islam, (5) freeing captives, (6) debtors, (7) for the cause of Allah and (8) the traveller.

[22] A Rano, 'A Treatise on Socioeconomic Roles of Zakah' MPRA Paper No 81155 (2017); MS Al-Uthaymeen, *Fiqh of Worship: Purification, Doctrines, Salat, Zakat, Siyam, Hajj,* trans. Abdallah Alaceri. (London: Al-Firdous Ltd, 2011); Powell (n 1) 43; S Bashear, 'On the Origins and Development of the Meaning of *Zakat* in Early Islam' (1993) *Arabica* 40, No 1, 84-113; Kahf (n 4).

[23] Al Sayyid (n 5).

[24] RA Musgrave and PB Musgrave, *Public Finance in Theory and Practice* (New York: McGraw-Hill, 1989).

a way to supplement state resources to address the healthcare needs of the population. Nonetheless, it is crucial to differentiate between the conceptualisation of conventional taxes and *zakat*.

Conventional taxes are typically rooted in the principles of public finance and are based on an individual's income, wealth, or consumption, without any religious or moral considerations.[25] In contrast, *zakat* is an Islamic religious obligation with specific rule, such as the categories of eligible recipients and the types of wealth subject to *zakat*. These distinctions underscore the unique nature of *zakat* as a form of religious giving, which differs from conventional taxation. Furthermore, it is important to note that the voluntary nature of *zakat* is a crucial aspect of its religious significance. If the state were to collect *zakat* as a mandatory tax, it could potentially compromise the religious freedom of Muslims who may object to the state's involvement in the collection and distribution of *zakat*. The implication of this argument in linking *zakat* to tax lies in the potential for utilising *zakat* as an additional financial resource to address the deficits in the health budget, while acknowledging and respecting its distinct nature and religious significance. By drawing parallels between the roles of tax and *zakat* in financing public health, the argument highlights the possibility of harnessing *zakat* in a complementary manner to conventional taxation.

There are two forms of *zakat*: *zakat al fitr*, which is specifically distributed in kind as food to the poor in *Ramadhan* before the *Eid* prayer, and *zakat al maal*, which is the annual tax on wealth. This book focuses on the latter, since it has a broader purpose aligned towards the social and economic improvement of the poor, and is usually paid out on cash savings, assets, shares, stocks, bonds, digital currencies, livestock, gold, and silver. These categories of *zakat* must be in the possession of an adult Muslim and must reach a specific threshold for a Muslim to be considered eligible for *zakat*. For example, in Kenya, Muslim clerics have advised that cash savings of more than KES 260,000 (GBP 1,761) incur *zakat* assessed at 2.5 per cent of total savings.

---

[25] JE Stiglitz, *Economics of Public Sector* (New York: WW. Norton & Company, 2000).

Is there a need for a scholarly contribution on *zakat*?

Muslims in Kenya comprise approximately 11 per cent of the entire population.[26] The majority of Kenyan Muslims ascribe to the *sunni* school of thought;[27] their understanding of *sunni* Islam has been shaped by scholars from the Middle East, Egypt and India,[28] and reference to *sunni* scholarship is also taken from foreign sources. Consequently, Muslim scholarship out of Kenya remains largely unknown and inaccessible. There are reasons for this. Islamic law in Kenya is taught in *madrassas* (Islamic schools) using prescribed texts based on the school of jurisprudence to which the *ustadh or ustadha* (male or female Islamic law teacher) ascribes. The *ustadhs* and *imams* confine themselves to verbally discussing Islamic law and its rulings during Friday sermons, through the media and when directly consulted. Some also publish booklets and newsletters to preach Islam and clarify misconceptions relating to Islamic law, but these are not widely available, and the content has not undergone the robustness of a peer review process.[29] In so doing, they reproduce the positions taken by medieval Muslim scholars, without reference to changes in time, place, and context.

---

[26] Government of Kenya, Kenya National Bureau of Statistics, '2019 Kenya Population and Housing Census Volume IV: Distribution of Population by Socio-Economic Characteristics' (Nairobi: Government Printers, 2020) 12, available: https://www.knbs.or.ke/?wpdmpro=2019-kenya-population-and-housing-census-volume-iv-distribution-of-population-by-socio-economic-characteristics

[27] The *sunni* and *shia* schools are two mainstream branches of Islam. There are a number of factions within each branch. Under the *sunni* school of thought, four prominent schools of jurisprudence guide *sunni* scholarship. These are, the Hanafi, Maliki, Shafi and Hanbali schools, taking after the names of their proponents. These schools distinguish themselves based on the jurisprudential principles they adhere to in interpreting normative Islam and issuing *fatawas* (legal rulings). The Hanafi school is considered as the most flexible when compared to the strict Hanbali school which adopts a literal and strict interpretation of normative Islam without recognising changes in time, place and context. See also: SJ Trimingham, *Islam in East Africa,* (Oxford: Clarendon Press, 1964).

[28] A Mazrui, 'Religion and Political Culture in Africa' (1985) *Journal of the American Academy of Religion,* Vol 53, No 4 (1985), 817-839, at 830; Trimingham, (n 27).

[29] Interviews with Islamic law experts.

There is utility in seeking to historicise, categorise and relativise Islamic scholarship, since it demonstrates a strong robustness in its claims of reliability and credibility. This helps in understanding the evolution and development of Islamic thought and jurisprudence overtime. By situating Islamic scholarship within its historical and social context, the book identifies the factors that shaped its formation, as well as the various debates, tensions, and contradictions that have arisen with it. This, in turn, sheds light on the diversity and complexity of Islamic thought and helps to challenge simplistic and essentialist notions of Islam.[30] This approach can also undermine the reliability and credibility of Islamic scholarship. By relativising Islamic scholarship and situating it within a historical and cultural context, scholars risk reducing it to a product of its time and place as seen from the approach taken by *ustadhs* and *imams* in Kenya, rather than an enduring and universal truth.[31] This approach is used to support a narrative that Islam is a static and outdated religion, rather than a living tradition that is constantly evolving and adapting to new circumstances. The goal of the book, therefore, in Chapter 4 is to demonstrate the plurality and complexity of interpretations that can emerge from the interaction between Kenyan law, human rights law and Islamic law. By doing so, the book aims to challenge simplistic and essentialist notions of Islam as static and outdated, and instead present it as a living tradition that is constantly evolving and adapting to new circumstances.

On this point, Kenyan Muslim clerics and scholars have held Islamic law to its historical origins, without attempting to apply the jurisprudence developed by the *sunni* schools to explore whether they can generate pluralistic responses to changing needs. This has limited the development of Kenyan Muslim scholarship. The only records where Islamic law is discussed in terms of its application to resolving disputes is through the *Kadhis'* court rulings, and judgements given by the *Kadhi* (a male Muslim magistrate who presides over Muslim disputes relying on Islamic sources

---

[30] W Hallaq, *Sharī'a: Theory, Practice, Transformations* (Cambridge, UK: Cambridge University Press, 2009).

[31] A An-Na'im, 'Complementary, Not Competing, Claims of Law and Religion: An Islamic Perspective' (2013) *Pepperdine Law Review,* Vol 39, Issue 5, 1231-1256, at 1250.

of law). These rulings relate to disputes arising out of personal status law and law relating to marriage, divorce, child custody and inheritance. Neither Kenyan Muslim scholarship nor the *Kadhis'* rulings have given thought to addressing the *maqasid al Islam* (the objectives to be achieved though Islamic law),[32] and in particular, the *maqasid* (objective) on health. The stance is similar insofar as scholarship on *zakat* is concerned. Kenyan Muslim scholarship has not explored how *zakat* can support the health *maqasid* and whether *zakat* can be given to Kenyan Government to support it in its duty towards achieving the right to health.

This is a significant gap – especially since the Ministry of Health in Kenya struggles towards the progressive achievement of the right to health. In general, public healthcare is not free. Certain healthcare services relating to maternal health and children's immunisation are either offered for free or are subsidised, while other services attract fees.[33] Certain donors also support the Ministry of Health and local NGOs to provide preventive healthcare services for patients. These are usually restricted to sexual and reproductive healthcare services and specific endemic diseases. Curative healthcare is usually subject to out-of-pocket payments by the patient. The poor seeking to access healthcare are conflicted between spending their limited wages on their economic wellbeing or paying hospital fees. Usually, they resort to home-based care or traditional medicine.[34] Their financial obstacles preventing their access to healthcare shows that there is a need to consider the progressive achievement of the right to health in the context of alleviating such financial hardship. It also pushed me to ask whether these financial obstacles of poor patients to seek medical assistance requires

---

32 Discussed in detail in Chapter 4. These objectives are the protection of religion, life, intellect, procreation, and property.

33 Government of Kenya, Ministry of Health, 'Kenya Health Policy 2014-2030: Towards Attaining the Highest Standards of Health' (Nairobi: Government Printers, 2014).

34 O Howland, 'Fakes and Chemicals: Indigenous medicine in contemporary Kenya and implications for health equity' (2020) *International Journal for Equity in Health* 19:199; J Harrington, 'Governing traditional medicine in Kenya: Problematization and the role of the Constitution', (2017) *African Studies* Volume 77, Issue 2; and B Ahlberg, 'Integrated Health Care Systems and Indigenous Medicine: Reflections from the Sub-Sahara African Region' (2017) *Front. Sociol.*

a re-examination of the health *maqasid*, to ask whether *zakat* can play a role in promoting health as part of normative Islam. Having set out these arguments, I now turn to address the scope of the book.

Scope of the Book

This book sets out to consider whether the normative scope of *maximum available resources* (MAR) under human rights law and scholarship can be extended to include *zakat* to be used towards the progressive achievement of rights. It focuses on the human right to health and its financing, using *zakat* to establish whether it is possible to interpret human rights law as requiring recourse to sources such as *zakat*, and to consider accepting Islamic law to govern its use in financing health. Relatedly, it examines the normative permissibility under Islamic law for the use of *zakat* to finance the core contents of the right to health and to make *zakat* available to the state. The book examines human rights and Islamic law scholarship to question the extent to which academia has engaged in scrutinising state responsibility towards expanding its fiscal space on two issues. First, to permit resource mobilisation from non-state actors and second, the use of those resources to support the progressive achievement of the right to health.

I argue that neither scholarship on human rights nor Islamic law has specifically addressed questions relating to how the normative content of the right to health and *zakat* can relate with each other. Human rights scholars, such as Elson et al,[35] Waris,[36] and Mcintyre[37] – whose scholarship focuses more on linking financial resources to the achievement of rights – have not explored sourcing such funds beyond taxation, borrowing, and

---

[35] D Elson, R Balakrishnan, and J Heintz, Public Finance, 'Maximum Available Resources and Human Rights', Nolan, A., O'Connell, R., and Harvey C. *Human Rights and Public Finance. Budgets and the Promotion of Economic and Social Rights* (Oxford: Hart Publishing Ltd, 2013), 13-39.

[36] A Waris, *Financing Africa* (Langaa RPCIG, Cameroon, 2019).

[37] Di Mcintyre, M Filip, and JA Røttingen, 'What Level of Domestic Government Health Expenditure Should We Aspire to for Universal Health Coverage?' (2017) *Health Economics, Policy, and Law* 12, No 2 (April): 125–37.

official development aid. Arguably, a state can make a political decision to mobilise additional sources of revenue by asking the Muslim community to donate their *zakat* towards the achievement of rights. However, the legal validity of such a decision by the state must be supported under human rights law, Islamic law, and the state's legal system.

Leading scholarship on *zakat* by Al Qaradawi,[38] Ramadan,[39] Kahf[40] and Powell[41] has been restricted to understanding the purpose of *zakat* and redistributing it in accordance with the rules set out under normative Islam. There is a need to extend Muslim scholarship to consider the usefulness of *zakat* under Islamic law to the realisation of social rights – in particular, the right to health. An academic and empirical contribution towards addressing these gaps is needed to explain how the content of human rights law and Islamic law is understood, and to demonstrate how these laws can work together towards supporting healthcare financially. The book takes Tamanaha's socio-legal positivist approach,[42] in investigating whether human rights law and Islamic law could generate legal responses that highlight their plurality and inbuilt transformative processes, to show that these laws are sensitive, susceptible, and responsive to varying interpretations.

Tamanaha's socio-legal positivist approach emphasises the importance of examining the role of law in society and how it operates within social, cultural, and political contexts. It recognises that the law is not just a set of rules, but a social practice that is influenced by social norms, values, and beliefs. Tamanaha's approach also emphasises the importance of studying the actual practices and experiences of law, as opposed to just the formal rules and doctrines. The book follows Tamanaha's approach because it recognises the importance of understanding the social, cultural, and political contexts in which Islamic law and human rights law operate. By

---

38 Al-Qaradawi (n 3).

39 T Ramadan, *Western Muslims and the Future of Islam* (Oxford University Press, 2005).

40 Kahf (n 4): 1–22.

41 Powell (n 4).

42 B Tamanaha, 'Socio-Legal Positivism and a General Jurisprudence', (2001) *Oxford Journal of Legal Studies*, Vol 21, No 1, 1-32.

taking a socio-legal positivist approach, the book seeks to understand how these laws are actually applied and experienced in practice, rather than just focusing on the formal rules and doctrines. This approach is useful in highlighting the plurality and inbuilt transformative processes of these laws, and how they can be responsive to varying interpretations.

However, the challenge is that human rights law and Islamic law do not unconditionally intertwine. This means that there are complexities and challenges in reconciling human rights law and Islamic law, as they do not always align unconditionally. Both legal frameworks have distinct historical, cultural, and philosophical underpinnings, which may lead to conflicting principles and norms. Human rights scholars distinguish between rights conceived as human rights, and those that emanate out of the norms taken from religious law – arguing that the latter is incapable of meeting the universality characteristic.[43] That is, they argue that human rights – as conceptualised under the Universal Declaration of Human Rights (UDHR)[44], the International Covenant on Civil and Political Rights (ICCPR)[45], the ICESCR[46], human rights treaties and resolutions – are capable of being shared by all people, and are applicable to all persons without exception, regardless of place.

---

[43] H G Ziebertz, and F Zaccaria (eds), *The Ambivalent Impact of Religion on Human Rights. Empirical Studies in Europe, Africa and Asia* (Springer, 2021); H Hannun, *Rescuing Human Rights. A Radically Moderate Approach* (Cambridge University Press, 2019); M H Tschalaer, *Muslim Women's Quest for Justice. Gender, Law and Activism in India* (Cambridge University Press, 2017); J Witte and C Green (eds), *Religion and Human Rights: An Introduction* (OUP, 2012); F Mervyn, *Constituting Human Rights: Global Civil Society and the Society of Democratic States* (London: Routledge, 2002); J Shestack, 'The Philosophical Foundations of Human Rights', in: Janusz Symonides, *Human Rights: Concepts and Standards* (Vermont, USA: UNESCO Publishing, 2000).

[44] UN General Assembly, Universal *Declaration of Human Rights*, 10 December 1948, 217 A (III).

[45] United Nations, Committee on Economic and Social Council. 'International Covenant on Civil and Political Rights, 16 December 1966.' United Nations, Treaty Series, December 16, 1966.

[46] (n 15).

The universality of human rights is a normative concept which is strongly related to that of equality and non-discrimination.[47] These refer to the intention of the norm-maker to guarantee to everyone, as part of a just society, all rights and freedoms set forth in the declaration, conventions, treaties, and resolutions without distinction. The complaint against Islamic law is that it conditions these principles of universality, equality and non-discrimination on its immutable sources of law, as set out in the *Qur'an* and the *sunnah* of the Prophet Muhammad (صلى الله عليه وسلم).[48] For example, Muslim women do not inherit equal to their male relative's share, a child born out of wedlock cannot inherit his father's estate, and LGBTQI[49] people are not given legal recognition nor permitted to marry. It is important to note here that Islamic law is not monolithic and there are diverse interpretations and practices among Muslims as well as ongoing efforts by Muslim scholars and activists to reinterpret Islamic law in more inclusive and egalitarian ways that uphold the principles of justice and equality without contradicting the letter and spirit of the *Qur'an*. Similarly, while claiming that the purpose of *zakat* is to promote an equitable society, where wealth is equally distributed to alleviate poverty, much of Islamic scholarship on *zakat* restricts its use for Muslims,[50] despite there being no such limitation imposed by the norms set out in the *Qur'an* on *zakat*.

---

47 E Brems, *Human Rights: Universality and Diversity* (Kluwer Law International, 2001).

48 The *sunnah* of the Prophet Muhammad (صلى الله عليه وسلم) documents his life. It refers to how he lived, what he did, the guidance given by him and his approach to addressing social, economic and political issues. The *sunnah* is comprised in a collection of verified reports by medieval Muslim scholars and jurists who documented narrations given by Muslim men and women who met and heard directly from the Prophet (صلى الله عليه وسلم) as well as those who indirectly came across the *sunnah*, hearing it from credible sources. The majority of *sunni* Muslims recognise the *sunnah* which is compiled by Bukhari and Muslim as authentic sources. The Arabic text written after mentioning the Prophet's name is translated as 'peace be upon him'. It is part of Muslim tradition to write the Arabic text every time the Prophet's name is mentioned.

49 Acronym for lesbian, gay, bisexual, transgender, queer and intersex.

50 ARM Qinâwî, *Fatâwâ al-Sawm* (Dâr Al-Amîn, Cairo, 1998), 59; Al Qaradawi (n 3); AR Al-Jaziri, *Islamic Jurisprudence According to the Four Sunni Schools, Volume I*, trans. Nancy Roberts (Fons Viate; Canada, 2009).

However, the universality of human rights has also been contested.[51] There have been arguments that human rights espouse European or western values which do not reflect Asian, African, Arabic, Hispanic, Islamic or Jewish conceptions of rights. Herskovits,[52] Shivji,[53] An-Naim and Deng,[54] Donnelly,[55] Brown,[56] Goodhart,[57] have argued that the exclusive nature of human rights undermines the values that people of different cultures and religions uphold and respect. While there are differences in how human rights law, cultures and religions conceptualise rights, entitlements and their enforcement, there are areas where they all intertwine. Health is one such entitlement, recognised as fundamental under both human rights law and Islamic law.[58] Therefore, I will demonstrate that the claim should not be generalised that human rights and Islamic law are not compatible. Rather, it should be considered from the perspective of how human rights and Islamic law can work together to address the shortages of funds for financing health. Some consideration on this is given next.

Human rights and Islamic law on the right to health

The claim, made by certain scholars, that Islamic law is incompatible with human rights – and therefore, incapable of supporting the realisation of those rights – depends on the context and content of rights being compared.

---

[51] P Magnarella, 'Questioning the Universality of Human Rights', (2003) *Human Rights and Human Welfare*, Volume 3, Issue 1, Article 6.

[52] M Herskovits, 'Statement on Human Rights,' (1947) *American Anthropologist*, 539-543, reprinted in Morton E Winston (ed), *The Philosophy of Human Rights* (Belmont, Wadsworth, 1989), 116-120.

[53] I Shivji, *The Concept of Human Rights in Africa* (CODESRIA, 1989).

[54] A An-Naim and F Deng (eds), *Human Rights in Africa. Cross Cultural Perspectives* (The Brookings Institution, 1990)

[55] J Donnelly, 'The Relative Universality of Human Rights' (2007) *Human Rights Quarterly* Vol 29, No 2 281-306.

[56] C Brown, 'Universal Human Rights: A Critique' (2007) *The International Journal of Human Rights*, Volume 1, Issue 2, 41-65.

[57] M Goodhart, 'Neither Relative nor Universal: A Response to Donnelly' (2008) *Human Rights Quarterly*, Vol 30, No 1,183-193.

[58] B H Aboul-Enein, 'Health Promoting Verses as mentioned in the Holy Qur'an (2016) *J Relig Health* 55(3):821-829; H Kamali, 'Maqāṣid al-Sharī'ah: The Objectives of Shari'ah' (1999) in *Islamic Studies Islamabad*: IRI, IIU, Vol 38, No 2.

The right of everyone to be healthy is recognised under both human rights law and Islamic law. The human right to health finds expression under article 12 of the ICESCR and has been interpreted authoritatively in General Comment 14 on the Right to the Highest Attainable Standard of Health.[59] Islamic law is to be understood from the context of *maqasid al shariah,* that is the common good to be achieved through practicing Islam. An understanding of this common good is derived from the application of *usul al fiqh,* principles of Islamic jurisprudence as developed by the different schools of Islamic thought.[60] Islamic law highlights the rationales, purposes and common good to be achieved in the observance of the Islamic faith.[61] Since the protection of health is one of the objectives intended to be achieved through Islamic law, Islamic scholarship considers health as a fundamental common good.

While the different schools of Islamic thought have applied their *usul* to develop methodological rules, guiding Muslims to understand the meaning and content of what constitutes the protection of health, they have also set out its limits. For example, under Islamic law, abortion is impermissible unless it is needed to protect the health and life of the mother.[62] Some Muslim jurists also dispute the provision of contraceptives.[63] Therefore, if *zakat* is to be used to support healthcare, it cannot finance the provision of health services related to sexual and reproductive healthcare that are considered *haram* (prohibited) or *makrooh* (disliked or offensive) under Islamic law. Conversely, human rights are indivisible. Therefore, denying women access to abortion services or contraception is linked to discrimination, and can constitute gender-based

---

[59] United Nations, Committee on Economic and Social Council. 'General Comment No 14: The Right to the Highest Attainable Standard of Health (Art. 12 of the Covenant), E/C.12/2000/4.' United Nations, November 8, 2000.

[60] H Kamali, *Principles of Islamic Jurisprudence* (Cambridge: Islamic Texts Society, 1991).

[61] Ibn Ashur, *Treaties on Maqasid al Shari'ah,* (trans.) Mohamed El Tahir El Mesawi (The International Institute of Islamic Thought, 2006).

[62] J Brockopp, (ed), *Islamic Ethics of Life: Abortion, War and Euthanasia* (University of California Press, 2003).

[63] D Atighetchi, 'The Position of Islamic Tradition on Contraception' (1994) *Med Law* 13(7-8):717-25.

violence, torture, and cruel, inhuman, and degrading treatment.[64] Under human rights law, access to safe abortion services is a human right. This is an example of the incompatibility of Islamic law with human rights, based on the context and content of how the right to health is understood and given meaning.

While human rights may be based on normative and theoretical arguments, their enforceability is rooted in law.[65] Most states have ratified the UDHR, ICCPR, ICESCR and related human rights treaties, which set out the norms through which human rights are guaranteed by states. Other states have guaranteed human rights in their constitutions, for example Chapter IV on the Bill of Rights under the 2010 Constitution of Kenya. The maximum available resources (MAR) obligation underpins such legitimacy. It places an obligation on the state as the primary duty bearer, guaranteeing the achievement of human rights. Article 2(1) of the ICESCR requires States:

> [T]o take steps, individually and through international assistance and co-operation, especially economic and technical, to the maximum of its available resources, with a view to achieving progressively the full realisation of the rights recognised [in the ICESCR] by all appropriate means, including particularly the adoption of legislative measures.[66]

Consequently, the book questions whether MAR is capable of being interpreted broadly to include *zakat*. It also asks whether MAR provides for an academic inquiry into drawing in Islamic law into human rights law. A question arises here on why MAR is even important to be considered

---

[64] UN Committee on the Elimination of Discrimination against Women (CEDAW), General Recommendation No 35 on Gender-Based Violence Against Women, Updating General Recommendation No 19 (2017). https://tbinternet.ohchr.org/Treaties/CEDAW/Shared%20Documents/1_Global/CEDAW_C_GC_35_8267_E.pdf

[65] A L Comstock, *Committed to Rights: UN Human Rights Treaties and Legal Paths for Commitment and Compliance* (Cambridge University Press, 2021); O De Schutter, *International Human Rights Law* (2nd Ed, Cambridge University Press, 2014); A Buchanan, *The Heart of Human Rights* (OUP, 2013); J Harrington and M Stuttaford, *Global Health and Human Rights: Legal and Philosophical Perspectives* (Routledge, 2010).

[66] Article 2(1) ICESCR

especially when economic, social, and cultural rights are often viewed as aspirational rather than obligatory. The MAR obligation is important because it provides the legal framework for assessing the extent to which a state is fulfilling its obligations under the ICESCR. It recognises that resources are limited, but also places an obligation on states to use the maximum of their available resources to realise economic, social, and cultural rights. This means that states must take steps to mobilise resources and allocate them in a way that ensures the greatest possible access to economic, social, and cultural rights for everyone. By including the ICESCR and the MAR obligation in its constitution, Kenya has committed itself to fulfilling its obligations under this treaty, such that it is no longer aspirational but legally binding.

The scope of article 2(1) of the ICESCR on maximum available resources

The MAR obligation specifies that human rights are progressive. As such, the state is under an immediate obligation to act towards achieving the right, so far as current circumstances permit. The state must strive to ensure the widest possible enjoyment of the right, under the prevailing circumstances, to the extent feasible, based on the available resources. The obligation requires the state to take steps. Human rights are not conditioned on the availability of resources, but on the state taking specific steps. Balakrishnan et al[67] place an emphasis on the financial aspects of the MAR obligation, whereas Robertson[68] and Skogly[69] also acknowledge those resources that can be made available in society through applying natural,

---

[67] R Balakrishnan, D Elson, J Heintz, and N Lusiani. *Maximum Available Resources and Human Rights: Analytical Report* (New Brunswick, NJ: Rutgers, 2011).

[68] RE Robertson, 'Measuring State Compliance with the Obligation to Devote the Maximum Available Resources to Realising Economic, Social, and Cultural Rights', (1994): *Human Rights Quarterly* 16:693–714.

[69] S Skogly, 'The Requirement of Using the Maximum Available Resources for Human Rights Realisation: A Question of Quality as Well as Quantity' (2012) *Human Rights Law Review* 12(3) 393-420.

human, educational and regulatory resources. Robertson[70] and Andersen[71] have also considered the role of non-state actors in supporting the state in its duty to achieve human rights. From the variety of resources available to a state, scholarship has focused on the critical role of taxation through which to achieve the progressive realisation of human rights.[72]

The argument in the book that MAR under human rights law should include non-state funds given to the state does indeed have implications for tax law. It could be argued that MAR was chosen because it allows the book to make the argument that *zakat* should be included in MAR. In identifying MAR, the aim of the book is to contribute to the broader field of human rights law by exploring the potential for convergence and innovation between different legal frameworks in addressing complex legal problems as well as highlighting the importance of understanding the political and social dynamics that shape the implementation and interpretation of this human right obligation. The argument that non-state funds such as *zakat* can be included in the MAR obligation under human rights law implies that the state may not be solely responsible for providing adequate resources for the realisation of the right to health. This may be seen as a departure from the traditional understanding that the state has the primary responsibility to provide for the right to health. However, the book also recognises the importance of constitutional law in determining whether *zakat* can be legally recognised as a source of revenue for public health in Kenya. This demonstrates the need to consider the specific legal

---

70 Robertson (n 68):693–714.

71 E Andersen, 'A New Approach to Assessing State Compliance with the Obligation to Devote Maximum Available Resources to Realise Economic, Social and Cultural Rights' (2010) DEV Working Paper 26.

72 Vageesh (n 1); P Alston and N Reisch, *Tax, Inequality and Human Rights* (OUP, 2019); B O'Hare, 'Tax and the Right to Health' (2018) *Health Humn Rights* 20(2):57-63; A Reeves, Y Gourtsoyannis, S Basu, Sanjay et al, 'Financing Universal Health Coverage – Effect of Alternative Tax Structures on Public Health Systems', (2015) *The Lancet*; A Waris and L. A. Latif. 'Financing the Progressive Realisation of Socio-Economic Rights in Kenya' (2015) UNLJ 8, No 1; A Waris, *Tax and Development* (Law Africa, 2013).

and political context in which human rights principles are applied, rather than relying solely on abstract doctrinal analysis.

However, taxes are not adequate sources of revenue through which to fulfil the state's obligation under the MAR norm. Most developing countries, and African states in particular, are often faced with budgetary constraints which affect their decisions regarding assigning resources to competing social, economic and development priorities. These budgetary constraints result from the low tax base available in developing countries, high levels of debt, and the problem of illicit financial flows that erode the fiscal capacity of African governments.[73]

Empirical evidence has also been documented by Lumina and Tamale demonstrating that African states are spending higher proportions of their budgets to service their external debts and are reducing their spending on the achievement of human rights.[74] The UN Independent Expert on debt, other international financial obligations and human rights has also observed the inadequacy of taxes towards financing the achievement of human rights.[75] As a result of these low tax bases, illicit financial flows and debt-servicing obligations, many African states have also been unable to achieve the 15 per cent budget share towards achieving the right to health, as set out in the Abuja Declaration 2001.[76]

---

[73] K Young, (eds) *The Future of Economic and Social Rights* (Cambridge University Press, 2019); I Bantekas and C Lumina (eds), *Sovereign Debt and Human Rights* (OUP, 2018); P Reuter (eds), *Draining Development? Controlling Flows of Illicit Funds from Developing Countries* (World Bank, 2012).

[74] C Lumina and N Tamale, 'Sovereign Debt and Human Rights: A Focus on Sub-Saharan Africa' (2021) *African Sovereign Debt Justice Paper Series.*

[75] A/HRC/49/47: 'Taking Stock and Identifying Priority Areas: A Vision for the Future Work of the Mandate Holder – Report of the Independent Expert on the Effects of Foreign Debt'.

[76] Organisation of African Unity. 'Abuja Declaration On HIV/Aids, Tuberculosis and Other Related Infectious Diseases, Abuja, Nigeria, 26-27 April 2001 OAU/SPS/ABUJA/3. Available at: Declaration.PDF (safaids.net)

These constraints were also recognised in the *travaux préparatoires* relating to the drafting of the ICESCR.[77] As a result, article 2(1) of the ICESCR requires states to also seek international assistance and cooperation to support their progressive achievement of human rights. The *travaux préparatoires* relating to the drafting of the ICESCR, contain no discussion or reference to the state taking steps through domestic assistance and cooperation under Article 2(1).[78] In Chapters 2 and 3, I will discuss whether the scope of article 2(1) can be extended to permitting the state to seek domestic financial assistance from the Muslim community by requesting their *zakat*. Even if article 2(1) permitted recourse to *zakat*, accepting the funds must be permitted under the state's legal system. Since *zakat* is governed by Islamic law, it is necessary to consider whether the Kenyan state whose Constitution requires separation of state and religion can accommodate or rejects the application of Islamic conditions for the use of *zakat*.

The Human Rights Committee has also placed constraints on the MAR obligation, by authorising states to limit elements of rights subject to resource constraints. Hence, subject to resource availability, a state can reduce spending on the progressive achievement of rights and avoid allocating 15 per cent of its total budget to the health sector, despite the Abuja Declaration. Balakrishnan and Elson explain that states enjoy a margin of discretion in selecting the means to carry out their obligations.[79] Greer explains further that such a margin relates to 'implementation discretion'[80] – meaning that the state can choose, for example, which health service to provide, and when and how, subject to resource availability. Such legal recognition of human rights and their subjection to resource

---

[77] *The International Covenant on Economic, Social and Cultural Rights: Travaux Preparatoires*, Volume 1, edited by Ben Saul (OUP, 2016), 723-758.

[78] ibid 723-857.

[79] R Balakrishnan and D Elson, *Economic Policy and Human Rights: Holding Governments to Account* (Zed Books, 2011).

[80] S Greer, 'The Margin of Appreciation: Interpretation and Discretion under the European Convention on Human Rights', (2000) *Human Rights Files* No 17, Council of Europe.

availability raises a concern over whether the human rights legal system is amenable to their financial maintenance.

While the ICESCR presents states as the duty bearers of guaranteeing human rights, at the same time it inevitably restricts the application of human rights due to the problem of resources, while establishing principles to ensure that some steps are taken by states to achieve, at least, a minimum core content of the rights. Scholarship is therefore needed on whether the ICESCR can then allow a state to extend the application of the MAR obligation to allow it to take *zakat* and finance health. This poses three legal issues.

The Legal Issues Arising

Pellissier has argued that resource constraints push states to set priority targets.[81] Arguing from the perspective of the right to health, he claims that setting priorities is helpful to states, in assessing what resources are available and releasing them accordingly. I question whether the 'margin of discretion' that states are allowed under General Comment No. 3 on The Nature of States Parties' Obligations[82] can be used to interpret the scope under article 2(1) of the ICESCR as permissible towards allowing a state to seek domestic assistance on mobilising additional sources of funds from the Muslims with which to finance the right to health. Islamic law is neither recognised nor included as part of the international and domestic legal framework guaranteeing the achievement of human rights. Neither is it expressly set out as part of the MAR obligation. Nor were any such considerations made in the *travaux preparatoires* relating to the drafting of the ICESCR. While scholars have addressed the dynamic nature of the

---

[81] A Pellissier, 'A Defence of the Human Right to Health' (2021) *Studies in Philosophy, Politics and Economics* 3(1), 27-31.

[82] UN Committee on Economic, Social and Cultural Rights (CESCR), General Comment No 3: The Nature of States Parties' Obligations (Art. 2, Para. 1 of the Covenant), 14 December 1990, E/1991/23.

MAR obligation,[83] there is very little academic scrutiny of whether it can accommodate a state's obligation to seek domestic assistance from non-state actors who can impose religious conditions on the use of the funds sought for achieving human rights. This presents the first legal issue investigated in this book.

The second legal issue is conceptualised around questions relating to the Islamic law governing the use of *zakat*. This is to assess whether Islamic law permits the use of *zakat* for health and allows *zakat* to be given to a non-Islamic Muslim minority state. This doctrinal analysis is complemented through empirical work. This is because the implementation and interpretation of legal principles are not solely determined by legal doctrine but also shaped by social, cultural, and political factors. Empirical work allows for an examination of the reality on the ground, revealing how legal principles are implemented and interpreted in practice. In the context of using *zakat* to finance public health in Kenya, fieldwork allowed for an understanding of the social and political dynamics that shape the implementation of *zakat*, which cannot be obtained through a doctrinal analysis alone.

Zakat is a fundamental pillar of Islam. It is, therefore, necessary to establish how Muslims understand and interpret the law on *zakat* to decide on the lawfulness of giving *zakat* to a non-Islamic state to finance health. This is significant since majority of Muslims prefer giving their *zakat* to Muslims. Offering it to the state would mean including non-Muslims as beneficiaries. Fieldwork therefore, became essential to discover and clarify the extent to which local actors are willing to consider the usefulness of *zakat* to finance

---

83 Latif, 'An Explication on Broadening the Definition and Scope of Maximum Available Resources under General Comment 14 of the ICESCR to Include Islamic Taxation in Financing the Right to Health', (2017) *Biomed J Sci & Tech Res* 1 (3); A Nolan, *Economic and Social Rights after the Global Financial Crisis* (Cambridge University Press, 2016); A Waris and L Latif, 'Towards Establishing Fiscal Legitimacy Through Settled Fiscal Principles in Global Health Financing' (2015) *Health Care Anal* 23(4):376-390; Elson et al (n 35) 13-39; Skogly (n 69) 395; M Dowell Jones and D Kinley, 'Minding the Gap: Global Finance and Human Rights' (2011) *Ethics & International Affairs*, 25, No 2, 183-210; Andersen (n 71).

health. The fieldwork reveals fresh insights into the Islamic law on *zakat* and academic literature discussing the compatibility between Islamic law and human rights.

The third legal issue relates to the Kenyan state, it questions the conditions under which Islamic law could permit the Kenyan state to take and use *zakat*. This, then, required an evaluation of the legal theory that guides the Kenyan state to consider accepting as part of its domestic law foreign norms sourced from a religious-based legal system. To do this, I explain the hierarchical legal structure organised under the Constitution to recognise and delimit the plurality of legal norms. This was needed to establish the compatibility of restrictions based on Islamic law on *zakat* with provisions of the Constitution. A book looking into how the Kenyan state can legally consider the use of *zakat* as part of its MAR obligation, acceptable under its constitutional order, supports interlinking scholarship on human rights and Islamic law. The structure of the book which is described next supports this discussion.

Structure of the Book

The book is written in three parts. It has six substantive chapters; each part contains two chapters. Chapter 2 demonstrates that the argument on broadening the scope of the MAR obligation under article 2(1) of the ICESCR to include *zakat* is acceptable under human rights law. In Chapter 3, the focus shifts to the Kenyan state, to consider how its obligation under human rights law to finance health are understood and implemented. The chapter reviews Kenya's health law and policies to consider how the state gives meaning to *maximum available resources* under human rights law and whether such meaning can justify recourse to sources such as *zakat*. The chapter justifies the need to source for additional funds to supplement the deficit in Kenya's health budget and resource limitations.

I then move on to show in Chapter 4 that it is acceptable under Islamic law to use *zakat* to finance healthcare and to give it to the Kenyan state, albeit with conditions. In so doing, I engage with the different schools of Islamic jurisprudence and the different methods of reasoning developed by these schools. Having made the argument that MAR could include *zakat,* that Islamic law permits this, and also permitted the use of *zakat* by the Kenyan state to finance health, I then turn to show how this premise would work within Kenya's constitutional order. So, in Chapter 5, I examined the 2010 Constitution of Kenya to understand the full legal effect of linking the MAR obligation to *zakat* and establishing what would be the Kenyan state's legal response. To present perspectives 'on the ground' regarding what would be practicable and empirically acceptable to rights holders, I interviewed key representative stakeholders, and discussed the findings in Chapters 6 and 7.

The following research questions are interrogated in the chapters:

i. Is it possible to interpret human rights law as requiring recourse to sources such as *zakat,* and to consider accepting Islamic law to govern its use in financing health?
ii. Does Islamic law permit a non-Islamic state to use *zakat* for the overall goal of financing healthcare, which would benefit both Muslims and non-Muslims?
iii. Is it acceptable under the Constitution of Kenya for the state to legally accept and use *zakat* to finance health with its Islamic law conditions?
iv. How are the norms and doctrine around the use of *zakat* and its feasibility in financing health interpreted, given context and content by stakeholders in Kenya?

Methodological Approaches Tailored to the Kenyan Context

An understanding of the right to health in the context of its MAR obligation provides an opening to explore the possibilities of links between human rights law and the *maqasid* on health under Islamic law. This allows me to introduce a discussion on the legality of a non-Islamic Muslim minority state taking and using *zakat* to finance the achievement of the right to health. This discussion involves two distinct legal systems which apply different methodological approaches to their sources. All doctrinal and normative-based inquiries under human rights law and Islamic law are made using the reliable and credible methods developed under these two legal systems. Therefore, I have relied on doctrinal analysis using deductive reasoning and analogy to interpret human rights law. In evaluating the Islamic norms on *zakat,* I have considered the use of *taqlid* (imitation: accepting as legally binding what previous classical and medieval Islamic scholars have ruled on a particular issue) and *isnaad* (a strictly regulated method of establishing the legitimacy of the *Sunna,* which requires tracing the information to Prophet Muhammed (صلى الله عليه وسلم) as its source).[84] Using these Islamic methods, I have applied *ijtihad* (independent reasoning) to make conclusions on the permissibility of *zakat* to finance health, and for it to be given to the Kenyan Government.

The main question that guided this study asks whether any conditions giving rise to legal permissibility exist under human rights law, Islamic law, and the Constitution of Kenya on the use of *zakat* to finance health. This question allowed me to make use of a combination of methods available under socio-legal research and Islamic jurisprudence. The use of *halaqa* gave me access to excluded voices from Muslim scholarship in Kenya: *halaqa* is a method of debating legal issues among Muslims to arrive at a normative consensus. The *halaqa* as a data collection method has not been used hitherto in socio-legal scholarship, much less in a project as designed by this book. *Halaqa* is different from focus group discussions. Its purpose is to create a community among Muslims whose ideas have been marginalised by getting them to engage on norms to solidify them and not to generate new norms. Relying on data based on the dialogic *halaqa* supported this research to exclusively include and hear from Muslim women who are experts on Islamic law, and those working as Government officers. My fieldwork did establish that there is a significant gender discrepancy when it comes to Islamic scholars in the country; it is heavily male dominated.

Through the use of *halaqa,* I ensured that my study provided a balanced gender perspective on the research questions, especially on how Muslim

---

84 Kamali (n 60) 3.

women understood and interpreted Islamic doctrine. By asking Muslim women the research questions, I got to hear their voice and reasoning on the use of *zakat* for financing public health. This method supported an understanding of doctrinal discussions from a women-only perspective since Islamic scholarship in Kenya has been dominated by Muslim men. The book is also written from a Muslim woman's perspective. Muslim women are central to the practice of Islam and its normative interpretations, but they are not listened to. Therefore, fieldwork was also necessary to fill this gap and include more Muslim women voices on the use of *zakat* for financing health. Therefore, I hope it also contributes towards the voice of women within the male-dominant perspective on the Islamic law on *zakat*. As a Muslim woman who understands Islam from a *sunni* perspective, with a legal and research background on finance and human rights, I was able to rely on my knowledge and expertise to confirm the many arguments made in the following chapters.

Interviews were conducted in Arabic, English, Swahili, Urdu, Punjabi, and Hindi, when gathering answers to questions asked of Muslim *zakat* payers.). As a native speaker of all these languages, I was able to engage with the interviewees in their own language. This allowed them to clearly express themselves and engage with me on a deeper evaluation of their views on *zakat* and the Kenyan Government. Having studied the *Qur'an* and Arabic grammar, I was also able to engage with scholars on the interpretation of the *Qur'an* in Arabic text. The methodology guiding this study was therefore carefully developed around doctrinal-based legal reasoning, taking into consideration a mixed-qualitative-methods approach, to engage with the norms, theory, and doctrine relevant to address the use of *zakat* to finance health. Since these discussions required the use of specific methodology to draw out the legal nuances in investigating the use of *zakat* to finance health, each of the six substantive chapters address their methodology separately.

The last chapter of the book is based on fieldwork carried out in Mombasa and Nairobi, from which I was able to appreciate the version and practice of Islamic law that guided Kenyan Muslims on *zakat* and provided me with an 'on the ground' position, from which to debate the argument my research was making. Obtaining the views of both state and non-state actors on how they interpreted and reconciled their understanding of Islamic law with the right to health, and the constitutional approach to law and religion, provides this study with rich socio-legal data, with which to understand scholarship on MAR and a state's duty to finance health.

A focused study such as this is not without limitations. The research is restricted to the right to health and its financing. It only considers the scope of the MAR obligation to the extent necessary to establish the state's financial obligation to achieve the right to health. The study avoids discussions relating to the state's obligation to take steps through seeking international assistance and cooperation. Significant contributions on this theme have already been extensively discussed by Meier et al., Van Ho, Karimova, Hunt, Salomon, Hammonds et al., and Sepulveda.[85] The research on Islamic law and *zakat* is sourced from the *sunni* schools of Islamic thought, with which I am familiar and because they dominate

---

[85] BM Meier, JB de Mesquita, and C Williams, 'Global Obligations to Ensure the Right to Health', (2022) *Yearbook of International Disaster Law Online*, *3*(1), 3-34; T Van Ho, 'Obligations of International Assistance and Cooperation in the Context of Investment Law', In: Erdem Turkelli, Gamze and Gibney, Mark and Krajewski, Markus and Vandenhole, Wouter (eds) *Routledge Handbook on Extraterritorial Human rights Obligations* (Routledge, 2021); T Karimova, 'The Nature and Meaning of 'International Assistance and Cooperation' under the International Covenant on Economic, Social and Cultural Rights.' *Economic, Social, and Cultural Rights in International Law: Contemporary Issues and Challenges.* (ed.) Eibe Riedel, Gilles Giacca, and Christophe Golay (Oxford University Press, 2016); P Hunt, 'Interpreting the International Right to Health in a Human Rights Based Approach to Health', (2016) *Health Human Rights,* 18(2): 109-130 ME Salomon, *Global Responsibility for Human Rights: World Poverty and* the *Development of International Law* (Oxford: Oxford University Press, 2008); ME Salomon, 'Is There A Legal Duty To Address World Poverty?' RSCAS Policy Papers 2012/03. Available online at: http://www.lse.ac.uk/law/people/academic-staff/margot-salomon/Documents/salomon3.pdf. R Hammonds, G Ooms and W Vanderhole, 'Under the (Legal) Radar Screen: Global Health Initiatives and International Human Rights Obligations' (2012) *BMC International Health and Human Rights* 12, 31, and M Sepulveda, 'Obligations of 'international assistance and cooperation' in an Optional Protocol to the International Covenant on Economic, Social and Cultural Rights,' (2006) *Netherlands Quarterly of Human Rights,* Vol 24/2, 271-303; M Sepúlveda, 'The Obligations of 'international Assistance and Cooperation' under the International Covenant on Economic, Social and Cultural Rights. A Possible Entry Point to a Human Rights Based Approach to Millennium Development Goal 8' (2009) 13 *The International Journal of Human Rights* 86.

Islamic thought in Kenya. *Shia* scholarship is not referred to. I restrict myself to utilising *ijtihad* (involving a process of deductive and inductive reasoning) as the Islamic methodological tool with which to understand and evaluate the Islamic norms regulating the use of *zakat.* I avoid discussions tracing the development of Islamic law and its schools, to focus instead on the dominant views on the use of *zakat,* by looking into the history of *zakat,* tracing its development and the legal rulings informing its practice.

My fieldwork was also limited to two sites (in Nairobi and Mombasa) where majority of Muslims live and to *sunni* Muslims groups (Somalis, Arabs, Swahilis, Indians, and Africans). My research did not aim to collect data on how much *zakat* has been paid by Muslims in Kenya as this would have required a national survey targeting the 11 per cent Muslim population and filtering who among them pay *zakat* and how much. Of significance to this book is that *zakat* is available in Kenya. I interviewed 150 Muslim respondents. From their accounts I was able to estimate that between 2018 and 2019, approximately KES 36 million (GBP 249,354) was paid out in *zakat.*[86] In its 2022/2023 Budget Report, the Government of Kenya estimated that constructing and equipping a health center would require at least KES 70 million (GBP 484,855).[87] My limited sample is indicative of the possibility of mobilising substantial *zakat.*

Part of my fieldwork was impacted by the government-imposed restrictions to curtail the COVID-19 pandemic during its peak in 2020-2021. This limited access to my research participants. I was forced to adapt my methods of inquiry to allow asynchronous interviews. Details on the robustness of the methods of inquiry facilitating my fieldwork are provided in Chapter 7. This focused study makes substantial contributions to the scholarship on human rights, the right to health, Islamic law, and

---

[86] Three FBOs were interviewed. One FBO indicated that it had collected KES 30 million (GBP 207,795) in *zakat.* Another explained that High Net Worth Individuals contribute at least KES 200,000 and that the organisation had received a total of KES 4 million (GBP 27,706) just from 20 'rich' Muslims. Another FBO received KES 2 million (GBP 13,853).

[87] Parliamentary Service Commission, *Budget Options for 2022/2023 and the Medium Term* (Parliamentary Budget Office, 2022), 54.

zakat. The findings provide in-depth insight into how Muslims, in the Kenyan context, make sense of their Islamic knowledge, and relate it to their duty as citizens to support their government to achieve the right to health. This provides students, academics, researchers, practitioners, policymakers, and all those interested in the themes addressed here to have a greater understanding of Muslim scholarship out of Kenya.

Having introduced the book, Part I begins with a critical evaluation of the MAR obligation under the ICESCR and its interpretation by the Government of Kenya.

PART I

FINANCING THE RIGHT TO HEALTH

Overview

This part comprises two chapters that explore how states interpret, promote, and fulfil their responsibility to utilise maximum available resources (MAR) to achieve the right to health. The primary focus is on determining whether the MAR obligation allows states to access *zakat* and facilitate its allocation towards health financing. To do so, it is essential to interpret the text of the International Covenant on Economic, Social, and Cultural Rights (ICESCR), which establishes the right to health, and its General Comment 14 on the Right to the Highest Attainable Standard of Health (GC14), which characterises the right. This approach is crucial for evaluating the extent to which the ICESCR and GC14 outline the range of financial resources available to states as part of the MAR obligation. Subsequently, an examination of the Kenyan state's understanding of its obligations under the ICESCR and GC14, as well as its financial commitments to these obligations, is conducted. The inquiry also explores whether Kenya has considered expanding its MAR obligation to encompass domestic private actors and the potential procurement of their funds.

Chapter 2
Financing The Right to Health - *Interpreting Maximum Available Resources*

Introduction

The right to health constitutes a fundamental human right, encompassing access to timely, appropriate, and quality healthcare, as well as addressing the underlying determinants of health, such as clean water, sanitation, adequate nutrition, and a healthy environment. This right transcends the provision of healthcare services, extending to the social determinants of health. It includes the right to access healthcare facilities, goods, and services; the right to prevention, treatment, and control of diseases; and the right to health-related education and information. The right to health incorporates both individual and collective aspects and must be accessible to all without discrimination. It requires that healthcare services are accessible, available, acceptable and of good quality.

The Universal Declaration of Human Rights recognises the right to health, which is safeguarded under the International Covenant on Economic, Social and Cultural Rights (ICESCR).[1] This right has a territorial scope, requiring each State Party to the ICESCR to adopt appropriate national measures to progressively realise the right to health. State Parties are also obligated to seek international assistance and cooperation to tackle cross-border health issues, such as the 2020-2021 reliance on regional and international cooperation to curb the spread of the coronavirus pandemic. This chapter addresses the national measures that State Parties are obligated to undertake to implement the right to health, with a particular

[1] United Nations General Assembly, Universal Declaration of Human Rights, 10 December 1948, 217 A (III); United Nations, Committee on Economic and Social Council, 'International Covenant on Economic, Social and Cultural Rights.' United Nations, Treaty Series, 16/121966.

emphasis on the state's financial obligation. It highlights the limited scope of human rights scholarship in exploring the types of resources contemplated as part of the *maximum available resources* (MAR) obligation, as stated under Article 2.1 of the ICESCR.

This chapter contends that scholarship on MAR typically associates the state's financial obligation with taxes, as the state bears the primary responsibility for implementing human rights and taxes represent the most consistent and significant form of revenue available. Although contemporary scholars, such as Elson et al[2], Waris[3] and McIntyre[4], advocate for an expanded fiscal space for financing health rights, their suggestions predominantly focus on public finance approaches for states to mobilise additional sources of revenue (e.g., indirect tax increases, the introduction of new taxes, and debt). Other scholars, including Skogly[5], Birsh and Gafni[6], concentrate on maximising existing revenue streams to finance health. While maximising current revenue streams is essential for the state to achieve its health priorities, this approach addresses only one aspect of implementing the right to health.

The other aspect relates to raising and allocating sufficient finances for healthcare, which cannot be accomplished solely through taxes or international assistance and cooperation. Instead, it must be achieved through national measures that mobilise additional funds to supplement

---

[2] D Elson, R Balakrishnan, and J Heintz, Public Finance, 'Maximum Available Resources and Human Rights.' In: A Nolan, R O'Connell, and C Harvey, *Human Rights and Public Finance: Budgets and the Promotion of Economic and Social Rights* (Oxford: Hart Publishing Ltd, 2013), 13-39.

[3] A Waris, *Financing Africa* (Langaa RPCIG, Cameroon, 2019).

[4] Di Mcintyre, M Filip, and J A Røttingen, 'What Level of Domestic Government Health Expenditure Should We Aspire to for Universal Health Coverage?' *Health Economics, Policy, and Law* 12, No 2 (April 2017): 125–37.

[5] S Skogly, 'The Requirement of Using the Maximum Available Resources for Human Rights Realisation: A Question of Quality as Well as Quantity' (2012) *Human Rights Law Review* 12(3) 393-420.

[6] S Birsh and A Gafni, 'Economists' Dream or Nightmare? Maximising Health Gains from Available Resources Using the NICE Guidelines', (2007) *Health Economics, Policy and Law,* Vol 2: 193-202.

the limited health budget (discussed further in Chapter 3). In this context, human rights scholarship has yet to explore the legal permissibility under human rights law or state acceptance of mobilising faith-based funds as part of the MAR obligation. This chapter contributes to the discourse by interpreting the ICESCR and its accompanying General Comment 14 doctrinally, examining the text of these human rights instruments to assess the validity of broadening the interpretation and meaning of MAR to encompass *zakat*.

This chapter's argument regarding the exploration of alternative sources of financing for implementing the right to health can be situated within a broader socio-legal perspective. Socio-legal scholarship seeks to understand the relationship between law and society and how law shapes social relations and outcomes. In the context of the right to health, socio-legal scholarship acknowledges that its realisation is not solely the state's responsibility but requires the involvement of various actors, including non-state actors. The range of actors engaged in implementing the right to health extends beyond the state. Private actors and recourse to traditional medicine are playing an increasing role.[7] Grover and Irwin also recognise the importance of local communities in advancing the right to health.[8] This recognition is crucial to this chapter's objective of exploring the possibility of linking community or social finance to MAR.

Digital health apps are also being developed, providing the public with free access to quick symptom diagnosis.[9] Dial Daktari, a Kenyan health app, offers paid subscribers 24/7 online access to a doctor and registered nurse to discuss their symptoms and treatment plans. Following the COVID-19 pandemic, several companies were registered by teams of doctors, nurses,

---

[7] OMJ Kasilo, C Wambebe, JB Nikema et al, 'Towards universal health coverage: advancing the development and use of traditional medicines in Africa', (2019) BMJ Global Health, Vol 4, Issue 9, 1-11; V Yilmaz, *Private Healthcare Provider Organisations as New Actors in the Politics of Healthcare* (Springer, 2017) 195-239.

[8] A Grover and A Irwin, 'The Power of Community in Advancing the Right to Health: A Conversation with Anand Grover', (2009) *Health and Human Rights*, Vol. 11, No. 1, 1-3.

[9] T Neumark and R J Prince, 'Digital Health in East Africa: Innovation, Experimentation and the Market' (2021) *Global Policy*, Vol 12, Issue S6, 65-74.

and medical equipment suppliers to provide healthcare packages based on home visits.[10] Nevertheless, private healthcare in Kenya is expensive, and most Kenyans rely on the public healthcare sector.[11] Thus, the state's role and involvement remain crucial. Access to finance by the state is therefore significant if the state is to discharge its ICESCR obligations. Moreover, by recognising the role of private actors and local communities in advancing the right to health, this chapter emphasises the importance of a collaborative approach to implementing the right to health as part of its contribution to socio-legal scholarship.

Kenya's current debt level, which has accumulated to KES 4.2 trillion (GBP 30.5 billion), may jeopardise the fulfilment of the right to health.[12] The state might face pressure to reduce public health expenditure to make debt repayments. Consequently, the challenge lies in extending the MAR obligation beyond traditional forms of domestic revenue mobilisation. In the following sections, this chapter discusses the right to health and the state's role as the principal actor responsible and accountable for its realisation. This discussion is necessary to determine whether there is a robust link obliging states to prioritise finances as part of their MAR obligation under the ICESCR and GC14. The chapter then addresses its central question: can the meaning of MAR be extended to include *zakat*? It focuses on this question within the rules of interpretation and the MAR scope conceptualised by human rights scholars.

State Obligations Relating to the Normative Content of the Right to Health

The ICESCR and its associated documents delineate the meaning and content to the right to health, addressing essential features that states must

---

[10] Dial Daktari, available: https://www.dial-daktari.com/

[11] N Mwenda, R Nduati, M Kosgei et al., 'What Drives Outpatient Care Costs in Kenya? An Analysis with Generalised Estimating Equations', (2021) *Front. Public Health*; O D Williams, 'COVID-19 and Private Health: Market and Governance Failure', (2020) *Development* 63, 181-190, 183.

[12] Lumina and Tamale (n 2).

prioritise for the realisation of this right. The ICESCR, which entered into force in 1976, imposes obligations on states to respect, protect and fulfil economic, social, and cultural rights. Implicit in these obligations is the requirement to finance the implementation of these rights.[13] The Committee on Economic, Social and Cultural Rights (CESCR: a body established by the United Nations Economic and Social Council) monitors states' implementation of rights and provides guidance through General Comments and Concluding Observations.[14] Though not legally binding,[15] these documents offer authoritative interpretations on individual rights and the legal nature of the human rights obligations enshrined in the ICESCR. Interpretation is, therefore, critical for understanding how states should implement the right to health. The 1969 Vienna Convention on the Law of Treaties is often applied in interpreting human rights treaties.

Article 31 of the Vienna Convention stipulates that treaties require continuous contextual interpretation.[16] This requirement allows for a broader interpretation of MAR in the context of Grover and Irwin's recognition of communities' role in advancing the right to health. A strong link to community funds as part of MAR has been suggested by Robertson who interpreted MAR to include marshalling of funds available from local communities.[17] CESCR, however, has not interpreted the MAR obligation to extend to taking funds from locally based non-state actors. Such an interpretation can be criticised as making 'unacceptable attempts to

---

[13] A Waris and LA Latif, 'Towards Establishing Fiscal Legitimacy Through Settled Fiscal Principles in Global Health Financing' (2015) *Health Care Analysis: HCA: Journal of Health Philosophy and Policy* 23, No. 4 (December): 376–90, 378.

[14] Established under the United Nations Economic and Social Council (ECOSOC) Resolution 1985/17 of 28 May 1985.

[15] H Keller and L Grover (eds), 'General Comments of the Human Rights Committee and their Legitimacy', in: *UN Human Rights Treaty Bodies: Law and Legitimacy* (Cambridge University Press, 2012) 116-198

[16] Vienna Convention on the Law of Treaties, 23 May 1969, S Exec Doc L 92-1 (1970), 1155 UNTS 331 (entered into force 27 Jan 1980). **Note: Kenya has signed but not ratified the Vienna Convention on the Law of Treaties.**

[17] ER Robertson, 'Measuring State Compliance with the Obligation to Devote the 'Maximum Available Resources' to Realising Economic, Social, and Cultural Rights', (1994) *Human Rights Quarterly* 16, 693-714.

attribute to treaty provisions a meaning which they do not have'.[18] Kenya has not ratified the Vienna Convention; therefore, its government is not strictly bound by the specific provisions delineated therein. Instead, Kenya may contemplate adopting an interpretation of MAR that encompasses the procurement of funds from locally based non-state actors to fulfil its obligations related to the right to health, notwithstanding the absence of CESCR endorsement for such an interpretation.

However, it is imperative to recognise that Kenya, despite its non-ratification of the Vienna Convention, remains subject to the principles of customary international law, which encompasses the general rule of treaty interpretation. This rule necessitates interpreting treaty provisions in good faith, while considering their ordinary meaning, contextual relevance, and alignment with the treaty's overall objectives and purpose. Therefore, Kenya must exercise caution in adopting an interpretation that deviates from the CESCR's stance.

Human rights treaties have also been interpreted through human rights scholarship and case law. However, in implementing rights, states do not refer to scholarship, they typically refer to doctrine and their political commitments.[19] States, when implementing the right to health, thus consider the ICESCR and the General Comments. The ICESCR and its General Comments present criteria for evaluating states' progress towards implementing human rights. Such evaluation is assessed through the periodic reporting by states made to the CESCR on their level of compliance. The CESCR consists of independent experts, who then examine State Party reports on compliance, and adopt specific 'Concluding Observations' in respect of them.

---

[18] P Alston, 'The Historical Origins of the Concept of 'General Comments' in Human Rights Law' in L Boisson de Chazournes and V Gowlabd Debbas (eds), *The International Legal System in Quest of Equity and Universality: Liber Amicorum Georges Abi-Saab* (The Hague: Martinus Nijhoff, 2001) 764

[19] SE Kreps and AC Arend, 'Why States Follow the Rules: Toward A Positional Theory of Adherence To International Legal Regimes', (2006) *Duke Journal of Comparative & International Law*, Vol. 16, 331-414.

These Concluding Observations are opinions – they impose no legal obligation on a state – but can influence State Parties on what measures to take towards promotion of the enjoyment of treaty rights. Lyons has noted the challenging limitations in conducting a legal analysis of Concluding Observations, since these are not documented on a thematic basis.[20] This presents a challenge in conducting an in-depth analysis of Concluding Observations, referring to the core MAR obligation that this chapter focuses on. Special Rapporteurs also play a role in interpreting human rights treaties, when 'they have encountered specific issues on which the existing jurisprudence gives no or scant guidance, they have offered their interpretations'[21] to provide treaty provisions with detailed normative and operational content.[22]

The CESCR is not a judicial body, its General Comments and Concluding Observations are therefore 'advisory and recommendatory',[23] giving room to the state to decide whether or not to adopt the recommendations given or to propose their own domestic measures. The extent to which states, such as Kenya, commit finances to implement the content of the ICESCR, General Comments and Concluding Observations depends on their understanding of the MAR obligation as primarily financial, which is essential for realising rights. Although aspirational, the ICESCR and the MAR obligation hold significant normative and political value, even without creating legally enforceable obligations. The implementation of aspirational human rights treaties is influenced by politics as states must balance their international commitments with their domestic priorities and political realities. This highlights the importance of understanding the

---

[20] D Lyons, 'Human Rights Derogations: Souring and Analysing the Concluding Observations of the International Human Rights Treaty Bodies', (2021) *Irish Studies in International Affairs*, Vol 32, No 1, 153-169, at 154

[21] P Hunt, 'Interpreting the International Right to Health in a Human Rights-Based Approach to Health', (2016) *Health and Human Rights Journal*, 1.

[22] J Harrington and M Stuttaford, 'Introduction; in J Harrington and M Stuttaford (eds), *Global health and human rights: Legal and philosophical perspectives* (London: Routledge 2010), 5.

[23] M O'Flaherty, 'Concluding Observations of United Nations Human Rights Treaty Bodies', (2006) *Human Rights Law Review* 6(1) 27-52, 33.

political context in which these commitments are made and implemented. Understanding the political context in which human rights commitments are made and implemented is crucial for social legal scholarship as it provides important insight into the challenges and opportunities for realising human rights in practise.

Thus, the next section discusses human rights law in the context of considering whether MAR can be interpreted to permit or require states to broaden its meaning and scope to include *zakat* and facilitate its transmission towards health finance. To do this, an understanding of how the right to health is characterised is necessary in order to determine precisely the points at which MAR becomes pertinent.

Core requirements and progressive realisation of the right to health linked to finance

The right to health is enshrined in article 12.1 of the ICESCR, which obligates states to 'recognise the right of everyone to the enjoyment of the highest attainable standard of physical and mental health'. This right largely depends on achieving the core primary healthcare requirements outlined in article 12.2, such as reducing stillbirth rates and infant mortality; improving environmental and industrial hygiene; preventing, treating, and controlling diseases and ensuring universal access to medical care. The right to health is also contingent upon securing its 'underlying determinants', which include access to food, sanitation, and education.[24] Financing is essential for fulfilling these core obligations and underlying determinants.

Four conditions are necessary for realising the right to health. Firstly, the *availability* of 'functioning public health and healthcare facilities, goods and services, as well as programmes, in sufficient quantity within the State

---

[24] United Nations, Committee on Economic, Social and Cultural Rights. 'General Comment No 14: The Right to the Highest Attainable Standard of Health (Art. 12 of the Covenant), E/C.12/2000/4.' United Nations, November 8, 2000, Paragraph 4 General Comment 14.

Party.'[25] Secondly, *accessibility* of 'health facilities, goods and services to everyone without discrimination, within the jurisdiction of the State Party'.[26] Thirdly, *acceptability,* meaning that 'all health facilities, goods and services must be respectful of medical ethics and culturally appropriate, sensitive to gender and life-cycle requirements as well as being designed to respect confidentiality and improve the health status of those concerned.'[27] Lastly, the *quality* of health and healthcare facilities, goods and services, which must 'be scientifically and medically appropriate and of good quality.'[28] These AAAQ conditions cannot be achieved without states ensuring adequate financial resources.

General Comment 14 on the Right to Highest Attainable Standard of Health outlines the underlying determinants and conditions necessary for realising the right to health, which form the minimum core content of the right. Regardless of their level of development and revenue constraints, states must immediately secure these through the MAR obligation. The ICESCR obligates states to fulfil MAR obligations without explicitly detailing the financial obligation and its implications. The MAR obligation requires states to 'take steps'. The meaning of to 'take steps' and whether it implies recourse to alternative financial sources beyond government revenue and international assistance will be discussed in the following section. In the context of realising the right to health, GC14 considers both the immediate obligations related to the right, and its progressive realisation as a state's general legal obligations. Article 2.1 of the ICESCR provides for the progressive realisation of rights, taking into account resource constraints that states may face in immediately securing the right:

> Each State Party to the present Covenant undertakes to take steps, individually and through international assistance and cooperation, especially economic and technical, to the maximum of its available resources, with a view to progressively achieving the full realisation

---

[25] ibid, Paragraph 12 (a).
[26] ibid, Paragraph 12 (a).
[27] ibid, Paragraph 12 (c).
[28] ibid, Paragraph 12 (c).

> of the rights recognised in the present Covenant by all appropriate means, including particularly the adoption of legislative measures.

The financial obligation of a state is contingent upon the availability of resources. The ICESCR does not impose a commensurate obligation on states to commit finances. Paragraph 31 of GC14 clarifies the concept of 'progressive realisation' by stating that states have a 'specific and continuing obligation to move expeditiously and effectively as possible towards the full realisation of article 12'. Progressive realisation acknowledges that full realisation of all rights is generally unattainable within a short time frame. Instead, rights are realised progressively over time, allowing states discretion in defining their understanding of rights and their implementation. Consequently, the obligation requires states to begin by securing the underlying determinants of health and its four conditions, some of which must be immediately ensured by states. To achieve this, states must commit to further obligations linked to MAR.

State obligations of conduct and result linked to finance

The right to health necessitates that states allocate MAR to fulfil three levels of obligations as interpreted by GC14: 'the obligations to *respect, protect* and *fulfil'* the right to health.[29]

> The obligation to respect the right to health requires states to refrain from interfering directly or indirectly with the enjoyment of the right to health. The obligation to protect requires states to take measures that prevent third parties from interfering with guarantees of article 12. Finally, the obligation to fulfil requires states to adopt appropriate legislative, administrative, budgetary, judicial, promotional and other measures towards the full realisation of the right to health.[30]

---

[29] ibid, Paragraph 33.

[30] ibid, Paragraph 33.

The obligation to fulfil commits the state to 'take steps' utilising the 'maximum of its available resources' to achieve the right to health. Within GC14, the content of MAR encompasses various state-led strategies, such as legislative and budgetary measures, to secure the right to health. However, neither the ICESCR nor GC14 explicitly suggest content nor provide interpretation regarding the budgetary aspects of MAR. Instead, human rights scholarship on MAR, discussed later on page 63, examines this issue. The obligation to fulfil using MAR is accompanied by the obligation to facilitate, provide and promote the underlying determinants of the right to health, such as access to health facilities, food, housing, and sanitation.[31] As these obligations can be constrained due to resource limitations, exploring the scope of MAR, and considering alternative sources of funding, such as Islamic funds such like *zakat*, could contribute to scholarship on enhancing access to and the enjoyment of the right to health. However, the formal language of the ICESCR obscures the fact that MAR primarily concerns financial resources at the disposal of the state.

To some extent, General Comment 3 (GC3) on 'The Nature of States Parties' Obligations' offers clarification on how states should achieve the MAR obligation.[32] GC3 paragraph 1 differentiates between two kinds of state obligations: obligations of conduct and obligations of result. These distinctions assist states in comprehending the precise nature of their MAR obligations. Before a General Comment is adopted, it goes through a 'contested and competitive process',[33] that results in shaping the quality and content of the recommendations it makes. This gives General Comments legal relevance for the steps states should undertake to ensure implementation of rights.[34] Consequently, the two obligations: of conduct and result are fundamental to how states interpret and implement their

---

[31] ibid, Paragraph 33.

[32] United Nations Committee on Economic, Social and Cultural Rights, General Comment No 3: The Nature of States Parties' Obligations (Art. 2, Para. 1 of the Covenant), 14 December 1990, E/1991/23.

[33] K Mechlem, 'Treaty Bodies and the Interpretation of Human Rights', (2009) 42 *Vanderbilt Law Review* 905, at 928.

[34] D McGoldrick, *The Human Rights Committee – Its Role in the Development of the International Covenant on Civil and Political Rights* (Clarendon Press, Oxford 1991) at 347.

MAR obligation concerning realising the right to health. Both types of obligations play a crucial role in guiding states' actions and strategies to fulfil their commitments.

Obligations of conduct require states to undertake actions or measures that are directly determined by the obligation itself. In this regard, states are expected to actively 'take steps' to secure at least the core content of rights. On the other hand, the obligation of result mandates that states ensure the attainment of 'a specified result and leaves it for that state to achieve such a result by means of its own choice'.[35] For instance, when addressing the right to health, a state may allocate sufficient finances towards providing accessible health facilities in marginalised areas. This action exemplifies the results that arise from the measures undertaken as part of the state's conduct. The obligation of result acknowledges the state's discretion in realising rights while considering its fiscal capacity, allowing for a tailored approach to implementation.

Understanding the interplay between obligations of conduct and result is vital for states when interpreting their MAR obligations. As outlined in paragraph 30 of GC 14, states must ensure that the steps taken to fulfil these obligations are "deliberate, concrete, and targeted" towards the full realisation of the right to health. Recognising the nuances between these two types of obligations allows states to develop coherent and robust strategies that effectively balance their commitments and capacities in the pursuit of realising the right to health'.

An interpretation of the terms 'deliberate, concrete and targeted' is not given under GC 14. They remain open ended and subject to varying interpretations. The assumption, which follows from paragraph 54 of GC14 is that a national health strategy should define these steps. Paragraph 53 of

---

35 R Wolfrum, 'Obligation of Result Versus Obligation of Conduct: Some Thoughts About the Implementation of International Obligations' in M H Arsanjani, J Cogan, R Sloane and S Wiessner (eds) *Looking to the Future: Essays on International Law in Honor of W Michael Reisman* (Brill | Nijhoff, 2010), 363-383, at 364.

GC14 also provides another conundrum to the meaning of to 'take steps' as part of the state's obligations of conduct and result. It states that:

> The Covenant, however, clearly imposes a duty on each State to take whatever steps are necessary to ensure that everyone has access to health facilities, goods, and services so that they can enjoy, as soon as possible, the highest attainable standard of physical and mental health.

The use of the term- 'whatever steps' which is included as part of the obligation of conduct and result that characterise the normative content of the right to health, suggests three things. One, that it is a mandatory duty on the part of a state to take whatever steps that are necessary to implement the right to health. Two, despite the mandatory duty imposed on a state, the state has discretion in considering whatever steps it can take. Three, the term 'whatever' does not limit a state from exploring for example religious funds that are mobilised locally. As long as these 'whatever steps' are available, appropriate, follow from every effort made and are within a state's disposal, the state can theoretically argue to justify extending its obligation of results towards broadly interpreting its MAR obligation to permit mobilising religious sources of funds.

The open-ended nature of these phrases has led to ongoing scholarly debate on the scope and parameters of MAR. Alston and Quinn view the phrase 'take steps'[36] as assuming an obligation of conduct. Eide has defined this obligation to mean the responsibility of a state under international law for the realisation of rights. Hence, to 'take steps' in Eide's estimation is for the state to take appropriate measures; to respect the freedom of the individual; to protect that freedom and other human rights against third parties; and, where required to provide access to welfare covering basic needs such as food, shelter, education and health.[37] To 'take steps'

---

[36] P Alston and G Quinn, 'The Nature and Scope of States Parties' Obligations under the International Covenant on Economic, Social and Cultural Rights', (1987) *Human Rights Quarterly* 9, 156-229.

[37] A Eide, 'Making Human Rights Universal: Achievements and Prospects. Human Rights', (1999) *Development Online*, Volume 6, Issue 1, xiii-50.

represents a clear legal undertaking of what a state can expect to do. It reflects the view held by the drafters of the ICESCR that each article should specify in detail the particular steps to be undertaken in order to implement the relevant right.[38] GC3 offers further insight by outlining the obligation to 'take steps' as being dependent on use of all appropriate means with a view to achieving progressively the full realisation of the rights recognised in the ICESCR. A definitional analysis of the term 'all appropriate means' is therefore necessary if we are to give effect to Article 31 of the Vienna Convention on Law of Treaties under which treaty terms require continuous contextual interpretation.

'All appropriate means,' is left open ended under paragraph 53 of GC14: 'the most appropriate feasible measures to implement the right to health will vary significantly from one State to another'. While GC14 does not make direct reference to the phrase 'all appropriate means', it specifically indicates where the term 'appropriate' is to be used. For instance, interpreting the right to health as extending to timely and 'appropriate' health care;[39] 'appropriate' treatment of prevalent diseases;[40] 'appropriate' measures to abolish harmful traditional practices;[41] the state to adopt 'appropriate' legislative, budgetary and other measures towards implementing the right to health[42] or 'appropriate' remedies for violations.[43] The term simply denotes suitability of the approach taken towards achieving something.

GC3 describes what is meant by 'all appropriate means.' It is first the obligation of a state to adopt legislative measures.[44] Second, for the state to

---

[38] United Nations General Assembly Official Records, Document A/2929 Annotations on the text of the draft International Covenants on Human Rights, Agenda item 28 (Part II) Annexes, Tenth Session, UN Doc A/2929 (1/7/1955). para. 19,

[39] Paragraph 11, GC 14 (n 24).

[40] Paragraph 17, GC 14 (n 24).

[41] Paragraph 22, GC 14 (n 24).

[42] Paragraph 33, GC 14 (n 24).

[43] Paragraph 59, GC 14 (n 24).

[44] Paragraph 3, GC 3 (n 32).

provide judicial remedies with respect to justiciable rights.[45] Third, for the state to give effect to the full and natural meaning of the phrase by deciding for itself which means are the most appropriate under the circumstances with respect to each of the rights, recognising that the 'appropriateness' of the means chosen will not always be self-evident.[46] Fourth, to consider other measures not limited to administrative, financial, educational and social measures. However, finance is not placed at par with legislative measures and judicial remedies. It is categorised as part of 'other measures', thus weakening its link to the MAR obligation in realising the right to health. To fully understand a state's MAR obligation, requires analysing what states interpret as appropriate towards implementing the right to health. This is considered in the next section.

In summary, the interpretation of MAR in the context of the right to health is characterised by ambiguity and ongoing scholarly debate, with key terms such as 'deliberate, concrete, and targeted,' 'take steps,' 'whatever steps,' and 'all appropriate means' remaining open-ended. The onerous and wide-ranging duties associated with realising the right to health necessitate significant financial resources and a creative approach that is both permissible under human rights law and compatible with domestic legislation. The lack of consensus on the scope and parameters of MAR implies that the obligation remains open for further political and scholarly engagement.

Re-interpreting the MAR Obligation to Give Recourse to *Zakat*

Human rights law gives states a wide margin of discretion in matters of economic and social policy, acknowledging that they are often faced with invidious choices regarding the resources to be assigned to competing social policy priorities within their existing budgetary constraints.[47] In this

---

[45] Paragraph 5, GC 3 (n 32).
[46] Paragraph 4, GC 3 (n 32).
[47] Paragraph 53, GC 14 (n 24).

regard, when CESCR supervises and monitors progress of State Parties' compliance with their obligations it makes recommendations to the state on the economic and social goals to prioritise commensurate to its fiscal capacity.[48] In so doing, CESCR plays a significant role in establishing the normative content of the right to health setting out the state's approach to its MAR obligation. CESCR has pointed out in various Concluding Observations for Kenya that inadequate efforts by the state to generate more resources can pose a serious obstacle to the realisation of rights.[49]

Whence and how are more resources for implementing the right to health to be mobilised from? The MAR obligation set out in the ICESCR, GC14 and GC3 provide no guidance on a normative or descriptive formulation for a state to consider in broadening its revenue base to allow recourse to non-state funds available domestically. The language is simple and open for each state to interpret it in its local context. In this regard, the ICESCR should also explicitly set out the conceptual and operational framework for MAR. This, however, has not been done. Legal permissibility to achieve a broadened interpretation of MAR can be achieved through articles 31 and 32 of the Vienna Convention on the Law of Treaties. These articles demand attention be given to the text, context, object, and purpose of a treaty in a systematic manner. According to Tobin, the articles permit an evolutive reading of human rights treaties.[50] Evolutive interpretation is both normative and descriptive. This is discussed on page 63 as the interpretative approach has received scholarly attention while CESCR has not provided direction on its use to discern the MAR obligation.

This does not prevent states from applying the evolutive interpretation since the ICESCR has a territorial scope, which means that every State Party to the ICESCR is under an obligation to take all appropriate national

---

[48] (n 33) 905.

[49] United Nations Committee on Economic Social and Cultural Rights, 'Concluding observations on the combined second to fifth periodic reports of Kenya' E/C.12/KEN/CO/2-5; also: E/C.12/KEN/CO/1, E/1995/22(SUPP) paras. 159-164, E/C.12/1993/6.

[50] J Tobin, *The Right to Health in International Law* (Oxford: Oxford University Press, 2012).

measures to progressively realise the right to health. This does not prevent states from applying article 31 and 32 of the Vienna Convention, in individually interpreting ICESCR and its normative content under GC14 to discover on its own how to characterise the MAR obligation for exacting a broad category of finances that can be made available to the state.

From the perspective of Kenya, which has not ratified the Vienna Convention on the Law of Treaties, the challenge lies in making use of the evolutive approach to interpret the MAR obligation within the ICESCR framework. However, it is important to note that Kenya is still bound by customary international law, which encompasses the general principles of treaty interpretation, including the systematic interpretation of treaty provisions based on their text, context, object, and purpose. In this context, the Kenyan government could utilise the evolutive approach to interpret the MAR obligation by considering its unique domestic circumstances and needs. This would involve a careful examination of the text of the ICESCR and General Comments 14 and 3, as well as the object and purpose of the right to health. By adopting this approach, Kenya could potentially develop a broader understanding of its MAR obligation that encompasses a wider range of financial resources, including those available from non-state actors within its territory, such as *zakat*.

MAR: A focus on taxes

In the quest for a deeper understanding of a state's obligation in financing the realisation of the right to health, this section embarks on a critical exploration of the scope of MAR with a focus on domestically mobilised financial resources, an area of scholarship that has primarily centred on taxation,[51] and the pivotal role of states in defining and implementing the normative content of the right to health as stipulated in the ICESCR and the General Comments.[52] The role of the state facilitates an understanding of how the right to health is promoted at the national level. Given the

---

[51] (n 2) – (n 5), (n 8), (n 13) and (n 17).

[52] MCR Craven, 'The International Covenant on Economic, Social and Cultural Rights – A Perspective on its Development', PhD thesis, University of Nottingham 1995, 144.

importance of states in implementing human rights, and the recognition of the non-binding nature of General Comments and Concluding Observations, it becomes important to consider how human rights treaties are to be interpreted, and the extent to which interpretation convinces and persuades states to accept the normative content of rights and to prioritise their financing.

Supporting this consideration, two basic rules are established in article 31(1) of the Vienna Convention. The first is on interpreting treaties in good faith, and the second, in applying the ordinary meaning of its terms. The ordinary meaning of a treaty's terms should be considered together with the context, the object and the purpose of the treaty.[53] This rule permits reference to materials related to the conclusion of the treaty.[54] This means that subsequent agreements regarding the interpretation of a treaty or subsequent practice in the application of a treaty are to be taken into account, together with the context.[55] In *Wemhoff v Federal Republic of Germany*, the court ruled that the objective in considering the object and purpose of a treaty is to seek the interpretation that is most appropriate to achieve the aims of a treaty.[56] This allows reference to be made to preparatory work (*travaux préparatoires)* of the treaty, to confirm the meanings it intended to give to its provisions.

Since the ICESCR imposes upon the state the obligation to fulfil the right to health, states have an interest in interpreting them restrictively[57] to retain discretion in domestic health policymaking, and thereby ease their burden. To prevent giving states a wide latitude to restrict their obligations, the responsibility for determining how the right to health can be realised and whether states have fulfilled their obligations primarily lies with CESCR. However, states can through 'subsequent practice' generated out of the

---

[53] (n 16) art 31(1).
[54] ibid, art 31(2)(a).
[55] ibid, art 31(3).
[56] *Wemhoff v Federal Republic of Germany*, 1 Eur Ct HR (ser A) 55, 75 (1968).
[57] L Henkin, 'The International Bill of Rights: The Universal Declaration and the Covenants' in R Bernhardt and JA Jolowics (eds) *International Enforcement of Human Rights* (1985) 8; (n 33) 919.

General Comments that CESCR publishes exercise discretion on whether or not to implement CESCR interpretations of the obligations states are bound to under the ICESCR. General Comments provide interpretive assistance to state bodies tasked with implementing the ICESCR and domestic legislation guaranteeing rights.[58]

In article 43(1)(a) of the Constitution of Kenya, the state recognises the 'right to the highest attainable standard of health', and in article 20(5), recognises the significance of resources towards its achievement. Under article 20(5), the state reveals its interpretative approach towards its MAR obligation stating that its responsibility depends on the adequacy of resources. This move by the Kenyan state is a confirmation of article 2.1 of the ICESCR and a recognition of GC14, that also bases the achievement of the right to health on the availability of resources. A literal interpretation of the ICESCR is noted. The Kenyan Constitution does no more to advance the meaning and scope of the resources to which it refers, nor on overcoming their limitations by expanding the scope of MAR. An identification of the resources referred to as part of the MAR obligation is made in GC14. They are identified as 'legislative, administrative, budgetary, judicial, promotional and other measures towards the full realisation of the right to health'.[59] These are the resources that states are obliged to secure as part of their MAR obligation.

The reference to the budget as part of the state's MAR obligation, therefore, establishes its fiscal responsibility towards securing the right to health. The budget is considered as the appropriate measure with which to finance the realisation of the right to health.[60] No further content on the state's fiscal responsibility is provided in GC14. The recognition of 'budgetary' measures as part of the MAR obligation suggests this to mean: all sources of revenue that a state can mobilise locally. Usually, budgetary references

---

[58] Makau wa Mutua, 'Looking Past the Human Rights Committee: An Argument for De-Marginalizing Enforcement', (1998) 4 *Buffalo Human Rights Law Review* 211, 231.

[59] Paragraph 33, General Comment 14 (n 24).

[60] BAM O'Hare, 'Tax and the Right to Health,' (2018) *Health Hum Rights*, 20(2): 57-63.

relate to taxes.[61] This is because the state is seen as the primary duty bearer in implementing rights. This seems to exclude religious sources of funds from the scope of MAR, because the primary duty bearer does not refer to religious institutions in carrying out its obligations, nor considers religious sources of funds as part of its fiscal space.

Neither do ICESCR and GC14 place the MAR obligation on third parties or non-state actors as opposed to State Parties. This has the effect of removing *zakat* from the scope of MAR when considering its ordinary meaning, since the purpose of the MAR obligation is on states to budget through the allocation of taxes towards the implementation of the right to health. GC3 on the Nature of State Parties Obligations seems to also suggest measures other than the budget. It states that each state must decide for itself which means are the most appropriate under the circumstances, with respect to each of the rights enshrined under the ICESCR.[62] However, the ultimate determination as to the appropriateness of measures remains one for the CESCR to make.[63]

No mention is made in the CESCR's General Comments on the appropriateness or suitability of including *zakat* as part of the state's budgetary measures under its MAR obligation, the focus is on taxes. Nor were any references to sources other than taxes that I found when searching the Concluding Observations issued to individual countries. I undertook a manual check of all Concluding Observations available on OHCHR's website[64] by downloading all the 514 pdf files, and individually searching for the terms: *zakat*, Islamic funds, religious funds, philanthropy, social finance, or community funds. This was necessary to confirm whether the CESCR included any of these terms or considered them appropriate in

---

[61] JR Hellerstein and W Hellerstein, *State Taxation* (Warren Gorham Lamont, 1998).

[62] Paragraph 4 General Comment 3 (n 32).

[63] S Leckie and A Gallagher, *Economic, Social and Cultural Rights: A Legal Resource Guide* (University of Pennsylvania Press, 2006) 287.

[64] OHCHR, United Nations Human Rights Treaty Bodies: UN Treaty Body Database, Available: https://tbinternet.ohchr.org/_layouts/15/treatybodyexternal/TBSearch.aspx?Lang=en&TreatyID=9&DocTypeID=5

specifying the scope of MAR, which would justify recourse to those funds by the state.

Clarity, therefore, in analysing the scope of MAR can be achieved through legislation relating to the implementation of rights or through evolutive interpretation which can allow states to consider alternative approaches to the meaning of treaty terms. Article 2.1 recognises the high desirability of adopting legislative measures, as these provide legal certainty. A sound legislative foundation for MAR is necessary to define its scope. Financing the right to health depends on such legal certainty as to the availability of funds. While this remains pending with CESCR, human rights scholarship over the years has contributed to analysing MAR.[65]

In interpreting the MAR obligations under the ICESCR, the use of evolutive interpretation is necessary to link its interpretation to permit alternative sources of revenue directed towards financing rights. This interpretative approach can give credibility to the possibility of widening the MAR scope to include *zakat*. It is futile to rely on the legal interpretation of MAR to analyse its scope, due to the doctrinal omission in ICESCR and the General Comments specifying scope. In instances such as these, the legal force and impact of advancing the scope of MAR to include *zakat* will depend on how convincingly and persuasively it is argued by the state seeking recourse to the funds as part of its obligation of conduct and of result. Whether the MAR obligation has the conceptual and operational potential to make a distinctive contribution towards recourse to *zakat* is analysed next.

MAR: Recourse to *zakat*

In exploring the scope of MAR, the General Comments provide limited guidance on the specific sources of revenue that can be made available to a state or are at its disposal. Moreover, there is no explicit mention of other resources that could potentially be mobilised by the state to fulfil its obligations. When interpreting the scope of MAR, GC14 refers to the

---

[65] (n 2) – (n 5), (n 8), (n 13) and (n 17).

budget,[66] whereas GC3 adopts a broader perspective by employing the term 'financial' measures.[67] By examining the ordinary meaning of the text, the reference to the budget implies the state's obligation to allocate tax revenue towards the realisation of the right to health, as taxes constitute a significant portion of a state's budget.[68] On the other hand, the ordinary meaning of 'financial measures'—considering the context of the right to health and the purpose of the ICESCR as elaborated in GC14—encompasses government initiatives such as promoting affordable health insurance, subsidising out-of-pocket payments, resorting to credit agreements, donor aid, and official development assistance aimed at financing the core obligations of the right to health.[69]

Given that the MAR obligation pertains to the state, its scope is limited to the sources of funds accessible by the state. Consequently, the MAR obligation is predominantly tied to taxes. This understanding of the MAR obligation presents an opportunity for further academic inquiry and debate, as scholars and policymakers explore alternative sources of funding and revenue generation to progressively realise the right to health.

The CESCR, in its Concluding Observations for Kenya, underscores the importance of raising national revenues and increasing reliance on domestic resources.[70] It also highlights the need to augment public funding levels to ensure the progressive realisation of health and other rights.[71] By acknowledging the allocation of taxes to finance health as part of a state's MAR obligation, the CESCR provides valuable insight into the scope of MAR. Furthermore, the CESCR recognises the significance of relying on

---

66 Paragraph 33, General Comment 14 (n 24).

67 Paragraph 7, General Comment 3 (n 32).

68 BAM O'Hare, 'Tax and the Right to Health,' (2018) *Health Hum Rights*, 20(2): 57-63.

69 Paragraphs 36, 39 General Comment 14 (n 24).

70 United Nations, Committee on Economic, Social and Cultural Rights, Concluding Observations on the Combined Second to Fifth Periodic Reports of Kenya, adopted by the Committee at its 57th session (22 February-4 March, 2016) E/C.12/KEN/CO/2-5, Paragraph 18.

71 United Nations, Committee on Economic Social and Cultural Rights, 'An Evaluation of the Obligation to Take Steps to the 'Maximum of Available Resources' under an Optional Protocol to the Covenant' UN Doc. E/C.12/2007/1 (2007).

domestic resources, although it does not elaborate on the nature of these resources.

Given that GC14 presents an abstract rather than contextual development of the right to health's content, it leaves ample room for persuasion and influence on national decision-makers when determining the extent to which they may consider broadening the scope of their MAR obligation to include, for instance, *zakat*. The argument put forth here is that the CESCR's recognition of domestic resources' reliance expands the financial scope of a state's MAR obligation to encompass the acceptance of *zakat*, which, as demonstrated in Chapter 7, constitutes a domestic resource. This recognition could potentially shape state practices in interpreting or elaborating on the scope of MAR.

The relevance of *zakat*, therefore, permits the state, as part of its obligation of result, to engage in dialogue with the Muslim community regarding the possibility of supporting the state in financing the implementation of health initiatives. This academic exploration encourages further discussion on the potential of alternative domestic resources, such as *zakat*, in contributing to the progressive realisation of the right to health, while emphasising the importance of an inclusive and comprehensive approach to understanding the scope of MAR obligations.

The understanding of MAR as the state's obligation of conduct and result, as indicated in GC3, highlights the potential avenues a state can explore when taking steps to ensure at least the core content of rights. The obligation of result necessitates that the state guarantees the attainment of a particular situation or specified outcome, while allowing the state the freedom to achieve such a situation through its chosen means.[72] This notion of choice provides the state with the opportunity to consider broadening its MAR obligation to include the acceptance of *zakat* as part of its fiscal strategy for financing health. However, the applicability of *zakat* within the context of article 2.1 of the ICESCR and the understanding of state obligations for financing health under GC14 remains ambiguous.

---

[72] (n 35) 364.

Considering that all obligations under the ICESCR are subject to resource constraints, which result from the state's diminishing fiscal space due to prevailing economic difficulties and debt servicing, the expansion of the MAR scope to encompass *zakat* is not inconsistent with the ICESCR's purpose.

In this academic exploration, I propose a more inclusive and comprehensive approach to understanding the scope of MAR obligations by considering the potential of alternative domestic resources, such as *zakat*, in contributing to the progressive realisation of the right to health. By examining the various possibilities within the state's obligations of conduct and result, I encourage further dialogue and research on the potential for integrating *zakat* and other non-traditional resources into the fiscal strategies aimed at financing health initiatives and fulfilling human rights obligations.

The ICESCR indeed focuses on the role of international assistance, without explicitly mentioning domestic assistance. Drawing an analogy between international assistance and the potential use of *zakat* as a domestic resource, however, can offer a broader perspective on the ways states can mobilise funds for the realisation of rights. While it is true that the treaty binds State Parties and extending the obligation of conduct and result to non-state actors might not be the ICESCR's intended purpose, exploring alternative domestic resources, such as *zakat*, can provide additional avenues for states to fulfil their human rights obligations.

Article 22 of the ICESCR acknowledges the potential contributions of international organisations and bodies in achieving rights, but it does not impose any obligations on them. As a result, one might argue that the scope of MAR under the ICESCR and GC14 is indeed restrictive. This argument finds support in the *Grootboom* and *Treatment Action Campaign* judgments, in which the South African Constitutional Court, while interpreting the ICESCR, ruled that a state is not obliged to go beyond its available resources.[73] However, the consideration of *zakat* as a potential domestic resource does not necessarily imply that states would be obligated to access these funds. Instead, it offers an additional option for states to explore in their efforts to fulfil their human rights obligations. In this context, recourse to *zakat* may be viewed as an opportunity, rather than an obligation, for states to expand their fiscal strategies and improve the progressive realisation of the right to health and other rights enshrined in the ICESCR.

As such, expanding the discussion on the scope of MAR to include alternative domestic resources, such as *zakat,* can promote a more comprehensive understanding of states' fiscal capacities and strategies in fulfilling their human rights obligations. This approach encourages further dialogue and research on the potential integration of non-traditional resources into fiscal strategies for financing health initiatives and realising human rights.

Although the state has some degree of flexibility in selecting and incorporating various sources of revenue into its financial strategy, the ultimate interpretative authority lies with the CESCR. As of now, the CESCR has not published a General Comment specifically addressing the content of MAR. In 2007, the CESCR issued "An Evaluation of the Obligation to Take Steps to the 'Maximum of Available Resources' under an Optional Protocol to the Covenant,"[74] with the primary goal of assisting the CESCR in monitoring State Parties' implementation of the ICESCR. The Optional Protocol focuses on providing the CESCR with criteria to assess the adequacy or reasonableness of measures undertaken by states as part of their MAR obligation, but it does not explicitly discuss the types of financial measures states should implement. The CESCR's reference to domestic resources in the Concluding Observations for Kenya is an indication that it is upon a state to consider what potential financial measures, such as *zakat,* that states could include as part of their fiscal

[73] *Government of the Republic of South Africa & Others v Grootboom,* 2000 (11) BCLR 1169 (CC), 94; and *Minister of Health & Others v Treatment Action Campaign & Others,* 2002 (10) BCLR 1033 (CC), 35 (South Africa)
[74] (n 71).

strategy. However, the scope of MAR under the ICESCR remains somewhat ambiguous and incomplete.

Consequently, turning to scholarly research is a justified approach to advancing an evolutive interpretation of MAR. Further exploration of the evolutive interpretation of MAR may provide valuable insights into the range of financial measures that could be considered within a state's fiscal strategy, including non-traditional sources such as *zakat*. Expanding the discussion on the scope of MAR in this manner encourages ongoing dialogue and academic inquiry, shedding light on novel approaches to resource mobilisation and fostering a more comprehensive understanding of states' obligations in realising human rights. As scholarship continues to evolve, it may eventually prompt the CESCR to refine its interpretation of MAR and provide clearer guidance for State Parties in fulfilling their obligations under the ICESCR.

Human Rights Scholarship on the Scope of MAR

The previous section elucidated the interpretation of the ICESCR and GC14 and discussed the right to health in the context of state obligations. This section posits that while the ICESCR introduced the MAR obligation, it is human rights scholarship that has played a crucial role in further clarifying its scope. However, such scholarship has largely avoided examining the potential contribution of Islam to the conceptualisation of MAR. To attain a more coherent understanding of MAR's scope, a deeper exploration of its interpretation is warranted.

The ICESCR does not comprehensively detail the financial obligations incumbent upon states; instead, these are deduced through interpretative rules. State practice demonstrates whether the MAR obligation is confined to allocating a specific proportion of taxes for the realisation of rights, or whether it entails linking other financial measures to such realisation. The following chapter examines this aspect, while the current chapter contends that interpretative scope exists within the ICESCR, GC14, and GC3 for an evolutive understanding of MAR's content. The CESCR's failure to expand MAR's scope to encompass *zakat* or other forms of religious funding results in vague state obligations and undermines a comprehensive articulation of MAR's scope and content. Consequently, there is an opening for academic scrutiny.

Although human rights scholarship has contributed significantly to clarifying MAR's scope, it has largely neglected to explore whether Islam can inform its conceptualisation. The right to health entails substantial resource implications, prompting scholars to scrutinise the extent to which the MAR obligation permits states to access funds beyond domestic taxes. Scholarship has also shaped the meaning of MAR. While the ICESCR and General Comments have elaborated on the substantive content of the right to health, scholarship has provided options for its realisation. The impact of scholarship on MAR depends on the quality of arguments and the degree to which the ICESCR is examined in a "serious, probing, and illuminating manner."[75] This may encourage states to incorporate academic insights into domestic law, guiding state practice of their MAR obligations.

Human rights scholarship on MAR oscillates between identifying additional funding sources to support states' MAR obligations and exploring ways to optimise already available resources. The former provides an avenue within scholarship to question the legality of incorporating *zakat* into the interpretation of MAR. This does not delve into considerations regarding the optimisation of resources already at the state's disposal; an area extensively investigated by Skogly.[76] Key insights into the development of MAR's scope have been offered by Robertson,[77] whose work serves as the primary foundation for this discussion. Tobin's[78] methodological approach aids in understanding how human rights are interpreted to support the legal analysis of state obligations and offers a

---

[75] H Steiner, 'Individual Claims in a World of Massive Violations: What Role for the Human Rights Committee', in P Alston and J Crawford (eds) *The Future of UN Human Rights Treaty Monitoring* (Cambridge: Cambridge University Press, 2000), 49.

[76] (n 5).

[77] (n 17).

[78] (n 50).

valuable framework for considering academic insights stemming from Robertson's contribution to the scope of MAR.

A comprehensive investigation of MAR's scope can be attributed to Robertson, who argued that MAR was a complex phrase, encompassing "two warring adjectives describing an undefined noun."[79] He elucidated that "maximum" represented idealism, while "available" signified reality. In his view, "maximum" constituted the "sword of human rights rhetoric," and "available" provided the "wiggle room" for the state.[80] Consequently, understanding Robertson's conceptualisation of MAR's scope is crucial. He begins by referring to article 2.1 of the ICESCR, which states that the state's obligation is "to take steps... to the maximum of its available resources." In this context, "steps" denote specific actions, and "resources" refer to the elements upon which the satisfaction of rights depends.[81] In implementing the right to health, a law mandating universal health coverage is a step, whereas hospitals, health workers, and essential medicines are the necessary resources for ensuring health provision.

Robertson contends that it is impossible to produce a truly definitive list of resources that a state must mobilise, as the ongoing processes of economic, digital, and social evolution continually generate different categories of resources. Instead, he identifies five traditional forms of resources that he believes delineate MAR's scope: financial, natural, technological, informational, and human resources.[82] These categories are also acknowledged by Skogly[83], Andersen[84], and Kendrick[85]. Robertson additionally recognises a sixth resource, the organisational resource

---

79 (n 17) at 694.
80 ibid.
81 (n 2).
77 (n 17) at 696-7.
83 (n 5).
84 E Andersen, 'A New Approach to Assessing State Compliance with the Obligation to Devote Maximum Available Resources to Realise Economic, Social and Cultural Rights' (2010) DEV Working Paper 26.
85 A Kendrick, 'Measuring Compliance: Social Rights and the Maximum Available Resources Dilemma', (2017) *Human Rights Quarterly*, Volume 39, Number 3, 657-679.

(discussed later), which is posited by UNICEF (a UN body reliant on voluntary contributions for supporting children's wellbeing).

While Robertson offers an indicative list of financial resources, subsequent scholars have largely confined this category to taxes. The financial scope of MAR, linked to taxes, is evident in the works of Balakrishnan[86], Elson[87], McIntyre[88], and Waris[89]. These scholars argue that MAR pertains to a state's tax base and tax policy, suggesting that the scope of MAR can be expanded by increasing taxes and introducing new taxes. Tomasevski, the Special Rapporteur on the right to education from 1998 to 2004, similarly highlights the reliance on taxes for financing health, education, water and sanitation, and assistance for those unable to work:

> 'It is hard to imagine how any state would raise the revenue to finance health, education, water and sanitation, or assistance for those too young or too old to work, were it not for taxation'.[90]

Olivier de Schutter, former Special Rapporteur on the right to food (2008-2014), has also emphasised the role of taxes within the scope of MAR.[91] Furthermore, Dowell-Jones and Kinley[92] have associated MAR's scope with public finance, proposing that the scope encompasses finances mobilised through securities exchange markets. As such, treasury bills and bonds should be considered within the scope of MAR, to be utilised for the realisation of rights. To date, a relatively narrow interpretation of the financial scope of MAR has prevailed in the academic literature.

---

86 (n 2).

87 ibid 13-39.

88 (n 4).

89 (n 3).

90 K Tomasevski, Background Paper submitted by Special Rapporteur on the Right to Education, Committee on Economic, Social and Cultural Rights, 19th Session (UN Doc E/C.12/1998/18) 5.

91 O Schutter, Report of the Special Rapporteur on the Right to Food – Mission to Brazil (UN Doc A/HRC/13/33/Add.6, 2009) para 36.

92 M Dowell Jones and D Kinley, 'Minding the Gap: Global Finance and Human Rights', (2011) *Ethics & International Affairs*, 25, No 2, 183-210.

Human rights scholars have acknowledged the significance of government revenues, including taxation and official development aid, as well as public expenditure within the scope of MAR. Notably, during the drafting of the ICESCR, American and Danish delegates agreed that resources should encompass both international and domestic sources.[93] Subsequently, in 1992, Danilo Turk suggested a broad interpretation of available resources. He argued that states, aware of their inadequacies, should allow various grassroots initiatives to flourish in order to address citizens' needs:

> People's movements, campaigns and initiatives aimed at satisfying citizen's needs… as perhaps one of the few means by which people who are organised can express themselves and create solutions for their many predicaments.[94]

Turk referred to this as the state "creating space" for the mobilisation of private resources, [95] recognising the value of local communities in supporting the state's MAR obligation to realize rights. This space recognises the value of local communities supporting the state in its MAR obligation to realise rights. Turk maintained that '[t]he issue of official legality should not be employed by a state to deny citizens the ability to fulfilling there [sic] own needs when the state is unwilling or incapable of doing so'.[96]

According to Turk, legal formalities should not be employed by a state to deny citizens the ability to fulfil their own needs when the state is unwilling or incapable of doing so. Based on these observations, it can be argued that the scope of MAR extends beyond the resources under the direct control of

---

[93] P Alston, and F Quinn, 'The Nature and Scope of State Parties' Obligations under the International Covenant on Economic, Social and Cultural Rights', (1987) 9 *HUM RTS Q* 156, 179-80.

[94] The Realisation of Economic, Social and Cultural Rights: Final Report Submitted by Danilo Turk, Special Rapporteur, UN Commission on Human Rights, Sub-Commission on Prevention of Discrimination and Protection of Minorities, 44th Sess, Prov Agenda Item 8, at 50, 192, UN Doc No E/CN4/Sub 2/1992/16 (1992).

[95] ibid.

[96] ibid.

the state. While article 2.1 of the ICESCR obliges states to consider recourse to resources available through international assistance and cooperation, there is no equivalent obligation to consider domestic assistance within MAR. Nevertheless, this obligation can be established by analogy with international assistance.

Robertson's identification of six forms of resources, including the organisational resource, provides the flexibility to consider whether the MAR obligation allows for the inclusion of domestic assistance, and consequently, access to funds not explicitly contemplated by the CESCR, such as *zakat*. Organisational structure encompasses community organisations, cooperatives, trade unions, religious organisations, and private sector institutions.[97] These organisational structures represent non-state actors as available resources from which states can seek assistance. Funds accessible by these organisations should therefore be considered within the scope of MAR.

While governments may not have direct control over private donations, they can encourage giving through tax policies that incentivise charitable contributions, such as *zakat*. Moreover, states can establish reliable mechanisms to collect and utilise such funds, aligning with their obligations of conduct and results discussed earlier. This chapter aims to bridge the gap in the literature by linking private sources of funds to the state's obligation of result as part of MAR, applying Tobin's interpretative methodology to demonstrate this connection.

Tobin argues that human rights law develops through an interpretative process capable of absorbing new meanings that advance the normative content of rights. This evolutive interpretation must be based on certain principles to ensure the legitimacy of new interpretations or the insertion of new content to advance the meaning of human rights obligations. To determine the legitimacy of *zakat* within the scope of MAR, it is necessary

---

[97] JR Himes, 'Implementing the United Nations Convention on the Rights of the Child: Resource Mobilisation and The Obligations of the State Parties' (Innocenti Occasional Papers, 2 Child Rights Series, 1992).

to conduct fieldwork to confirm stakeholders' acceptance of linking *zakat* to health financing and allowing state recourse to these funds.

While the General Comments provide interpretative guidance to states, the margin of discretion allows states to define a set of financial measures they perceive as useful towards the realisation of rights.[98] Given their discretion, states can interpret their obligations restrictively.[99] I argue that the use of the term "margin of discretion" in Tobin's approach should be seen as creating positive, not restrictive, obligations for the state, permitting states to contribute to new and evolutive interpretations or insert new content to advance the meaning of their human rights obligations.[100] This expands the scope of MAR to include resources that can be made available through non-state actors (organisational structure). While this position is compelling, there is limited evidence of state practice, except for the Kenyan state expressing its intention in its health policy to rely on non-state resources (discussed in Chapter 3). In Chapter 7, fieldwork accounts are presented to explore the practicability of this position.

The full potential of MAR will be realised over time, necessitating an interpretive approach beyond the Vienna Convention's rules of interpretation. Tobin's criteria for interpreting the scope of MAR under the ICESCR and GC14 allows for testing the evolutive interpretive approach. Focusing on the margin of discretion given to states, Tobin's approach addresses local context peculiarities and acknowledges the importance of non-state actors in implementing the right to health. This margin of discretion aligns with the views of Balakrishnan, Elson, and Greer, who highlight states' discretion in selecting means to carry out their obligations, including the provision of health services subject to resource availability. Balakrishnan and Elson note that states enjoy a margin of discretion in selecting the means to carry out their obligations.[101] Greer explains further

---

[98] Paragraph 53 General Comment 14 (n 24).

[99] ibid.

[100] (n 57) 8; (n 33) 919.

[101] R Balakrishnan and D Elson, *Economic Policy and Human Rights: Holding Governments to Account* (Zed Books, 2011).

that such a margin relates to 'implementation discretion'[102] – meaning that the state can choose, for example, which health service to provide, and when and how, subject to resource availability. Such legal recognition of human rights and their subjection to resource availability raises a concern over whether the human rights legal system is amenable to their financial maintenance. The MAR obligation must emphasise that rights require financial resources for their implementation.

By connecting the margin of discretion with the principle of public participation, Tobin allows non-state actors, at the state's discretion, to join the ICESCR's "interpretative community" and offer recommendations on the scope of MAR.[103] This interpretive approach creates the flexibility – the 'wiggle room'[104], that Robertson foresaw, extending the scope of MAR to potentially include faith-sourced funds like *zakat*. Advancing the scope of MAR should be influenced by state practice, with every state having a margin of discretion in assessing suitable measures for their specific circumstances.[105]

States have accepted their MAR obligation under the ICESCR through ratification and submission of periodic reports to the CESCR.[106] This chapter contends that refining the scope of MAR to encompass faith-sourced funds, such as *zakat*, is essential. However, the inclusion of religious sources in human rights scholarship is lacking, primarily due to the conceptual and institutional separation between Islamic law and human rights. This separation stems from the secular/separationist approach and the argument that Islamic law is incompatible with human rights. Nonetheless, this situation is evolving, with many Muslim donors and development NGOs mobilising *zakat* to fund projects that advance human rights. Despite these practical developments, Islamic law has yet to

---

[102] S Greer, 'The Margin of Appreciation: Interpretation and Discretion under the European Convention on Human Rights', (2000) *Human Rights Files* No 17, Council of Europe.

[103] (n 50) 78.

[104] (n 17) 694.

[105] Paragraph 53, General Comment 14 (n 24)

[106] (n 15).

find its place within human rights discourse. The challenge lies in building bridges between these two fields in theory, as well as in practice.

While there is no legal obligation for the Muslim community to assist the state in achieving the right to health, health and well-being are priorities under Islamic law. *Zakat* is not owned or controlled by the state, presenting a new dimension to MAR and state obligation. Although calling it a "new dimension" might be misleading, the argument for recognising and including community resources as part of the MAR obligation can be traced back to the Declaration on the Right and Responsibility of Individuals, Groups, and Organs of Society to Promote and Protect Universally Recognized Human Rights and Fundamental Freedoms[107] that was adopted[108] by all State Parties in 1999. This Declaration asserts that everyone has the right to promote and strive for the protection and realisation of human rights and fundamental freedoms at national and international levels.

Article 7 of the Declaration states that: 'Everyone has the right, individually and in association with others, to develop and discuss new human rights ideas and principles and to advocate their acceptance'. Article 13 asserts that: Everyone has the right, individually and in association with others, to solicit, receive and utilise resources for the express purpose of promoting and protecting human rights and fundamental freedoms…' Scholarship following the Declaration is limited towards addressing two main issues. First, the legal recognition and protection of human rights defenders to work in a safe, supportive environment and to be free from attacks,

---

[107] United Nations Office of the High Commissioner for Human Rights (OHCHR), *Commentary to the Declaration on the Right and Responsibility of Individuals, Groups and Organs of Society to Promote and Protect Universally Recognized Human Rights and Fundamental Freedoms,* July 2011. Available at: https://www.refworld.org/docid/4e2fc3f02.html

[108] United Nations General Assembly. *Fifty third Session, 85th plenary meeting,* A/53/PV.85 adopted on Wednesday, 9th December 1998, 3pm, New York. Proceedings available at: https://digitallibrary.un.org/record/265554?ln=en. Kenya delegation present. Declaration adopted without vote. No objections from Kenya.

reprisals and unreasonable restrictions.[109] The second issue addresses the misgivings over who is responsible for adhering to the morals prescribed within the Declaration.[110] Specific academic engagement in inquiring into the Declaration as the fecund for discourse on the role of local communities mobilising financial resources for rights is non-extant. The closest discussion on local community revenue mobilisation is contained in the work of Sanchez who emphasised the importance of communities in being responsible for realising and achieving human rights.[111]

Later, Giacomazzi argued that the concept of the community being responsible for the achievement of rights is not new to the world.[112] She explained that some cultures operate upon the understanding that people also have duties to themselves, each other, their communities and their world. She contends that it is, therefore, important to revisit the issue of community responsibility towards the realisation of rights. Similarly, Clarke picked up on this and argued from the perspective of faith-based organisations (FBOs) as 'agents of transformation' mobilising the moral energy of faith communities in support of the (now expired) Millennium

---

[109] K Bennet, D Ingleton, AM Nah et al., 'Critical Perspectives on the Security and Protection of Human Rights Defenders', (2015) *The International Journal of Human Rights,* Vol 19, No.7, 883-895.

[110] H Kung, 'Don't be Afraid of Ethics! Whey we need to talk of responsibilities as well as rights', (n.d) *InterAction Council.* Available at https://www.interactioncouncil.org/publications/dont-be-afraid-ethics-why-we-need-talk-responsibilities-well-rights

[111] OA Sanchez, 'Some Contributions to a Universal Declaration of Human Obligations', (1997) *InterAction Council.* Available at https://www.interactioncouncil.org/publications/some-contributions-universal-declaration-human-obligations. Sanchez referred to rights as obligations. According to him, many societies have traditionally conceived of human relations in terms of obligations rather than rights. This is true, in general terms, for instance for much of Eastern thought. While traditionally in the West the concepts of freedom and individuality have been emphasised, in the East, the notions of responsibility and community have prevailed.

[112] M Giacomazzi, 'Human Rights and Human Responsibilities: A Necessary Balance', (2005) *Santa Clara J. Int'l L.* 3:164.

Development Goals.[113] According to Clarke, Wilson[114] and Herbert[115] development studies have traditionally neglected the role of religion, and its role in the lives of the poor throughout the developing world. They argue that this neglect was heavily influenced by secularisation theory, the belief that religious institutions, actions and consciousness lose their social significance over time as societies modernise. Accordingly, academics and policy makers ignored the role of religion as an analytical lens through which FBOs can help solve the limited resources dilemma that states face in financing rights. This situation has now begun to change but has had limited impact in looking at FBOs linking religious funds to the MAR obligation.

Casanova also argued that religion traditionally focused on the private sphere, on the moral and spiritual regulation of individual conduct. Since the late 20th century, however, religious discourse has developed a new concern with the conduct of public life, and religious leaders and organisations have become more willing to tread the public stage and to highlight the moral and spiritual import of public policy.[116] Subsequently, academic literature has examined growing engagement between donors and faith communities,[117] and the role of such communities in supporting the poor.[118] Research has also examined the relevance of religion in

---

[113] G Clarke, 'Agents of Transformation? Donors, faith-based organisations and international development', (2007) *Third World Quarterly*, Vol. 28, No. 1, 77-96.

[114] B Wilson, *Religion in Sociological Perspective* (Oxford: Oxford University Press, 1992) 49.

[115] D Herbert, *Religion and Civil Society: Rethinking Public Religion in the Contemporary World* (Aldershot: Ashgate, 2003).

[116] J Casanova, *Public Religions in the Modern World* (Chicago, IL: Chicago University Press, 1994).

[117] D Belshaw, R Calderisi & C Sugden (eds), *Faith in Development: Partnership between the World Bank and the Churches in Africa* (Washington, DC: World Bank and Oxford: Regnum Books, 2001); K Marshall & R Marsh (eds), *Millennium Challenges for Development and Faith Institutions* (Washington, DC: World Bank, 2003); and K Marshall & L Keough (eds), *Mind, Heart and Soul in the Fight Against Poverty* (Washington, DC: World Bank, 2004).

[118] D Narayan, R Chambers, MK Shah & P Petesch, *Voices of the Poor: Crying out for Change* (Washington, DC: World Bank and New York: Oxford University Press, 2000).

development and the work of FBOs.[119] What is missing in such examination is linking religious sources of funds to the realisation of the right to health.

Conclusion

This chapter articulates the right to health and looks at scholarship discussing the financial obligations on the state to achieve this right. It argues that human rights law permits an evolutive interpretation of the obligations guiding state responsibility towards the progressive realisation of the right. In particular, the *maximum available resources* (MAR) obligation, if interpreted broadly, offers states with the capacity to source faith-based funds such as *zakat* to supplement their health budget deficits. The permissibility given to a state under ICESCR and GC14 to apply its discretion in setting out its responsibilities boosts the application of evolutive interpretation to broaden the meaning and understanding of MAR. Overall, it can be argued that state obligation under the MAR principle is still under construction. The principle should be further clarified. Support for MAR to include *zakat* can be demonstrated by state practice at a national level. The next chapter, therefore, turns to consider how the Kenyan state implements the right to health, and understands its MAR obligations to discover the potential of opening up MAR to consider recourse to *zakat*.

This chapter reflects a consensus on how the provisions of ICESCR should be interpreted. Legal rules of interpretation have not been employed to formulate or advance the content of MAR, by permitting interpretations that extend the MAR obligation of a state to accepting *zakat* as part of its fiscal approach to financing health. This is because CESCR has not yet extensively set out a comprehensive financial MAR scope, so there is not much to interpret. However, a closer look at human rights scholarship assumes the possibility of broadening the financial scope of MAR and prompting this chapter to make its contribution: human rights scholarship

---

[119] W Tyndale, 'Faith and economics in development: A bridge across the chasm?', (2000) *Development in Practice*, 10 (1), 9 – 18; and KA ver Beek, 'Spirituality: A development taboo', (2000) *Development in Practice*, 10 (1), 2000, 31 – 43.

can accept the inclusion of recourse by a state to *zakat* as part of its MAR obligation. However, this is one part of the argument, under human rights law. Consideration must also be given on whether Islamic law permits the use of *zakat* to finance health and to give it to a non-Islamic state. By focusing on Kenya, it also becomes necessary to question whether its constitutional legal system permits the state to accept *zakat* to finance health in accordance with its Islamic rules. The conditions of legal permissibility are examined in Chapters 4 and 5.

Finally, the chapter highlights the importance of considering political factors in the implementation of the MAR obligation. The potential inclusion of faith-based funds, such as *zakat,* in the fulfilment of MAR obligations, raises important constitutional and political concerns which are explored further in the next chapters. The chapter's main takeaway is that the MAR obligation under human rights law is still under construction, and there is a need for a comprehensive financial MAR scope.

Chapter 3
The Kenyan Approach to Financing Health - *Giving Meaning to Maximum Available Resources*

Introduction

Considering the critical role that states play in implementing human rights, it is essential to examine the interpretation of the maximum available resources (MAR) obligation by the Kenyan state. This chapter investigates whether the Kenyan state has considered adopting an evolutive interpretation of MAR. As demonstrated in Chapter 2, the scope of MAR under the ICESCR remains ambiguous and requires further clarification. This chapter seeks to determine whether the Kenyan state has given MAR a more precise scope. By analysing the development of health policy and law in Kenya, this chapter demonstrates that the ratification of the ICESCR did not necessarily compel the state to adopt legislative measures that mirrored the ICESCR's characterisation of its MAR obligation in implementing the normative content of the right to health. Instead, the state underwent a process of defining its domestic approach to MAR in relation to realising the right to health. The Kenyan approach has been shaped by its colonial history and the 2010 Constitution, which commits the state to guarantee every citizen the highest attainable standard of health.

The significance of this chapter lies in its attempt to address, at least partially, the issue of revenue limitations in financing health in Kenya. The Kenyan state has struggled to meet the financial commitment agreed upon under the 2001 Abuja Declaration, which calls for allocating 15 per cent of its total budget towards improving health.[1] The budget allocated to the health sector between 2000 and 2018 consistently fell short of the 15 per cent target (see Figure 1 below). In the fiscal years 2019-2020 and 2020-2021, the health budget increased to 9.1 per cent and 11.1 per cent, respectively, in response to the COVID-19 pandemic.[2] The health budget shown in Figure 1 includes international assistance (Official Development Assistance, or ODA) and philanthropy extended to the government, through which specific health goals, such as child immunisation, prenatal maternal healthcare, and sexual and reproductive healthcare, are met.[3] Without this external support, the health budget fluctuates between 3 and 6 per cent.[4] This can be attributed to the limited fiscal capacity of the state in mobilising sufficient revenue sources to prioritise public services.[5]

---

[1] Organisation of African Unity, 'Abuja Declaration on HIV/AIDS, Tuberculosis and other Related Infectious Diseases' Adopted at a Special Summit held in Abuja, Nigeria 24-27 April 2001 (OAU/SPS/ABUJA/3), clause 26.

[2] Government of Kenya, Ministry of Health, 'National and County Health Budget Analysis' (Nairobi: Government Printers, 2022), vi.

[3] D Kibira, C Asiimwe, M Muwonge et al., 'Donor Commitments and Disbursements for Sexual and Reproductive Health Aid in Kenya, Tanzania, Uganda and Zambia', (2021) *Front Public Health* 9:645499

[4] LA Latif, 'Can you reap what you don't sow? Health Finance in Kenya's Progress towards Universal Health Coverage', (2019) *Financing for Development* Vol 1, Issue 3, 41-67.

[5] A Kairu, S Orangi, B Mbuthia et al., 'Examining health facility financing in Kenya in the context of devolution', (2021) *BMC Health Services Research* 21:1086.

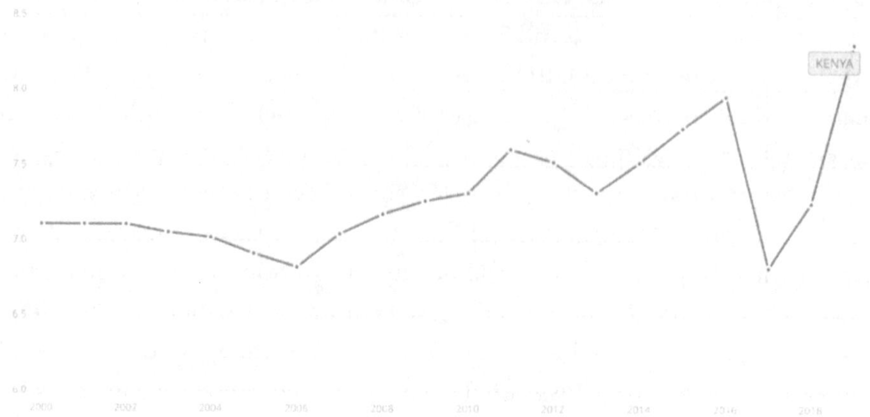

Figure 1: *Health Budget (2000-2018) as percentage of national GDP*

Source: World Bank NHA Database (2022)

The problem of revenue constraints has frequently been cited by governments as a justification for their failure to meet their right to health obligations.[6] Consequently, in 2001, a special African Summit organised by the African Union (AU, then known as the Organisation of African Unity), led to the adoption of the Abuja Declaration. All African countries agreed to address the problem of limited health funds by increasing investments and financing for the sector, which signalled a more robust normative commitment towards health finance. The Abuja commitment has been reiterated in several subsequent African instruments, signed by the Government of Kenya, emphasising the need for a stronger normative commitment to health finance. The Addis Ababa Declaration of 2006 on Community Health in the African Region,[7] the 2008 Ouagadougou Declaration on Primary Health Care and Health Systems in Africa,[8] the

---

[6] L Gostin, K Klock, H Clark et al., Financing the Future of WHO (2022) *The Lancet*, Vol 399, Issue 10334, 1445-1447.

[7] The Addis Ababa Declaration on Community Health in the African Region, 20-22 November 2006. http://www.afro.who.int/publications/addis-abeba-declaration-community-health-african-region-20-22-november-2006

[8] Regional Committee for Africa, Adoption of the Ouagadougou Declaration on primary health care and health systems in Africa: achieving better health for Africa in the new

2012 Tunis Declaration on Value for Money, Sustainability and Accountability in the Health Sector[9] all underscore the necessity to increase health financing. The Abuja Declaration also influenced Aspiration 1 of AU Agenda 2063 of the *Africa We Want* –which outlines Africa's investment priority areas for the next four decades and requires African governments to commit to financing health by increasing its budget.[10]

On 31st January 2015, Kenya endorsed Agenda 2063 at the 24th AU Ordinary Assembly. However, the continental target of allocating 15 per cent of the total budget to the health sector, is not explicitly mentioned in Agenda's Financing and Resource Mobilisation Strategy, which serves as the agenda's operational framework.[11] The strategy remains silent on providing such estimates, it instead acknowledges the fundamental challenge in mobilising finances to achieve the implementation of Africa's priority areas at a national level. The strategy suggests increasing national efforts to mobilise between 75-90 per cent of domestic sources of revenue, primarily through taxes. Agenda 2063 recognises the critical importance of finance in achieving the goals it outlines and proposes the mobilisation of resources from all existing funding mechanisms on the continent.[12] The agenda places the obligation of result (discussed in Chapter 2) on the state to explore and unlock new sources of finance.

As a result, this chapter seeks to investigate the extent to which the Kenyan Government, in fulfilling its MAR obligation, has explored accessing new

---

millennium (World Health Organization. Regional Office for Africa, 2008). http://www.who.int/iris/handle/10665/19989

9 Ministerial Conference on Value for Money, Sustainability and Accountability in the Health Sector. Tunis 4-5 July 2012. http://www.who.int/workforcealliance/media/news/2012/hhaconf2012story/en/

10 African Union Commission. 'Agenda 2063: A Shared Strategic Framework for Inclusive Growth and Sustainable Development'. (2013).

11 The Africa Union Commission, 'A Shared Strategic Framework for Inclusive Growth and Sustainable Development, First Ten-Year Implementation Plan 2014-2023' (2015). Available at: https://www.un.org/en/africa/osaa/pdf/au/agenda2063-first10yearimplementation.pdf

12 Africa Union, Agenda 2063 The Africa We Want (Africa Union Commission, 2015) Clause 72, Sub-clause; o, 20.

sources of finance to realise of the right to health. The Parliamentary Budget Office (PBO) has estimated a health financing revenue gap of KES 32 billion (GBP 221 million) in its Budget Options for 2022/2023 and has warned that resource limitations could hinder the full realisation of the right to health.[13] PBO attributes the shortfall to a steady decline in income tax and value added tax collection over the past five years, which has constrained the state's fiscal capacity to allocate sufficient funds to the health sector.[14] However, the PBO does not offer any recommendations on seeking alternative sources of funding.

Similar to the ICESCR and GC14, the 2010 Constitution of Kenya assigns the responsibility of implementing the right to health to the state while allowing the state to limit this responsibility by demonstrating that 'the resources are not available'.[15] This suggests that finance does not strongly underpin the MAR obligation as strongly as it could. Instead, the constitutional right to health in Kenya should be interpreted more broadly through the adoption of legislative measures.[16] The ICESCR also emphasises the need for states to adopt such measures.[17] Consequently, the Kenyan Parliament passed the 2017 Health Act, providing normative clarification for the right to health.

The Health Act articulates the state's understanding of its obligation to achieve the right to health. Section 86 of the 2017 Health Act outlines the state's health financing strategy – the first since gaining independence in 1963.[18] This chapter contends that the Kenyan state is advancing the MAR obligation by centring its health policy and law around a financing strategy.

---

[13] Parliamentary Service Commission, *Budget Options for 2022/2023 and the Medium Term* (Parliamentary Budget Office, 2022), 54.

[14] ibid, 27.

[15] Republic of Kenya, Constitution of Kenya, 2010 (Nairobi: National Council for Law Reporting, 2010), article 20(5)(a)

[16] ibid, article 21(4).

[17] United Nations, Committee on Economic and Social Council, 'International Covenant on Economic, Social and Cultural Rights.' United Nations, Treaty Series, 16/12/1966, article 2.1

[18] Republic of Kenya, The Health Act, No 17 of 2017 (Nairobi: National Council for Law Reporting, 2017).

By implementing this strategy, the state can legally evaluate whether its financial responsibility towards health can encompass accepting faith-based funds, such as *zakat,* to supplement health budget deficits. A health financing strategy is typically based on the health outcomes identified by the state and follows the state's interpretation of the obligations it must fulfil to implement the right to health.

To delve deeper into this matter, the chapter examines how the Government of Kenya has conceptualised, interpreted, and understood the meaning of the right to health and its MAR obligation. The chapter's discussion is limited to the state's obligation to provide finances and facilitate their allocation towards realising the right to health. The inquiry into the Kenyan state's MAR obligation focuses on determining whether the obligation permits the government to access domestically sourced faith-based funds, such as *zakat*. Each section of the discussion identifies distinct phases between health, its financing, and the role of the state by tracing these aspects through colonial (where necessary) and contemporary periods. The latter part evaluates state-led fiscal policies for health, underscoring the importance of introducing new revenue streams to increase health funding.

In conclusion, the chapter evaluates whether the state's approach to financing health, based on the health strategies and instruments guiding the state in understanding its financial obligations, endures a broadened meaning and understanding of MAR, to possibly include *zakat*. The chapter demonstrates that the Kenyan government is taking strides towards advancing the MAR obligation by developing a health financing strategy centred on identifying health outcomes and reflecting on its financial responsibilities towards public health. This implies that the government is open to considering new sources of finance, such as faith-based funds like *zakat,* to supplement the health budget. However, this is not merely a policy proposal concerning *zakat* donations but rather an illustration of how political commitments and legal frameworks can generate innovative solutions to complex legal problems.

Financing: Role of Institutions, Actors and Health Law

The evolution of the Kenyan health system is historically intertwined with the country's colonial policies aimed at addressing the health needs of the population.[19] The colonial policies were shaped by the necessity to protect European settlers from infectious endemic diseases,[20] and subsequently, to respond to the growing demand for healthcare services from Africans.[21] The establishment of institutions for implementing health policy and financing healthcare services mirrored colonial interests and outcomes, focusing on facilitating the creation of a market centred around African labour that catered to the needs of the British Empire and European settler community.[22] Healthcare services and their financing were assessed against this backdrop.

Upon achieving independence in 1963, the Kenyan government pledged to restructure its institutions to provide welfare services for all citizens.[23] Access to affordable and subsidised healthcare services was normatively committed to as part of the nation's image, driven by African socialism. However, health financing was made contingent upon the state's economic status and revenue capacity.[24] Typically, the pool of revenue mobilised by the state is distributed across various public sectors, with the health sector receiving smaller budget allocations compared to education, debt service, and defence.[25]

---

[19] G Ndege, *Health, State and Society in Kenya: Faces of Contact and Change* (USA: University of Rochester Press, 2001).

[20] A Beck, *A History of the British Medical Administration of East Africa, 1900-1950* (Cambridge, Massachusetts, 1970).

[21] (n 19).

[22] A Mohiddin, *African Socialism in Two Countries* (Croom Helm, 1981).

[23] Republic of Kenya, Sessional Paper No 10 of 1965: African Socialism and Its Application to Planning in Kenya (Nairobi: Government Printed, 1965).

[24] ibid, 24.

[25] Republic of Kenya, Comprehensive Public Expenditure Review: From Evidence to Policy (National Treasury and Planning State Department for Planning Monitoring and Evaluation Department, 2018), 12.

In light of these observations, the subsequent sub-sections delve into the development of the Kenyan health sector, examining the institutions responsible for delivering and funding healthcare services. The aim is to clarify how the state implements healthcare, whether it perceived as an obligation or a necessity arising from prevailing social and economic circumstances. This analysis elucidates the characterisation of health and its financing, revealing what can be expected from the government. A more in-depth discussion of the history of colonial rule and Kenyan politics following decolonisation is not provided, except where necessary to contextualise developments in health policy.

Colonial period: 1895-1963

During the colonial era, beginning with the annexation of Kenyan territory in 1895 and its establishment as a protectorate of the British Empire,[26] public health strategies primarily focused on controlling infectious tropical diseases. This was achieved through the provision of appropriate vaccines and medicines,[27] as well as implementing proper sanitation measures to shield European settlers from contamination. The health of Africans was of little concern, and they were often regarded as sources of risk.[28] Consequently, Africans were subjected to zoning powers and segregated into separate zones away from Europeans.[29] The colonial medical department was established with the primary objective of supporting medical initiatives aimed at protecting Europeans.[30]

To accomplish its goal of securing Kenyan territory against the spread of infectious disease, the colonial medical department conducted routine

---

26 LH Gann, and P Duignan, *Rulers of British Africa, 1870-1914* (London: Croom Helm, 1978); See also Chapter 6 of the thesis where colonial history in the context of Muslims and the later British colonisation is discussed.

27 MS Chaiken, 'Primary Health Initiatives in Colonial Kenya', (1998) *World Development* Vol 26, No9, 1701-1717, 1704.

28 (n 26) Ch 2.

29 ibid, 38-9.

30 H Tilley, 'Medicine, Empires, and Ethics in Colonial Africa' (2016) *AMA Journal of Ethics*, Vol 18, No 7:743-753, 745.

medical safaris, which provided remote African communities with diagnostic and curative services, immunisation, and tropical diseases screening.[31] Obstacles such as uncleared forests, inadequate communications channels, and shortages of manpower and materials made it difficult for colonial medical service officers to reach African populations.[32] As a result, the department depended on Christian missionaries who engaged local African communities to disseminate western medicine in areas with significant African populations.[33] This example demonstrates a political power relying on non-governmental organisations to address the needs of a subjugated population. In contemporary times, such support is viewed as a shared responsibility in delivering essential services, such as healthcare, where various actors collaborate to ensure the well-being of the community. Christian medical missions offered medicine-philanthropy in rural African areas that the colonial medical department had not yet reached.[34] This reliance on missions eventually became an established state practice in independent Kenya. From a human rights perspective, permitting non-state actors to contribute to addressing health needs represents one way of fulfilling the MAR obligation.

During colonial rule, the colonial administration determined the necessary for providing healthcare. Given the limited funds available for administering the protectorate, the medical department was under prioritised.[35] In his 1901 report, Sir Charles Eliot (Commissioner and Consul General between 1901-1904) documented that approximately £3,892 had been spent by the medical department in 1898-99; £4,010 in 1899-1900; and £4,712 was budgeted for 1900-01. In comparison, the military spent £32,663, £50,513 and £38,005 respectively during the same period in

---

[31] (n 22) 223, 205; and B Robertson, *Angels in Africa: A Memoir of Nursing in the Colonial Service* (London: Radcliffe Press, 1993).

[32] (n 20) 102-104.

[33] M Vaughan, *Curing Their Ills: Colonial Power and African Illness* (Palo Alto, Stanford University Press, 1991), 288.

[34] J Iliffe, *East African Doctors: A History of the Modern Profession,* (Cambridge University Press, 1998), 19.

[35] ibid, 92.

Kenya.[36] Between 1895 and 1920, health financing was not a prioritised outcome of the colonial administration. Limited health services were provided through the colonial medical department and missionaries. In 1915, the Headquarter Medical Stores, under the stewardship of a Principal Medical Officer (PMO), was established to address the health needs of the protectorate.[37] The resources required for the PMO to 'civilise', 'improve' and 'develop' the African population would be achieved through governance structures later established by the colonial administration.[38]

In 1920, the protectorate transitioned into a colony.[39] A legal distinction is made between the East African Protectorate and the Kenya Colony, as it pertains to the provisions of healthcare services and the justifications for delivering health needs alongside financial commitments. As a protectorate, the British Empire assumed the responsibility and cost of administering the territory.[40] During this period, the colonial administration consolidated agreements with their allies: the Maasai and the Sultan of Oman, from whom the Empire gained control of the Rift Valley[41] and the ten-mile coastal strip (discussed in Chapter 6).[42] The

---

36 East Africa Protectorate, Report for 1901-02. London.

37 A Crozier, *Practising Colonial Medicine: The Colonial Medical Service in British East Africa* (I. B. Taurius, 2007) 1-14.

38 Tilley (n 30) 744.

39 G Bennett, *Kenya: A Political History: The Colonial Period* (Oxford University Press, 1964).

40 Mwangi Wa-Githumo, 'Land and Nationalism in East Africa: The Impact of Land Expropriation and Land Grievances Upon the Rise and Development of Nationalist Movements in Kenya 1884-1939' 200-04 (1974) (PhD. Dissertation, Faculty of Education, New York University).

41 M Shanguhyia and MM Koster, 'Land and Conflict in Kenya's Rift Valley: Historical and Contemporary Perspectives', in T Falola and M M Heaton (eds) *Contemporary Africa: Challenges and Opportunities* (Palgrave MacMillan, 2014), 191. The Rift Valley is Kenya's most productive agricultural area with fertile lands and lush pastures, it was alienated for European settlement.

42 The ten-mile coastal strip which comprised the territory along the Indian Ocean starting southwards from the Tanzania border and moving northwards towards the Somali border was under the administration and control of the Sultan of Oman (more on this in Chapters 5 and 6). This location was strategical as it housed a fortress (Fort Jesus) along the coastline near Mombasa and was the main trading route connecting East Africa to the Indian subcontinent and the Arabian Peninsula along the Red Sea.

control of these regions was crucial towards establishing colonial rule in Kenya, securing the Empire's economic interests by controlling and eliminating obstacles to trade and influencing the migration of European settlers.[43] This control aimed to create conditions for resource exploitation, efforts that were frequently undermined by patterns of noncompliance by Africans. The declaration of the Kenyan colony was therefore central to the colonising process and subjugation of the Africans, forcibly extracting land from them and creating a wage-labour force. Control was asserted through law and taxation, with limited commensurate social benefits.[44] Laws were enacted to 'regulate labour contracts, land tenure, vagrancy, desertion and to control social activities that impinged on work'.[45]

The governance structures established in the Kenyan colony consisted of a combination of laws, including colonial, customary and Islamic (discussed in Chapter 6). These laws were situated within an institutional framework designed to recognise plural norms while subjecting their legality to British standards of justice and morality.[46] The governor represented the Crown in the Kenya Colony, which was divided into eight provinces, each overseen by a Provincial Commissioner. These provinces were further subdivided into districts, headed by District Commissioners, which were then divided into locations and sub-locations where District Officers and chiefs were appointed to maintain law and order.[47] This political organisation mirrored the system through which the colonial administration planned the

---

[43] G Gokmen, WN Vermeulen and PL Vezina, 'The Imperial Roots of Global Trade', (2020) *Journal of Economic Growth*, 25, 87-145.

[44] S Stichter, *Migrant Labour in Kenya: Capitalism and African Response 1895–1975* (London: Longman, 1982) 82.

[45] SE Merry, 'Review: Law and Colonialism', (1991) *Law and Society Review*, Vol 25, No 4, 889-922, 892.

[46] S Constantine, *The Making of British Colonial Development Policy, 1914-1940* (London: Frank Cass 1984) 164-194.

[47] O Chitere, 'The Provincial Administration in Kenya: A Study of its Characteristics and Potential for Sustainment under Devolved System of Government', Institute of Policy Analysis and Research, No. DP 05/074, Proceedings of the Kenya National Academy of Sciences (Heinrich Boll Foundation, 2005); YP Ghai, JPWB McAuslan, and P McAuslan, *Public Law and Political Change in Kenya: A Study of the Legal Framework of Government from Colonial Times to the Present* (Oxford University Press, 1970).

development of the health sector and enacted health laws. Healthcare services, particularly preventive measures aimed at controlling infectious diseases, were provided at all levels of governance.

At the lowest levels of governance (sub-locations and locations), healthcare services were accessible through dispensaries. District level healthcare services were provided through health clinics, while provincial hospitals offered treatment to patients and extended the scope of healthcare services to include rehabilitative and promotive healthcare practices.[48] Medical supplies were delivered to provinces for distribution to districts, locations, and sub-locations. Doctors were primarily available in hospitals, which largely catered to European settlers.[49]

The Public Health Ordinances of 1913 and 1921 predominantly embodied 'colonial sanitarianism'.[50] The Ordinance aimed to segregate and sanitise, as part of the health promotion activities envisioned by the colonialist administration. This legislation authorised the creation of zones in townships, separating European settlers from Africans and Indians. Efforts to promote the welfare of Africans were limited,[51] resulting in a justification for reduced spending on meeting their health needs, aside from preventing the outbreak of infectious diseases. In 1924, the Headquarter Medical Stores (renamed in 1927 to Medical Stores and Equipment) introduced a Senior Medical Officer position alongside the existing Principal Medical Officer. Additionally, the office of the Director of Medical Services was established.[52] These institutions were responsible for procuring, storing, and distributing medicine and supplies, primarily to provincial hospitals and subsequently to health centres and dispensaries. Healthcare hinged on the budget allocated by the colonial government and was based on

---

48 (n 37) 1701-1717.

49 (n 19) 53.

50 J Harrington, *Health,* in *Oxford Handbook on International Law and Development* (2022) 4.

51 F Cooper, 'Modernising Bureaucrats, Backward Africans, and the Development Concept; in F Cooper and RM Packard (eds), *International Development and the Social Sciences: Essays on the History and Politics of Knowledge* (Berkely, LA, University of California Press, 1996), 64.

52 (n 37) 1-14.

considerations of affordability.[53] Between 1910-1924, the colonial administration spent £0.01 per capita on health, constituting 0.04 per cent of the total budget.[54] Financing health was not a primary priority of the colonial administration, which focused instead on improving economic growth.

In 1926, the Britain's Colonial Development and Welfare Act established funds to provide services such as health, education, water, and housing. Despite this, the colonial government in Kenya was reluctant to prioritise and meet these needs. In the same year, Archdeacon Owen, a missionary who had been protesting against the unfair practices imposed on Africans, pressurised the colonial government to provide resources to fund welfare programmes.[55] In turn, this led the colonial government to impose harsh new demands on the Africans, for example, by increasing hut taxes.[56] By this time, those Africans upon whom taxes had been imposed (starting with the hut tax [a colonial tax on a per hut or household basis] assessed at 1 Rupee [currency used in Kenya during colonial rule], gradually increasing to 8 Rupees) questioned why the provision of social services was not commensurate with the taxes the colonial administration collected from them.[57]

Through the Young Kavirondo Association, formed in 1921 and renamed the Kavirondo Taxpayers Welfare Association in 1923, a group of educated Africans demanded accountability from the colonial government. They sought an explanation of how African taxes were being redistributed to

---

[53] (n 19) 32-55

[54] Expenditure data obtained from various issues between 1910 and 1926 of the Blue Book of the British East Africa Protectorate, Nairobi: changed into Blue Book for the Colony and Protectorate of Kenya, Nairobi.

[55] D Wylie, 'Confrontation over Kenya: The Colonial Office and its Critics 1918-1940' (1977) *The Journal of African History* Vol 18, No 3, 427-447, 441.

[56] BJ Berman and JM Lonsdale, 'Crises of Accumulation, Coercion and the Colonial State: The Development of the Labour Control System in Kenya, 1919-1929' (1980) *Canadian Journal of African Studies* Vol 14, No 1, 55-81.

[57] H V Moyana, 'Underdevelopment in Kenya and Southern Rhodesia, 1890-1923: A Comparative Study' (1976) *Journal of Eastern African Research & Development*, Vol 6, No 2, 269-293.

secure access to social services,[58] as healthcare services still primarily served European settlers. At this time, Africans trained by the colonial medical department in lower clinical roles, under the supervision of Indian doctors, served large and remote areas.[59] This demand for accountability led to their strategic deployment in remote African areas to quell the agitation over increased taxation without corresponding access to healthcare services. To further address these concerns, the colonial government created Local Native Councils (LNC)[60] in 1924, intending 'to give Africans more involvement in the allocation of funds regarding their locality but were also intended to function as forums to redirect African political agitation'.[61]

The LNCs represented the colonial government's political response to decentralising and shifting healthcare responsibility to Africans in their localities. This shift placed the burden of health finance at the local level upon the beneficiaries. Out of pocket payments at the point of use in provincial hospitals, district clinics and location-based dispensaries added further burden to the African people.[62] The colonial approach to health policy, developed on a needs basis (prevention of infectious diseases), functioned as a tool for managing African discontent (through the LNCs), was based on considerations of affordability, and was driven by missionaries. There was no obligation, per se, on the colonial government to meet health needs proportionate to the taxes being paid by African people.

In the 1940s, a Colonial Medical Research Committee in Britain was established to administer funds from the research allocation of the Colonial

---

[58] (n 19) 100-103.

[59] A Greenwood and H Topiwala, Indian Doctors in Kenya, 1895-1940: The Forgotten History (London: Palgrave Macmillan, 2015).

[60] Composed of African chiefs, headmen and elders of the community and were chaired by the District Commissioner. They passed resolutions relating to agriculture, health, education.

[61] O Okia, *Communal Labor in Colonial Kenya: The Legitimization of Coercion*, 1912-1930 (Palgrave MacMillan, 2012) Ch 6, 108.

[62] (n 19) Ch 5.

Development and Welfare Act. To justify new health proposals for the colonies between 1945 and 1952, the Committee relied on models already operational in Britain.[63] During the 1940s, the social medicine movement[64] in Britain gained prominence. This movement advanced the view that it was not sufficient to achieve the state of health merely through preventive and curative medicine. Instead, the attainment of positive health also depended on the cultural, physical and social environment.[65] Positive health lay in 'recreation, physical education, housing, nutrition, eugenics, education, employment, town-planning and perhaps, by far the largest factor of all, mental health'.[66] This influenced the reconceptualization of health policy in colonial Kenya, as reflected in the 1945 Ten-Year Programme proposed by the colonial medical department for the development of health and hospital services. However, this programme was fiscally linked to the political and economic situation in the country.[67]

Browne observed that 'in a country with primitive standards, where the commonest diseases are preventable and where the methods of preventing them are known it is of the utmost importance to invest the limited financial resources available in a wise preventive policy'.[68] Consequently, health policy in colonial Kenya remained restricted to sanitation measures and infection prevention. Health started receiving more attention in colonial policymaking following the establishment of the World Health Organisation (WHO) in 1948. Underlying the WHO were its policies on less

---

[63] S Clarke, 'The Research Council System and the Politics of Medical and Agricultural Research for the British Colonial Empire, 1940-51', (2013) *Medical History*, Vol 57, Issue 3, 338-358, 340.

[64] J Pemberton, 'Origins and Early History of the Society for Social Medicine in the UK and Ireland' (2002) *Journal of Epidemiology & Community Health* 56:342-346.

[65] RC Browne, 'Social Medicine in England and East Africa', (1950) *East African Medical Journal*, Vol 27, No 2, 70.

[66] GVW Anderson, 'Medical Practice after the War', (1942) *East African Medical Journal*, Vol 19, No7, 208.

[67] HJ Diesfeld and HK Hecklau, *Kenya: A Geomedical Monograph* (Berlin: Springer-Verlag, 1978), 26.

[68] (n 66) 171.

costly investments for protecting health, such as protein-based nutrition,[69] construction of the sewage system, and the availability of clean water. These policies also shaped colonial health policy. The Public Health Ordinance was revised in 1948 to include the last two goals for health, as part of the colonial government's legal commitment to achieving preventive health services. The Ordinance was adopted as the Public Health Act at independence in 1963.[70]

Several general conclusions can be drawn from this section regarding the question of whether finances played a role in defining the structure of the colonial health sector or conversely, whether the structure determined its financing. Finances indeed played a primary role in defining the colonial health structure. The lack of finances initially led the colonial administration to permit missions to provide healthcare until it was in a better financial position to assume responsibility. Furthermore, finances dictated the level at which healthcare was provided and identified the health needs against which finances were mobilised.

The primary aim of the colonial administration was to focus on trade by extracting raw materials for export earnings and maintaining a labour force for that purpose.[71] Additionally, it aimed to raise local revenue through the imposition of hut taxes[72] and alienate land for European settlement to engage in production to recover the £6,000,000 spent on constructing the railway.[73] The administration did not prioritise increasing financing for the delivery of health services in the colony. Consequently, a cost sharing strategy between the colonial administration and the LNCs was formulated, placing the burden of extending health services at the community level on Africans. Without the additional finances brought in by the LNCs, the health sector would have stagnated. This colonial approach to limiting finances for health in favour of economic growth and

---

[69] J Nott, 'No One May Starve in the British Empire: Kwashiorkor, Protein and the Politics of Nutrition Between Britain and Africa', (2021) *Soc His Med* 34(2):553-576.

[70] ibid, 27.

[71] (n 20).

[72] (n 19).

[73] (n 20), 32.

sharing health financing responsibility with non-state actors persisted into the post-independence period.

Independence and current period: 1963-2022

Upon gaining independence, the Ministry of Health (MoH) was established as the primary institution responsible for proposing health policy and legislation, identifying the country's health needs, and developing strategies to address those needs. MoH incorporated the colonial Medical Stores and Equipment, which underwent several name changes: including Central Medical Stores (CMS), Central Medical Store Management Information System (CMS/MIS), Medical Supplies Coordinating Unit (MSCU) and finally Kenya Medical Supplies Agency (KEMSA).[74] Two institutions were created under MoH to support healthcare service delivery in the country: KEMSA and the National Hospital Insurance Fund (NHIF). KEMSA was responsible for the procurement and distribution of medicines and supplies nationwide, reflecting the government's financial commitment to health. Established in 1966, the NHIF provided medical insurance coverage to its members, as part of the government's efforts to alleviate the financial burden of out-of-pocket payments (OPP) when accessing healthcare services. A financial commitment towards health was emerging, which would shape the state's obligations.

At independence, the central government planned to establish 250 rural health clinics but initially did not allocate financial resources to this endeavour due to affordability concerns.[75] By 1970, however, the MoH operated 195 health centres and 603 dispensaries across the country. The central government funded 88 per cent of these health facilities, with municipalities financing an additional 9 per cent.[76] There was only one

---

[74] KEMSA, Historical Background, available at: https://www.kemsa.co.ke/about-us/historical-background/

[75] R Wamai, T Veintie and P Virtanen, *Healthcare Policy Administration and Reforms in Post-Colonial Kenya and the Challenges for the Future* (Helsinki: The Renvall Institute for Area and Cultural Studies, 2009)

[76] (n 67) 35.

national referral and teaching hospital located in Nairobi, with each province having a provincial hospital. Health centres were set up across the districts, and dispensaries were spread across sub-districts. Healthcare access was structured in tiers:

Level 1: dispensaries (lowest level of care)

Level 2: health clinics

Level 3: health centres

Level 4: district hospitals

Level 5: provincial hospitals

Level 6: referral hospital (highest level of care)

However, the MoH faced significant challenges financing these tiers due to the abolition of user fees after independence, a low-taxable population and high costs associated with meeting the infrastructure development needs of a newly independent country.[77] The institutional structure for health facilities established during colonial rule, which included provincial hospitals, district clinics and location-based dispensaries, was integrated into independent Kenya's governance structure.[78] These public health facilities were funded by central government,[79] and the allocation of

[77] K Munge and AH Briggs, 'The Progressivity of Healthcare Financing in Kenya' (2014) *Health Policy and Planning*, Vol 29, Issue 7, 912-920.

[78] (n 67) 26-30.

[79] The 1963 Independence Constitution altered the political structure that was in place during colonial rule in Kenya. The newly independent state was to adopt *majimboism*, which meant political and fiscal autonomy of regions from the central government, in other words devolution. However, in the years that followed after independence, the constitution was amended in favour of a centralised government and *majimboism* was dropped. With this the colonial government brought back the colonial political structure with the central government now at the apex of the hierarchy delegating certain powers and functions to the Provincial Commissioners who further delegated functions to the District Commissioners. The latter then required District Officers and area chiefs to implement orders at their locational and sub-locational levels.

resources for healthcare provision was based on affordability considerations, as it had been during the colonial period. In fulfilling its commitment to healthcare provision, the government also subsidised medical missions.[80] As the government bore the responsibility for funding healthcare, it determined its own obligations towards achieving health goals. Consequently, healthcare was subject to fiscal decisions made at the central-government level.

At independence, the only normative commitment towards financing health was articulated in Sessional Paper No 10 of 1965 on African Socialism and Its Application to Planning in Kenya (Sessional Paper No 10). This document bound the government bound to provide medical coverage to reduce out-of-pocket payments, offer free maternity services and ensure child immunisation,[81] contingent upon the availability of funds. Sessional Paper No 10 outlined the blueprint for the independent government's organisation, emphasising that while social services and welfare are essential, economic growth took precedence.[82] It posited that the provision of social services and welfare would depend on available funds, and that adopting a liberal, free market model would help sustain the new economy, eventually transitioning into a welfare state guaranteeing healthcare.[83]

The commitment expressed in Sessional Paper No 10 subtly echoed the colonial approach of removing social services and welfare provision from the core of the government's fiscal obligation to taxpayers. This stance seemed to contradict the struggle for independence, which was founded on principles of self-rule, equality, non-discrimination, access to social services and welfare, land use, and economic participation.[84] The health commitments in Sessional Paper No 10 were not enshrined in new

[80] FO Barasa, 'The Church and the Healthcare Sector in Kenya: A Functional Analysis of its Development through Evangelisation' (2020) *International Journal of Innovative Science and Research Technology*, Vol 5, Issue 9, 1058-1064, 1061.

[81] Republic of Kenya, Sessional Paper No 10 of 1965: African Socialism and Its Application to Planning in Kenya (Nairobi: Government Printed, 1965) 30, 47.

[82] (n 22), 26-30.

[83] ibid.

[84] C Hornsby, *Kenya: A History Since Independence* (Bloomsbury Academics, 2013).

legislative measures; instead, the colonial Public Health Ordinance (with its various amendments over the colonial period) was passed as the Public Health Act of 1963,[85] addressing similar colonial concerns such as infection control and sanitation relating to housing, water supplies and food. While health considerations evolved over time, the government did not assume significant open-ended financial obligations.

The promulgation of the new Constitution of Kenya in 2010 introduced a devolved form of governance, replacing the centralised system (power concentrated with the central government).[86] The eight provinces established during colonial rule were restructured into 47 sub-national governments (counties), each with an executive governor and a legislative county assembly. Under this devolved governance, healthcare service delivery shifted from the MoH to the county governments, which assumed fiscal responsibility for healthcare provision, akin to the colonial LNCs. The Constitution recognised health as a human right, justifying a positive claim on state resources. Access to healthcare under devolution was also structured in tiers:

Level 1: community facilities (lowest level of care)

Level 2: health dispensaries

Level 3: health centres

Level 4: county hospitals

Level 5: county referral hospitals

Level 6: national referral hospital (highest level of care)

The MoH retained the functions of formulating health policy, health regulation and providing technical assistance to counties. National referral

---

[85] Republic of Kenya, Public Health Act, Chapter 242 LN142/1963 (Nairobi: Government Printers, 1963).

[86] (n 67) 26.

health facilities are also managed under MoH. KEMSA continues to procure and distribute medicine and supplies to county governments.[87] Each county government is fiscally responsible for providing county health services.[88]

Health up to the point of independence was framed as part of welfare services and not seen as a human right. The legal recognition of the right to health came later in 1972, when Kenya ratified the ICESCR (discussed in the next section) and accepted its role as the principal duty bearer responsible and accountable for its realisation. But until the right to health received domestic articulation under the Constitution and the Health Act No 21 of 2017, it was not mentioned in various Development Plans, the 1994 Kenya Health Policy, and the National Health Sector Strategic Plans (discussed in 3.3). The phrase 'MAR' also did not appear in these documents.

There has been a notable increase in the involvement of private actors and the use of traditional medicine.[89] While this chapter acknowledges the growing role of non-state actors in healthcare service delivery it contends that the state's role remains critical and has not diminished, as private healthcare in Kenya is expensive and most Kenyans rely on the public healthcare sector.[90] Consequently, the institutional role and involvement of the state are essential for fulfilling its MAR obligations, as discussed in Chapter 2.

---

[87] KEMSA, Legal Mandate available at: https://www.kemsa.co.ke/legal-mandate/

[88] Republic of Kenya, Constitution of Kenya, 2010 (Nairobi: National Council of Legal Reporting) Fourth Schedule: Part 2 (2).

[89] J Harrington, *Traditional Medicine and the Law in Kenya* (Routledge Handbook of Complementary and Alternative Medicine, 2015).

[90] N Mwenda, R Nduati, M Kosgei et al., 'What Drives Outpatient Care Costs in Kenya? An Analysis with Generalised Estimating Equations', (2021) *Front. Public Health*; O D Williams, 'COVID-19 and Private Health: Market and Governance Failure', (2020) *Development* 63, 181-190, 183.

Fulfilling Health Obligations Through Public Health Strategies

This section evaluates various public health strategies formulated by the Kenyan government to provide healthcare services, aiming to understand how the state determines its level of obligation. The assessment focuses on the financial aspect of the state's MAR obligation and examines whether the state fulfils this obligation through the implementation of these strategies and whether the obligation is explicitly articulated.

Post-independence, the Government of Kenya prepared several Five-Year Development Plans outlining its approach to delivering healthcare services, among other objectives. The Development Plans of 1966-1970, 1970-1974, and 1974-1978 are crucial in comprehending how the state conceptualised its commitment to healthcare.[91] These initial plans illuminate the development stages of health characterisation in Kenya and the obligations placed on the state. The first Development Plan (1966-1970) introduced free outpatient treatment; free board and lodging for all in-patients, and free hospital treatment for children under the age of 18.[92] The second Development Plan (1970-1974) detailed the financial burden imposed on the state by its commitments under the first Development Plan. It acknowledged that the free healthcare envisioned in the first plan resulted in a 'significant overloading of the medical facilities without at the same time any corresponding increase in means for staff, buildings, equipment and medicament'.[93]

The third Development Plan (1974-1978) saw the government commit to considering the 'appointment of a Special Commission to examine financing of the nation's health service and to make recommendations for

---

[91] Republic of Kenya, Development Plan 1966-1970 (Nairobi: Government Printers, 1965); Development Plan 1970-1974 (Nairobi, 1969); Development Plan 1974-1978 (Nairobi: Government Printers, 1974).
[92] Republic of Kenya, Development Plan 1966-1970 (Nairobi: Government Printers, 1965), 3.
[93] Republic of Kenya, Development Plan 1974-1978 (Nairobi: Government Printers, 1974), 15.

their improvement'[94]. This Development Plan was formulated after Kenya became a State Party to the ICESCR in 1972. However, this did not necessarily entail domestic legal consequences since the ICESCR does not explicitly require State Parties to take legal measures.[95] The health proposals in the plan provide no insight into how the government conceptualised its MAR obligation. Instead, the Development Plan delineated the following health obligations, conditional on the availability of funds, outlining what could be expected from the state:

(1) Construction of urgently needed new facilities, to the extent they can be staffed
(2) A substantial programme of renovating and up-grading existing facilities and technology
(3) Major investments in training at all levels of medical skills
(4) More emphasis and awareness of preventive and promotive programmes
(5) Substantially increased assistance to church health services

The Development Plan corresponds with the types of resources identified by Robertson, discussed in Chapter 2 within the scope of MAR: financial, natural, technology, information, and human resources.[96] It associated healthcare service delivery with the extent permissible by the availability of funds. Elements of the government's MAR obligation can be discerned from the third Development Plan (1974-1978). The government acknowledged that financing the establishment of health facilities also necessitated a commensurate 'increase in means for staff, buildings, equipment and medicament'.[97] Such expenses would burden the state.

---

[94] Republic of Kenya, Development Plan 1974-1978 (Nairobi: Government Printers, 1974), 489-490.

[95] P Alston and G Quinn, The Nature and Scope of State Party Obligations under the International Covenant on Economic, Social and Cultural Rights (1987) *Human Rights Quarterly*, Vol 9, No 2, 156-229, 166.

[96] ER Robertson, 'Measuring State Compliance with the Obligation to Devote the 'Maximum Available Resources' to Realising Economic, Social, and Cultural Rights', (1994) *Human Rights Quarterly* 16, 693-714.

[97] Republic of Kenya, Development Plan 1974-1978 (Nairobi: Government Printers, 1974), 15.

Consequently, by recommending an increase in financial assistance for church health services, the government maximised its approach to health finance. It relied on existing infrastructure, equipment and human resources maintained by the Catholic and Protestant churches, thereby reducing the financial burden it would otherwise have incurred. This can also be interpreted as the state recognising itself as the primary duty bearer for delivering healthcare, justifying the financial assistance given to non-state actors to provide healthcare services. The third Development Plan (1974-1978) does not use the phrase *maximum available resources* but refers to the simultaneous use of 'health planning' followed by 'financial limitations'.

The MAR obligation requires states to 'take steps' (Chapter 2).[98] This action can be gleaned from the fourth Development Plan (1978-1982), in which the government focused extensively on regional distribution of healthcare services. It recognised the underlying determinants of health in providing effective and accessible medical services,[99] and the four conditions necessary to secure health: *availability, accessibility, acceptability* and *quality* of public health and healthcare facilities, goods, and services (discussed in Chapter 2).[100] While not expressly stated, the recommendations outlined in the Development Plan (1978-1982) resonated with the state's obligation of conduct.

Chapter 2 explained that obligations of conduct must be implemented through actions determined by the obligation itself. The state must 'take steps' to secure at least the core content of rights. The obligation of result requires the state to 'ensure the obtainment of a particular situation – a specified result and leaves it for that state to achieve such a situation or result by means of its own choice'.[101] The proposal under the fourth

---

[98] (n 95) 156-229, 158.

[99] Republic of Kenya, Development Plan 1978-1982 (Nairobi: Government Printers, 1977) 3-7.

[100] Paragraph 12 (a) General Comment 14.

[101] R Wolfrum, 'Obligation of Result Versus Obligation of Conduct: Some Thoughts About the Implementation of International Obligations' in M H Arsanjani, J Cogan, R

Development Plan (1978-1982) was to increase access to healthcare at district levels by deploying more healthcare workers, improving the medical staff/population ratio, and deploying specially trained nurses at village level. The Development Plan also identified the financial difficulties in meeting the health needs of the population across the different tiers of healthcare. As such, it proposed decentralising healthcare. In so doing, the government demonstrated its approach to delivering on its health commitments.

In 1982, the government formulated its health financing strategy under the District Focus Rural Development Plan (DFRDP).[102] While article 2.1 of the ICESCR obliges State Parties to seek international assistance, the DFRDP outlined the government's approach to procuring domestic assistance for financing healthcare at district level. This plan marked a shift in the state's approach to delivering on its health commitments. Under the third Development Plan (1974-1978), the state financially supported mission-led health services, acknowledging itself as the primary duty bearer for health. However, with the introduction of '*harambee*' (political slogan used by Jomo Kenyatta: the first President of independent Kenya, to get citizens to share the cost of financing the state) financing in the DFRDP, the state extended the duty to achieve healthcare to its beneficiaries. This approach mirrored that of the colonial administration, which shifted its fiscal responsibility for providing healthcare services to the Local Native Councils. Under *harambee* financing, local communities at the grassroots level were asked by District Officers to collectively contribute to their local healthcare projects.[103]

During the 1980s, the government faced fiscal distress due to high debt levels, worsening trade terms, and the oil glut that had pushed the Kenyan economy towards recession and reliance on debt. To support economic recovery, the IMF proposed structural adjustment programmes for the

---

Sloane and S Wiessner (eds) *Looking to the Future: Essays on International Law in Honor of W Michael Reisman* (Brill | Nijhoff, 2010), 363-383, 364.

102 Republic of Kenya, District Focus Rural Development (Nairobi: Government Printers, 1982).

103 CO Oyaya, and SB Rifkin, 'Health Sector Reforms in Kenya: An Examination of District Level Planning' (2003) *Health Policy* 64: 113-127.

country. Consequently, the government needed to reduce social spending and impose user fees for public services.[104] As a result, the DFRDP proposed *harambee* financing as an alternative source of revenue to fund health. This proposal, as part of historical state practice, demonstrates how the Kenyan state conceptualised and understood its policy commitment towards healthcare provision.

The sixth Development Plan (1982-1986), aimed to revive the Kenyan economy.[105] Following DFRDP's *harambee* health financing, the latter Development Plan connected the achievement of health needs to the mobilisation of local resources, characterised as human, physical and financial.[106] The mobilisation of financial resources was discussed exclusively in the context of *harambee* financing. The Development Plan (1982-1986) re-introduced the position under Sessional Paper No 10, prioritising finances towards economic activity and reducing social spending. Thus, to alleviate the state's financial burden over social spending, the Development Plan justified resorting to *harambee* financing.[107] Health was recognised as a 'basic human need' linked to 'safe, sanitary and secure shelter, adequate diets, adequate and accessible health services and safe drinking water'.[108] While the state's MAR obligation is not explicitly mentioned, the plan acknowledged that state capacity to meet health needs was constrained[109] and that commitments towards financing health would necessitate 'new ideas in low cost effective health delivery systems with a strong rural orientation'.[110] The Development Plan (1982-1986) envisaged international assistance, primarily from the United States, to support health finance.

---

104 D Sahn and R Bernier, 'Have Structural Adjustments Led to Health Sector Reform in Africa?' (1995) *Health Policy*, Vol 32, Issues 1-3, 193-214.

105 Republic of Kenya, Development Plan 1982-1986 (Nairobi, 1982), p ii.

106 ibid, 19.

107 ibid, 23.

108 ibid, 43.

109 ibid, 44.

110 ibid.

Harambee financing, a government-backed fiscal measure, was implemented to support the state in providing healthcare. Under General Comment 3, the state's obligation of conduct and of result in understanding its MAR obligation is emphasised, drawing attention to the potential avenues states can explore when undertaking steps to deliver healthcare. The obligation of result necessitates the state to 'ensure the obtainment of a particular situation or a specified result and leaves it for that state to achieve such a situation or result by means of its own choice' (Chapter 2).[111] The element of choice is reflected in the sixth Development Plan (1982-1986). By seeking *harambee* financing, the state can be perceived as extending its MAR obligation to beneficiaries, which is crucial to underscore as it demonstrates acceptable state practice in resorting to social finance.

Similarly, recourse to *zakat* can be considered a matter of choice for the state to include as part of its fiscal approach to financing health. Given that all health commitments under the discussed Development Plans are subject to resource limitations – resulting from the state's shrinking fiscal space due to economic difficulties and debt service – expanding the scope of MAR to encompass *zakat* is not inconsistent with the Kenyan state's approach to financing health. The Development Plans only mention *harambee* financing, and no other category of financial measures that the state implement.

The sixth Development Plan (1982-1986) represents the first substantive political document where health was conceptualised as a basic need, with its financing shared by the state and its beneficiaries – a strategy unlikely to succeed under the ICESCR, which solely binds State Parties as primary duty bearers. *Harambee* financing seems to have been excluded from the state's fiscal measures in the seventh and eighth Development Plans (1986-1990 and 1990-1994). The severe social and economic consequences of HIV/AIDS are discussed in these Development Plans, along with the magnitude of resource gaps in combatting the spread of HIV/AIDS and

---

[111] (n 101).

managing the public health crisis concurrently.[112] Under the 1986-1990 Development Plan, the government signalled the need for a comprehensive national health policy and financing strategy, if 'targeted and measurable steps towards achieving health for all is to be realised'.[113] However, the scope of these measures is not elaborated upon.

The state's understanding of its obligation towards healthcare is outlined in the inaugural 1994-2010 Kenya Health Policy.[114] The Policy specified the country's health needs[115] and emphasised the urgency of resources for delivering those needs. It recognised the problem of limited resources, and therefore divided the implementation of the identified health needs into two-time bound National Health Sector Strategic Plans I (NHSSP I) and II (NHSSP II)[116] implemented between 1994-2004 and 2005-2010 respectively. The government's 'fiscal obligations towards increasing and diversifying financial flows to the health sector'[117] were expressly acknowledged. Resources were to be mobilised through:

(a) Social financing mechanisms
(b) Encouraging private investments
(c) Beneficiary contributions through cost sharing
(d) Mobilising resources from communities[118]

[112] Republic of Kenya, Development Plan 1986-1990 (Nairobi: Government Printers, 1986); Development Plan 1990-1994 (Nairobi: Government Printers, 1989).
[113] Development Plan 1986-1889, 89-91.
[114] Government of Kenya. *Ministry of Health. Kenya's Health Policy Framework* (Nairobi: Government Printer 1994).
[115] ibid, 32-49: see Part III – The Agenda for Reform (Reduce by at least half the infant, neonatal and maternal deaths; reduce by at least 25% the time spent by persons in ill health; improve by at least 50% the levels of client satisfaction with services; reduce by 30% the catastrophic health expenditures).
[116] Government of Kenya, Ministry of Health, *The First National Health Sector Strategic Plan of Kenya 1994-2004* (Nairobi: Government Printer, 1994); and Government of Kenya, *Ministry of Health. The Second National Health Sector Strategic Plan of Kenya 2005-2010* (Nairobi: Government Printer, 2004).
[117] Government of Kenya, Ministry of Health, *The First National Health Sector Strategic Plan of Kenya 1994-2004*, 31.
[118] ibid, 39.

Though not legally binding, the Policy expanded the state's fiscal reach to non-state actors' resources. However, the discussions in the Policy were not connected to the state's MAR obligation under human rights law, and the phrase 'MAR' had not yet featured in the state's health policy. Health was not referred to as a right in the Policy, a deliberate omission to limit the justiciability of the 'right to health'.[119] In determining the resources to be allocated for financing the health needs identified in the Policy, the state granted itself extensive discretion. The state was not obligated to use all its resources, but rather the maximum amount that could be allocated towards financing health. Its discretion extended to mobilising the funds listed under categories (a) through (d) above.[120] The crucial aspect to note within the Policy is the acknowledgement of alternative sources of funding that the state could mobilise from society. *Zakat* represents one such social financing mechanism. Consequently, the Policy makes significant contribution to health financing, considering the conditional acceptability under the ICESCR for states to exercise their discretion in fulfilling their MAR obligation. The acceptability within Kenya's health policymaking to seek funds from non-state actors for financing health suggests a broader scope of the MAR obligation.

Upon reviewing the Development Plans and the Kenya Health Policy, it becomes evident that the MAR obligation is closely tied to the health budget. Between 1994 and 2004, health allocations ranged from 3-6.8 per cent of the total budget.[121] Firstly, this was insufficient to implement the NHSSP I and II. Secondly, the budget allocations were not aligned with the health priorities outlined under the NHSSP I and II.[122] Basing the financial capacity of the state's MAR obligation on a fluctuating health budget –

---

[119] LA Latif, F Simiyu, and A Waris, 'A Case Study on the Application of Human Rights Principles in Health Policy Making and Programming in Cherangany Sub County in Kenya', (2017) *Integrative Journal of Global Health* 1, No 1.

[120] (n 116), 39.

[121] PK Kimalu, et al. (2004) A Review of the Health Sector in Kenya. *Kenya Institute for Public Policy Research and Analysis*, 24.

[122] AH Glenngard and TM Maina, 'Reversing the Trend of Weak Policy Implementation in Kenya Health Sector? A Study of Budget Allocation and Spending of Health Resources Versus Set Priorities' (2007) *Health Research Policy Systems*, Vol 5, No 3.

rather than establishing it within a health financing framework that precisely delineates which available sources of funds will finance specific health needs – undermines the realisation of the right to health.

A critical observation regarding the characterisation of health in Kenya is that its financing necessitated a coordinated response from various partners. Nevertheless, the state assumed responsibility for defining public health objectives and providing resources to attain them. As the government could not predict its future fiscal capacity, it avoided committing itself to uncertain and open-ended levels of expenditure. The Development Plans, the Kenya Health Policy and the NHSSP I and II projected the government's intention to promote better healthcare by setting aspirational goals. This approach demonstrates how the Kenyan state understood health and determined the threshold of its obligations.

In 2010, the state declared health a constitutional right, contingent on the availability of public resources. Its legislative content was further delineated in 2014. This section has shown that through its health policy and law, the Kenyan state has pivoted towards accessing new sources of finance to support its health commitments. State practice has also informed the MAR obligation. The subsequent section investigates whether such state practice has been incorporated into the state's legislative approach, delineating its MAR obligation, and justifying its interpretation to extend the scope of MAR to include non-state actor funds. This finding would validate giving MAR an evolutive interpretation, linked to state practice, and potentially encompassing *zakat*.

The Constitutional and Legislative Approaches to the Right to Health and its MAR obligation in Kenya

The 2010 Constitution of Kenya explicitly recognises the right to health. As a fundamental right, the determination of the state's obligation towards its realisation is still in the early stages of development. Article 43(1)(a) of the Constitution guarantees every citizen the 'enjoyment of the highest attainable standard of health'. Article 21(2) places the burden on the state to take legislative, policy, and other measures to achieve the progressive realisation of the right to health. While the right asserts a positive claim on the state's resources, article 20(5) hinges the right on considerations of affordability. The constitutional text does not express the normative content of the right to health; rather, reference to the ICESCR is implied under article 2(5), which recognises as part of Kenyan law all treaties signed by the state.

Before the 2010 Constitution, the 2003 and 2004 draft Constitutions also included economic and social rights (ESR) as part of their bill of rights. The inclusion of ESR, encompassing health, housing, sanitation, and social security, resulted from 'domestic pressure to compel the government to take bolder action to address widespread poverty and inequality'[123] by committing to the judicial enforcement of ESR. During the debates surrounding the 2003 and 2004 draft Constitutions, no issues were raised against their inclusion in the Bill of Rights.[124]

The 2010 draft encountered more controversial issues. In the context of health, the inclusion of reproductive health as part of the state's conceptualisation of 'the highest attainable standard of health' was extensively debated by faith-based organisations seeking clarity on whether the right permitted abortion. A group of members of parliament sought the removal of ESR from the Constitution, claiming ESR as 'unenforceable'.[125] Although the normative content of the right to health and the obligations to which the state would be bound were not specifically addressed, the Committee of Experts tasked with drafting the Constitution 'was categorical that no debate on these rights was to be entertained'.[126]

---

[123] Committee of Experts on Constitutional Review, 'Final Report of the Committee of Experts on Constitutional Review', 11 October 2010, 108.

[124] J Harrington, 'Framing the National Interest: Debating Intellectual Property and Access to Essential Medicines in Kenya' (2014) The Journal of World Intellectual Property, Vol 17, Issue 1-2, 16-33.

[125] M Wachira et al, 'Human Rights Group Protests Clause Exclusion', Daily Nation, 22 January 2010, available at www.nation.co.ke/News/politics/-/1064/847716 /-/wsc3i5z/-/index.html S Anyangu-Amu, 'Kenya: Proposed Constitutional Amendment Sets Back Women's Rights', Inter Press Service, 11 March 2010, available at www.globalissues .org/news/2010/03/11/4821

[126] (n 123) 345.

Instead, the content of the right to health was to be clarified through legislation and judicial decisions.

Following the promulgation of the 2010 Constitution, the government prepared Sessional Paper No 10 of 2012 on Kenya Vision 2030, outlining its proposals for implementing the 2010 Constitution.[127] Regarding health, Vision 2030 delineated the thresholds the state must meet to discharge its obligations towards the realisation of the right to health. These obligations were to:

(a) Provide an efficient integrated and high-quality affordable healthcare system
(b) Establish a decentralised national healthcare system
(c) Improve access to healthcare for all through a robust health infrastructure network, improving the quality of health service delivery to the highest standards, promotion of partnerships with the private sector and providing access to those excluded from healthcare for financial or other reasons.[128]

In Vision 2030, no explicit reference is made to the normative content outlined in General Comment 14. Instead, the Vision aims to explain the government's interpretation of the right to health and its understanding of the obligations it carrics. Vision 2030 asserts that the right to health encompasses access to affordable care, improved governance, and better management of health delivery systems, enhanced access and equity in the availability of essential healthcare, reduced incidence of preventable diseases, and control of environmental threats to health.[129] The Vision 2030 acknowledges that these determinants of the right to health would subject the state to significant open-ended financial obligations, and thus, makes them dependent on government budget decisions. Consequently, an

---

[127] Republic of Kenya, Sessional Paper No 10 of 2012 on Kenya Vision 2030 (Office of the Prime Minister, Ministry of State for Planning, National Development and Vision 2030).

[128] ibid, vi.

[129] ibid, 104.

obligation is placed on the state to develop a fiscal plan that considers affordability, allocates funds and assigns responsibility for healthcare delivery.[130]

Subsequently, the state formulated the Kenya Health Policy (KHP) 2014-2030, which delineated its comprehensive health governance plan, connecting the achievement of health to the budget.[131] The KHP acknowledged that the constitutional right to health was subject to progressive realisation, contingent on the availability of public resources.[132] It interpreted this as imposing an obligation on the state to develop defined, achievable, 'priority cost effective healthcare interventions and services addressing the high disease burden, that are acceptable and affordable within the total resource envelope of the sector'.[133] These healthcare interventions and services, referred to as the Kenya Essential Package for Health (KEPH), were outlined in the Kenya Health Sector Strategic and Investment Plan 2014-2018 (KHSSP). The KHSSP presented the national government's fiscal plan, illustrating how it allocated its health budget for delivering the country's specific health needs under the KEPH. Through the KHSSP, the state demonstrated its obligation towards achieving the right to health by creating a predictable fiscal space.[134] Since health was a devolved function, the obligation to ensure healthcare service delivery also rested with the county governments, which in turn prepared their County Health Sector Strategic and Investment Plan (CHSSP), outlining their fiscal commitments to KEPH.

Through the KHP and KHSSP, the state began to shape its constitutional commitment to healthcare delivery and characterise its obligations. Through these policy initiatives, which shaped the state's characterisation of the right to health, indicated a departure from the initial

---

130 ibid, 105.

131 Republic of Kenya, Kenya Health Policy 2014-2030: Towards Attaining the Highest Standard of Health (Ministry of Health, 2014), 18, 61.

132 ibid, 30.

133 ibid.

134 Republic of Kenya, Kenya Health Sector Strategic and Investment Plan 2014-2018 (KHSSP) (Ministry of Health, 2014), 63-64.

conceptualisation of health and its financing under colonial rule. A strong connection between health and the government's fiscal obligation towards it was being established, which later manifested in the 2017 Health Act. This legislative text commits the state to 'observe, respect, protect, promote and fulfil the right to the highest attainable standard of health'.[135] It articulates the state's understanding of the normative content of the right to health, and places finance at the centre of the state's MAR obligation. The Health Act binds the government to 'ensure progressive financial access to universal health coverage by taking measures', such as developing a national health insurance system and defining a standard health package financed through prepayment mechanisms.[136]

The state's confirmation of its financial obligation towards the realisation of the right to health relies on a future defined list, referred to as a 'standard health package'. The Act realistically reflects the state's expectations in financing health and explicitly calls upon the state to implement legal measures that would entail domestic legal consequences. The current KHSSP 2018-2023 was developed following the enactment of the Health Act. This plan reflects the state's legal commitment to realising health and the benchmarks it must meet in fulfilling its obligations. The plan extends the obligations delineated in KHSSP 2014-2018, demonstrating continuity over the obligations (a)-(c) mentioned earlier. Furthermore, while the plan elaborates on the state's financing commitments outlined in the Health Act, it reemphasises the state's dependence on private sector funds to alleviate the financial burden carried by the publicly financed health system.[137]

KHSSP 2018-2023 illustrates how the state has comprehended and interpreted its MAR obligation. It updates the government's obligations under KEPH, aligning them with the targets and indicators set forth in

---

135 Republic of Kenya, Health Act, No 12 of 2017 (Nairobi: National Council of Legal Reporting), section 4.

136 ibid, section 86.

137 Republic of Kenya, Kenya Health Sector Strategic and Investment Plan 2018-2023 (KHSSP) (Ministry of Health, 2018) 21, 69.

Sustainable Development Goal 3 on Good Health and Wellbeing.[138] The standard health package mentioned in the Health Act is developed around SDG3.[139] KHSSP addresses the challenges of limited funds by emphasising the importance of 'maximising the availability of resources'[140]. This marks the state's first reference to MAR. The MAR obligation is outlined as follows[141]:

(a) To increase government budget allocation to health with an increase from 6 per cent to 13 per cent
(b) To increase health insurance coverage through instigation of mandatory contributions
(c) To set up institutional mechanisms for pooling health revenue
(d) To promote private sector investment in the health sector
(e) To identify potential poor and vulnerable beneficiaries of health insurance subsidies
(f) To collaborate with donors

The state's MAR obligation to health is realised through finance, secured via budget increments, health insurance schemes, and reliance on assistance. Approximately KES 2.6 billion (GBP 179 million) is required to fund the implementation of KHSSP between 2018-2023. Out of this sum, the government confirms its capacity to generate KES 1.9 billion (GBP 131 million).[142] The remaining balance can be financed by accessing new sources of funds from donors. In its understanding of MAR, the state extends its fiscal responsibility to seek financial assistance from non-state actors. This book is particularly interested in the state linking its MAR scope to providing health insurance subsidies for the poor and vulnerable. In the context of the state seeking collaboration with non-state actors as part of *maximising the availability of resources,* which can be mobilised and

---

[138] Republic of Kenya, Kenya Health Sector Strategic Plan 2018-2023: Mid Term Review Synthesis Report (2021) 25.
[139] KHSSP 2014-2018, 12.
[140] ibid, 69.
[141] ibid, 69-70.
[142] ibid, 82.

identifying poor and vulnerable beneficiaries to access health insurance subsidies, it resonates with the objective of *zakat* under Islamic law (discussed in Chapter 4). Based on this, the chapter confirms the possibility of accepting faith-based funds – such as *zakat* – to supplement health budget deficits as part of the state's understanding of its MAR obligation. References to funds that can be availed by non-state actors continue to appear in Kenya's health policies and strategic plans. The government has shown its openness towards exploring its MAR obligation.

The Government of Kenya's potential to source for additional domestic revenue is contingent on its population's economic conditions. 49 percent of the urban population and 53 percent of the rural population in Kenya live below the poverty line.[143] Since they do not earn adequate income, they are not taxed, limiting the tax revenue that the government can collect from its population. Instead, formal sector employees earning taxable salaries bear the burden of taxation. Taxable profits declared by private corporations also provide the government with a revenue source. However, not all private corporations are transparent with their profit declarations and operate various tax avoidance schemes that result in loss of revenue for the government.[144] In sourcing additional funds, increased taxation would only burden the working class and deter the private sector from investing domestically. Consequently, generating additional domestic revenue targeted for health would then have to be sourced from alternative means.

Identifying additional domestic revenue sources for health is therefore essential in steering the health sector towards self-sustainability. In 2020, 36 percent of sick Kenyans did not access healthcare due to financial

---

143 Government of Kenya, Kenya National Bureau of Statistics, '2019 Kenya Population and Housing Census Volume IV: Distribution of Population by Socio-Economic Characteristics.' (Nairobi: Government Printer, 2020).

144 RN Misati, K Ngoka, A Kamau et al., *Profit Shifting by Multinational Corporations in Kenya: The Role of Internal Debt* (United Nations University World Institute for Development Economics Research, 2022).

constraints.[145] Data from the Ministry of Health in Kenya revealed that in 2020, there were 1.4 hospital beds per 1000 people, 0.868 nurses and midwives per 1,000 people, and 0.199 physicians per 1,000 persons.[146] In Kenya, the Maternal Mortality Ratio stands at 362 maternal deaths per 100,000 live births, with the target being to reduce MMR to 147 per 100,000 live births. Funding shortages prevent midwives from reaching pregnant women in rural areas or in villages.[147] In terms of regional distribution of health facilities, the Rift Valley region maintains the highest number, followed by the eastern region. The north-eastern region continues to have the lowest concentration of health facilities out of the 10,506 public health facilities operated by the government countrywide.[148] As of October 2021, these facilities lacked drugs, health workers, and medical equipment.[149] Additional sources of domestic revenue for health would aim to reduce these disparities.

Conclusion: General Framing of Health Finance and MAR Obligation

Given the crucial role of states in implementing human rights, it was essential to examine how the ICESCR is interpreted by the Kenyan state and to what extent its interpretation aligns with the normative content and meaning of the right to health under General Comment 14. This chapter has demonstrated that ratification of the ICESCR does not necessarily oblige the state to adopt legislative measures that mirror the ICESCR's characterisation of the normative content of the right to health. Instead, the

---

[145] P Njagi, W Groot and J Arsenijevic, 'Impact of household shocks on access to healthcare services in Kenya: a propensity score matching analysis', (2021) *BMJ Open*, Vol 11(9): e048189.

[146] Government of Kenya, Ministry of Health, 'Pathways to optimal health infrastructure in Kenya' Policy Brief, n.d.

[147] E Langat, L Mwanri and M Temmerman, 'Effects of implementing free maternity service policy in Kenya: an interrupted time series analysis', (2019) *BMC Health Services Research*, 19, 645

[148] Kenya Master Health Facility List, http://kmhfl.health.go.ke/#/home

[149] Open Africa, https://africaopendata.org/dataset/health-facilities-in-kenya/resource/0257f153-7228-49ef-b330-8e8ed3c7c7e8

state underwent a process of defining its domestic approach to healthcare delivery and determining the extent of its obligations. This process involved the government's evolving understanding of health, initially as part of its budget decisions, and later shaped by political commitments and legislation.

During the colonial period, the allocation of revenue towards health budgets prioritised the interests of European settlers, seeking to create an infection free environment conducive to their wellbeing. After independence, public health strategies were decentralised to address healthcare needs at the community level, as healthcare demands within the colony expanded beyond the needs of Europeans. The colony's fiscal constraints justified this shift. Financing healthcare delivery was not a primary objective of the colonial government when determining the resources required for the colony's economic growth; instead, it was viewed as a shared responsibility between the government and healthcare beneficiaries. This logic persisted after independence, with healthcare delivery depending on the availability of public resources and recourse to other forms of domestic assistance. The characterisation of health as a right asserting a positive claim on state resources only materialised with the promulgation of Kenya's new 2010 Constitution. The subsequent health policies and strategic plans reflected the government's commitment to defining and budgeting for its financial obligations concerning the realisation of the right to health.

The Kenyan state has played a significant role in establishing the normative content of the right to health and defining what it considers as its domestic obligations.[150] Since independence, the state has politically expressed its intention to access additional funding from Kenyan citizens. The Kenya Health Sector Strategic and Investment Plan 2018-2023 rearticulates the scope of the state's maximum available resources obligation by linking it to pooling health revenue from the private sector and donors. The KHSSP 2018-2023 implies an obligation to seek domestic assistance, allowing the

---

150 MCR Craven, 'The International Covenant on Economic, Social and Cultural Rights—A Perspective on its Development', (PhD thesis, University of Nottingham 1995), 144.

government to explore and include available revenue sources at its disposal and those that can be made accessible to it as part of its financial strategy. This suggests the possibility of accessing *zakat* as a domestic resource, reflecting an evolutive interpretation of MAR.

However, the potential use of *zakat* as a domestic resource raises questions about the relationship between the state and religious communities. Relying on religious non-state actors to support state budgets can be complex and may led to concerns about religious bias or exclusion of non-members of a specific faith. In the Kenyan context, utilising *zakat* to supplement the state health budget could be perceived as prioritising the interests of the Muslim community over other groups, potentially exacerbating existing religious tensions in the country. Furthermore, it raises questions about the authority, consent, control, legality, and trust in the state's management and distribution of *zakat* for healthcare. These concerns will be explored in the following three chapters.

PART II

LEGAL SYSTEMS

Overview

In Part I, this academic work delved into the state's obligations to fulfil the right to health (Chapter 2). It subsequently explored the Kenyan Government's comprehension and execution of its duty under human rights law to finance healthcare (Chapter 3). In the process, a concise history of the Kenyan health sector's evolution was presented, highlighting the issue of resource constraints. This reinforces the argument presented in Chapter 2 for broadening the interpretation of *maximum available resources* under human rights law, warranting recourse to sources such as *zakat*. As a result, Chapters 2 and 3 established the potential for interpreting human rights law to encompass *zakat*. These chapters also underscored the necessity to examine two additional issues: first, the feasibility of employing *zakat* to fund healthcare within Islamic law; and second, whether recourse to *zakat* could also be acceptable under the Kenyan legal system and to Kenyan Muslims. These questions are scrutinised both in this chapter and in Part III.

Part II of this book focuses on the permissibility of utilising *zakat* to finance healthcare under Islamic law and the Kenyan Constitution. Chapter 4 probes whether Islamic law permits a non-Islamic state to use *zakat* for the overarching goal of funding healthcare, benefitting both Muslims and non-Muslims alike. Chapter 5 investigates the acceptability of the Kenyan Constitution permitting the state to legally accept and utilise *zakat* for healthcare financing while adhering to Islamic law conditions. This chapter analyses the circumstances under which the Kenyan Government can lawfully accept and use *zakat* for healthcare financing or be restricted from accessing these funds. Two legal sources (Islamic law and the Kenyan Constitution) are examined to identify these conditions, which are delineated and analysed to facilitate understanding the legal intricacies arising when Islamic law norms governing *zakat* are presented before the Kenyan Constitution for recognition and inclusion as a legal source. The potential conditions imposed by Islamic law when offering *zakat* to the Kenyan Government for healthcare financing, and conversely, whether those conditions are permissible under the Kenyan Constitution to justify the acceptance and use of *zakat,* are discussed as part of the state's responsibility to utilise *maximum available resources* for healthcare financing.

By examining these questions, normative, doctrinal, and theoretical clarity is achieved regarding the interplay between Islamic law and the Kenyan legal system. The concept of resource limitation within human rights scholarship acknowledges the challenges faced by states in fully realising the right to health. Limited sources of revenue pose one of the most significant obstacles to achieving this right. This book furthers academic scrutiny by analysing the role of Islamic law in healthcare financing, utilising the normative and methodological approaches provided by Islamic law for using *zakat* to address limited funding issues. This is further examined through fieldwork to comprehend how the Kenyan public understands Islamic law and constitutional conditions, supporting or rejecting the government's access to *zakat*.

Furthermore, it is important to draw the reader's attention to two well established traditional Islamic considerations; using the *salawat* (صلى الله عليه وسلم)[1] in parenthesis each time Prophet Muhammad's (صلى الله عليه وسلم) name is mentioned and the significance of Arabic in Islamic scholarship. The *Qur'an* was revealed in Arabic, and Prophet (صلى الله عليه وسلم), as well as most of his close *sahaba* (companions) were Arabs. Traditional Muslim scholarship, the development of legal doctrine and practice in medieval Islam, and the *hadith* collections (the authentic and reliable collection of the sayings and actions of the Prophet (صلى الله عليه وسلم) reported by his *sahaba* and documented by Imam Bukhari and Imam Muslim[2]) are all in Arabic. Translations are now available, but the *Qur'an* and the *hadith* collections are best understood from reading the Arabic script. The *fiqh* (science of using methodological principles to ascertain Islamic law) that Muslims refer to

---

[1] The *salawat* is translated as 'peace be upon him'. It is a custom with Muslims to mention the *salawat* immediately after referring to Prophet Muhammad (صلى الله عليه وسلم). Since this thesis applies Islamic methodologies, it follows the Islamic customs.

[2] Under *sunni* Islam, the *hadith* collections by Imams Bukhari and Muslim are regarded as authentic and reliable secondary sources of Islam.

from the four *sunni madhabs* (schools of Islamic thought[3]) is also in Arabic. To understand and make rulings based on Islamic law, one should be well versed in Arabic, *fiqh*, *hadith* and its *isnaad* (chain of transmission);[4] and *ijma* (consensus of the scholars) on Islamic doctrine and jurisprudence.

This knowledge is grounded in the Arabic language of the *Qur'an* and Islamic texts, the historical context of the *Qur'an's* revelation, and the explanations provided by Prophet Muhammad (صلى الله عليه وسلم) and the *fuqaha* (Muslim jurists). If this knowledge is lacking, one must consider the opinions and documented rulings of previous jurists, their debates, and adopt the most flexible rulings from their conclusions.[5] This is the starting point for understanding Islamic law on *zakat*. This methodology ensures the robustness of Islamic legal research, guaranteeing the reliability of Islam's doctrinal interpretations and legal rulings.

This method is characteristic of Islamic legal research, which links reliability of findings to the *Qur'an*, the *isnaad* of *hadiths* and *ijma*. There can be no deviation from rulings explicitly set out in the *Qur'an*, rulings sourced from *hadith* with an *isnaad* authenticated by jurists or rulings confirmed through *ijma* of jurists. Islamic norms must also be adhered to. These norms can be identified through historical enquiry, examining the documented comprehensive accounts of legal practice by Prophet Muhammad (صلى الله عليه وسلم), his *sahaba*, and later by individual jurists. The *ummah* (Muslim society) has played a crucial role in the construction and preservation of Islamic norms, developing a social conscience around these norms (for example, paying *zakat* exclusively to impoverished Muslims).

---

3 Generally, there are four dominant schools of Islamic thought under *sunni* Islam. These are the *Hanafi*, *Maliki*, *Shafi'e* and *Hanbali madhabs*. Discussed later in the chapter.

4 *Isnaad* is a form of Islamic methodology to test the authenticity of what is claimed as *sunnah*. It protects the reliability of Islamic law by tracing the claim to either the Prophet (صلى الله عليه وسلم), his *sahaba* or those persons who heard the claim from a *sahaba* as source of information.

5 T Ramadhan, *Western Muslims and the Future of Islam*, (Oxford: Oxford University Press, 2004); MH Kamali, *Principles of Islamic Jurisprudence* (Cambridge: Islamic Texts Society, 1991) and NJ Coulson, *A History of Islamic Law* (Edinburgh University Press, 1964), 182-200.

With this overview in mind, Chapter 4 begins by addressing whether Islamic law permits giving *zakat* to a non-Islamic state for the general purpose of financing healthcare, benefitting both Muslims and non-Muslims. Chapter 5 then advances the discussion by determining whether it is acceptable under the Constitution of Kenya for the state to legally accept and use *zakat* to finance healthcare while adhering to Islamic law conditions. Part II demonstrates how the norms and doctrine of these inter-legal approaches to revenue mobilisation for healthcare financing can be interwoven to alleviate the healthcare budget crisis in Kenya. A subsequent discussion explores the existence of any legal parameters within which *zakat* can be used to finance healthcare and be made available to the Kenyan state. This discussion is predicated on Islamic law as a discipline and source of scholarship on revenue mobilisation beyond the Islamic world.

Chapter 4
Legal Permissibility under Islamic Law on the use of *Zakat* by A Non-Islamic State to Finance Health

Introduction

This chapter investigates the legal foundations within Islamic law and scholarship on *zakat* to determine the permissibility of providing funds to a non-Islamic state for healthcare financing and the inclusion of non-Muslims as beneficiaries. The chapter commences by examining the interpretive flexibility of the *Qur'an* and legitimacy of its interpretation. It contends that the consensus of a group of individuals on a single interpretation or reading does not render it authoritative, and that Muslims are at liberty to interpret or extract from the text whatever is necessary and convenient to their individual and collective wellbeing.

The chapter establishes two primary points. First, despite differing opinions among jurists regarding the allocation of *zakat* to non-Muslims, Islamic law permits the utilisation of *zakat* for healthcare purposes, including non-Muslims beneficiaries, and as a source of revenue for a non-Islamic state, provided that it adheres to the Islamic conditions regulating its use. Second, Islamic law exhibits the capacity for evolution, dynamism, responsiveness, and multidimensionality, capable of generating responses from its diverse and rich traditions, emphasising its plurality and inherent transformative processes. The chapter advocates for the employment of *zakat* as a revenue source to support healthcare financing in Kenya, while cautioning that the *Qur'an* and *hadith* must provide answers on the permissibility of granting *zakat* to the Kenyan state and utilising it for non-Muslim healthcare.

This chapter seeks to clarify certain Islamic doctrinal and scholarship limitations and ambiguities concerning *zakat*. The *Qur'an* delineates eight categories of *zakat* beneficiaries:

> Zakat expenditures are only for the poor, for the needy, for those employed to collect (zakat), and for bringing hearts together (for Islam) and for freeing the captives (or slaves) and for those in debt and for the cause of Allah and for the (stranded) traveller – an obligation (imposed) by Allah. And Allah is Knowing and Wise.[1]

The *Qur'an* does not explicitly specify the purposes for which *zakat* must be allocated. Islamic scholarship has addressed this issue, with Al-Qaradawi, the late leading contemporary authority on *zakat,* stating that *zakat* must be directed towards poverty alleviation;[2] Kahf,[3] Ahmed,[4] Mahmud and Shah[5] also corroborate this assertion. Consequently, the majority of *zakat*-related studies have concentrated on its role on reducing household poverty rates, with landmark empirical research conducted by Kahf and Powell.[6] Additionally, the *Qur'an* does not explicitly restrict *zakat* payment to Muslims. *Sunni* scholarship, however, appears to have reached a consensus that *zakat* should only be made available to Muslim beneficiaries.[7]

---

[1] *Qur'an*: Chapter 9, verse 60.

[2] Y Al-Qaradawi, *Fiqh al Zakah, Vol. II: A Comparative Study of Zakah, Regulations and Philosophy in the Light of Quran and Sunna* (trans.) Monzer Kahf (Jeddah, Scientific Publishing Centre, 1999).

[3] M Kahf, '*Zakat*: Unresolved Issues in the Contemporary Fiqh' (1989) *Journal of Islamic Economics*, Vol 2, No 1.

[4] H Ahmad, 'Role of Zakah and Awqaf in Poverty Alleviation', (2004) Islamic Development Bank, *Occasional Paper* No 8.

[5] MW Mahmud and SS Shah, 'The Use of *Zakat* Revenue in Islamic Financing: Jurisprudential Debate and Practical Feasibility', (2009) *Journal on Studies in Islam and the Middle East*, vol 6, no 1.

[6] Kahf (n 8); and R Powell, '*Zakat*: Drawing Insights for Legal Theory and Economic Policy from Islamic Jurisprudence', (2010) 7 PITT. Tax Review. 43.

[7] For a detailed discussion of these four schools on *zakat* see: ARn Al-Jaziri, Islamic Jurisprudence According to the Four Sunni Schools, Volume I, (trans) Nancy Roberts. Fons Viate; Canada, 2009.

This chapter highlights the limitations imposed by scholarship on *zakat* as a financing source exclusively for Muslim use and posits that Islamic law, though historically grounded, can evolve in tandem with societal progress of across time and place. Accordingly, this chapter questions whether the *sunni* Islamic scholarship consensus, which confines the eight categories of *zakat* beneficiaries to Muslims, is strongly supported by historical evidence in excluding non-Muslims from these categories. Furthermore, it probes the extent to which Islamic law permits the allocation of *zakat* to a non-Islamic state and allows a non-Islamic state to implement Islamic norms on *zakat*.

Historically, Muslims have considered Islamic governments or Muslim jurists as the legitimate sources for the application and enforcement of Islamic law, rather than a non-Islamic state.[8] This is due to 'the religious significance of compliance with a religious obligation'[9] inherent in Islamic law, whereas a non-Islamic state, such as Kenya, employs its own authority for compliance, not based on the *Qur'an* or *sunnah* (the sayings and actions of the Prophet (صلى الله عليه وسلم) recorded in *hadith* collections). This distinction raises challenges within Islamic law to restrict the allocation of *zakat* – a fundamental pillar of Islam – to a non-Islamic state for healthcare financing and the inclusion of non-Muslim beneficiaries, testing the adaptive capacity of Islamic law. An-Naim contends that Islamic law and state law function as complementary normative systems, with each operating 'on its own terms and within its field of competence and authority'.[10]

An-Naim's argument implies that while each legal system must remain distinct, Islamic law can influence the development and interpretation of state law and be incorporated as modern legal codes for application by a

---

[8] AS Mousalli, *The Islamic Quest for Democracy, Pluralism, and Human Rights* (University of Florida Press, 2001); A An-Naim, 'The Compatibility Dialectic: Mediating the Legitimate Coexistence of Islamic Law and State Law' (2010) *The Modern Law Review*, Vol 73, No 1, 1-29.

[9] A An-Na'im, 'Complementary, Not Competing, Claims of Law and Religion: An Islamic Perspective' (2013) *Pepperdine Law Review*, Vol 39, Issue 5, 1231-1256, at 1250.

[10] Ibid, at 1250.

non-Islamic state.[11] The extent to which this argument affects state norms will be considered in the following chapter. The present discussion focuses on whether Islamic law permits the giving of *zakat* to a non-Islamic state for healthcare financing and the implementation of Islamic norms on *zakat*. The inquiry does not concern Islamic law influencing state law to incorporate *zakat* norms; rather, it pertains to the permissibility under Islam for *zakat,* as a religious obligation, to be offered to a non-Islamic state for governance and utilisation. The subsequent chapter will explore how state law can incorporate Islamic law as positive law instead of religious law. To convincingly argue this position, this chapter must first demonstrate that Islam, operating 'on its own terms and within its field of competence and authority',[12] allows *zakat* to be used in a manner proposed in the book.

A recent study investigated the feasibility of using *zakat* to finance health insurance in Sudan; however, this research focused exclusively on a Muslim-majority state and did not address whether *zakat* could be employed to fund health insurance for non-Muslims.[13] Beyond Muslim-majority states, Muslim scholarship has not addressed the question of offering *zakat* to a non-Islamic state with a Muslim-minority population. This gap in scholarship is addressed by examining three questions:

i. Whether there exist any legal parameters within Islamic law governing the use of *zakat* for healthcare financing;
ii. Whether non-Muslims can be considered as beneficiaries of *zakat*-funded healthcare; and
iii. Whether *zakat* can be made available to a non-Islamic state.

These questions are analysed through Islamic doctrine, *fiqh*/scientific methodology, and scholarship. To examine these questions, the chapter is divided into five subsections and a conclusion. The discussion begins with an explanation of the methodology for studying, analysing and deriving

---

[11] ibid, at 1250-1251.

[12] ibid, at 1250.

[13] FM Idris, M Seraj and H Ozdeser, 'Assessing the possibility of financing social health insurance from *zakat*, case of Sudan: ARDL bounds approach', (2022) *Journal of Islamic Accounting and Business Research*, Vol 13 No 2, 264-276.

legal rulings under Islamic law. The discussion then moves to provide an overview of the history of *zakat* and its governance. Thereafter, the rest of the discussion delves into a critical analysis of the questions. The proposal to use *zakat* as a source of revenue that can be made available to a non-Islamic state to support healthcare financing is introduced with the following cautionary statement taken from one of the interviewees:

> Answers must be found from the Qur'an and hadith on whether our zakat can be given to the Kenyan state and whether our zakat can be used to finance healthcare of non-Muslims. It does not matter, even if under the Constitution, it is acceptable to take and use zakat or even if the President says this is ok and can be done. It must be permitted under our law, our shari'ah (Islamic law). We must ask ourselves what the Qur'an says, is there hadith on this, is there evidence from the past that zakat was given to non-Muslims.[14]

The Methodology of Studying Islamic Law

Deliberations within the realm of Islamic law, pertaining to any legal point, question, or issue, are contingent on the rigour and robustness of the methodology employed. This methodology enables scholars to establish the context in which Islamic law operates, offering the normative framework and doctrine that addresses all legal inquiries. Distinct principles are also employed in deriving Islamic norms and doctrine. Consequently, reference to the sources of Islamic law, its various schools, and the methodologies they employ, is of paramount importance in the development of a comprehensive approach to the study of Islamic law. The ensuing discussion will elaborate on these aspects.

Sources of Islamic law

The *Qur'an* serves as the primary reference in the study of Islamic law and the derivation of legal rulings. The *sunna,* which encompasses the sayings

---

[14] Interviewee No. 137. Interview date 15.02.2020 Nairobi

and actions of the Prophet (صلى الله عليه وسلم) further explicates the *Qur'an*. The *sunna* is documented in *hadith* collections,[15] which through a chain of reliable authorities has been handed down from generation to generation of Muslims. *Hadith* also shows what the *sahaba* (the close companions of the Prophet (صلى الله عليه وسلم) held to be exclusively correct in matters of religion and law and could therefore properly serve as a norm for practical application.[16]

Both the *Qur'an* and *hadith* are considered fixed texts, indisputable nor apocryphal.[17] Classical and traditional jurists have maintained that the *Qur'an* should be interpreted literally, with minimal room for variation.[18] In contrast, modern Muslim scholars such as Kamali,[19] Ramadhan,[20] and Ali[21] argue that the *Qur'an* should be understood contextually, considering the time and place, allowing for diverse interpretations. Ali, who views Islamic law as an immutable source, posits that it can be an 'evolutionary, dynamic, responsive and multidimensional phenomenon capable of generating responses from within varied and rich traditions, highlighting its plurality and its inbuilt transformative processes'.[22] Consequently, this chapter examines whether the verses on *zakat* are amenable to such transformative interpretations.

---

[15] I Goldziher, *Introduction to Islamic Theology and Law* (trans.) Andras and Ruth Hamori (Princeton University Press, Princeton, New Jersey, 1981) 37.

[16] For studies on *hadith* see GHA Juynboll, *The Authenticity of the Tradition Literature: Discussions in Modern Egypt* (Leiden, 1969).

[17] Goldziher (n 20), 31.

[18] RM Gleave, 'Interpreting Scriptures in Judaism, Christianity and Islam' in M Z Cohen and A Berlin (eds) *Overlapping Inquiries* (Cambridge University Press, 2016), Chapter 8, 183-203; C Melchert, 'Ahmad Ibn Hanbal and the Qur'an', (2004) *Journal of Qur'anic Studies*, Vol 6, No 2, 22-34.

[19] Kamali (n 5).

[20] Ramadhan (n 5).

[21] SS Ali, *Modern Challenges to Islamic Law* (Cambridge: Cambridge University Press, 2016).

[22] ibid., at 10.

In the absence of a direct *Qur'anic* verse or *hadith* addressing a legal issue or question, scholars employ *qiyas* (deduction).[23] The presence of a *hadith* on a matter is not disregarded when it appears to provide solid grounding; however, *ijtihad* (the unfettered exercise of intellect) is accepted and even required as a justifiable means of determining the law.[24] This intellectual pursuit contributed to the development of *fiqh*/scientific methodology and the emergence of the *fuqaha* (scholars of jurisprudence).[25] Differences among the *fuqaha* led to the formation of scholarly factions and schools, which primarily diverged in specific legal rulings and occasionally in methodological points.

Schools of Islamic thought

In the exercise of *qiyas/deductive reasoning,* reference is made to Islamic schools of thought when their doctrine and practice support the reasoning. Four predominant traditional schools of *sunni* Islamic thought exist, each with minor variations in ritual and law.[26] The *Hanafi* school, prevalent among Muslims in Turkey, Central Asia, and the south Asian subcontinent, is the first. The *Maliki* school, which gained followers in parts of Egypt, North and West Africa, followed. The *Shafi* school dominates regions such as parts of Egypt, East and Southern Africa, South Arabia and Malaysia. Lastly, the *Hanbali* school is represented by a relatively small number of

[23] A Hasan, 'The Principle of Qiyas in Islamic Law – An Historical Perspective', (1976) Islamic Studies, Vol 15, No 3 201-210, 202 and 205.

[24] TJ Al-Alwani, 'Ijtihad' (1991) *Occasional Paper Series, No 4,* International Institute of Islamic Thought, 6-9.

[25] There are numerous schools of jurisprudence in Islam. Some of these schools have disappeared (e.g., Mutazilites), some are waning (e.g., Bahai); new ones are emerging, and the existing ones are diversifying. However, the main schools of Islamic jurisprudence are two, the Sunni and Shi'a schools, which have survived in their traditional forms to date.

[26] There are two dominant sects in Islam: The *sunni* and *shi'a*. Most of the Muslims subscribe to the *sunni* sect. The distinction between the two sects' centres around Imam Ali; the Prophet's (صلى الله عليه وسلم) cousin and son-in-law. Both sects are divided in their understanding on who among the Prophet's (صلى الله عليه وسلم) *sahaba* should have succeeded him. The *shi'a* believe that the leadership was lawfully Imam Ali's.

adherents in the Middle East, particularly in Saudi Arabia.[27] Most Muslims in Kenya are *sunni* who subscribe to either the *Shafi* or *Hanafi* school. These schools are named after their founders.

The distinguishing feature of these schools is the methodological tools they employ to derive legal rulings from the *Qur'an* and *hadith*. The *Hanafi* school is considered the most flexible, while the *Hanbali* school is attributed with rigidity. All four schools oppose giving *zakat* to non-Muslims.[28] However, their scholarship does not address the permissibility of offering or providing *zakat* to non-Muslims or a non-Islamic state for purposes such as healthcare.

Since the 8th century, doctrinally based legal analysis has been conducted within these schools of thought. Each school represents centuries of legal thought and experiences, shaping the way Islamic scholars identify and elucidate Islamic law.[29] While they engage with specific reasoning methods and interpretation rules when examining the sources of Islamic law, they all concur on the significance of *ijma* (juristic consensus), *shura* (consultation) and *ijtihad* (reasoning).[30] Despite these diverse reasoning methods, *ijtihad*/intellectual reasoning, a well-established tool for discovering Islamic doctrine, is widely employed.[31] It encompasses all three

---

[27] Goldziher (n 20) 49.

[28] MA Mahajneh, I Greenspan and M M Haj-Yahia, '*Zakat* Giving to Non-Muslims: Mufti's attitudes in Arab and Non-Arab Countries (2021) *Journal of Muslim Philanthropy & Civil Society*, Vol V, No II, 66-86 at 71-73.

[29] Kamali (n 5): 3; Coulson (n 5), 21-35.

[30] D Vishanoff, *The Formation of Islamic Hermeneutics: How Sunni Legal Theorists Imagined a Revealed Law* (Ann Arbor: American Oriental Society, 2010): MY Faruqi, *Development of Usul al Fiqh: An Early Historical Perspective* (Adam Publishers, 2007); S Lucas, *Constructive Critics, Hadith Literature, and the Articulation of Sunni Islam: The Legacy of the Generation of Ibn Sa'd,Ibn Ma'in and Ibn Hanbal* (Leiden: Brill, 2004); W Hallaq, *A History of Islamic Legal Theories: An Introduction to Sunni Usul al Fiqh* (Cambridge: Cambridge University Press, 1997) 19, 23, 28; C Melchert, *The Formation of the Sunni Schools of Law, 9th – 10th Centuries CE* (Leiden: Brill, 1997); W Hallaq, 'On The Authoritativeness of Sunni Consensus', International Journal of Middle East Studies 18, no 4 (1986): 427-454.

[31] Kamali (n 5): 3.

doctrinally-based research methods (deductive, analogy and inductive) within socio-legal scholarship.

These four schools situate Islamic methodology firmly within a theological framework grounded in revelation and reason. Revelation classifies actions as obligatory, forbidden, and permissible, while reason, through the application of *fiqh*/scientific methodology, elaborates on these legal categorisations.[32] Thus, the law on *zakat,* as described in the *Qur'an,* is examined in this context to determine whether revelation and reason permit its allocation to a non-Islamic state for financing healthcare for both Muslims and non-Muslims. The efficacy of these methods is discussed next.

Islamic methodology

Islamic scholarship is historical in nature, with norms preserved through centuries of scholarly transmission. These norms have either been fortified against change or have evolved in response to changing circumstances. Modern perspectives on Islam and its law must align with historically established norms agreed upon by scholars, leaving little room for contention.[33] The law is mostly irrefutable, with limited scope for reinterpretation or reconstruction of historical Islamic norms under orthodox Islam.[34]

However, this does not mean that the exposition of Islamic norms, fundamentally medieval in spirit and outlook, cannot be re-examined today to inform the political, economic, and social development of both

---

32 A El Shamsy, 'The Wisdom of God's Law: Two Theories' in Kevin Reinhart and Robert Gleave (ed), *Islamic Law in Theory: Studies on Jurisprudence in Honor of Bernard Weiss* (Brill, 2014) 19-38, 23.

33 Abu Hanifa, Imam Malik, Imam Shafi and Imam Ahmad ibn Hanbal – the mainstream orthodox jurists of *Sunni* Islam – also hold these views. Khalil Mohamed Ibrahim, Islam and the Challenges of Modernity. Georgetown Journal of International Affairs, Vol 5, No 1 (2004), 97-104.

34 WB Hallaq, *Sharī'a: Theory, Practice, Transformations* (Cambridge, UK: Cambridge University Press), 2009; Joseph Schacht, *An Introduction to Islamic Law* (Oxford, 1964); Coulson (n 5).

Muslims and non-Muslims. This is where the three Islamic methods of *ijma/juristic consensus, shura/consultation,* and *ijtihad/intellectual* reasoning become useful. By employing these methods on the *Qur'an* and *hadith,* several meanings can be drawn. The goal is not to produce a view starkly at variance with the Muslim view on *zakat,* or against historical facts known to general readers of Islamic law, but rather to rely on these methods to draw conclusions on the law on *zakat* as set out in the *Qur'an* and refer to reliable historical sources.

Muslim scholars, through *ijma*/juristic consensus, have predominantly maintained that only Muslims are eligible to receive *zakat*.[35] This consensus has established a norm within Islamic law regarding the lawful recipients of *zakat*. However, it can be argued that this view contradicts practice during the Islamic classical and medieval periods, which served as the foundation for the development of Islamic law. Moreover, there is limited Islamic scholarship available discussing the legal aspects of *zakat* as a source of revenue to finance health, leaving room for *shura* (consultation) and *ijtihad*/intellectual reasoning.[36] To address this gap, the present chapter examines the three questions outlined in the introduction. Although *zakat* has been extensively studied as an economic tool to reduce poverty and ensure equitable wealth distribution within local groups,[37] it has not been linked to achieving the right to health. Exploring the answers to these questions will provide valuable insights.

---

[35] Al Ghazali, *Ihya Ulum al-Din,* (trans.) K Honerkamp, *Revival of Religion's Sciences,* Volume 1 (Fons Vitae, 2016); Ibn Mundhir, *Al Ijma,* (trans.) S Abd al Hamid (The Islamic Literary Foundation 2014) 174. Views by Ahmad Al Layth and Abu Thawr cited in Al Qaradawi (n 7).

[36] L Latif, 'An Explication on Broadening the Definition and Scope of Maximum Available Resources under the General Comment 14 of the ICESCR to include Islamic Taxation in Financing the Right to Health', *Biomed J Sci & Tech Res 1(3)-2017;* and L Latif, 'Framing the Argument to Broaden Kenya's Limited Fiscal Space for Health Financing by Introducing *Zakat*', *Biomed J Sci & Tech Res 5(5)-2018.*

[37] Kahf (n 8); Powell (n 11); N Hoque, MA Khan, and KD Mohamed, 'Poverty alleviation by *Zakah* in a transitional economy: a small business entrepreneurial framework', (2015) *J Glob Entrepr Res.*

During his lifetime, Prophet Muhammad (صلى الله عليه وسلم) not only legitimised the textual sources for law, the *Qur'an* and the *sunna*, but also sanctioned the three methods of *ijma*/juristic *consensus, shura*/consultation and *ijtihad*/intellectual reasoning to guide interpretation and development of the law. After his death, the caliphs engaged in *shura*/consultation with the *sahaba* on specific issues raised, leading to *ijma*/juristic consensus, which the caliph would adopt as the legal ruling. If they did not agree, the caliph would make an independent ruling through *ijtihad* (independent reasoning). Differences were legitimate, and multiple views were standard.

Despite the *ijma*/juristic consensus of the four schools of thought opposing the distribution of *zakat* to non-Muslims, the process of *shura*/consultation with local Muslim scholars and *zakat* payers in Kenya allows for the exercise *ijtihad*/intellectual reasoning to explore the Islamic permissibility of extending *zakat* to non-Muslims and to a non-Islamic state. Historical evidence highlights that the second caliph of Islam, Umar ibn Al-Khattab, issued a decree instructing Muslim governors to rule first by the *Qur'an* and the *sunna* and subsequently by employing *ijtihad*/intellectual reasoning on matters upon which the *Qur'an* and the *sunna* remained silent.[38] As the *Qur'anic* verses on *zakat* do not explicitly state that the funds are exclusively for Muslims, nor is there a *hadith* outlining such restrictions, the use of *ijtihad*/intellectual reasoning is justified. Al-Khattab's decree serves as a precedent for employing *ijtihad* to interpret the *Qur'an,* provided it is contextualised and does not contradict other parts of the *Qur'an* or the *sunna*.

Ibn Khaldun, a prominent 13th century Muslim scholar, clarifies the methodology applicable to addressing questions related to Islamic law. He contends that while the *Qur'an* and the *sunna* represent the only authoritative sources, *ijma*/juristic consensus holds equal authority. He regarded *ijma* as infallible and binding.[39] Umar ibn Abdul Aziz, the eighth

---

[38] AB Al-Jassas, *Al-Ijma: Dirasa fi Fikratihi: Bab al-Ijtihad,* (ed.) Zuhayr Kibi (Beirut: Dar al-Muntakhab, 1993) 9-10.

[39] Ibn Khaldun, *The Muqaddimah: An Introduction to History,* (trans.) F Rosenthal (Princeton University Press, 2015) 53.

caliph of Islam, saw the impossibility of a universal *ijma*/juristic consensus. Therefore, he accepted the *ijma* of a specific country.[40] This sets a valuable precedent for attempting to establish *ijma* on *zakat* among Kenyan Muslims and their scholars. However, dissenting opinion exist. The *Shafi* school, predominant in Kenya, acknowledges the formative role of consensus and the legitimacy of divergent views. This permits research into the possibility of offering *zakat* to a non-Islamic state for healthcare financing, thereby including non-Muslims as beneficiaries, irrespective of the *ijma*/juristic consensus of the four schools.[41]

The *Shafi* school perceives *ijma* as a consensus encompassing the entire community, both scholars and the public. The school acknowledges that attaining such consensus is challenging, which, in turn, enhances the reliability of the derived ruling. Goldziher opposes this view, arguing that *ijma*/juristic consensus should only be exercised by acknowledged Islamic scholars of a given period, as it is their role to interpret and deduce law and doctrine.[42] Since a majority of Kenyan Muslim scholarship is rooted in the *Shafi* school, this chapter does not limit *ijma* to the consensus of Muslim scholars alone. *Ijma* under the *Shafi* school also stems from *shura/consultation* within the community, leading to an acceptable opinion. Consequently, the chapter's deliberations are supplemented by fieldwork to assess the *ijma*/juristic consensus and *shura*/consultation of the Muslim public on *zakat* as addressed in Part III.

Individual Muslims exercise *ijtihad*/intellectual reasoning to form an opinion, which is subsequently deliberated upon and either accepted or rejected. *Ijtihad* is crucial for comprehending the scope and significance of a text. It has been utilised in various ways: first, for generating new opinions on issues lacking textual authority; second, for formulating legislation to keep up with social development; and finally, for the

---

[40] Al-Jassas (n 43) 15-16.

[41] (n 33) 71-73.

[42] Goldziher (n 20) 52.

theoretical renewal or development of the legal system, enabling Islamic law to adapt to different times and conditions.[43]

In conclusion, this section highlights two essential points. Firstly, when addressing the question of using *zakat* to finance health and include non-Muslims, it is crucial to adhere strictly to the precedents established under Islamic law. Subsequently, the operational principles of *ijma*/juristic consensus, *shura*/consultation, and *ijtihad*/intellectual reasoning are employed as methodological tools available to Islamic scholarship in reaching a well-reasoned conclusion. *Ijtihad* endows Islam with capacity for evolution. Collectively, these three methods indicate that there is scope for re-examining the *fiqh*/scientific methodology on *zakat,* assessing its suitability for financing health by offering *zakat* to a non-Islamic state and non-Muslims who fulfil Islamic criteria. Although the four schools of thought may oppose giving *zakat* to non-Muslims, an alternative perspective permitting this can be found in the *ijtihad*/intellectual reasoning of the caliph Umar ibn Al-Khattab. As a *sahaba,* he is considered a more reliable source for justifying an expanded application of Islamic law.[44]

With the methodological framework for analysing legal questions under Islamic law established, the subsequent sections delve into the inquiry concerning *zakat* as a potential source of revenue for financing health, accessible to non-Muslims and a non-Islamic state.

---

[43] MF Al-Durayni, *Al-Ijtihad wa al-Tajdid fi al-Fikr al-Islami*. (Valetta, Malta: Islamic World Studies Center, 1991) 12-14.

[44] MN Musharraf, *A Roadmap for Studying Fiqh: An Introduction to the Key of the Four Madhabs* (Australian Islamic Library, 2020)

Zakat: Background

The beneficiaries of *zakat*

Surah Al Tawbah (the Chapter on Repentance), verse 60 of the *Qur'an,* is often cited by Muslim scholars when discussing *zakat*. This verse identifies eight types of recipients:

1. the poor;
2. the needy;
3. those employed to collect zakat;
4. those whose hearts are to be inclined towards Islam/bringing them towards Islam;45
5. for freeing captives;
6. debtors;
7. for the cause of Allah;46
8. the traveller.

Among these 8 categories of beneficiaries, the poor and needy receive priority.

Zakat is not *sadaqa*

A discerning observer of linguistics may question the translation of the word *sadaqa* (charity) in *Surah Al Tawbah* verse 60 as '*zakat*'. Although the Arabic word used in the verse refers of *sadaqa,* it is considered the standard for identifying persons to whom *zakat* must be paid or on whose behalf it must be distributed. An examination of the historical context of this verse is necessary to clarify why the literal text mentions *sadaqa* but implies *zakat*.

---

[45] Scholars have addressed this to also mean those who are not aggressive towards Islam and those whom, if assistance is given, may incline towards Islam.

[46] Muslims perform acts with the hope and reward from God and hence their actions are towards gaining the pleasure of God; as such they pay for infrastructure through which people receive assistance, such as building hospitals, schools or constructing water wells.

The *Qur'an* is divided into Meccan and Medinan verses. Before the *Hijra*,[47] the Prophet (صلى الله عليه وسلم) received revelation concerning theology and eschatology,[48] referred to as 'Meccan *surahs*' since they were revealed in Mecca. Several Meccan verses also discussed *sadaqa*, which was sought from Muslims' voluntary charitable endeavours on behalf of poor and needy Muslims.

After the Prophet (صلى الله عليه وسلم) migrated to Medina, revelation focused on legislation, strict enforcement of doctrine, and codes of conduct for structuring society.[49] *Surah Al Tawbah* was revealed in Medina when the Prophet (صلى الله عليه وسلم) was establishing an Islamic government. Verse 60 carried a mandatory instruction on the payment of *sadaqa*. In my opinion, this transformed the discretionary nature of *sadaqa* into an obligation. Its obligatory nature required Muslims to annually pay this tax according to the prescribed criteria. Some of these criteria are found in the *Qur'an*, while others are established through the *sunna*.[50] The *Qur'anic* criteria are linked to verse 60, which identifies eight categories of *zakat* beneficiaries. Consequently, the word *sadaqa* has dual implications due to this verse: charity, based on voluntary giving (with no prescribed formula for *sadaqa*, even a smile is considered charity[51]), and mandatory *sadaqa*, also referred to as *zakat*, which is prescribed under a regulatory framework. *Surah Al*

---

47 The *hijra* is used to describe the start of the Muslim calendar after migration of the Prophet from Mecca to Medina in 622CE.

48 MM Al Azami, 'The History of the Quranic Text from Revelation to Compilation. A Comparative Study with the Old and New Testaments (UK Islamic Academy Leicester: UK, n.d); M Shafi, The Qu'ran – How it was Revealed and Compiled' (n.d.) http://www.daralislam.org/portals/0/Publications/TheQURANHowitwasRevealedand Compiled.pdf; MM Pickthall, *The Meaning of the Glorious Qu'ran*. (Birmingham: Islamic Dawah Centre International, 2013).

49 Goldziher (n 20).

50 The *sunna* contains references to the instructions, sayings and actions of the Prophet. The *sunna* has been codified in the collection of *hadith* by Bukhari and Muslim. The *hadith* refers to the collection of the *sunna* and the traditions established by the *sahaba* (the companions of the Prophet who lived with him and who were in or had direct contact with him).

51 S Al Sayyid, *Fiqh us Sunnah: Az Zakah and As Siyam* (trans.) Muhammad Saeed Dabas and Jamal al Din Zarabozo (Islamic Printing & Publishing Co, Egypt, 2000) 98.

Tawbah, verse 60, is thus considered to refer to this mandatory form of *sadaqa* as *zakat.*

Zakat is the Islamic form of tax on wealth

An examination of the meaning and scope of *zakat* reveals hermeneutic disputes among scholars, resulting in the establishment of two main positions. The first position regards *zakat* a form of tax (discussed in Chapter 1), while the second position views it as charity or alms. A third stance, primarily advanced by modern scholarship, perceives *zakat* as a financial instrument and a source of revenue. However, all scholars concur on the obligatory nature of *zakat,* differing on its description, scope, and categories of wealth subject to *zakat.*

Those scholars opposing the characterisation of *zakat* as tax argue that the term 'tax' implies the existence of a political authority imposing and collecting *zakat* for redistribution. They contend that since most Muslims reside in non-Islamic states where *zakat* is neither imposed nor collected by the state, its payment in these contexts is discretionary and voluntary, rendering the tax analogy weak.[52] Conversely, scholars who equate *zakat* with tax emphasise its obligatory nature, dismissing the discretionary and voluntary aspect.[53] They argue that the absence of a political authority imposing or forcibly collecting *zakat* does not dilute its mandatory nature. As the third pillar, *zakat* is compulsory.

Similarly, modern scholars assert that *zakat* should not be described as charity or alms, as it is a higher obligation and a financial form of worship on surplus on wealth.[54] Although no political authority enforces payment, eligible Muslims self-assess *zakat,* making it self-enforcing due to its

---

[52] MS Ibn Al-Uthaymeen, *Fiqh of Worship: Purification, Doctrines, Salat, Zakat, Siyam, Hajj.* (trans.) Abdallah Alaceri. (London: Al-Firdous Ltd, 2011).

[53] Pickthall (n 52); Kahf (n 8); Powell (n 11) 43; ASU Rano, 'A Treatise on Socioeconomic Roles of Zakah', MPRA Paper No 81155 (2017).

[54] M Zulfiqar, *Zakat According to the Qur'an and Sunna* (Riyadh: Darussalam, 2011); Al Qaradawi (n 7).

religious obligation.[55] These positions clearly distinguish *zakat* from *sadaqa* (charity). While *zakat* is mandatory, *sadaqa* is not. Bashear posits that the *Qur'anic* revelation on *sadaqa* preceded those on *zakat*, leading to the interchangeable use of the terms and distorting their distinct meanings.[56] This chapter treats *zakat* as tax, as its mandatory nature renders it a consistent financing source for health.

Understanding *zakat* as tax highlights the significance of defining tax and its relationship to religious communities. While the state imposes tax, the *Qur'an* imposes *zakat* as a religious obligation for Muslims. This raises questions about normative claims in tax law and the state's role in collecting specific taxes from religious communities. Key questions include whether *zakat* can be considered a tax if collected by the state, even if voluntarily submitted as a donation. This depends on how tax is defined, and whether it includes religious obligations such as *zakat*. If tax is defined as any compulsory payment made to the state, *zakat* may not fall under this definition. However, if tax is defined more broadly as any payment to the state for public goods and services, *zakat* could be considered a tax.

The convergence between *zakat* and tax has crucial implications for understanding the relationship between law and politics, highlighting the tension between religious obligations and state power, and the challenges of accommodating religious diversity within a secular state. It also raises questions about the state's legitimacy in collecting taxes from religious communities, and the role of religious obligations in shaping tax policy. This discussion on *zakat* and tax contributes to socio-legal scholarship by emphasising the complexity of the relationship between law, religion, and the state. It underscores the importance of examining how religious norms intersect with state law and policy, and the implications for religious minorities and their interactions with the state. This resonates with

---

55 Mazni Abdullah, (n.d). 'The Role of *Zakat* on Muslims' Tax Compliance Behaviour – From Qualitative Perspectives' https://pdfs.semanticscholar.org/b46b/a63b1ae70135e2daabb12ac8ecf7864455a8.pdf.

56 S Bashear, 'On the Origins and Development of the Meaning of *Zakat* in Early Islam', (1993) *Arabica* 40, No 1, 84-113.

Redding's work on India,[57] which illustrates the complexity of the relationship between religion and state governance in contemporary contexts and the ways in which states may rely on religious communities to support their own survival.

The discussion also raises vital questions about the extent to which the Kenyan state may need to engage with Islamic non-state actors to effectively implement its health policies and fulfil its obligations under international human rights law. These questions relate to broader debates within socio-legal scholarship about the role of non-state actors in the implementation of human rights and the potential for religious communities to play a meaningful role in shaping public policy.

Categories of *zakat*

In Chapter 1, it was noted that *zakat* is levied on specific categories of wealth that meet the prescribed threshold. Examples of these traditional categories include income savings, livestock, shares, gold and silver. Savings and shares exceeding Kenya Shilling (KES) 260,000 (GBP 1,761),[58] or gold and silver over 80g are subject to 2.5 per cent of the total amount in *zakat*. The *zakat* on livestock varies, and Al-Sayyid Sabiq provides a list of thresholds for cows, goats, sheep and camel.[59] Some scholars object to imposing *zakat* on savings and shares, drawing a distinction between visible and non-visible wealth.[60] They argue that *zakat* is only applicable to visible wealth. Conversely, other scholars do not make this distinction and include all the traditional wealth categories under *zakat*. Muslim scholars in Kenya advise that the payment of *zakat* be made on both forms of wealth,[61] and most Muslims in Kenya pay *zakat* on their savings and gold.

---

[57] JA Redding, *A Secular Need: Islamic Law and State Governance in Contemporary India* (University of Washington Press, 2020).

[58] Using the rate of 1GBP to 147KES, as at May 2022.

[59] Al Sayyid (n 56) 275.

[60] NP Aghntdes, *Mohammedan Theories of Finance* 527 (1916); Powell (n 11).

[61] Interviewee No. 144. Interview date 20.02.2020 Nairobi

The differing perspectives on *zakat*-eligible wealth categories have been addressed by Imam Malik, Al-Qaradawi and Powell.[62] Kahf discusses the views of various Islamic schools of thought on extending *zakat* to other wealth categories, such as stocks and bonds, while Gapur Oziev and Magomet Yandiev explore *zakat* on cryptocurrencies.[63] *Zakat* eligibility applies to every adult Muslim of sound mind who possesses these wealth categories, provided the threshold is met.

State involvement in collecting *zakat*

Currently, governments in countries such as Egypt, Jordan, Kuwait, Iran, Bangladesh, Bahrain, Lebanon, Indonesia, and Oman[64] facilitate *zakat* collection and distribution through voluntary state intervention schemes. While many Islamic governments support state-level *zakat* collection, the Tunisian government diverges from this view. In December 2019, the Tunisian Parliament debated a draft finance law for 2020 introduced by the Al Nahda political party, which called for a government established *zakat* fund supervised by the Ministry of Finance. The Tunisian parliament rejected the idea of state involvement, arguing that no state should administer or manage a religious obligation.[65] To date, no secular or non-Islamic state receives, collects, or distributes *zakat*, or facilitates the process.

---

[62] Imam Malik ibn Anas, *Al-Muwatta of Imam Malik Ibn Anas: The First Formulation of Sharia 93-110* (trans.) Aisha Abdurrahman Bewley (2001); Kamali (n 5); Al-Qaradawi (n 7); Powell (n 11).

[63] Kahf (n 8); G Oziev and M Yandiev, 'Cryptocurrency from *Sharia* perspective' (2017) *Al Shajarah* 23(2), 315-338.

[64] Egypt: Law No. 66 of 1977 (establishing the Nasser Social Bank); Jordan: *Zakat* Act of 1978; Kuwait: Law No. 5 of 1982 (establishing the *Zakat* House) – not yet mandatory; Iran: http://irandataportal.syr.edu/welfare-social-security/imam-khomeini-relief-foundation-2 ; Bangladesh: Ordinance No. VI of 1982; Bahrain: Decree Law No. 8 of 1979 (establishing the *Zakat* Fund); Lebanon: Lebanon's *Zakat* Fund https://www.*zakat*.org.lb/ Indonesia: Law of *Zakat* Management No. 38 (1999); Oman: Administered by the Ministry of Religious Affairs and Endowments. https://www.mara.gov.om/home.aspx

[65] A Al Hilali, 'It was presented by Al-Nahda Movement. Why did the Tunisian parliament drop the "*Zakat* Fund"?' Teller Report, 12 December 2019.

Muslim scholars have striven to articulate the main principles of *zakat* assessment, collection, and disbursement, and have investigated individual Muslim countries to examine how these principles are applied, and how the general *zakat* system is put in place.[66] Among these scholars are those who argue that *zakat* is unlike the other four pillars of Islam,[67] in that its practice is not entirely left up to the individual's conscience. Government intervention is required to manage both *zakat* collection and disbursement.[68] State authorities have the power to force an individual to pay.[69] For this reason, Al-Qaradawi explains that some Muslim jurists categorise *zakat* as *'fiscal worship'*, reflecting the fact that it must be performed by individuals in accordance with governmental or fiscal mechanisms. The truth of this assertion, however, is limited to countries with an Islamic form of government, and not, for example, a non-Islamic state with a Muslim-minority population.

As the prerogative to tax lies with the state and *zakat* is a form of tax, there is no reason within Islamic law why a state cannot impose or receive it. Historical accounts further clarify this position. Ishmawi recounts that following the Prophet's (صلى الله عليه وسلم) death, the question of giving *zakat* to the state became disputed. Dissenting Arab tribes contended that taxes due during the Prophet's (صلى الله عليه وسلم) lifetime were not payable to the caliph or the Islamic government. Caliph Abu Bakr maintained that the state held the right to exact that tax, establishing a precedent when he compelled dissenting tribes to comply. That precedent allowed the caliph to intervene in the interpretation of verses linked to the execution of state financial policies.[70] Consequently, although Islamic law serves as the

---

66 Al Sayyid (n 56); Al-Qaradawi (n 7); Kahf, (n 8) 22; Powell, (n 11); Hoque et al (n 42).

67 Of the five foundation tenets of Islam, *zakat* is regarded as the third most important act of piety after the *shahada* (professing belief in Allah and acknowledging Muhammad as the Messenger of Allah) and the five daily *salaats* (prescribed prayer). The fourth and fifth tenets refer to *saum* (fasting during the month of Ramadhan- this is the ninth month of the Islamic calendar), and the *hajj* (performing the circumambulation of the Ka'aba in Mecca).

68 Al-Qaradawi (n 7), 59.

69 ibid.

70 MS Ishmawi, *Al-Khilafa al-Islamiyya*. (Cairo: Sina li al-Nashr, 1992) 105-9.

supreme law for Muslims, the absence of explicit injunctions on numerous issues, both old and new, granted rulers considerable latitude in implementing their interpretations.

There are Muslim scholars who argue that *zakat* can only be given to an Islamic government.[71] In contrast, others contend that the obligation of *zakat* should be discharged by eligible individuals without state interference.[72] Extensive literature addresses these viewpoints; however, it lacks a discussion from the perspective of a non-Islamic state. In addressing this gap in Islamic scholarship, this chapter situates itself within the context of contemporary Kenya, building upon its strong Islamic historical ties. Islamic scholarship on *zakat* has explored its benefits to the Muslim community but has not considered the potential benefits for non-Muslims or the utilisation of *zakat* by a non-Islamic state for healthcare financing. This oversight may stem from the notion that *zakat,* as a financial form of worship, is exclusively for Muslims' benefit. Moreover, the *ulama* (Muslim scholars) interpret of *Surah Al Tawbah* verse 60 as referring solely to Muslims.

As scholars continue to explore *zakat* as a revenue source for the poor and needy and establish rules for modern wealth sources, subsequent sections of this work adopt a different perspective on *zakat* discourse. It is posited that the four traditional Islamic schools of thought have established *zakat* rules.[73] The following sections respectfully acknowledge these claims while drawing attention to the fact that none of the four schools have fully addressed *zakat* jurisprudence in the context of its use by a non-Islamic state and its minority-Muslim population to finance healthcare for all.

---

[71] S Qutb, *Social Justice in Islam,* (trans.) John B Hardie. (USA: Islamic Publications International 1953); A Rahnema, *Pioneers of Islamic Revival. Studies in Islamic Society* (London: Zed Books Ltd); Al-Qaradawi (n 7).

[72] BA Malik, 'Philanthropy in Practice: Role of *Zakat* in the Realization of Justice and Economic Growth', (2016) *International Journal of Zakat* 1(1): 64–77; A Al Ghofeeli, *Nawazel Al Zakat* (Al Maiman and Bank Al Bilad, Riyadh 2008); M Khadduri, (trans.) (n.d.), 'The *Zakat* (Legal Alms)', in al Shafi'i's Risala, *Treatise on the Foundation of Islamic Jurisprudence,* n.p., Islamic Text Society.

[73] (n 33) 71-73.

Undoubtedly, it is essential to link *zakat* to Muslims' needs, as the tax must first address the problems facing the believers before being allocated to other purposes or non-Muslims. Consequently, *zakat* has been assigned an economic objective: of reducing poverty and ensuring equitable wealth distribution within society. However, the *Qur'an* does not restrict *zakat's* application solely to addressing economic issues. The eight categories of beneficiaries encompass broader goals, aiming to tackle social problems as well. Thus, in such instances, *zakat's* purpose would be to address the social needs of the poor and needy.

Permissibility of Using Zakat to Finance Health

This section explores the permissibility of utilising *zakat* to finance healthcare within the context of Islamic law. The subsequent sections will delve into the legality of giving *zakat* to non-Muslims and non-Islamic states. Islamic law aims to foster justice and enhance the wellbeing of humankind, with its foundation rooted in the attainment of core objectives. These objectives, known as *maqasid ul shari'ah ul islamiyyah* (objectives of Islamic law), are articulated and expounded upon by Al Ghazali. He asserts that Islamic jurists must first discern the objective to be attained before issuing a legal ruling.[74] Moral and legal actions within Islam are justified through these objectives, which are derived from the *Qur'an* and the *sunna*. Ibn Taymiyyah describes these objectives as means to achieve justice,[75] while Ghazali further elaborates that they 'exist for the achievement and realisation of the very benefits of a human being'.[76] Ghazali classifies these objectives into five categories: religion, life, intellect, procreation, and property, referring to them as *daruriyat* (necessities).[77]

---

[74] AH Al Ghazali, *On Legal Theory of Muslim Jurisprudence* (trans.) Ahmad Zaki Mansur Hammad. Volume 1. (Dar ul Thaqafah MaktabaIslamia Publications, 2018).

[75] Ibn Taymiyyah, *Maqasid Ash Sharia* (Sifatu Safwa Publications n.d).

[76] Al Ghazali (n 79) 37.

[77] Kamali (n 5); H Kamali, 'Maqāṣid al-Sharī'ah: The Objectives of *Sharia*' (1999) *Islamic Studies Islamabad*: IRI, IIU, Vol 38, No 2.

Islamic law offers a lucid framework for identifying objectives that warrant protection from both the state and individuals, thereby justifying state intervention in achieving these goals. *Daruriyat* represent the vital necessities that a state must provide for its citizens to enable them to engage in religious worship, intellectual pursuits, life preservation, procreation, and property protection. *Hajiyat* (complementary needs) and *tahsiniyat* (embellishments/luxuries) are supplementary aspects, providing additional benefits without being essential to securing a high quality of life. The state is under no obligation to provide these luxuries. Similar to contemporary human rights obligations, a state's duty under Islamic law is to ensure *daruriyat*; or the minimum core obligations.

The combined understanding of *daruriyat* and the principle of *ijtihad*/intellectual reasoning allows jurists the flexibility to incorporate health as an objective protected by Islamic law, aligning with the *maqasid* that aim to safeguard life. Various *Qur'anic* verses and *sunna* support this view, with Aboul-Enein highlighting 28 *Qur'anic* verses emphasising the significance of a healthy lifestyle for preserving life.[78] Moreover, a *hadith* documented in the *musnad* (collection) of Imam Hanbal underscores the importance of valuing health.[79] In this *hadith*, the Prophet (صلى الله عليه وسلم) advises individuals to prioritise their health and prevent illness. Health plays a crucial role in maintaining life, making it the state's responsibility to protect health by financing healthcare provisions. Consequently, this validates the allocation of *zạkat* to people living in poverty, who are identified as *zakat* beneficiaries and cannot afford healthcare. The permissibility of using *zakat* to finance health within Islamic law is established through the law's objective of preserving life, and by extension, healthcare, by classifying it as part of *daruriyat*.

While various schools of Islamic thought have applied their principles to devise methodological rules guiding Muslims in comprehending the meaning and content of protection of health, they have also established its

---

[78] BH Aboul-Enein, 'Health Promoting Verses as mentioned in the Holy Qur'an', (2016) *J Relig Health*. Jun; 55(3): 821-829.

[79] Imam Ahmed bin Hanbal, *Musnad* (trans.) Nasiruddin Al-Khattab (Darussalam 2012).

boundaries. For example, Islamic law prohibits abortion unless the mother's health and life are at risk.[80] Muslim jurists also debate the provision of contraceptives.[81] Thus, *zakat* cannot be employed to fund health services associated with sexual and reproductive healthcare that are deemed *haram* (prohibited) or *makrooh* (disliked or offensive) under Islamic law, such as accessing abortion services or contraception.

Permissibility of Extending Zakat to Cover Health Finance for Non-Muslims

A liberal interpretation of *Surah Al-Tawbah,* verse 60, could be argued not to confine the allocation of *zakat* exclusively to Muslims. Ibrahim al-Nakha'i, a distinguished Muslim jurist of the 7th century, adhered to the principle of refraining from declaring anything as absolutely mandated or prohibited. Instead, he maintained that it was only possible to assert that 'the *sahaba* disapproved of this, they recommended that'.[82] Similarly, Abdallah ibn Shubrama would only pronounce certainty on matters deemed permissible by the law. He believed that determining the forbidden was impossible unless it was explicitly prohibited.[83] An objective interpretation of *Surah Al-Tawbah,* verse 60 would struggle to discover a clear prohibition against non-Muslims. The verse's content stipulates an essential condition that *zakat* must be distributed among eight specific categories of beneficiaries, without explicitly or unequivocally mentioning the recipients' religious beliefs.

A comprehensive understanding of Islam as it has unfolded throughout history cannot be achieved solely through the *Qur'an,* despite its

---

[80] J Brockopp, (ed), *Islamic Ethics of Life. Abortion, War and Euthanasia* (University of California Press, 2003).

[81] D Atighetchi, 'The Position of Islamic Tradition on Contraception' (1994) *Med Law* 13(7-8):717-25.

[82] Cited in Goldziher (n 20) 36.

[83] AAM Ibn Sa'd, *Kitab al-tabaqat al-kabir* (Leiden, n.d). VI, 244:20 (in as much as Darimi and Sa'd were making reference to dietary regulations, these principles that they established can be applied towards determining rules on *zakat*).

indispensable role. Prophet Muhammad (صلى الله عليه وسلم) established the proportional rate for levying *zakat*. Given the circumstances of his time, it was likely necessary to transform *zakat* from a rudimentary form of collective charity into a mandatory tax, collected in fixed amounts by the emerging state. *Zakat* regulations were further developed during the caliphate of Umar ibn Al-Khattab in Medina around the 6th century.[84] Due to their inherent importance, these regulations gained prominence following the Prophet's (صلى الله عليه وسلم) death, with subsequent caliphs exercising discretion on whether to collect *zakat* at the state level. It is crucial to recognise that legal development in Islam, which evolved in response to public needs, commenced immediately after the Prophet's (صلى الله عليه وسلم) death. Muslims were scattered across remote lands, and those who were not part of Medina's religious sphere lacked a clear understanding of *zakat's* modalities. As a result, they required rules for administering *zakat* at the state level. Their challenge was to develop these regulations to offer a legal perspective on the relationship between Islam and its subjects regarding *zakat*.[85]

To a certain degree, caliph Umar ibn Al-Khattab codified the rules concerning *zakat*. He implemented accounting and auditing principles to guide *zakat* collectors in its collection, administration, management, and distribution. What remains unclear from the written records during Umar ibn Al-Khattab's caliphate is whether *zakat* was intended solely for the benefit of Muslims. However, evidence, suggests that he did not discriminate between Muslims and non-Muslims in the allocation of *zakat*, as he instructed that a poor Jewish man be supported using funds from the *bait al maal* (treasury where *zakat*, *ushr*/land tax, spoils of war were deposited).[86] The extent to which the practice of distributing *zakat* to non-Muslims continued after this incident is uncertain. Consequently, historical

---

[84] A Fauzia, 'A History of Islamic Philanthropy in Indonesia', in M Ricklefs and B Lockhart (eds) *Faith and the State* (Leiden: Brill, 2013) at 47; A Zallum, *Funds in the Khilafa State* (Milli Publications, 2002).

[85] M Iqbal, 'Challenges to Islam and Muslims: What is to be Done?', (2003) *Islamic Studies*, Vol 42, No 4, 595-637.

[86] Zallum (n 89) 205.

evidence on *zakat* practices is quite limited. In the absence of state enforcement of *zakat*, it can be assumed that Muslims paid it directly. Thus, the question arises: is there a reliable source on the payment of *zakat* to non-Muslims?

Actions by caliph Umar Ibn Al-Khattab indicate that *zakat* can be allocated to non-Muslims.[87] Upon entering Syria, Al-Khattab ordered that the taxes, including *zakat* collected for the general needs of the Muslim community, also be used to support helpless and sick Jews and Christians. This directive was issued to the Syrian governor, who represented the Islamic state and was responsible for addressing the needs of its citizens. Another caliph, Umar Ibn Abdul Aziz, also commanded his lieutenants to identify needy non-Muslims and provide assistance using *zakat* funds.[88]

Al-Tabari, an eminent Muslim historian, recorded in his *Tafsir* that Muslim jurists permitted non-Muslims to serve as tax collectors.[89] Islamic fiscal law comprises four categories: *zakat, jizya, ushr, and kharaj*.[90] Tax collectors were granted the authority to collect any of these four types of taxes. *Surah Al-Tawbah*, verse 60, states that tax collectors are among the beneficiaries of *zakat*. If non-Muslims were appointed as tax collectors, they would also be recipients of *zakat*. Al-Tabari does not specify whether non-Muslim officers' tax collection responsibilities included *zakat* or were limited to *jizya* or *ushr*, for instance. Therefore, it cannot definitely be concluded that non-Muslim tax collectors also benefitted from *zakat*. This assertion, however, is based on a narrow foundation. A more robust and comprehensive justification,

---

[87] AY Al-Baladhuri, *Futuh al-buldan*, (Beirut: Dar al-Kutub al-Illmiya, 1981), 129 (trans.) H Kennedy (*Conquests of The Lands*).

[88] ibid, 177.

[89] Al-Tabari, *Tafsir*, (Beirut: Dar al Ma'rifa, 1989) Chapter 4: 63-64 (trans.) W F Madelung and A Jones (1989) 63-64.

[90] *Jizya, ushr,* and *kharaj* are different from *zakat*. Unlike *zakat*, these other taxes are not required to be paid to a prescribed list of beneficiaries, they are also subject to different conditions and rates. Some of these taxes (*jizya*) are no longer applicable. *Jizya* was taken from non-Muslims living in Islamic States in exchange for protection, the Ottomans later abolished this tax in 1856. *Ushr* and *kharaj* are levies on land and its agricultural produce.

grounded in *fiqh*/scientific methodology, is needed for this claim to gain merit among Muslims and Muslim scholars.

Regrettably, Muslim scholarship has not extensively explored the deeper grounding of this claim. Sheikh Saqr, the former head of Al Azhar's Fatwa Committee in Egypt, contends that the majority of scholars prohibit extending *zakat* for the benefit of non-Muslims.[91] Al Ghazali also explicitly restricts the recipients of *zakat* to Muslims.[92] Supporting this stance, Ibn Al-Mundhir asserts that there is unanimity among scholars against utilising *zakat* to benefit non-Muslims.[93] Additionally, Al Qaradawi, citing traditionalists such as Ahmad, Al-Layth and Abu Thawr, also advises against allocating *zakat* to non-Muslims.[94] Collectively, the four schools of *sunni* Islam - *Hanafi, Maliki, Shafi* and *Hanbali,* also limit the availability of *zakat* to Muslims, stipulating Muslim status as a condition for receiving or benefiting from *zakat*.[95]

These views are contested by reports indicating that caliph Umar ibn Al-Khattab provided *zakat* to a non-Muslim, and another *sahaba* (Amr Ibn Maymun) also allowed *zakat* to be given to Christian monks.[96] Based on this, Ibn Sirin and Az-Zuhri, *hadith* narrators, further reinforce the position that it is permissible to use *zakat* to benefit non-Muslims within Muslim-majority states.[97] Ibn Abi Shaybah, a prominent and reliable *sunni* scholar of the late 7th century, reports that Jabir ibn Zaid (a student of the Prophet's

---

91 Cited in 'Giving *Zakat* to Non-Muslims', IslamOnline 13th September 2003, https://fiqh.islamonline.net/en/can-i-give-zakah-to-non-muslims/

92 Al Ghazali, *Ihya Ulum al-Din*, (trans.) K Honerkamp, 'Revival of Religion's Sciences, Volume 1 (Fons Vitae, 2016).

93 Ibn Mundhir, *Al Ijma*, (trans.) S Abd al Hamid (The Islamic Literary Foundation 2014) 174.

94 Cited in Al Qaradawi (n 7).

95 For a detailed discussion of these four school on *zakat* see: AR Al-Jaziri, *Islamic Jurisprudence According to the Four Sunni Schools, Volume I*, (trans.) Nancy Roberts. (Fons Viate; Canada, 2009).

96 Cited in M As-Sallabi, *Biography of Umar bin Abdul Aziz* (Darussalam Publishers) (n.d).

97 Al-Qaradawi (n 7), 40.

(صلى الله عليه وسلم) wife, Ai'sha) permitted *zakat* to be used for the benefit of non-Muslims.[98] Shaybah cites this evidence:[99]

> Jabir ibn Zaid was asked, 'where should we distribute our zakat?' He replied, "to the destitute amongst Muslims and Dhimmis (a non-Muslim citizen of the Islamic state). He then stated, 'God's Messenger would distribute to the Dhimmis from both zakat and khums'.

This narration by Zaid verifies that the Prophet (صلى الله عليه وسلم) provided *zakat* to non-Muslims. Although this narration is not documented in the authentic hadith collections by Bukhari and Muslim, rendering it a weak source, its citation by Shaybah suggests a strong possibility of authenticity. The four schools also do not include Zaid's narration, indicating its perceived lack of cogency.

Thus, the general tendency in the development of Islamic law holds greater relevance for this book than the specific details, which vary among different schools. Islam derives its beliefs and practices from its definitive sacred text, the *Qur'an*. The exegesis dedicated to the *Qur'an* simultaneously illustrates the legal and dogmatic evolution of the religion. Consequently, historical research becomes essential. The history of Islam also represents a history of *Qur'an* interpretation. Accordingly, history is one of the acceptable methods of inquiry in Islamic law for understanding the *Qur'an's* meaning. It is the author's opinion that scholars did not intend to hinder the development of *zakat* by confining it within a stockade of legal restraints.

From the outset, Muslim jurists emphasised adherence to the words of the *Qur'an*. The jurist Sufyan Al-Thawri, for example, asserted that: 'knowledge means that you are able to grant a permission and base it on

---

[98] Ibn Abi Shaybah, *Al-Musannaf*, Volume 3 (trans.) M Awwamah (Dar ul Islam Publishers, n.d) 178

[99] Ibid, 178.

the authority of a reliable traditionist. Anyone can find a restriction easily enough'.[100]

Moreover, the following principle of dietary regulation exemplifies the argument being made here to determine whether Islamic law prohibits *zakat* from being given to non-Muslims:

> When it is uncertain whether a thing should be declared as forbidden or as permitted, permission prevails. It is a principle that everything is permitted, prohibition is something superadded, and in the case of doubt one should fall back on the principle.[101]

Islam, as a religion, addresses all of humanity. Consequently, delineating distinctions between Muslims and non-Muslims concerning the scope of *zakat* confines Islam as an insular religion. The absence of explicit prohibition under Islamic law, combined with the varied responses from Muslim jurists and *hadith* narrators, indicates that there is room within Islamic law to permit giving *zakat* to a non-Muslim who meets the criteria outlined in verse 60. The task of interpreting the *Qur'an* and regulating life in accordance with the *Qur'an* should not be 'lost in absurd sophistry and exegetical trifling',[102] detached from the real world. A fitting example would be a minority-Muslim population in a non-Islamic state residing in a particular area with limited access to healthcare facilities; such a population should not debate the allocation of *zakat* for building a health clinic based on the intricate doctrinal reasoning that the clinic would also be accessible by non-Muslims. The subsequent section is dedicated to understanding the Islamic stance on whether *zakat* can be provided to a non-Islamic state to finance healthcare.

---

[100] Ibn Abd Al Barr, *Jami bayan al-ilm wa fadlihi* (trans.) M Al Misri, *Knowledge and its Virtue* (Darul Imam Bukhari, 2010), 115:9.

[101] M Damiri (1906), *Hayat al-hayawan al-kubra,* (trans.) A S G Jayakar (Bombay, 1937), 41.

[102] Goldziher (n 20) 85.

Permissibility of Giving *Zakat* to a Non-Islamic State

The potential recognition of *zakat* as a viable resource under human rights law, pursuant to article 2.1 of the International Covenant on Economic, Social and Cultural Rights (ICESCR), is rendered legally impotent if Islamic jurisprudence does not explicitly place it within the purview of the non-Islamic state. Any deviation from established norms in the administration and utilisation of *zakat* would directly influence its character as the third pillar of Islamic worship, thus raising questions about the locus of authority. Is it permissible, according to Islamic jurisprudence, to allocate *zakat* to a non-Islamic state? To address this query, one must examine *ijma* (juristic consensus) and *shura* (consultation) to ascertain the presence of any legal provisions within Islamic law that would allow for such an allocation.[103] The exploration of *zakat's* potential to finance healthcare in a non-Islamic state, through the direct transfer of funds to the state, remains inadequately investigated.

Hashim posits that the body of Islamic law is a product of human intellectual endeavour[104], and as such, certain aspects may evolve in tandem with the progression of human thought. This evolution can be facilitated through the employment of *ijma* and *shura,* which have historically served as interpretive tools in adapting Islamic law to evolving contexts, governing relations with non-Muslims in Muslim-majority states, engaging with non-Islamic states, and addressing societal needs.[105] Nevertheless, Muslim jurists have largely refrained from scrutinising the application of these interpretive mechanisms to gain insight into the permissibility of allocating *zakat* to non-Islamic states in order to address social needs. The question, then, is whether such allocation is permissible under Islamic law. To address this issue, it is necessary to conduct a historical analysis of the conceptualisation of a state within the framework of Islamic jurisprudence. Central to this analysis is the determination of whether professing the Islamic faith is a prerequisite for a state to be eligible

---

[103] Kamali (n 5).

[104] ibid.

[105] S Helfont, *Yusuf Al-Qaradawi: Islam and Modernity* (Tel Aviv University Press, 2009), 89.

to receive *zakat*. In this investigation lies the resolution to the question of whether Islamic law permits the allocation of *zakat* to a non-Islamic state.

Islamic law concerns

The challenge lies in the fact that the majority of Muslim jurists' historical deliberations have focused on circumstances in Islamic countries where Muslims constituted the majority, and the legal system was informed by their religious sources. It is now crucial to shift the discourse toward the nature of states receiving Muslims and granting them citizenship. Can Islamic law permit the allocation of *zakat* to such states? This allocation cannot be dissociated from the adherence to Islamic norms governing *zakat* utilisation. Consequently, the issue hinges on whether Islam permits a non-Islamic state to implement Islamic law.

Historically, the authority to apply Islamic law was first exercised by the Prophet Muhammad (صلى الله عليه وسلم) and subsequently by the caliphs. As Muslims migrated to secular states and as Muslim-majority countries transitioned from Islamic to secular states in the post-colonial era, the authority to apply Islamic law shifted to the decisions of the *kadhi* (judge) and the *fatwas* (decrees) of the *mufti* (jurist) in matters of civil law exclusively.[106] The transfer of authority from the state to the *kadhi* or *mufti* demonstrates the adaptability of Islamic law through different authorities. Although the authority to apply Islamic law has historically been vested in Muslims, Islamic law would still be applied among Muslims even if the state authority neither professes Islam nor regards Islamic law as a source of law. This raises the question of whether the state authority must profess Islam to accept *zakat*.

Scholars such as Bayhaqi and Ibn Sa'd argue that during the Umayyad caliphate, it was not a requirement for the state authority to practice Islam

---

106 B Tibi, *The Challenge of Fundamentalism: Political Islam and the New World Disorder* (Berkeley and Los Angeles: University of California Press, 1998).

in order to apply Islamic law.[107] They contrast this with the successor Abbasid caliphate, which maintained that the mandate to apply Islamic law was exclusive to the religious Islamic state.[108] For the Umayyads, religion was not a prerequisite for legitimacy in applying Islamic law.[109] Accordingly, a non-Islamic state could potentially qualify to apply Islamic law on *zakat* and thus be eligible to receive *zakat* for healthcare financing.

However, both the Umayyads and Abbasids presented the state as led by Muslims, thus constraining the discussion on the authority to apply Islamic law to Muslims. Consequently, scholars have not concentrated on examining the legality or permissibility under Islamic law of authorising a non-Islamic state led by a non-Muslim to apply Islamic law on *zakat*. The acceptance of *zakat* is linked to the permission to apply Islamic law. As such, there is no evidence to test and confirm the legal possibility under Islamic law of allocating *zakat* to a non-Islamic state, nor is there evidence of a non-Islamic state directly accepting and utilising *zakat*.

Historically, relations between Muslims and non-Muslims under the Islamic caliphates reveal that non-Muslims held positions as state employees, including high-level roles in government, across various Islamic caliphates. During the Umayyad period (late 7th and 8th centuries), Christians twice commanded the Muslim army.[110] Later, Abbasid caliph Al-Mutawakkil issued a decree prohibiting the employment of non-

---

[107] Bayhaqi, *Al-Mahasin wa'l-masawi*, (ed.) Friedrich Schwally (Giessen 1902), 392; AM Ibn Sa'd, *Kitab al-tabaqat al-kabir*, (ed.) Eduard Sachau et. al 9 vols. (Leiden, 1904-1940).

[108] ibid.

[109] There was a belief among the Muslims during the Umayyad rule that the Umayyads stood in rigid and conscious opposition to the demands of Islam and governed accordingly. The rulers of that dynasty, and their governors and administrators, were made out to be no less than the heirs of the enemies of nascent Islam, and it was thought that their attitude toward religion was a new guise in which the old Quraysh spirit of animosity – or at best indifference – to Islam had survived. The Umayyads were aware that as caliphs they stood at the head of an empire whose foundations had been laid by a religious upheaval: they were conscious of being true adherents of Islam. This cannot be denied them.

[110] Ibn Qutayba, *Uyun al-Akhbar* (trans.) L Kopf, *[Book of Choice Narratives]* (Cairo: Al-Mu'assa al-Misriyya, 1963) 99.

Muslims in departments concerning Muslim affairs. Another Abbasid caliph in the 9th century, when Christians held numerous state administration positions, ordered their removal.[111] However, some caliphs, such as al-Ta'i[112] and ministers like Iz al-Dawla[113] maintained Christian employees.[114] This demonstrates that previous Muslim rulers did not oppose the application of Islamic law by non-Muslims, as long as the law's continuity was maintained, irrespective of the religion of those applying it.

Historical Islamic states did not prohibit the employment of non-Muslims, nor did the *Qur'an* and *sunna*. The Prophet (صلى الله عليه وسلم) himself employed non-Muslims to educate Muslims. Muslim jurists permitted non-Muslims to serve as executive ministers, tax collectors, and advisors.[115] Umayyad caliph Muawiya appointed a Christian to oversee the Muslim revenue department in Syria.[116] In practice, non-Muslims participated alongside Muslims in administering the Islamic state. When Muslims occupied Egypt in the late 7th century, they entrusted state administration to non-Muslims. These instances demonstrate that non-Muslims have been involved in administering the Islamic state and implementing Islamic law. It appears that there is no prerequisite for a state officer to profess the Islamic faith in order to receive *zakat* and to apply the Islamic norms regulating its use.

What then of non-Muslims in non-Islamic states, seeking to apply Islamic law by accepting *zakat* and using it to finance health? The discussion thus far has shown that non-Muslims collected *zakat* as employees of the Islamic state. Their roles as heads of revenue departments and tax collectors suggest that they can receive and administer *zakat* if they do so in

---

[111] Al-Tabari, *Tarikh* (trans.) E Yarshater (Cairo: Al Maktaba al-Husayniyy, 1999) 1389-90, 1438.

[112] ibid, 363-381.

[113] ibid, 357.

[114] AH Al-Ghazali, *Mishkat al-Anwar* (Aleppo: Al-Dar al Ilmiyya, 6 vols, 1927). 6:310, 511. [*The Niche for Lights* (trans.) WHT Gairdner (1998)].

[115] Al-Tabari (n 94) 63-64.

[116] A H Siddiqi, *The Origins and Development of Muslim Institutions* (Jamiyat Ul Fallah Publications, 1962) 100.

accordance with Islamic law. The authority to do so originates from the Islamic state or a Muslim leader. Intellectuals like Abbas Mahmud al-Aqqad,[117] Taha Husain[118] and Muhammad Husayn Haykal[119] contend that the religion of a state should not be a determining factor, nor should it be in allocating *zakat* to a non-Islamic state.

It appears that, since the *Qur'an* specifies the recipients of *zakat*, the permissibility within Islamic law of allocating *zakat* to a non-Islamic state is contingent upon this stipulation. The non-Islamic state would need to apply Islamic law. The notion that a non-Islamic state can apply Islamic law is contested by Qutb, who asserts that only an Islamic state can legitimately apply Islamic law. [120] The Islamic state both symbolises the community's submission to God based on Islamic law and embodies political and ideological obedience to God. Qutb posits that without such submission and obedience, a state forfeits its legitimacy.[121] Such a state cannot apply Islamic law and consequently becomes ineligible to receive *zakat*. It can be argued, then, that Islamic law provides no authority to a non-Islamic state to apply or exercise any aspect of its law or rules. *Zakat* can therefore only be given to a legitimate government, with legitimacy seemingly derived from submission to God based on Islamic law. The distinction between a state with Islam as its supreme law and a non-Islamic state lies in the submission aspect. Both forms of states can apply Islamic law – the crux of the matter appears to centre around submission and obedience to God. This can be expressed by accepting *zakat* and using it in accordance with *Surah Al-Tawbah*, verse 60.

---

[117] Discussed in James Toth, *Sayyid Qutb: The Life and Legacy of a Radical Islamic Intellectual* (Oxford University Press, 2013).

[118] A Mahmoudi, *Taha Husain's Education. From the Azhar to the Sorbonne* (Routledge 1998).

[119] CD Smith, *Muhammad Husayn Haykal: An Intellectual and Political Biography* (University of Michigan Press, 1968).

[120] S Qutb, *Al-Salam al-Alami wa al-Islam* (Beirut: Dar al-Shuruq, 1983); S Qutb, *Milestones.* (ed.) AB al-Mehri (CreateSpace Independent Publishing Platform, 2017).

[121] S Qutb, *Milestones.* (ed.) AB al-Mehri (CreateSpace Independent Publishing Platform, 2017).

If belief in God is a critical factor influencing permissibility under Islamic law to allocate zakat to a non-Islamic state, the preamble to the Constitution of Kenya acknowledges the supremacy of the 'Almighty God of all creation.'[122] The preamble offers the ultimate political, legal, and social recognition of God that Islamic law demands from a state. Although the Kenyan state recognises God, it is not obliged to recognise and apply Islamic law. In accepting *zakat*, the state can choose to disregard *Surah Al-Tawbah*, verse 60, resulting in the rejection under Islamic law of allocating *zakat* to a non-Islamic state. If a non-Islamic state adopts *ijma* (juristic consensus) and *shura* (consultation), do these methods ensure the permissibility criteria under Islamic law?

Use of Islamic methods

In assessing the potential for Kenya, a non-Islamic state, to lawfully accept *zakat*, it is essential to examine Islamic methods within a secular context. This investigation involves exploring the similarities between the Kenyan democratic system of devolved governance and the Islamic principles of *ijma* (juristic consensus) and *shura* (consultation). As these principles cannot be confined to historical contexts, their practical implications must be considered in relation to evolving socio-economic circumstances and changing political conditions. A legitimate state institutionalisation of *ijma* and *shura* provides a normative role for the state in making fundamental decisions on behalf of the populace. Consequently, the question arises: do democracy and participation reflect a contemporary application of *ijma* and *shura* in a non-Islamic state?

Al Ghazali contends that the moral legitimacy of political power must be grounded in the people's free choice and support, which is represented by the public approval of Muslims.[123] In this sense, *shura* or consultation symbolises a democratic (consultative) government, advocating for people's equality, individual rights, and the limitation of state functions to

---

[122] Republic of Kenya, Constitution of Kenya (Nairobi: National Council of Law Reporting, 2010).

[123] AH Al-Ghazali, *Al-Iqtisad fi al-Itiqad* (Cairo: Al-Matba'a al-Mahmudiyya, n.d.) 215.

serve the interests and development of the people. Permissibility under Islamic law to allocate *zakat* to the Kenyan state necessitates the application of Islamic law, legitimising its reception and utilisation for health financing.

The Kenyan democratic system of devolved governance curtails government powers by channelling them through popular avenues and representative bodies. This system fosters a tolerant political environment, encouraging the development of intellectual, religious, social, and ethical interactions. In contrast, Muslims generally concur that the common political function of conducting people's affairs belongs to the community at large rather than the ruler.[124] In a democratic setting, this function is carried out through elected parliamentarians, embodying a form of *shura* or consultation. In non-Islamic states, Muslims seeking to address the issue of limited health finances through state involvement must work within the parameters of Islamic law. To achieve this, certain commonalities must exist between Islamic law and the non-Islamic state.

Historically, *shura* has been employed by the Islamic state to elect state authorities through a selective consultative body comprising state officers, with its modern-day equivalent being the parliament. *Ijma,* on the other hand, was exclusive to jurists who exercised *ijtihad* (intellectual reasoning) to resolve legal issues. Consensus among different jurists on similar legal problems created the *ijma,* which was not open to the public. Therefore, how can these historical methods apply to authorise the allocation of *zakat* under Islamic law to the Kenyan state?

The Umayyad dynasty, in distinguishing between religious and political authority, expanded the use of *ijma* and shura to address social, ethnic, and religious organisations, political and economic development, and human aspirations and needs. *Ijma* came to symbolise political authority, becoming legitimate when the community, as the holder of such power, deemed it so. Political rule is based on the people's power to form a contract, and in this regard, *shura* evolved into a significant source of communal power. *Shura* represents a form of democratic interaction that allows for differing and

---

124 Tibi (n 111).

even divergent understandings concerning the nature of power, government, and, most importantly, the state-society relationship. Consequently, the permissibility under Islamic law to allocate *zakat* to a non-Islamic state depends on the presence of *ijma* and *shura* within that state. Through these methods, actions can be developed to provide the non-Islamic state with the lawful authority to administer *zakat* for health financing, with legitimacy derived from the people's choice.

While *shura* and democracy share denotative similarities, both advocating for public participation and representation in political decision-making, their connotations differ significantly. Democracy attributes ultimate sovereignty to the people, whereas *shura* grounds its authority in God's revelation, making God the supreme sovereign. It can be argued that under Islamic law, allocating *zakat* to a non-Islamic state can meet the criterion of legal permissibility, provided the state adheres to the relevant Islamic law governing the use of *zakat*. Such authority under Islamic law should also be guided by the *ijma* and *shura* of the Muslims whose *zakat* is proposed to be offered to the state.

Historical practice does not present any restrictions within Islamic law that would justify refusal in allocating *zakat* to a non-Islamic state. However, the necessity for *ijma* and *shura* to establish this permissibility calls for conducting interviews with Kenyan Muslims, their scholars, and other stakeholders. By engaging these individuals in dialogue, a deeper understanding of the complexities involved in applying Islamic principles within a non-Islamic state can be gained. Furthermore, these discussions can help identify potential areas of convergence between Islamic law and the Kenyan democratic system, providing a framework for the lawful allocation of *zakat* for health financing.

In conclusion, the permissibility of allocating *zakat* to a non-Islamic state such as Kenya depends on the presence of *ijma* and *shura* within the state, as well as the state's adherence to relevant Islamic law governing the use of *zakat*. Although there are significant differences between *shura* and democracy, their shared emphasis on public participation and representation in political decision-making suggests potential common ground. Further research and engagement with Kenyan Muslims and their scholars can help determine the feasibility of applying these Islamic principles within the context of Kenya's democratic system of devolved governance.

Conditional permissibility exists under Islamic law to give *zakat* to a non-Islamic state

The consensus among the four *sunni* Islamic schools of thought posits that the authority to implement Islamic law resides solely with an Islamic state or Muslim government.[125] Consequently, it can be argued that the administration of *zakat*, which is governed by Islamic law, cannot fall under the purview of a non-Muslim administration. Under this premise, the Kenyan state, as a non-Islamic constitutional entity, may only be granted the authority to apply Islamic law if the government is led by Muslims. Nevertheless, this is not the definitive conclusion under Islamic law. In order for the Kenyan state to be eligible to receive *zakat*, it must adhere to the fundamental assumption of the Islamic juridical theory of the state. Scholars such as Khaddhuri and Ahmed elucidate that according to the Islamic juridical theory, authority—irrespective of the entrusted party—must emanate from a divine source, and the constitution must acknowledge this.[126]

For the Kenyan state to meet this criterion, it must recognise God as the sovereign. Indeed, the preamble of the Constitution of Kenya acknowledges the supremacy of God and safeguards the freedom of religion under article 32(1). This recognition, however, may not fulfil the requirements of Islamic law for the state to guarantee the protection of its norms, as article 8 of the Kenyan Constitution also asserts that there shall be no state religion. While Islamic law would permit the allocation of *zakat* to a non-Islamic state, provided it complies with the provisions of *Surah Al-Tawbah* verse 60, the answer also hinges on the legality within the Kenyan

---

[125] Mousalli (n 13).

[126] M Khadduri, (1951) 'The Juridical Theory of the Islamic State' *The Muslim World*, Vol 41, No 3, 181-185; I Ahmed, (1968). 'Sovereignty in Islam' *Pakistan Horizon*, Vol 11, No 4, 9 December) 244-257.

legal system of accepting and utilising *zakat* in accordance with its Islamic stipulations. Additionally, the state's approach to collecting *zakat* and directly allocating it to finance healthcare needs deemed acceptable under Islam, as previously discussed, must be considered. This may not be feasible, as states typically pool and consolidate revenue sources during the budget process.

In Kenya, the authority of norms is derived from the Constitution, which delineates the authority of law. Islamic law is only invoked in the context of resolving disputes pertaining to marriage, divorce, and inheritance between consenting Muslim parties. Article 32, which enshrines the freedom of religion, does not explicitly introduce *zakat* within the public domain; it remains implicitly confined to private Muslim practice. Consequently, the Kenyan state's taking, accepting or collecting of *zakat* presents a conundrum, as its utilisation depends on an authority that the state does not officially recognise but instead subordinates. Nevertheless, permission under Islamic law to allocate *zakat* to the Kenyan state can be legally granted if the state guarantees adherence to its Islamic conditions (restricting *zakat* to the beneficiaries listed in the *Qur'an* and refraining from financing healthcare that violates Islamic law). The acceptability of this condition is examined in the subsequent chapter, which focuses on the Kenyan Constitution.

Conclusion

The authority of the *Qur'an* and *hadith* to legitimise one opinion over another on *zakat* is never entirely conclusive, as the meaning of the *Qur'an* and the validity of the *hadith* may be subject to debate and reinterpretation. The malleability of the *Qur'an*, rather than its specificity, is what keeps it relevant; any attempt by a group of Muslims to assert exclusive validity for their interpretation of the *Qur'an* has historically been countered by other groups and claims. The *Qur'an* does not lend itself to being controlled, particularly at an epistemological and philosophical level, by specific claims or interpretations. *Qur'anic* legitimacy cannot be monopolised by one group of people. In this chapter, it has been demonstrated that, in principle, every Muslim can be a legitimate interpreter and reader.

The question of whether Muslims individually interpret the *Qur'an* or accept the interpretations provided by their scholars is explored through fieldwork in Chapter 7. The findings reveal that interpretations are referred to Muslim scholars who, adhering to the *Shafi* and *Hanafi* schools, oppose the allocation of *zakat* to non-Muslims and the Kenyan state. This occurs despite normative and doctrinal clarity in permitting such use of *zakat*. How Islamic law is interpreted by Muslim communities living in different geographical areas is crucial in understanding how local views also influence the development of Islamic law. In the context of this book, fieldwork is essential to comprehend these local views and assess the willingness of Muslims in Kenya to offer *zakat* for health to non-Muslims and the Kenyan state. Fieldwork is fundamental to advance the discussion on the political and practical feasibility of the book's proposal: the availability of *zakat* financing health in Kenya and the permissibility of giving it to the state.

This chapter has demonstrated that the consensus of a group of people on one interpretation or reading does not render it authoritative. As long as the reader does not explicitly deny the *Qur'anic* text or interpret it contrary to the text itself, they are free to read from or into the text whatever is necessary and convenient for their individual and communal well-being. Divergent interpretations and understandings, as well as methodological differences, are natural outcomes of the text's nature. Muslims tend to follow the views of jurists, which is not textually mandated but driven by adherence to specific schools. The *Qur'an* does not preclude new readings. While Islam's original objective was to unite the community and facilitate its development and change in practical terms, narrow interpretations limiting *zakat* for Muslims undermine and contradict its significance. This chapter has examined the debates surrounding the use of *zakat* to benefit non-Muslims, evaluated the normative framework within which legal questions pertaining to Islamic law are addressed, and drawn two conclusions.

Firstly, although there is a difference of opinion among jurists regarding the allocation of *zakat* to non-Muslims, an inquiry into the interpretation of the primary source of Islamic law, the *Qur'an*, reveals that it does not restrict its scope in addressing the general welfare of both Muslims and non-Muslims alike. By connecting the *maqasid* (objective) of life with the interpretation of *Surah Al-Tawbah*, verse 60, Islamic law permits the use of *zakat* for health, encompassing non-Muslims who fall within any of the eight categories of beneficiaries.

Secondly, the fact that jurists are divided supports Ali's assertion that Islamic law is capable of being 'evolutionary, dynamic, responsive, and a multidimensional phenomenon capable of generating responses from within varied and rich traditions, highlighting its plurality and its inbuilt transformative processes.'[127] This allows for a re-evaluation of the applicability of Islamic law outside the Islamic world. Islamic law provides *zakat* as a means to finance health, including non-Muslim recipients, and offers *zakat* as a source of revenue to a non-Islamic state, on the condition that it adheres to the Islamic regulations governing its use.

As a result, this chapter proposes the utilisation of *zakat* as a source of revenue that can support financing healthcare in Kenya, with the following caution taken from one of the respondents interviewed in Nairobi:

> It is not for Islamic law to panel-beat itself so that it can be regarded as acceptable under the Constitution of Kenya. The Constitution is not at par with Islamic law to order that Muslims water down or change what the Qur'an and sunnah say on a specific subject so that it is consistent with state law. Answers must be found from the Qur'an and hadith on whether our zakat can be given to the Kenyan state and whether our zakat can be used to finance healthcare of non-Muslims.[128]

The next chapter completes the argument conceived here. Permissibility within Islamic law partly suffices to establish recourse to *zakat* as a source of revenue to finance health. This argument must also meet the legal threshold, set out as part of the Kenyan legal system, through which religious norms can be recognised as sources of law capable of binding the

---

[127] Ali (n 26) 10.

[128] Interviewee No. 137. Interview date 15.02.2020 Nairobi

state. The next chapter addresses permissibility concerns, by reference to the Constitution of Kenya, to discover the capacity of the domestic legal system to be bound by Islamic conditions to qualify for *zakat*.

Chapter 5
The Kenyan Legal System and its approach to accepting Zakat – *Permissibility under The Constitution of Kenya*

Introduction

This chapter embarks upon a pioneering theoretical exploration of incorporating Islamic law on *zakat* within the Kenyan legal framework. Utilising Tamanaha's socio-legal positivism as the guiding legal theory to characterise the Kenyan legal system,[1] this chapter combines An-Naim's civic reasoning approach[2] with socio-legal positivism. This fusion demonstrates that Islamic law can provide the Kenyan state with acceptable norms capable of functioning within its legal system. The chapter's argument is inspired by Massoud's insightful observation in his seminal work, which posits that legal systems 'might not only be reconciled with religion, but counterintuitively be nourished by it'.[3] Although Massoud's scholarship focuses on Muslim-majority countries, it can be employed to envisage the potential for expanding socio-legal research horizons, elucidating how Islamic law can 'seep into the architecture'[4] of Muslim minority states.

The crux of this chapter lies in comprehending the manner in which the Kenyan constitutional order perceives the relationship between law and religion. Kenyan scholars examining this relationship have predominantly

---

[1] B Tamanaha, 'Socio-Legal Positivism and a General Jurisprudence', (2001) *Oxford Journal of Legal Studies,* Vol 21, No 1, 1-32.

[2] A An-Naim, 'The Compatibility Dialectic: Mediating the Legitimate Coexistence of Islamic Law and State Law', (2010) *The Modern Law Review,* Vol 73, No 1, 1-29, 2.

[3] MF Massoud, *SHARI'A INSHAALLAH: Finding God in Somali Legal Politics* (Cambridge University Press, 2021), 2

[4] ibid, 4.

focused on the *Kadhis'* courts (Islamic courts), debating the legality of their constitutional basis.[5] They have also explored whether the inclusion of Muslim personal law in the Constitution constitutes discrimination against other religions that are not explicitly mentioned.[6] Academic scrutiny of the Islamic religion in Kenya has, thus far, adhered to the constitutional principle of separation of state and religion expressed under article 8. However, Kenyan scholarship has not thoroughly investigated whether the state, by opting to apply Islamic law outside the *Kadhis'* court system, contravenes this principle. This is vital because, aside from the constitutional recognition of Muslim personal law, the Kenyan state has also permitted the application of Islamic law to Islamic forms of contract.[7]

---

[5] A Cussac, Muslims and Politics in Kenya: The Issue of the Kadhis Courts in the Constitution Review Process (2008) *Journal of Muslim Minority Affairs* 28 (2): 289-302, JM Isanga, 'Kadhi's Courts and Kenya's Constitution: An International Human Rights Perspective'. (Kenya Section of the International Commission of Jurists, ed, 2009) 29, 47; J Chesworth, *Kadhi's Courts in Kenya: Reactions and Responses* (South Africa: National Research Foundation, 2010) 3-17; H Ndzovu, 'Is the Inclusion of the Kadhi Courts in the Kenyan Constitution against the Principle of a Secular State?' (2013) NP Available at: https://papers.ssrn.com/sol3/papers.cfm?abstract_id=2327775

[6] M Ngugi, and S Ngugi, 'Kadhi Courts Exceed Limits of the Law' *Africa News Service, Opposing Viewpoints in Context* Issue: 17 August 2009; OG Mwangi, 'Religious Fundamentalism, Constitution-Making and Democracy in Kenya: The Kadhis Courts Debate' (2012) *The Round Table* 101 (1):41-52; T Abdelkader, 'Kadhis Courts in Kenya's Constitutional Review (1998-2010): A Changing Approach to Politics and State Among Kenyan Muslim Leaders' (2013) *Islamic Africa* 4(1):103-124; S Hirsh, (n.d) 'Religion and Pluralism in the Constitution: Expanding and Transforming the Kenyan Kadhis Courts'. Katiba Institute. Available at: http://www.katibainstitute.org/wp-content/uploads/2018/02/Religion-and-Pluralism-in-the-Constitution-Hirsch-.pdf

[7] In Kenya for example, the Banking Act (Chapter 488) and the Capital Markets Act (Chapter 485A) have been amended to give recognition to Islamic banking, as well as trading and transacting through Islamic financial products. Pluralism in Kenya's political and governance framework has facilitated the easy transition of the market into one that also offers Islamic financial products to the diverse society without restricting its use exclusively to the minority Muslim population. To give further effect to the recognition of the principles of Islamic finance within the commercial and real estate sector, the Kenyan Income Tax Act (Chapter 470) and the Stamp Duty Act (Chapter 480) have been amended to remove double taxation on stamp duty and value added tax once the ownership under a '*Mudarabah*' (partnership in profit) contract is being transferred to the client following payment in full to the financier.

In Kenya, the Constitution serves as the primary source of law, with all other laws mandated to align with it. This would ostensibly exclude the integration of Islamic law as an additional source. Nevertheless, the Kenyan Constitution indeed acknowledges legal pluralism,[8] recognising Muslim law as part of domestic law, ensuring its judicial enforcement through the establishment of the *Kadhis'* courts (Islamic courts), and allowing Muslim personal law to supersede specific fundamental freedoms outlined in the Constitution. This apparent contradiction - whereby the state is simultaneously prohibited from involving itself in religion, yet actively participates in implementing Islamic law as part of state law - demonstrates that the interaction between the Constitution and Islamic law seems not to be normatively closed. This creates an opportunity to explore the implications of integrating the Islamic law on *zakat* within the framework of the Kenyan constitution. This chapter seeks to elucidate the position of Islamic law in the Kenyan legal system, starting with an examination of the constitutional issues emerging from this complex interplay.

The Constitutional Issues Arising

This chapter investigates the competing normative claims the Kenyan state must consider in deciding whether to accept and utilise *zakat* alongside its Islamic conditions. The question presupposes that the creation of hierarchies among norms in the Constitution of Kenya, which modifies the separation between state and religion, implies that the state can legally apply Islamic law if it chooses to do so. This proposition facilitates an inquiry into the legal theory that characterises the nature and essence of law in Kenya, allowing for an examination of whether Kenyan law can accommodate the co-existence of multiple legal systems. The chapter further questions whether the legal enforcement of religious norms at the state level contradicts Kenya's commitment to legal centralism.

---

[8] MC Green, 'Religious and Legal Pluralism in Recent African Constitutional Reform', (2012) *Journal of Law and Religion*, Vol 28, No. 2, 401-439.

General jurisprudence in Kenya concerning law and legal phenomena is built upon HLA Hart's thesis,[9] which reduces our understanding of the law to the union of primary and secondary rules.[10] This union, Hart posited, delineates the fundamental elements that constitute law. Although Hart acknowledged various sources of law, he also asserted an overarching norm to which all other legal rules and social norms are subordinate.[11] This overarching norm stems from state law characterised by legal positivism and structured around legal centralism. While legal positivism elucidates the legal theory, legal centralism describes its operation. Centralism excludes all laws and norms that do not originate from the state, thus ousting religious norms from the basic elements that form legal theory. However, when state law grants constitutional legality to a religious norm, effectively rendering it state law, where does one draw the distinction between law originating from the state and that originating from a divine source? Can the primary rules of an external legal system with divine origins be applied as the primary rules of a constitutional state? Hart's thesis, despite its clarity on the hierarchy of norms from which rules are derived, does not provide an answer to this question.

It is challenging to precisely pinpoint the nature of Hart's concept of law when examining legal theory in Kenya, particularly when certain aspects of Islamic law are incorporated into the normative legal order established by the Constitution. This is because, while Kenya adheres to Hartian jurisprudence, it simultaneously combines legal pluralism within its legal positivist constitutional order.[12] As a historically plural society, Kenya has developed robust legal, and social normative institutions, some of which are based on the divine as their source of law. Consequently, this chapter argues that such a context deconstructs Hart's thesis and reconstructs it by modifying the legal positivism approach in Kenya to Tamanaha's socio-

---

[9] J O Rachuonyo, 'Kelsen's Grundnorm in modern Constitution Making: The Kenya Case,' (1987) *Law and Politics in Africa, Asia and Latin America*, Vol 20, No 4.

[10] HLA Hart, *The Concept of Law* (Clarendon Law Series, 1961).

[11] ibid, 204-5.

[12] (n 9).

legal positivism.[13] This amalgamates the methodological approaches of legal centralism and legal pluralism to describe how the Kenyan legal order incorporates Islamic norms both above and subordinate to state law within the constitutional framework. This chapter delves into the validity of these arguments.

Questions regarding the constitutional validity of the state's application of Islamic law arise when the state opts to apply, implement, and enforce Islamic law beyond Muslim personal law. Such action may either restrict or limit the exercise of state power and authority, thus contravening the separation principle. Would the Kenyan state choose to do so? The state bears a legal responsibility to mobilise all locally available revenue sources to finance human rights. The scarcity of healthcare funds in the country necessitates that the state seeks additional or alternative funding sources. The MAR obligation allows for the inclusion of *zakat* as a potential source of finance, thereby obligating the state to consider *zakat*. In doing so, the state must first ascertain the legal permissibility of implementing law derived from a religious text. Essentially, it must scrutinise whether article 8 precludes it from accepting and utilising *zakat*. This central question underpins the chapter, with the constitutional issues highlighted herein discussed in greater detail. A foundational understanding of the Constitution is essential to set the stage for a more profound analysis.

Background to the Constitution and Shaping of its Norms

Kenya's genesis essentially lies in the British colonial conquest, and the development of its state apparatus and laws originated from authoritarian structures rooted in the colonial power's ideology of legal centralism.[14] The coastal region of pre-colonial Kenya had already been subjected to foreign control and dominion, with the Sultan of Oman establishing an administrative framework for the economic exploitation and political

---

13 (n 1).

14 YP Ghai, JPWB McAuslan, and P McAuslan, *Public Law and Political Change in Kenya: A Study of the Legal Framework of Government from Colonial Times to the Present* (Oxford University Press, 1970).

domination of the Kenyan coast (elaborated further in Chapter 6). The emerging bourgeoisie Arab society, alongside the indigenous population with whom Arabs intermarried to form the Swahili people, created a plural society founded on distinct and robust normative structures.[15] The British inherited this plural amalgamation, and the Arabs of Omani and Yemeni origin, who were Muslims, employed Islamic law to govern their public legal relations and personal status law. To ensure enforcement, the Sultan of Oman, who controlled the Kenyan coast, established *Kadhis'* courts.[16]

Subsequently, the British colonialists, who sought control over the Kenyan hinterland, negotiated administrative authority over the coast from the Sultan, who granted it on the condition that Muslim personal law continued to be enforced by the colonial administration. The British, aiming to characterise their new colony along the lines of legal centralism, later made the application of Muslim personal law contingent upon the consent of all involved parties. Similarly, the Constitution prepared for Kenya's transition from a colony to an independent state conditioned Muslim personal law to consistency with constitutional norms and objectives and incorporated the historic *Kadhis'* courts into the state's judicial system.

It was during the period of 2003-2010, when discussions surrounding the creation of a new constitution were underway, that Kenyan Christians voiced their concerns that the inclusion of *Kadhis'* courts and reference to Muslim personal law in the draft constitution was discriminatory and violated the constitutional principle separating state and religion. They sought judicial determination. While the High Court ruling acknowledged the importance of the *Kadhis'* courts, the majority of judges concurred that their existence as a state institution was unconstitutional and breached the secular principle.[17] The 2010 referendum, resulting in the adoption of the current Constitution, resolved the legality of the *Kadhis'* courts, which,

---

[15] SJ Trimingham, *Islam in East Africa,* (Oxford: Clarendon Press, 1964).

[16] A Mazrui, 'Religion and Political Culture in Africa,' (1985) *Journal of the American Academy of Religion,* Vol 53, No 4, 817-839, at 830.

[17] *Joseph Kimani & 2 others v Attorney General & 2 others* (2010) eKLR, full decision available at: http://kenyalaw.org/caselaw/cases/view/70143/

along with Muslim personal law, now form part of the state's judicial institution and law. In summary, this brief background demonstrates how law has both tolerated and limited religion within the state, as well as exhibited a preference for Islamic religion over others. This raises the question of the type of legal system the Constitution of Kenya presents for legal and religious norms and their interaction.

The Constitution delineates a comprehensive and definitive legal system, with article 2(1)-(4) outlining the framing principles of this order:

> the Constitution is the supreme law of the country and binds all persons and all state organs, no person may claim or exercise state authority except as authorized under the Constitution, the validity or legality of the Constitution is not subject to challenge by or before any court or other state organ, and any law that is inconsistent with the Constitution is void to the extent of the inconsistency and any act or omission in contravention of the Constitution is invalid.

Unlike Zambia's Constitution, which proclaims the Republic a Christian nation,[18] Kenya's Constitution, under article 8, asserts that there shall be no state religion. Generally, this signifies that the state shall neither enact laws respecting the establishment of religion, nor ascribe to or propagate religion or apply religious principles. However, exceptions are made for Islamic law, which is enforced as part of state law. This divergence is significant in explaining the varying relationships between state and religion in Kenya, which this chapter endeavours to construct.

Article 27(1) of the Constitution confirms that every person is equal before the law and has the right to equal protection and equal benefit of the law. Article 27(4) asserts that the state shall not discriminate directly or indirectly against any person on any ground, including religion. Yet, article 24(4) limits the application of equality to the extent strictly necessary for

[18] Zambia is the only African country whose constitutional preamble declares that it is a Christian nation. *Zambia: The Constitution of Zambia* [Zambia], 1991, available at: https://www.refworld.org/docid/3ae6b5610.html

the application of Muslim law before the *Kadhis'* courts to persons who profess the Muslim religion in matters relating to personal status, marriage, divorce, and inheritance.[19] Arguably, such limitation is justified by the state's commitment to protecting freedom of religion under article 32.

Article 32(1) states that every person has the right to freedom of religion and further clarifies under article 32(4) that a person shall not be compelled to act or engage in any act that is contrary to their religious beliefs. This commitment is further supported by the establishment of *Kadhis'* courts under article 169(1)(b). Article 170(5) recognises the application of Muslim law relating to personal status, marriage, divorce, or inheritance, in proceedings in which all the parties profess the Muslim religion and submit to the jurisdiction of the *Kadhis'* courts. While this article does not suggest a religion for the Kenyan state contrary to article 8, it does indicate that the state has recognised the application of law that does not originate from the state and has enacted law establishing a religious institution and religious law. Moreover, the state also enforces Muslim personal law. Since this is formulated in law, it expresses the national will.

Five core principles can be discerned from this constitutional background that resonate with a liberal constitutional democracy. First and second are the principles of *limitation* and *conditionality*: the application of Muslim personal law is limited and conditional (all parties must be Muslim and must consent to its application), and the jurisdiction of the *Kadhis'* court is also limited (to personal law) and conditional (Muslim parties must not contest jurisdiction). Third is the principle of *exclusivity*, whereby the *kadhi* must be a Muslim and the dispute must involve only consenting Muslims. Fourth is the principle of *non-interference*, with the state refraining from interfering in the application and interpretation of Muslim law. The fifth principle relates to *derogation*, whereby the right to equality can be qualified by Islamic law when necessary.

Why provide this background and identify these principles? How do they relate to the question at hand? The argument is that these principles furnish

---

[19] Collectively referred to as personal law.

the chapter with a starting point for its inquiry into whether the Kenyan state can legally accept *zakat* to finance health without contravening article 8. These five principles contain the legal criteria to assist the state in deciding whether to accept *zakat* and how to use it (conditionally, limitedly, exclusively for health, non-interferingly and non-derogating from Islamic law on the use of *zakat*).

Collectively, the principles curtail the state's power concerning *zakat* usage, analogous to the conditions imposed for receiving foreign aid. The distinction between the conditions of *zakat* and foreign aid lies in the former deriving its authority from a divine source. Can the Kenyan state legally recognise the divine as a source of authority? Would such recognition violate article 8? The fact that Muslim law is expressly identified in the Constitution and considered part of state law suggests that the state recognises divinity as a source of law. Is there then a problem for the state to accept *zakat* together with its Islamic conditions? Moreover, can the state reject those conditions but accept *zakat*? Can it do so within its legal framework? These questions are examined next.

Complex Constitutional Hierarchies

My contention here is that receiving and accepting *zakat* may not present any significant difficulties for the state. However, embracing it with its Islamic conditions might prove complex, as this subjects state authority to a religious source of law. Furthermore, another legal challenge arises when a state committed to separation from religion opts to receive and subsequently administer *zakat* using its institutions. While political and economic justifications may exist for the Kenyan state accepting *zakat*, several complexities emerge from a doctrinal and academic standpoint.

Firstly, the prohibition against state-religion fusion under article 8 of the Constitution constitutes the most significant obstacle. Secondly, since Islamic law prescribes regulation on *zakat* (indicating that it is subject to an entirely different legal system), how will the Kenyan state justify the application of Islamic law within its constitutional framework – and should it? Given that under article 2(1), the Constitution recognises only itself as the supreme law, and under article 2(4) it nullifies all laws inconsistent with the Constitution, this also encompasses Islamic law. *Zakat* targets specific recipients to the exclusion of all others, contravening the principle against discrimination in the Constitution. Thirdly, since taxation is compulsory and forcibly extracted by the state, can the state compel Muslims to remit *zakat*? In other words, can the Kenyan state legally legislate on *zakat* and submit *zakat* to its authority? Must the Kenyan state accept *zākat* with its conditions? The subsequent discussion delves into each of these legal challenges, employing legal pluralism as the methodological tool of inquiry.

Determining whether the Kenyan legal system can permit the government to accept *zakat* to finance healthcare necessitates an initial examination of the Kenyan Constitution, which encompasses the religion policy adopted by the state. Articles 8 and 32[20] are of paramount importance, advocating for a neutral political public sphere that neither favours a specific religion nor restricts its presence. The declaration that there shall be no state religion under article 8 raises the question of whether the establishment of subordinate *Kadhis'* courts issuing legal decisions based on Islamic law elsewhere in the Constitution (under articles 169(1)(b) and 170[21]) suggests

[20] Article 8: There shall be no State religion. Article 32 (1): Every person has the right to freedom of conscience, religion, thought, belief and opinion; (2) Every person has the right, either individually or in community with others, in public or in private, to manifest any religion or belief through worship, practice, teaching or observance, including observance of a day of worship; (3) A person may not be denied access to any institution, employment or facility, or the enjoyment of any right, because of the person's belief or religion; (4) A person shall not be compelled to act, or engage in any act, that is contrary to the person's belief or religion.

[21] Article 169 (1) (b): The subordinate courts are – the Kadhis' courts.
Article 170: (1) There shall be a Chief Kadhi and such number, being not fewer than three, of other Kadhis as may be prescribed under an Act of Parliament; (2) A person shall not be qualified to be appointed to hold or act in the office of Kadhi unless the person— (*a*) professes the Muslim religion; and (*b*) possesses such knowledge of the Muslim law applicable to any sects of Muslims as qualifies the person, in the opinion of the Judicial Service Commission, to hold a Kadhi's court; (3) Parliament shall establish Kadhis' courts, each of which shall have the jurisdiction and powers conferred on it by legislation, subject to clause (5); (4) The Chief Kadhi and the other Kadhis, or the Chief Kadhi and such of the other Kadhis (not being fewer than three in number) as may be

a preference for Islam, or whether this contradicts the article 8 declaration. Addressing the principle that arises from this seemingly contradictory constitutional stance is crucial, as it may provide the answer to whether the Kenyan state can receive and utilise *zakat*. A complex state-religion model is at play in this context.

The constitution on religion

The typical method by which the state articulates and implements its approach to religion is through the law.[22] Consequently, the Kenyan constitutional state-religion model manifests in three forms that shape the relationship between the state and religion. The first form is the constitutionally prescribed separation of state and religion under article 8. Article 8 presents consequentialist justifications for non-intervention by the state in internal religious matters or intervention in the affairs of religious organisations. Doe and Jeremy contend that separating the state from religion is essential to protect individuals' autonomy from the state and allow them to practice their faith freely.[23] It may be argued that article 8 represents a form of deference to religious law, enabling the enjoyment of its own sovereignty without state interference.

Esbeck and Kuru maintain that this form of separation necessitates that the state neither supports nor hinders any religion.[24] Fox elucidates that this represents the most extreme form of neutrality, precluding any

---

prescribed under an Act of Parliament, shall each be empowered to hold a Kadhi's court having jurisdiction within Kenya; (5) The jurisdiction of a Kadhis' court shall be limited to the determination of questions of Muslim law relating to personal status, marriage, divorce or inheritance in proceedings in which all the parties profess the Muslim religion and submit to the jurisdiction of the Kadhi's courts.

22 N Doe and A Jeremy, 'Justifications for Religious Autonomy, Law and Religion' R O'Dair and A Lewis (eds), *Current Legal Issues*, (Oxford University Press 2001), 421-442.

23 ibid, 424.

24 CH Esbeck, 'A typology of church-state relations in American thought' (1988) *Religion and Public Education*, 15, 1, 43-50; AT Kuru, *Secularism and State Policies Towards Religion: the United States, France and Turkey* (Cambridge, Cambridge University Press, 2009); J Fox, 'Separation of Religion and State and Secularism in Theory and in Practice', (2011) *Religion, State and Society*, 39:4, 384-401.

government involvement or interference in religion.[25] Thus, under article 8, the state cannot accept *zakat,* with or without its conditions. This strict separation stance overlooks the state's role in imposing limits on religious practice. The state can restrict religion to prevent it from becoming a source of conflict or dispute in society. The rule is that there shall be no state religion – not that the state cannot intervene in religious matters.

Arguably, however, article 8, does not preclude the state from supporting the expression of religion in public life. Kuru cites the example of a state funding religious schools as compatible with this form, 'as long as the state does not favour one particular religion at the expense of others'.[26] Similarly, Esbeck argues that the term separation of state and religion is mythical, as it is permissible for a state to support religion in general without preferring one religion over others.[27] This implies that the Kenyan state can assist religious institutions but not seek assistance from them. In contrast, several missionary-funded healthcare centres in Kenya receive ongoing government subsidies, contrary to article 8.

The second form, identifiable under article 32, allows for the public expression of religion in the country. This form presents an integrationist justification and is addressed within the context of fundamental rights. Freedom of religion contributes to the attainment of social justice, political stability, and harmony.[28] The state permits the integration of religion in a pluralistic society because it is necessary for social justice. Religion influences culture, convictions, organisational structures, and social relations. Guaranteeing freedom of religion is a sign of tolerance corresponding to the duty of non-interference by the public authority.[29]

---

[25] Fox, (n 24) 385.

[26] Kuru (n 24) 44-45.

[27] Esbeck (n 24) 48.

[28] K Boyle and J Sheen (eds), *Freedom of Religion and Belief: A World Report* (London, 1997), 12.

[29] SC van Bijsterveld, 'Freedom of Religion: Legal Perspectives, Law and Religion' R O'Dair and A Lewis, (eds) Current Legal Issues, Volume 4 (Oxford 2001) 299-309

According to Madeley, this state-religion relationship 'requires that government action should not help or hinder any life-plan or way of life more than any other and that the consequences of government action should therefore be neutral'.[30] Both Esbeck and Fox contend that this form allows the state to support or restrict religion, provided the outcome is equitable for all religions.[31] Jacobsohn clarifies that this is simply means the government genuinely commits to religious freedom, demonstrated by the legal and political safeguards implemented to enforce that commitment.[32] This relationship influences the role of religion in society – the relationships between religion and law, and religion and politics. It thus provides the legal space to examine the fundamental question regarding the state's involvement in *zakat* or accepting it with its conditions.

While article 8 aims to prevent state interference in religion, article 32 invites the state to manage religions contrary to Madeleys' approach on government neutrality. What legal space do these articles create for the state's acceptance and use of *zakat*? Under articles 8 and 32, the availability and distribution of *zakat* in Kenya seem free from state regulation. Article 8 explicitly prevents the state from contemplating the acceptance and use of *zakat* since it would necessitate the application of Islamic law in governance.

Article 32 blurs the boundary between religion and state. It sits between the double periphery of religion's everyday presence in society and its legal restrictions. Article 32 permits faith-based organisations (FBOs) to become duty bearers on behalf of the government in providing socio-economic rights, to a certain extent. In exercising such duty, FBOs have complete autonomy. Karner and Aldridge confirm that religion responds to the

---

30 JTS Madeley, 'European Liberal Democracy and the Principle of State Religious Neutrality' (2003) *West European Politics*, 26, 1, 1-22, 5-6.

31 Esbeck (n 24), Fox (n 24), 386.

32 GJ Jacobsohn, *The Wheel of Law. India's secularism in comparative constitutional context.* (Princeton: Princeton University Press, 2003) 28.

socio-economic situation in a country.[33] Religious institutions assist in delivering social services.

Norris and Inglehart also assert that when a state can no longer deliver services, religious movements provide necessary support, prompting states to have a 'direct interest in promoting or controlling such religious institutions in order to maintain their power and legitimacy'.[34] An engagement between the state and religion under this form does not entirely violate article 8, but it does reveal that the separation between religion and state is more complex. By utilising *zakat,* the state enables religious institutions to voluntarily assist in realising its obligation under article 43(1)(a) of the Constitution (guaranteeing every citizen the right to health). This does not present any problem.

However, should the state exert its authority to direct these institutions to compulsorily give *zakat,* it infringes upon their article 32 freedom and violates article 8. Consequently, it could be argued that the state may also infringe upon article 32 rights when it chooses to accept *zakat* without applying its Islamic conditions. Moreover, if the state were to attempt to submit funds mobilised by religious institutions as part of its fiscal budget, it would violate article 32. Additionally, in extending its jurisdiction to require eligible Muslims to remit their *zakat* to the state to finance health, the state would not contravene article 32 – it will contravene article 8. The state must balance the constitutionally guaranteed fundamental freedom to practice religion with its duty under article 43(1)(a).

No constitutional provision grants the state unhindered power to dispense with the religious autonomy, under article 32, to capture religious sources of revenue to finance rights. Thus, whether the state can receive or involve itself in the mobilisation of *zakat* can only be at the request of Muslims or their religious institution. This would properly feature under political

---

[33] C Karner and A Aldridge, 'Theorizing Religion in a Globalizing World', (2004) *International Journal of Politics, Culture and Society* 18 (1), 5-32, 11.

[34] P Norris and R Inglehart, *Sacred and Secular: Religion and Politics* Worldwide (Cambridge: Cambridge University Press, 2004) 230.

negotiations rather than law. However, the negotiation process is not as straightforward as it seems, as Muslim representation in Kenya is fragmented, and different schools of thought inform the understanding of *zakat* and their interactions with the state.[35]

The third form of state-religion relationship contemplated under the Kenyan Constitution, which expressly problematises the neutrality presented under articles 8 and 32, is introduced under articles 169(1)(c) and 170 of the Constitution (the so-called '*Kadhis'* court' provisions). The latter admits the exclusive operation of Islamic law as part of state law enforced by the state's judicial institutions. This poses a direct conflict with article 8 and was the subject of repeated opposition during the making of the 2010 Kenyan Constitution.

Since this chapter aims to engage in the broader debate on the separation between state and religion within the context of Kenya, a brief discussion on the constitutional process in retaining *Kadhis'* courts as part of state institutions is necessary. This may help to clarify the legality surrounding state acceptance and use of *zakat* to finance healthcare. Isanga explains that some Christian groups have opposed the establishment of these courts, arguing that the state is discriminating against other religious bodies by exclusively permitting the setting up of *Kadhis'* courts, which are run on non-Muslim taxpayers earnings and introduce Islamic law as part of state law.[36] The Kenyan judicial system recognises and enforces the implementation of Islamic law, limited to the 'determination of questions of Muslim law relating to personal status, marriage, divorce or inheritance in proceedings in which all parties profess the Muslim religion and submit to the jurisdiction of the *Kadhis'* courts'.[37]

Does this form of relationship suggest a preference for Islam by the Kenyan state? Does it contradict article 8? Or is this form simply reflecting the promise before independence between Kenya's first president, Jomo

---

[35] This is discussed in Chapter 7.

[36] Isanga (n 5) 47

[37] Article 170 (5), Constitution of Kenya, 2010.

Kenyatta, and Mr Shamte, the Prime Minister of Zanzibar, to secure the Islamic judicial system that was already entrenched in pre-colonial Kenya?[38] In light of these questions, article 169(1)(c) was the subject of extensive deliberations during the Constitution of Kenya Review Commission (CKRC), established to draft the new Kenyan Constitution.[39] Chesworth documents the history of including the *Kadhi's* courts clause in the draft constitutions, arguing that the opposition to *Kadhis'* courts resulted from three arguments strongly advanced by some Christian organisations.[40]

First, that state and religion shall be separate; second, there shall be no state religion; and third, that all religions will be treated equally.[41] Ndzovu explains that the inclusion of *Kadhi's* courts against the arguments advanced resulted in a section of Christian leaders petitioning the constitutional court to rule on the legality or otherwise of *Kadhi's* courts.[42] In May 2010, a three-judge bench pronounced that the inclusion of the *Kadhi's* courts in the draft Constitution was illegal, ruling that religious courts should not form part of the judiciary.[43] The judges effectively relied on the principle of separation of state and religion. This decision was, however, overturned on appeal to the High Court. Can it thus be argued that the Constitution endorses an official religion under articles 169(1)(c) and 170? Does it allude to a specific intent to support a specific religion and accept its norms as part of Kenya's legal system, which by extension would justify or restrict the application of the conditions of *zakat*? Arguably, this is a matter of interpretation. Or does it demonstrate the contradictions within the Constitution on the controversial relationship between law and religion? The answer to these questions lies in how we interpret the Constitution.

---

[38] More on this in Chapter 6.

[39] Committee of Experts/Reference Group. Progress on the Constitution Review Process by the Committee of Experts (CoE) and Reference Group (RE) as at October 2009.

[40] Chesworth (n 5) 7.

[41] ibid 9.

[42] Ndzovu (n 5).

[43] *Joseph Kimani & 2 others v Attorney General & 2 others* (n 17).

Interpreting the constitution

Several interpretive methods, such as textualism, purposivism, structuralism, and originalism have been developed to guide the reading and understanding of constitutions.[44] Goldsworthy and Mutunga argue that controversy in the interpretation of constitutions surrounds two central issues:[45] whether interpretation should be governed mainly by the letter or the spirit of the law, and whether the meaning of the Constitution can and should be determined by its founders' original intentions, purposes, or understandings.

Both Goldsworthy and Mutunga, in narrowing down these two issues, provide helpful guidance in resolving the dilemma posed by the three interrelated articles 8, 32 and 169(1), read alongside 170. Effectively, under article 8, the state should not accept *zakat* if it means to apply its conditions, which are governed by Islamic law (textualism), since applying Islamic law would contradict the theory of sovereignty enshrined under article 2(1) of the Kenyan Constitution.[46] Should the Muslims choose to utilise their pooled *zakat* funds and apply them towards financing private healthcare, no state involvement is required (purposivism). The fact that the Constitution recognises and establishes Muslim religious courts does not impact the governance of *zakat* or permit state interference since the Constitution limits the jurisdiction of the *kadhi's* courts (structuralism) to only adjudicating Muslim personal law. The latter, however, does provide wiggle room for the state to consider accepting *zakat* and applying its conditions in adding *zakat* proceeds to its healthcare budget. There already exists domestic precedent in the application of Islamic law over Muslim personal law. However, the problem in applying Islamic law-based

---

[44] J Goldsworthy, *Interpreting Constitutions: A Comparative Study*. (Oxford: Oxford University Press, 2007); BJ Murrill, 'Modes of Constitutional Interpretation' (USA: Congressional Research Service Report 2018)'.

[45] ibid, Goldsworthy; W Mutunga, 'The 2010 Constitution of Kenya and its Interpretation: Reflections from the Supreme Court Decisions', (2015) *Speculum Juris Volume* 19 (1), 1.

[46] Article 2(1): This Constitution is the supreme law of the Republic and binds all persons and all state organs at both levels of government.

principles for *zakat* is distinct from existing application of Muslim personal law since the use of *zakat* for funding healthcare is also to include non-Muslims.

Articles 169(1)(c) and 170 can be said to endorse the recognition of a historic religious institution that traces its introduction and development along Kenya's coastline during its pre-colonial era, and which also influenced the decolonisation political architecture to be adopted at independence (originalism). It does not, therefore, indicate preference for Islam by the state, but a legal recognition of a geographic Muslim judicial system independently existing on territory brought under the sovereignty of Kenya at independence. This form of state and religion relationship emphasises the view that the state can put in place infrastructure and institutions based on which a specific religion can exercise legal authority. However, the state must not become an active participant; it must only get involved or interfere when called upon or on public interest concerns.

Similarly, by analogy, an argument can be made that the state can authorise institutional support at state level for the mobilisation of *zakat,* but it is far more problematic to identify *zakat* as part of its domestically available revenue base. The state may put in place institutions[47] to receive *zakat,* together with its conditions, if such institutions will be administered by Muslims for Muslims. This is analogous to the system in Germany. Although Germany does not have an established church, Protestantism and Catholicism are recognised as official religions, and most citizens pay a state-collected church tax, which is remitted to the church and not the state.[48]

---

[47] For example, the Kenyan State has established the Wakf Commission under the Wakf Commissioners Act (Chapter 109) to administer Muslim endowments. The Wakf Bill 2018 aims to revise the previous act which since its enactment during colonial rule has not been amended, neither does it reflect the socio-economic realities of the Muslims. The bill is under currently under discussion.

[48] G Halmai, 'Varieties of State-Church Relations and Religious Freedom Through Three Case Studies' (2017) Mich St L Rev 175-207.

The interpretive methods guide us towards understanding why the *Kadhis'* courts and Muslim personal law were included in the Constitution. The methods also guide us to appreciate the law of the state on religion. Islamic law is part of state law since it is enforced by its judicial system (textualism and structuralism). This creates an exception to the general rule under article 8. This exception permits treating Islamic law as an authoritative text to determine Muslim personal law. Hence, can the Islamic law on *zakat* also become part of state law, if the state so chooses? The answer to this is not so obvious as one might think. It can only be discovered by an examination of the legal theory that guides the Kenyan state. Discovering the Islamic law on *zakat* will require scriptural interpretation; the Kenyan state will have to consult the *Qur'an* in deciding how to use *zakat* and will have to treat the *Qur'an* as authoritative – or as we lawyers often say, binding. The difficulty becomes evident when we follow the constitutional hierarchisation of norms. The law on *zakat* and the *Qur'an* do not feature there. Does the Constitution permit the state to interpret scripture? Does legal pluralism help explain this?

Relatedly, where a broader aim, beyond the religious institution is envisioned, such as financing health using religious funds, could its conditions be subject to the state's authority? The legality of the latter position will be discussed in the next section. What can be gathered from these discussions is that the *'wall of separation'* aptly referred to by Madan[49] between state and religion, prescribed by the modern Western models such as in France, Turkey, and the United States of America, do not feature within the Kenyan legal system. From the explanations offered by

[49] TN Madan, 'Secularism in Its Place' (1987) *Journal of Asian Studies* 46: 4, 747-759.

Hooker,[50] Woodman,[51] Pimentel,[52] Gebeye[53] and Swenson,[54] it can be suggested that this is because of the ubiquitous phenomenon of the co-existence of different normative orders defining state and society relationships within a plural socio-political space. In its modern post-colonial context, Kenya has evolved from the co-existence of different social normative systems, with different ideologies and forms of validity, that the Constitution seeks to protect. In this respect and with deference to Islam, articles 32, 169(1)(c) and 170 of the Kenyan Constitution acknowledge the legitimacy of Islamic law and its claim to select its own principles for application to certain fields of the Muslim social life. As such, separation of Islam from the state and its law would give rise to obstacles to justice.

Similarly, should the state choose to accept *zakat* without its conditions, it would result in a conflict of claims to legality. This draws out the context within which the chapter explores the question on whether and to what extent the Kenyan legal system permits the government to accept *zakat* to finance health, in accordance with the rules prescribed under Islamic law. Legal pluralism provides the methodological approach to determine the situation in which the availability of funds for financing health are within the field of operation of two bodies of legal norms: the Kenyan Constitution and the Islamic law on *zakat*.

The use of legal pluralism to explain the Kenyan state's relationship with Islam under the Constitution suggests four things. First, there is no

---

[50] BM Hooker, *Legal Pluralism: An Introduction to Colonial and Neo-Colonial Laws* (Oxford: Clarendon Press 1975).

[51] G Woodman, 'Legal Pluralism and the Search for Justice' (1996) *Journal of African Law* Vol 40, No 2 152-167.

[52] D Pimentel, 'Legal Pluralism in Post-Colonial Africa: Linking Statutory and Customary Adjudication in Mozambique' (2011) *Yale Human Rights and Development Law Journal*, 14 (1): 59-104.

[53] B Gebeye, 'Decoding Legal Pluralism in Africa', (2017) *The Journal of Legal Pluralism and Unofficial Law*, 49:2, 228-249.

[54] G Swenson, 'Legal Pluralism in Theory and Practice', (2018) *International Studies Review*, 20(2), 342.

exclusive hegemony of the state in the legal sphere.[55] Second, there exists within the state a recognition of non-state law. Third, there is some sort of contact between state and non-state law. Fourth, the Constitution alone is seen to confer on these state and non-state law sources both authority and effectiveness. The effect of this last point describes that the law on *zakat*, therefore, is to be accommodated as part of an overall hierarchical arrangement and cannot be exclusively assigned to a particular legal order – since it must meet the test of both state law and Islamic law, when used by a non-Islamic state. The Kenyan Constitution only recognises Muslim personal law. Various statutes have been enacted giving recognition to Muslim trust and financial services law, but none on *zakat*.[56] This means that in the absence of law guiding the state, the state has no legal obligation to accept the Islamic conditions that accompany *zakat*. This calls into question the legal nature of the law on *zakat* in Kenya.

The Kenyan Legal System and its Relationship with Islamic Law

The Constitution of Kenya acknowledges that norms do not derive their legal character solely from state ordination. It recognises customary law,[57] international law,[58] traditional forms of dispute resolution,[59] and Muslim personal law[60] as additional sources of norms. Consequently, the Constitution accommodates these diverse forms of norms within a vertically structured conceptual framework, which elucidates the manner in which the Constitution characterises the law and its legal system. It

---

[55] Not only is the limited scope of Islamic law recognised under articles 169 and 170, but articles 159 also recognises traditional forms of dispute resolution mechanisms.

[56] For example, the Banking Act (Chapter 488) and the Capital Markets Act (Chapter 485A) have been amended to give recognition to Islamic banking, as well as trading and transacting through Islamic financial products. The Income Tax Act (Chapter 470) and the Stamp Duty Act (Chapter 480) have been amended to regulate the tax on transactions pursuant to Islamic forms of contracts.

[57] Article 2(4).

[58] Article 2 (5) and (6)

[59] Article 159(2) (c).

[60] Article 170(5).

acknowledges norms promulgated by the state in accordance with the Constitution,[61] presenting a normative model of law reminiscent of a pyramid. At the apex of the structure lies the rule of consistency, akin to Hart's rule of recognition,[62] which legally validates and identifies the remaining norms of the system. This rule of consistency ensures that, although multiple normative orders can co-exist in society, the Constitution alone asserts its supremacy over these norms.[63] While the Constitution of Kenya adopts a sympathetic stance towards legal pluralism, it engenders what may be termed a *reductive legal pluralism.* This descriptive methodology posits that if social and religious norms are to possess any legal effect and be regarded as part of the state's law, such norms must be reconciled with the Constitution's rule of consistency and be enforced as part of state law.

Thus, it is evident that the normative order of law in Kenya repudiates the 'top-down' jurisprudence of Hobbes, Bentham, and Austin, which favoured a robust state-centric view of law. However, it does present a top-down consistency rule. As expressed in article 2(1), 'the Constitution is the supreme law of the Republic and binds all persons and all state organs at both levels of government'.[64] Article 2(4) mandates the consistency of all law with the Constitution: 'Any law, including customary law, that is inconsistent with this Constitution is void to the extent of the inconsistency, and any act or omission in contravention of this Constitution is invalid'. The term 'law' is employed, rather than 'norms', suggesting that the Constitution situates social norms (customary practice, religion) within its legal system, enabling the state to recognise, as law, the normative ordering co-existing within its socio-political space, by reference to its consistency rule.

---

[61] Article 1(3)

[62] (n 10) 204-5.

[63] Article 2(4): Any law, including customary law, that is inconsistent with this Constitution is void to the extent of the inconsistency, and any act or omission in contravention of this Constitution is invalid.

[64] At both the national and county level.

Hence, according to article 2(4), the law need not be official law promulgated by the state or state officers. Implicit in article 2(4) is the understanding that society unifies in officially accepting the rule of consistency as containing the criteria of validity for Kenya's legal system. In conjunction, articles 2(1) and 2(4) provide a logical approach to understanding the normative order of law in Kenya. Based on this understanding, if the Kenyan state were to accept and utilise *zakat* to finance health in accordance with Islamic law, these articles would necessitate that such use and the application of Islamic law be consistent with the declaration under article 8, which separates state and religion. It thus follows that it would be illegal for the Kenyan state to accept *zakat* on the condition that Islamic law be applied to determine its use and governance. This constitutes a strict textual interpretation of article 8. In principle, article 8 precludes reference to Islamic law as the governing law for the use of *zakat*, should it be donated to the state.

Nevertheless, articles 169 and 170(5) seem to qualify article 8. Article 169 establishes the *Kadhi's* courts, while article 170(5) recognises the application of Muslim personal law as a source of Kenyan law. Both articles mitigate the rigid separation of state from religion under article 8. Muslim personal law has been granted official recognition as a form of law, and the status of law has also been conferred upon it. However, the criteria for determining the validity of Muslim personal law are conferred upon the *Kadhi* to the extent that article 27, when read in conjunction with article 24(4) of the Constitution, is qualified by Islamic law.

Article 27 states that 'Every person is equal before the law and has the right to equal protection and equal benefit of the law'. Meanwhile, article 24(4) elucidates that 'equality shall be qualified to the extent strictly necessary for the application of Muslim law before the *Kadhis'* courts, to persons who profess the Muslim religion, in matters relating to personal status, marriage, divorce and inheritance'. Consequently, the spirit of article 8 is thereby diminished. The Kenyan normative order of law demonstrates the capacity to accommodate pluralist possibilities. The rule of consistency under article 2(4) is challenged by article 24(4). The application of Muslim personal law before the *Kadhis'* courts can qualify and limit the application of article 27 by invoking article 24(4). Both are constitutional provisions, and the limitation of one by the other does not impact article 2(4) – the rule of consistency. This is because such limitation applies solely to Muslims litigating before the *Kadhis'* courts. What implications does this discussion have on the legality of the state accepting and taking *zakat* and utilising it in accordance with Islamic law?

The legal application of Islamic law

The Kenyan Constitution, as a self-referential document, asserts that its 'validity or legality… is not subject to challenge by or before any court or other state organ.'[65] In this context, the sources of Muslim personal law are not explicitly outlined within the Constitution, nor codified by the state. Instead, Muslim personal law exists as an external point of reference for the state. As a consequence, since Muslim personal law forms part of the Constitution's conceptual framework of the law, its validity or legality is not subject to challenge. Thus, Islamic law – limited to Muslim personal law – becomes part of state law, which in turn blurs the separation of state and religion as articulated in article 8. This understanding implies that if the application of the Islamic law regarding the use of *zakat* is a precondition for donating funds to the state, the state would not contravene article 8 by accepting these conditions. However, just as Muslim personal law finds explicit mention in the Constitution to be considered part of the legal system, Islamic law on the use of *zakat* must also be expressly set out in the Constitution; otherwise, article 8 would be violated. Such is the nature of the relationship between law and religion, as established by the Constitution of Kenya. This approach confirms Doe's view that the 'ordinary means which the state employs to express and implement its approach to religion is law'.[66]

The qualification of the constitution's rule of consistency by article 24(4) confirms its pluralistic view of law. It integrates, under a single system of rules, the historical Islamic normative order that existed along the Kenyan

[65] Article 2(3).

[66] (n 22) 421.

coast before British colonisation – and imposes its limits. Insofar as Islamic law can be legally applied by the Kenyan state, it is restricted to matters of Muslim personal law. *Zakat,* however, does not appear within the constitutional provisions or as part of the Muslim personal law mentioned in the Constitution. Consequently, a general conclusion may be drawn that if the acceptance of *zakat* is contingent upon the application of Islamic law in governing its use, the Kenyan state is not permitted to accept it. Given the *Qur'an's* status as the most authoritative source of norms in Islam, the state must exercise caution when venturing into such a sensitive area for Muslims, as it necessitates scriptural interpretation. The Kenyan state would need to consult the *Qur'an* when determining how to utilise *zakat* and treat the *Qur'an* as authoritative, potentially crossing the well-established divide between state and religion.

This chapter contends that if the normative order of law in the Constitution of Kenya acknowledges legal pluralism, then the portion of Islamic law governing the use of *zakat* can be considered a source of law under article 2(4): 'Any *law,*[67]... that is inconsistent with this Constitution is void to the extent of the inconsistency...'. It can then be argued that, under article 2(4), Islamic law is subordinate to the Constitution. There are evident principles for both its subordination[68] and recognition.[69] Although the Constitution does not create the legal status of Islamic law within itself (it is created by the *Qur'an*), Islamic law is subject to the Constitution's overarching rule of consistency. This rule determines the relationship between Islamic law and the state.

Islamic law forms part of Kenya's social normative order. A portion of it (Muslim personal law) is recognised by the state (article 170(5)), while the

---

[67] Emphasis is mine.

[68] Article 2(1): This Constitution is the supreme law of the Republic and binds all persons and all State organs at both levels of government.

[69] Article 2(4): Any law, including customary law, that is inconsistent with this Constitution is void to the extent of the inconsistency, and any act or omission in contravention of this Constitution is invalid.

rest is subject to article 2(4) and article 32 (freedom of religion).[70] The Kenyan Constitution assumes harmony in identifying, separating, accepting, and rejecting different normative orders. The approach is guided by the principle outlined in article 2(4) – the rule on consistency, which can be seen as the Constitution's principle of legal science. Simultaneously, article 2(4), when read in conjunction with articles 24(4), 32 and 170(5), challenges the notion that the presentation of a legal system and legal theory in the Constitution is settled. It invites scrutiny of Kenya's true legal system and whether this system, despite article 8, can recognise and apply Islamic law on *zakat*. Addressing this issue is arguably one of the most pressing concerns for contemporary Kenyan scholars.

Turning to Hart for guidance, he suggests that certain customs may fall outside the scope of law: 'The meaning and good sense of the denial that custom, as such, is law lie in the simple truth that, in any society, there are many customs which form no part of its law'.[71] In the Kenyan context, this could mean that parts of Islamic law not explicitly recognised by the Constitution are excluded from the conception of law. However, Hart emphasises the importance of a group's acceptance of a rule,[72] allowing for the potential recognition of Islamic law, beyond Muslim personal law, as part of Kenya's legal system under article 2(4). While Hart's theory could accommodate legal pluralism, he stresses the importance of unified or shared official acceptance of the rule of recognition containing the system's criteria of validity: 'what is crucial is that there should be a unified or

[70] Article 32 (1): Every person has the right to freedom of conscience, religion, thought, belief and opinion. 32 (2): Every person has the right, either individually or in community with others, in public or in private, to manifest any religion or belief through worship, practice, teaching or observance, including observance of a day of worship. (3) A person may not be denied access to any institution, employment or facility, or the enjoyment of any right, because of the person's belief or religion. (4) A person shall not be compelled to act, or engage in any act, that is contrary to the person's belief or religion.

[71] (n 10) 44.

[72] (n 10) 63-4.

shared official acceptance of the rule of recognition containing the system's criteria of validity'.[73]

According to Hart, the criterion of validity is to be identified by officials.[74] His 'Concept of Law' does not require these officials to be state officials. Scholars such as Teubner, Tamanaha, and Cotterrel argue that Hart was not concerned with accommodating legal pluralism within his theoretical framework.[75] Instead, he focused on the nature of law rather than what it should be (what law *is* rather than what it ought to be). Thus, we move from norms to law. Normative Islam is part of Kenya's social order, and the only aspect of normative Islam considered part of state law pertains to Muslim personal law.

Islamic law represents a comprehensive legal system akin to Hart's 'developed' legal system, with secondary rules and institutions.[76] The question then arises: how does one legal system recognise another and allow its enforcement? Can these two legal systems be reconciled? Does the Kenyan legal system view Islamic norms as binding or legally effective? Under article 2(4), only norms consistent with the Constitution are recognised. However, the Constitution provides no further guidance on where these norms can be found or whether external sources not expressly mentioned in the Constitution can be considered part of state law. This constitutional ambivalence necessitates a clear understanding of Kenya's legal system, in order to establish the boundaries of what constitutes law in the country. A systematic approach must be employed to clarify the relationship between Islamic law and state law, ultimately reducing the extent of legal pluralism within the state (reductive legal pluralism). Failing

---

[73] (n 10) 111.
[74] ibid 117.
[75] G Teubner, 'How the Law Thinks: Toward a Constructivist Epistemology of Law' (1989) 23 *Law & Society Review* 727; B Tamanaha, 'The Folly of the "Social Scientific" Concept of Legal Pluralism', (1993) 20 JL & Soc'Y 192, 201, and R Cotterrell, *Law, Culture and Society: Legal Ideas in the Mirror of Social Theory* (Routledge 2006) 37.
[76] (n 10) 91-9.

to do so may result in difficulties managing a dual legal system without significant friction.

Can the Kenyan legal system then legally permit the use of *zakat* in accordance with Islamic law without contravening article 8, despite the potential recognition of Islamic law under article 2(4)? Legal pluralism, characterised by its reliance on multiple overlapping norms and institutions, cannot provide a method to resolve this conflict between law and religion. The following section will discuss why legal pluralism, with its emphasis on a multiplicity of norms and institutions, distorts the concept of law and the legal system in Kenya concerning the extent to which Islamic law can be accommodated by the state. The limitation of legal pluralism in providing clarity on the concept of law in Kenya are addressed by turning to socio-legal positivism and the process of civic reason. This approach aims to present a unified yardstick for determining the concept of law in Kenya. By doing so, it is hoped that a clear answer can be provided as to whether the Kenyan legal system can legally permit the government to accept and utilise *zakat* while applying Islamic law governing its use.

Socio-legal positivism emphasises the importance of understanding law in its social context, focusing on the relationships between law, society, and the state. This perspective acknowledges the coexistence of multiple normative orders within a society and the influence of societal values and beliefs on the legal system. By examining the Kenyan legal system through the lens of socio-legal positivism, a more nuanced understanding of the interplay between Islamic law and state law can be achieved. The process of civic reason, on the other hand, refers to a deliberative approach in which different viewpoints and values are considered in the formation and interpretation of law. This method allows for a more inclusive legal framework that respects diverse perspectives and accommodates varying normative orders while maintaining a sense of unity and coherence within the legal system.

By employing socio-legal positivism and the process of civic reason, the Kenyan legal system can better address the challenges posed by the coexistence of Islamic law and state law. This approach can help establish clear boundaries and criteria for the recognition and application of Islamic law within the state's legal framework, particularly concerning the use of *zakat*. In conclusion, the Kenyan Constitution's inherent legal pluralism necessitates a more nuanced understanding of the relationship between Islamic law and state law. Utilising socio-legal positivism and the process of civic reason can provide valuable insights into this complex relationship and offer a clearer path for the legal system to accommodate Islamic law while respecting the Constitution's principles. By establishing clear boundaries and criteria for the recognition and application of Islamic law, the Kenyan legal system can more effectively address the challenges posed by legal pluralism and the coexistence of multiple normative orders.

Can Islamic law on *zakat* be accommodated?

A complex legal problem arises with respect to the relationship between the Kenyan legal system and Islamic law, particularly in terms of its inclusion within the legal framework. Article 170(5) of the Kenyan Constitution acknowledges Muslim personal law as part of state law, but it does not codify its content. Instead, the task of interpreting Muslim personal law is delegated to the *Kadhi,* a state officer, who consults external sources of law to discern its substance. Consequently, scriptural interpretation becomes a state function, and Islamic law is incorporated into state law through the process of judicial decision-making.

The Islamic law on *zakat* could potentially follow a similar approach if it were considered part of Muslim personal law. In that case, the *Kadhi* would determine its application at the state level. However, *zakat* is not currently included under Muslim personal law. Given that Islamic law on *zakat* could be viewed as part of article 2(4) of the Constitution, one could argue that it ought to be applied within the consistency rule. The challenge that arises, which article 2(4) does not resolve, is determining who at the state level would interpret the *Qur'an* to extract the relevant law on *zakat*? Legal pluralism does not provide a clear answer to this question, as it only reaffirms that Islamic law is part of the diverse social normative orders in Kenya but does not clarify how these multiple legal orders interact within the Constitution's consistency rule. Swenson's analysis comes close to offering a solution, but his approach does not sufficiently address the unique problem presented by the Kenyan Constitution.[77]

Swenson proposes four approaches to explain the interaction and relationship between state and non-state law, which can be categorised as *combative, competitive, cooperative,* or *complementary*.[78] He further identifies five strategies that have been commonly employed by states in their interaction with non-state actors: *bridging, harmonisation, incorporation, subsidisation,* and *repression*.[79] These strategies serve to summarise the various methods through which states have accommodated or rejected non-state law, either by integrating it into state law or by recognising its legal effect.

The Kenyan Constitution adopts a cooperative approach to Islamic law by allowing the application of Muslim personal law and the establishment of the *Kadhis'* courts. This approach aligns well with the strategies of incorporation and harmonisation. Through incorporation, article 170(5) of the Constitution blurs the distinction between state and Islamic law – at least from the state's perspective, since Muslim personal law is enforced as state law by state officers. Incorporation enables the establishment of religious courts with state support and regulation. Harmonisation seeks to ensure that the decisions made by the *Kadhis'* courts align with the Kenyan Constitution, implicitly recognising that Islamic law maintains a considerable degree of autonomy and independent legitimacy. While Swenson's summary of approaches for legal pluralists' sheds light on how different normative orders can legally function within a state, it does not resolve the dilemma posed by article 2(4). Perhaps an answer lies within legal positivism?

Legal positivism posits that for Islamic law to be part of the Kenyan legal system, it must either be expressly stated in the Constitution or under statutory law. It also suggests that Islamic law may be considered part of

[77] See generally, Swenson (n 54) 342.
[78] ibid.
[79] ibid.

Kenyan law under article 2(4) of the Constitution if it falls within the scope of 'any law, including customary law' and meets the criteria for constitutional validity. However, legal positivism does not address how to interpret the phrase 'any law' within a legally pluralistic environment. Why is this important?

In my view, attaining a more precise conceptual and analytical understanding of the Kenyan legal system will facilitate the identification, description and comprehension of the relationship between law and Islamic law. Article 2(4) challenges the institutional nature of law in Kenya, prompting me to consider that the Constitution has reconfigured legal positivism, rendering it compatible with a sociological approach. Drawing on Tamanaha's socio-legal positivism, I will argue that the answer to whether the Kenyan legal system permits the government to take and utilise *zakat* in accordance with Islamic law can be found within this theoretical framework. Article 2(4) implies that the Constitution epitomises law and accommodates socio-legal phenomena by effectively subordinating all such normative orders to the Constitution. It presents a distinctive aspect of legal positivism, which must be examined by first discussing how the Kenyan state characterises legal pluralism and then exploring Tamanaha's theory as a potential solution to the question posed in this chapter.

Legal pluralism: Is there a confusion in applying Islamic law?

Legal pluralism is defined as a 'situation in which two or more legal systems co-exist in the same social field.'[80] It 'describes and characterises the existence of several distinct legal systems, or perhaps legal sub-systems, within a single independent political community, like a nation-state.'[81] The Kenyan legal system acknowledges and accommodates this phenomenon. The central question is how much of legal pluralism is part of the Kenyan legal system? To address this query, I will first briefly introduce various

---

[80] SE Merry, 'Legal Pluralism', (1988) 22 *Law & Society Review* 869, 870.

[81] J Waldron, 'No Barking: Legal Pluralism and the Contrast between Hart's Jurisprudence and Fuller's'. Colloquium: The Hart-Fuller Debate 50 Years On, Australian National University College of Law, 2008.

legal pluralism theorists and their characterisation of the phenomenon, before explaining how the Kenyan legal system conceptualises legal pluralism.

Theorists of legal pluralism, such as Allot, Hooker, Griffiths, Woodman, Pimentel and Gebeye, have discussed legal pluralism in the context of imperialism.[82] They have confined legal pluralism to an examination of cases where European colonial powers superimposed their legal systems on the pre-existing systems within their colonies. Conversely, other theorists of legal pluralism, including Pospisil, Engels, Vanderlinden, Menski, Jackson, Gunther, Douglas-Scott, Oomen, Crowe, and Sandberg, adopt a broader perspective.[83] They argue that legal pluralism is a characteristic of every society, regardless of whether it has a colonial past. They approach legal pluralism as a 'model of the legal universe' to borrow the words of Barber,[84] in which legal systems and institutions can conflict and overlap. These theorists perceive legal pluralism as a means of recognising normative orders as law that do not derive their legal character

---

[82] AN Allot, *Essays in African Law* (London: Butterworths, 1960) Chapter 7; B Hooker, *Legal Pluralism: An Introduction to Colonial and Neo-Colonial Laws.* (Oxford: Clarendon Press, 1975); J Griffiths, 'What is Legal Pluralism?' (1986) 24 *Journal of Legal Pluralism* 1, 5-8; G Woodman, 'Legal Pluralism in Africa: The implications of state recognition of customary laws illustrated from the field of land law', (2011) *Acta Juridica*, 35-58, 39; Pimentel (n 52) 59-104; and Gebeye (n 53) 228-249.

[83] L Pospisil, Anthropology of Law: A Comparative Theory of Law (New York: Harper and Row, 1971) 107 Merry (n 74) 869; J Vanderlinden, 'Return to Legal Pluralism: Twenty Years Later', (1989) *Journal of Legal Pluralism* 28: 149-157; W Menski, *Comparative Law in a Global Context: The Legal Systems of Asia and Africa* (Platinum Publishing, 2000); S Jackson, 'Legal Pluralism Between Islam and the Nation-State: Romantic Medievalism or Pragmatic Modernity?' (2006) *Fordham International Law Journal* 30(1), 157-176; K Gunther, 'Legal Pluralism or Uniform Concept of Law?' (2008) *NoFo* 5; S Douglas-Scott, *Law after Modernity* (Hart: Oxford. 2013); B Oomen, 'The Application of Socio-Legal Theories of Legal Pluralism to Understanding the Implementation and Integration of Human Rights Law', (2013) *European Journal of Human Rights'* 471-495; J Crowe, 'The Limits of Legal Pluralism', (2015) *Griffith Law Review*, Vol 24, No 2, 314-331; R Sandberg, 'The Failure of Legal Pluralism', (2016) *Ecclesiastical Law Journal* 137-157 and Swenson, (n 54) 342.

[84] N Barber, 'The Rechtsstaat and the Rule of Law', (2003) 53 *University of Toronto Law Journal* 443, 450.

from state ordination. In essence, legal pluralism acknowledges law on the ground.

While these theorists provide a descriptive approach to understanding legal systems, intriguing normative questions arise (dealt with later under this chapter). The primary question here is whether legal pluralism assists in identifying a legal theory or defining the concept of law in Kenya. This question is essential to determine if the Kenyan legal system can legally allow the government to take and use *zakat* while adhering to the conditions imposed under Islamic law. As demonstrated in the next section, the legal pluralism acknowledged in article 2(4) of the Constitution problematises article 8 concerning the application of Islamic law. Thus, legal pluralism does not aid in identifying a legal theory representative of Kenya's legal system concerning law and religion. In fact, legal pluralism is controversial in the context of the interplay between Islamic law and state law. This controversy is best elucidated using Griffith's categorisation of legal pluralism as deep and weak.

Deep legal pluralism, as initially defined by Griffiths, was developed to challenge the prevailing ideology of legal centralism, which has become the dominant theory regarding law and was antagonistic to all notions of legal pluralism.[85] Legal pluralism differentiates between state law and non-state law. According to Griffiths, deep legal pluralism refers to, and results from, two facts. First, not all law is state law. Second, not all law is administered by a single set of state-sponsored institutions.[86] Conversely, weak legal pluralism, as explained by Griffiths, refers to situations in which the state recognises, validates, and backs different bodies of law for different groups in society.[8] The question then arises: how do both forms manifest in the Kenyan context?

The emergence of legal pluralism in Kenya has historical connotations. Lewin suggests that it resulted from the recognition granted by the colonial

---

85 Griffiths (n 82); and Jackson (n 83).

86 ibid.

powers to 'customary' laws in the territories they came to dominate.[87] The British colonial power encountered existing regulatory institutions in the East Africa Protectorate (modern day Kenya) over which they could not exercise complete control (*Kadhis'* courts, the *Wakf*[88] institution) nor had the ability to eradicate (African customary law).

Such legal pluralism challenged the British colonial administration's state-centric ideology, according to which all law is and should be state-sponsored law, uniform for all persons, equally applied across all social groups, and emphatically superior to, if not exclusive of, any and all other systems or repositories of law.[89] Confronted with different forms of regulatory institutions (such as the *kadhis, liwalis* and *mudhirs* subservient to the Sultans of Oman and later Zanzibar), and social normative structures (African customary law), the colonial administration had to determine how to maintain its commitment to legal centralism while also ensuring a functional and uninterrupted application of Islamic law and African customary law. This response first classified the type of legal pluralism emerging in the Kenya colony. The colonial administration exhibited both forms of legal pluralism.

Kadhis' courts, the *Wakf* Commission, and the native courts were granted appropriate powers, and the necessary degree of autonomy for their operation was respected. On one hand, the colonial administration acknowledged the parallel operation of Islamic law and African customary law alongside state law, conceding that the colonial administration did not have exclusive hegemony over law. On the other hand, the colonial administration secured monopoly over the social normative structures by subordinating the non-state law to the state, effectively integrating them part of state law. I contend that this approach transformed weak legal pluralism into a reductive legal pluralism that sought state backing for legal effect, ultimately becoming part of state law pluralism. In effect, this

---

[87] J Lewin, 'The Recognition of Native Law and Custom in British Africa', (1938) 20 *J. Comp. Legis & Int'l L.* 16.

[88] Islamic endowment.

[89] Griffiths (n 82) 3.

returned the legal system to legal centralism. This approach was later adopted by the independent Kenyan state.

Legal centralism emerged as the dominant theory during the 19th and 20th centuries Kenya, a time when the country was under colonial occupation. The concept did not accept the recognition of non-state law or social normative orders unless they were made subordinate to the colonial state law. This is because both the colonial state and the subsequent independent state were seen as the sole sources of the law. However, this position has been challenged. As previously discussed, the acceptance of Islamic law as part of Kenyan law resulted from the historical development of the state, revealing instances of pluralism in which state law is one element. Despite this, it is necessary to distinguish between pluralism in which state law is one element (not applicable to Kenya), and pluralism within state law (relevant to Kenya).

Building on Vanderlinden's suggestion that pluralism within state law can always be reconciled into a self-consistent scheme,[90] once can deduce that Vanderlinden conceptualises legal pluralism as a legal method. In line with Vanderlinden's position and Swenson's five strategies for understanding state and non-state law interaction, legal pluralism can be characterised as a method to bridge, harmonise, incorporate, subordinate, or repress the existence of different laws to a higher authority – the Constitution. This approach, taken by the British colonial administrators in Kenya and later continued by the country during and after independence, resonates well with Vanderlinden and Swenson's positions. In Kenya, there is now a definitive legal system that constructs a hierarchy for legal norms, with all such norms required to be consistent with a higher overarching norm, such as article 2(4) of the Constitution, which demands the unconditional acceptance of the Constitution's supremacy over all other norms.

Consequently, any law inconsistent with the Constitution is void to the extent of the inconsistency, and any act or omission in contravention of the Constitution is invalid. Similarly, the conditions of Islamic law for the use

---

90 Vanderlinden (n 83) 149-157.

of *zakat* can only be accepted by the Kenyan state if they are consistent with article 2(4). However, article 2(4) would require reference to the *Qur'an*, which effectively contravenes article 8. While social normative orders are recognised, they are only binding at state level when recognised as legal by the state (reductive legal pluralism). The practice of *zakat* by Kenyan Muslims is not given any legal effect by the state. How then can *zakat* be used at state level when it sits between two competing constitutional claims (articles 2(4) and 8)? How can this dilemma to be resolved? Legal pluralism offers no answer, and Hart's legal positivism further complicates this dilemma.

This section demonstrates that Hart's hegemonic influence persists, despite the presence of legal pluralism. All law in Kenya should either be state law or state-sponsored law. Nevertheless, other forms and systems of regulatory regimes, over which the Kenyan state neither exercises complete control nor has the ability to eradicate, continue to exist within the Kenyan legal system.[91] I argue that these forms and systems are inextricably woven into the fabric of the modern post-colonial Kenyan state. Consequently, it can then be argued that the juristic definition of a legal system in Kenya appears to be under-inclusive, a reality minimised by the Hartian legal positivist perspective. Does Tamanaha provide a solution to legal positivism's failure to adequately capture the complexity of contemporary legal systems? This question is addressed in the following section.

Socio-legal positivism: Accommodating Islamic law?

Article 2(4) of the Kenyan Constitution underscores that in Kenya, law is determined by reference to its sources.[92] This Hartian perspective is arguably confirmed by the article's consistency rule, which also presents a unified yardstick of legal validity. As such, it appears that legal positivism is firmly entrenched in Kenya's legal discourse, considering that it is 'hard to find a contemporary legal scholar who seriously questions the centrality

---

[91] Jackson (n 83) 157-176.

[92] Article 2(5) The general rules of international law shall form part of the law of Kenya. Article 2(6) Any treaty or convention ratified by Kenya shall form part of the law of Kenya under this Constitution.

of social sources in determining legal validity'.[93] The primary question regarding whether Islamic law can be applied in the use of *zakat* by the Kenyan state depends on whether it belongs to Kenya's normative system. Earlier, I argued that article 2(4) demands consistency of all law with the Constitution: 'Any *law*, including customary law, that is inconsistent with this Constitution is void to the extent of the inconsistency, and any act or omission in contravention of this Constitution is invalid'. The reference is made to the word *law*, not *norms*. This suggests that the Constitution places social norms (customary practice, religion) as part of its legal system, enabling the state to recognise as *law* the normative ordering that co-exists within its socio-political space, based on its consistency rule.

However, characterising Kenya's legal system as grounded in legal positivism renders it incapable of addressing the cross references within the Constitution that recognise Muslim personal law, referenced in scripture, as part of its legal system. The Kenyan state would have to consult the *Qur'an* when deciding how to use *zakat,* treating the *Qur'an* as authoritative and part of its normative and legal system. This implies crossing the well-established divide between state and religion. The unresolved problem is determining who at the state level would interpret the *Qur'an* to deduce its law on *zakat*.

This question falls within the realm of how two legal systems interact. In the context of clarifying the relationship between state law and Islamic law, the consistency rule under article 2(4) appears vague, uncertain, and indicative of an internal tension when read alongside articles 8 and 170(5). Islamic law, as a form of law under article 2(4), is characterised by cross references (articles 8, 170(5)), and is subject to two types of hierarchies: the consistency rule and an inverted hierarchy. This latter form is evident in how article 24(4) treats Muslim personal law. Under article 27, the Constitution guarantees every person the right to equality, but article 24(4) suspends this right concerning the application of Muslim personal law. This places Muslim personal law above the law of equality in Kenya.

---

93 Crowe (n 83) 321.

This analysis reveals the interaction between two separate legal systems: one constitutional and the other of divine origin. Thus, legal positivism's monist claim is proven incorrect in this context. Consequently, there arises a need to consider Kenya's legal system from a sociological perspective. A sociological approach may offer a means to understand and explain how the Kenyan legal system recognises Islamic law as part of the Islamic legal system and permits its enforcement. A question that arises is whether these two legal systems can be reconciled? Does the Kenyan legal system regard Islamic law on *zakat* as binding or having legal effect? Under article 2(4), only those laws that are consistent with the Constitution are recognised. Other than this, there is no other indication in the Constitution on where these laws are to be found. Are their external sources to be consulted? Can such external sources, not explicitly mentioned in the Constitution, be considered part of the law of the state or its legal system? This constitutional ambivalence necessitates understanding of Kenya's legal theory to establish clear boundaries of what constitutes law in the country. A systematic approach is required to determine the relationship between Islamic law and Kenyan law.

If the Islamic law on *zakat* is to be legally recognised by the Kenyan state, a multidisciplinary approach to the interpretation of article 2(4) must be pursued. Such an approach should be neither insular nor inward looking, but rather should seek to employ doctrinal methods as part of a broader attempt to understand its concept of law, alongside an array of methods compatible with a sociological approach. Article 2(4) should, therefore, be subject to a flexible interpretative power. The former Chief Justice of Kenya, Willy Mutunga, has deliberated on this point, arguing that the Constitution provides an interpretative space that permits us 'to even go beyond the minds of the framers whose product, and appreciation of the history and circumstances of the people of Kenya, may have been constrained by the politics of the moment'.[94] Mutunga opposes the Constitution's legal-centric letter and text interpretation, asserting that its content is not solely

[94] W Mutunga, 'Developing Progressive African Jurisprudence: Reflections from Kenya's 2010 Transformative Constitution'. Lameck Goma Annual Lecture, July 27, 2017., 31.

reflective of legal phenomena. Instead, its content serves to facilitate the social, economic and political growth of Kenya, as long as its interpretation is coherent, certain, harmonious, predictable, uniform and stable.[95]

Mutunga's reflections indicate that doctrine-based work alone is insufficient to understand law in Kenya. For him, it is crucial to comprehend legal interpretation as transformative.[96] Consequently, interpreting the Constitution should also result in transformative law making. However, his thinking falls short of considering the relationship between the Constitution and Islamic law, in further exploring the understanding of law in Kenya and clarifying the tension between article 2(4), which potentially accepts the application of Islamic law by the state, and article 8 that rejects such claim.

Tamanaha[97] has developed a transformative approach to understanding law, and his thesis helps to clarify the problem between articles 2(4) and 8, addressing whether Islamic law can be applied by the Kenyan state as part of its law and legal system. As conceptualised by Tamanaha, socio-legal positivism, introduces cross-disciplinary work into law, breaking down the self-contained discipline of law and encouraging its engagement with sociology. The intersection between these two disciplines facilitates the introduction and application of Islamic law under article 2(4) and also helps reconsider the separation of law and religion under article 8. Socio-legal positivism, akin to Hart's Concept of Law, acknowledges that there is more than one way to conceptualise law. Unlike Hart, it posits that the source of law is not exclusively institutional. The theory accepts that law is both an institutionalised normative system and a non-institutionalised form of normative order. Hart only recognises the former concept of law, as it gives privileges the state as the source of law. The Kenyan Constitution, as

---

95 ibid, 33.
96 Of inducing large scale social change grounded in law, ibid, 3.
97 (n 1) 1-32.

previously discussed, manifests this view under article 2(1)[98], but article 2(4) opens it up for the challenge.

The Constitution asserts its authority over law making, and its legal system claims supremacy over all other institutionalised normative systems in the country while maintaining and supporting various forms of normative orderings. Likewise, Islamic law possesses these three features, but it does not exert such authority within the nation except through express authorisation by the state (article 170(5)). In applying the Islamic law on *zakat* as part of article 2(4) of the Constitution, the initial consideration will identifying the legal official who possesses the capacity to interpret and apply the Islamic law concerning the use and governance of *zakat.* Arguably, this could be the *kadhi,* but such responsibility does not appear under article 170(5). *Zakat* is not part of Muslim personal law. However, it is part of what is construed under article 2(4) as 'any law…'. Yet, since it is part of religious law, applying it as part of state law would contravene article 8.

Socio-legal positivism that, suggests that for a contravention under article 8 to occur, Hart's rule of recognition, expressed under article 2(4), necessitates a co-ultimate social convention regarding *whose* actions have the status of law. If the state refrains from interpreting the Islamic law on *zakat* but merely utilises the *zakat* to finance health initiatives as advised by a Muslim scholar authorised to interpret Islamic law, then no contravention of article 8 occurs. The state is merely implementing the conditions of the donated funds, analogous to the conditions accepted by a state in return of international aid. Tamanaha posits that socio-legal positivism places social sources at the heart of legal positivism. According to him, social actors 'can be engaged in producing and reproducing a legal system through secondary rules, regardless of their efficacy in generating widespread conformity to the primary rules'.[99] Article 2(4) recognises that law in Kenya is the product of complex social practices. The practice of *zakat* can give rise

---

[98] The 'Constitution is the supreme law of the Republic and binds all persons and all State organs at both levels of government'.

[99] (n 1) 15.

to law under article 2(4), and through its practice, we can identify the existence and content of Islamic law.

Nevertheless, the Islamic law on *zakat* must comply with the consistency rule under article 2(4). Undoubtedly, Islamic law will regulate and limit the Kenyan state's power in utilising *zakat*. *Zakat* is only available for the beneficiaries outlined under Chapter 4 and cannot be availed for procuring abortions, except to protect the mother's health; providing contraception to unmarried persons; sex change operations; or other medical practices deemed as inappropriate under Islamic law. These conditions are not unreasonable when compared with the greater aim of mobilising funds to provide poor Kenyans with medical care and essential medicines. With careful consideration, the Islamic law on *zakat* can operate under article 2(4).

Getting to constitutional permissibility in applying the Islamic law on zakat using civic reasoning

The argument for integrating Islamic law on *zakat* into article 2(4) can be substantiated by An-Naim's civic reasoning framework, which may plausibly enable the Kenyan legal system to undertake functions associated with Islamic law.[100] An-Naim contends that a secular state can adopt Islamic law, provided that the reasoning process adheres to a civic standard.[101] The incorporation of Islamic law on *zakat* into state decision-making must be grounded in civic deliberation, deliberately eschewing arguments framed in religious truth assertions. This poses a challenge, as Islamic law analysis typically employs a doctrinal approach for Muslims, while certain non-Muslim Kenyan factions have exhibited an exaggerated response to Islam, particularly regarding the inclusion of *Kadhis'* courts in the Constitution,[102] the wearing of headscarves[103] and the performance of

---

[100] (n 2) 1-29, 2.

[101] A An-Na'im, *Islam and the Secular State. Negotiating the future of Shari'a.* (Cambridge, Massachusetts, and London: Harvard University Press 2008), 138-9; (n 2), 1-29, 2.

[102] Mwangi (n 6) 41-52; Cussac (n 5) 289-302.

[103] *Methodist Church in Kenya v Mohamed Fugicha & 3 Others* (2019) eKLR. Available at: http://kenyalaw.org/caselaw/cases/view/165289/

congregational prayers at schools.[104] Absolute religious truth assertions exclusive nature is often invoked when providing rationales based on Islamic law, and as Malik astutely observes, this can potentially intimidate adversaries and stifle debate.[105] Consequently, An Naim endorses civic reason, rather than explicit religious language, as a foundation for determining how to alleviate tensions between law and religion.

Examining article 8 through a civic reasoning perspective suggests that this approach facilitates dialogue on how Islamic law on *zakat* can be integrated into the Kenyan legal system, exemplifying the transformative interpretation championed by Mutunga. Civic reasoning aims to foster unity by emphasising that dialogue, mutual understanding and collaboration are essential in diverse societies where religious law is a component of the social structure. An-Na'im posits that individuals share universal human values and principles, despite differences in knowledge, tradition, practices, and beliefs. Civic reasoning encompasses reasons and rationale accessible to most citizens, irrespective of their background. The right to health serves as a common foundation for initiating discussions on appropriate claims regarding *zakat* usage for healthcare and resolving conflicting claims. Civic reasoning necessitates the development of a shared language to facilitate the translation of diverse knowledge, beliefs, values, and interests into acceptable and pragmatic forms of collaboration. By employing civic reasoning, individuals with distinct cultural or religious values and social practices strive to reach agreements for peaceful coexistence, while preserving their differences.[106]

Civic reasoning safeguards the process of upholding the normative expectations of Muslims who contribute *zakat* to the state for healthcare purposes. The civic reasoning process allows for the identification expectations that will receive social approval, ensuring that articles 2(4) and

---

[104] Maureen Kakah, Kenya: Parents Sue Over Ban on Islamic Prayers at School. *allAfrica*, 11 March 2019. Available at: https://allafrica.com/stories/201903110212.html

[105] A Malik, *Polycentricity, Islam, and Development: Potentials and Challenges in Pakistan* (USA: Lexington Books 2018.), Ch 3, 122.

[106] An-Na'im (n 101).

8 are not violated if the state accepts *zakat* and implements Islamic law governing its usage. The application of civic reasoning can be regarded as a component of the societal response to law, which can be generated and perpetuated through meaningful reasoning processes.

Civic reasoning can be directly linked to the determination of legality or illegality through the rule of consistency. As the Constitution confers all sovereign authority to the people, they hold the power to dictate the extent to which their legal system can engage with religious law. Employing civic reasoning as a means to derive such rationale or interpretation, Kenyan citizens can delineate the limits of their legal system and establish the demarcations. In this way, article 8 can be addressed to tackle the challenge of incorporating Islamic law on *zakat* into the Kenyan state's practices, reconstructing the historical connection between law and Islamic law in Kenya by integrating *zakat* alongside Muslim personal law as a component of the Kenyan legal system. Civic reasoning offers a mechanism through which legal pluralism can be acknowledged while simultaneously distinguishing between law and religious norms. This approach creates an opportunity for the Kenyan legal system and Islamic law to recognise health financing as a shared belief.

Conclusion

This chapter has demonstrated that the Constitution offers the Kenyan state acceptable rules that can permit the inclusion of Islamic law on *zakat* to function as part of its legal system. The Kenyan legal system produces its own legal norms, by which it can lend Islamic law normative quality – through which it would be possible to constitutionally permit the state to accept *zakat* with its Islamic conditions. The chapter has shown that since the creation of hierarchies among norms in the Constitution of Kenya modifies the separation between state and religion, it then follows that the state can legally apply Islamic law if it so chooses.

While the doctrinal analysis and legal theory thus far have provided a solid framework for understanding the permissibility of using *zakat* to finance health, the reality on the ground may not always match up to these ideals.

Accordingly, the next chapter discusses its findings from fieldwork which uncover the issues surrounding the reluctance of local stakeholders to endorse the use of *zakat* as a source of revenue. The real-world application of *zakat* is complex and requires an understanding of the social, cultural, and political context in which it is being implemented. Fieldwork allowed for the collection of rich and nuanced data that could not be obtained through doctrinal analysis alone, thereby revealing the realities of implementing *zakat* in the Kenyan context.

Thus far, the book has offered a deep understanding of how the implementation of Islamic law intersects with the politics of healthcare financing in Kenya. By undertaking phenomenological accounts from local stakeholders, including Muslim leaders and faith-based organisations, Chapters 6 and 7 unveil the mistrust of the state and the insularity of Muslim groups that hinder the implementation of *zakat* for healthcare financing. This original contribution sheds light on how the practice of Islamic law is embedded in the socio-political realities of Kenya, which is often neglected in the doctrinal and legal analysis.

PART III

PHENOMENOLOGICAL ACCOUNTS

Men make their own history, but they do not make it
just as they please; they do not make it under self-selected
circumstances, but under circumstances existing already,
given and transmitted from the past.
–Karl Marx[1]

[1] K Marx, and D De Leon, *The Eighteenth Brumaire of Louis Bonaparte* (New York: International Pub. Co, 1898) Chapter 1, 1.

Overview

Chapters 3, 4 and 5 have systematically explored the potential for *zakat* to finance health in Kenya, drawing upon normative, doctrinal, and theoretical perspectives from both human rights and Islamic law. The following two chapters seek to complement these discussions with empirical evidence, providing insights into the interpretations and implementation of *zakat* financing norms and doctrine by local actors within the Kenyan socio-political context. The chapters also demonstrate the process by which these norms and doctrine acquire meaning in the Kenyan socio-political setting. The main question asked is whether Kenyan Muslims and non-Muslim actors consider it feasible to use *zakat* to finance health. Will Kenyan Muslims accept to remit their *zakat* to the Kenyan state?

Answers to this question reveal the representative feelings of the actors about giving *zakat* to a non-Islamic constitutional state with a Muslim minority committed to separating the state from religion. It will also suggest reforms that could potentially result in giving legal recognition under human rights law, Islamic law, and the Kenyan legal system to permit the use of *zakat* to finance health. Moreso, the interviews with local actors assisted with the understanding of Islamic law from a Kenyan perspective.

The research for the two chapters was conducted in Mombasa and Nairobi, by face to face and online interviews with government and Muslim clerics, on what it is possible to learn from them of the legal doctrinal issues surrounding the taking and use of *zakat* by the state, under the current Kenyan constitutional framework and Islamic scholarship. Focus group discussions were also held alongside the use of *halaqa* (a method of debating doctrinal issues among Muslims to arrive at a normative consensus). The *halaqa* as a data collection method is used here to analyse clearly how Muslims understand and interpret the possibility of making *zakat* available to the Kenyan state to finance health.

Relying on data based out of the dialogic *halaqa* supported this research to exclusively include and hear from Muslim women who are experts on Islamic law and government officers. There is a discrepancy in terms of gender when it comes to Islamic scholars in Kenya – it is heavily male dominated.[1] Hence, the need to design a research methodology using a gender perspective. The *halaqa* method, therefore, supported an understanding of doctrinal discussions from a women-only perspective. A comparison of *halaqa* with 'western' methods is discussed later. The book is also written from a Muslim woman's perspective, and therefore contributes towards the voice and position of a woman within the dominant male perspectives on Islamic law (discussed under Chater 6).

The chapters that follow set up the fieldwork findings. Chapter 6 starts by first providing a background on the historical linkages between Islam and the modern Kenyan state; it highlights the common themes that constitute Islamic scholarship in Kenya, to reveal the dearth of literature on *zakat* capable of supporting an understanding of how to relate the body of Islamic scholarship on *zakat* to finance healthcare under human rights law. Such historical discussion provides an insight into the social context within which the fieldwork was carried out, so that careful analysis can be made when considering *zakat* as a source of revenue for the Kenyan government with which to finance health. It also discusses the political tensions between the Muslims and the state, in order to ask whether these tensions influenced the Muslim view on giving *zakat* to the state.

Chapter 7 presents phenomenological accounts on the possibility of giving *zakat* to the Kenyan government to finance health. Such an inquiry has not been previously made by scholars. I was unable to find any literature on this issue on library databases. Nor has this inquiry been, in the words of an interviewee *'conceived by Kenyan Muslims'*.[2] Will Kenyan Muslims allow this? It is worth then speaking to these Muslims, their scholars, and the

---

[1] H Ndzovu, 'Broadcasting Female Muslim Preaching in Kenya: Negotiating Religious Authority and the Ambiguous Role of the Voice', (2019) *The African Journal of Gender and Religion*, vol 25, no 2, 14-40.

[2] Interviewee No. 132. Interview date 13.02.2020 Nairobi.

Muslim leaders in Government, on their views of norms informing *zakat*, on the feasibility of using *zakat* to finance public health in Kenya and of their willingness to accept this idea. The *ulema* (Muslim scholars) in Kenya have been greatly influenced by external literature on *zakat*. This is not to say that Muslim scholars in Kenya do not provide *fatwas* based on their *ijtihad* (deductive reasoning).[3] They apply the *Qur'an* and *sunna* to determine who qualifies as a beneficiary of *zakat* and the purposes towards which *zakat* can be utilised.[4] However, answers to questions (other than the *Qur'anic* prescription of who the *zakat* beneficiaries should be) are discussed through established precedents by traditional schools of thought, and reference to external scholarship.[5]

The problem with this approach is that, as a result, Islamic scholarship advanced by Kenyan Muslims is at a nascent stage, and is male dominated. This means that women's perspectives on *zakat* have been neglected. I found no written sources on *zakat* by Muslim women at the Jaamia Mosque library in Nairobi which houses Islamic literature. I did find limited literature on library databases by Muslim women documenting the use of *zakat* to reduce poverty levels among Muslims in Muslim countries and on the contemporary uses of *zakat*.[6] Their literature was generally focused on empirical work and literature reviews rather than doctrinal or normative inquiries relating to *zakat*.

---

[3] K Kresse, (ed), 'Guidance (Uwongozi) by Sheikh al-Amin Mazrui: Selections from the First Swahili Islamic Newspaper', (2017), *African Sources for African History*, volume 14.

[4] Jamia Mosque, The Friday Bulletin, Issue 796 (2018); see also Issue 888 (2020).

[5] M Mwakimako, *Mosques in Kenya: Muslim Opinions on Religion, Politics and Development* (De Gruyter, 2021).

[6] AM Yuniar, A Natasya, RA Kasri et al, 'Zakat and Digitalisation: A Systematic Literature Review', (2021) paper presented at the 5th International Conference of Zakat Proceedings; ASR As Salafiya, 'A Scientometric Analysis of Zakat Literature Published in times of COVID-19 Pandemic', (2021) *International Journal of Zakat*, Vol 6, No.2, 1-14; NMA Zaaba and R Hassan, 'A Systematic Literature Review on Zakat', (2021) *Journal of Islamic Finance*, Vol 10, No. 2, 101-111; R Rini, 'A Review of the Literature on Zakah between 2003 and 2019', (2020) *International Journal of Economics and Financial Issues* Vol. 10, No. 2. 156-164; H Zainal, 'Reputation, Satisfaction of Zakat Distribution, and Service Quality as Determinant of Stakeholder Trust in Zakat Institutions', (2016) *International Journal of Economics and Financial Issues*, Vol 6, Issue 7, 72-76.

During the *halaqa* with Muslim women participants,[7] it was explained that the problem is not that there are few Muslim women scholars who advice other women on *zakat,* but they have not attempted to publish their perspectives. This is because most *zakat* payers are Muslim men, and they seek advice from male Muslim scholars. The *halaqa* participants explained that a male Muslim scholar is seen as a more authoritative figure than the female Muslim scholar. This view does not reflect the growing literature by Muslim women scholars challenging the traditional and post-classical interpretations of Islamic law.[8] This view is reinforced by referring to male Muslim scholars as *imams* (male Muslim who leads in congregational prayer), *sheikhs* (title to respect given to an elderly scholar) and *alim* (knowledgeable in religious matters), while the female Muslim scholar is referred to as *ustadha* (Muslim female teacher). The difference in these terms indicates that more value will be attached to writings and *fatwas* by a *sheikh* or an *alim,* rather than an *ustadha.* This could potentially be the reason why there is limited Islamic scholarship from Muslim women in Kenya. The next two chapters provide empirical insights offering answers to these gaps in Islamic scholarship on *zakat* and dominant perspectives that influence the Kenyan thinking on the use of *zakat* to finance health.

---

[7] Interviewee nos. 133,134,135,136. Interview date 15.02.2020 Nairobi

[8] F Shahin, 'Islamic Feminism and Hegemonic Discourses on Faith and Gender in Islam', (2020) *International Journal of Islam in Asia,* 1(1), 27-48; M Siddqui, *My Way. A Muslim Woman's Journey* (I.B. Tauris, 2014); AA Hidayatullah, Feminist Edges of the Quran (Oxford University Press, 2014); SS Ali, *Gender and Human Rights in Islam and International Law: Equal Before Allah, Unequal Before Man?* (The Hague: Boston: Kluwer Law International, 2000); M Siddiqui, *How To Read The Quran* (Granta Books, 2007); H Moghissi, *Feminism and Islamic Fundamentalism: The Limits of Postmodern Analysis* (Zed Books, 1999)

Chapter 6

Muslims in Kenya - *Their History, Schools of Jurisprudence and Social Groupings*

Introduction

There are four key concerns with respect to the Muslim society in Kenya: first, their history and interaction with the modern Kenyan state; second, how their schools of jurisprudence influence their understanding and interpretation of Islamic norms and doctrine; thirdly, the social structures within which they identify and make decisions collectively. Finally, consideration must be accorded to the content of Islamic scholarship that Muslim scholars and non-Muslim academics have extensively written on – revealing the lack of literature on normative and doctrinal issues around the use of *zakat* to finance health in a non-Islamic country. These are discussed next.

Muslim History, Religion, Politics and Social Groupings

Understanding the past

Chapter 4 discussed how Islam is rooted in a sense of dependency on the *Qur'an,* and the *sunna* of Prophet Muhammad (صلى الله عليه وسلم), which contributed to its law and dogma. Islam is also rooted in a sense of dependency on its schools of jurisprudence and their *ulama* (Muslim scholars). As a system of law, Islam reached in its definitive, orthodox form along the coast of East Africa in the early 7th century, and much earlier elsewhere.[1] Arab traders from Yemen and Oman settled along the littoral

---

[1] *The Periplus of the Erythrean Sea.* While the author of the book and its exact date of publication is unknown, the following historians have attempted to discuss and present

fringe of the Indian Ocean, that is now part of the territorial sea of modern-day Kenya. Islam in Arabia was *sunni* in nature.[2] In southern Arabia, Islam was characterised by the *Shafi* school of jurisprudence, which was also brought to East Africa with the arrival of the Yemeni and Omani Arabs.[3] By the 9th century, two small groups – from Shiraz in Persia, modern-day Iran, and *Ibadis* from Oman – had also settled along the East African coast.[4] The Shirazi were *shia;* the *Ibadis,* a third sect of Islam. They too brought to East Africa their version of Islam. Being few, they were unable to match the growing Arab *sunni* influence in the region.[5]

Around this time, a few Indian traders (I refer to Indians here but later also include Pakistanis following the partitioning of British India into India and Pakistan) were also residing in East Africa.[6] The Muslim Indians depended on the *Hanafi* school of jurisprudence to guide their practice of Islam. Following this historical association with the two schools of jurisprudence,

---

their analysis of the book and placed its date between 40 and 70 CE: WH Schoff, (ed,) *The Periplus of the Erythraean Sea: Travel and Trade in the Indian Ocean by a Merchant of the First Century,* (New York: Longmans, Green, & Co Hill, 1912); JE Hill, *Through the Jade Gate to Rome: A Study of the Silk Routes during the Later Han Dynasty 1st to 2nd Centuries CE,* (Book Surge Publishing, 2009). GWB Huntingford, (ed,) *The Periplus of the Erythraean Sea, by an unknown author: With Some Extracts from Agatharkhides 'On the Erythraean Sea'* (London: Hakluyt Society, 1980); W Vincent, *The Periplus of the Erythrean Sea, Containing an Account of the Navigation of the Ancients, from the Sea of Suez to the Coast of Zanguebar, Vols. I & II,* (London: A. Strahan Printers Street, 1800), 139-222 and Appendix No IV.

[2] J McHugo, *A Concise History of Sunnis and Shi'is* (Washington DC: Georgetown University Press, 2017); L Louer, *Sunni and Shi'a. A Political History of Discord,* (trans.) E Rundell (Princeton: Princeton University Press, 2017); A Hughes, *Muslim Identities* (New York: Columbia University Press, 2013).

[3] A Lodhi, 'Muslims in Eastern Africa – Their Past and Present', (1994) *Nordic Journal of African Studies* 3(1): 89-98, 89; CH Stigand, *The Land of Zinj: Being an Account of British East Africa, its Ancient History and Present Inhabitants* (London, 1966), 4; LP Harries, *Islam in East Africa* (London: Universities' Mission to Central Africa, 1954), 15.

[4] G Mathews, 'The East African Coast until the Coming of the Portuguese', in R Oliver, and G Mathew (eds) *History of East Africa* Vol. 1, (Oxford, 1963), 94-95.

[5] A Jaffer, 'Conversion to Shi'ism in East Africa', (2013) *Journal of Shi'a Islamic Studies* 6, 131-154.

[6] E Alpers, 'Gujarat and the Trade of East Africa, c.1500-1800' (1967) *International Journal of African Historical Studies,* 9, 22-44; JS Trimingham, *Islam in East Africa* (London, 1954); Mathews (n 13), 94-95;

my fieldwork sought to understand whether adherence to the schools persisted. Historically, these schools applied the use of *qiyas* (deductive analogy), which permitted new interpretations of the Islamic sources to consider legal questions that were not examined under classical or medieval Islam. However, historical Islamic rulings continue to apply precedent, and this sometimes has had the effect of restricting new interpretations on *zakat*.[7]

Since the arrival of the Arabs along the Kenyan coastline, they have generally practiced and preached *sunni* Islam; the Arabs built the first mosques in East Africa. The Great Mosque of Kilwa in Zanzibar, an archipelago off the Tanzanian coast, and Shanga Mosque in Kenya's Pate Island have been identified as the first mosques built in East Africa by the Arabs in the 12th century.[8] The Arab presence, however, remained confined to the coastal region of Kenya (see Figure 2 and Figure 3 below).

---

[7] W Hallaq, *Sharī'a: Theory, Practice, Transformations* (Cambridge, UK: Cambridge University Press, 2009); W Hallaq, 'Was the Gate of Ijtihad Closed?' (1984) *Int. J. Middle East Stud.* 116; 3-41.

[8] P Bahn, *Great Sites of the Ancient World* (Frances Lincoln, 2020), 227; HM Conn, 'Islam in East Africa: An Overview', (1978) *Islamic Studies,* Vol17, No 2, 75-91, 84; P Garlake, *The Early Islamic Architecture of the East African Coast* (British Institute of History and Archaeology in East Africa, 1966) 77-83.

Figure 2: *The entire geography of the East Africa Protectorate (later referred to as the Kenya Colony) of the British Empire*

Source: Duignan, O and Gann LH, Colonialism in Africa 1870-1960: Volume 5 A Bibliographical Guide to Colonialism in Sub Saharan Africa (Cambridge University Press, 1973), 1054.

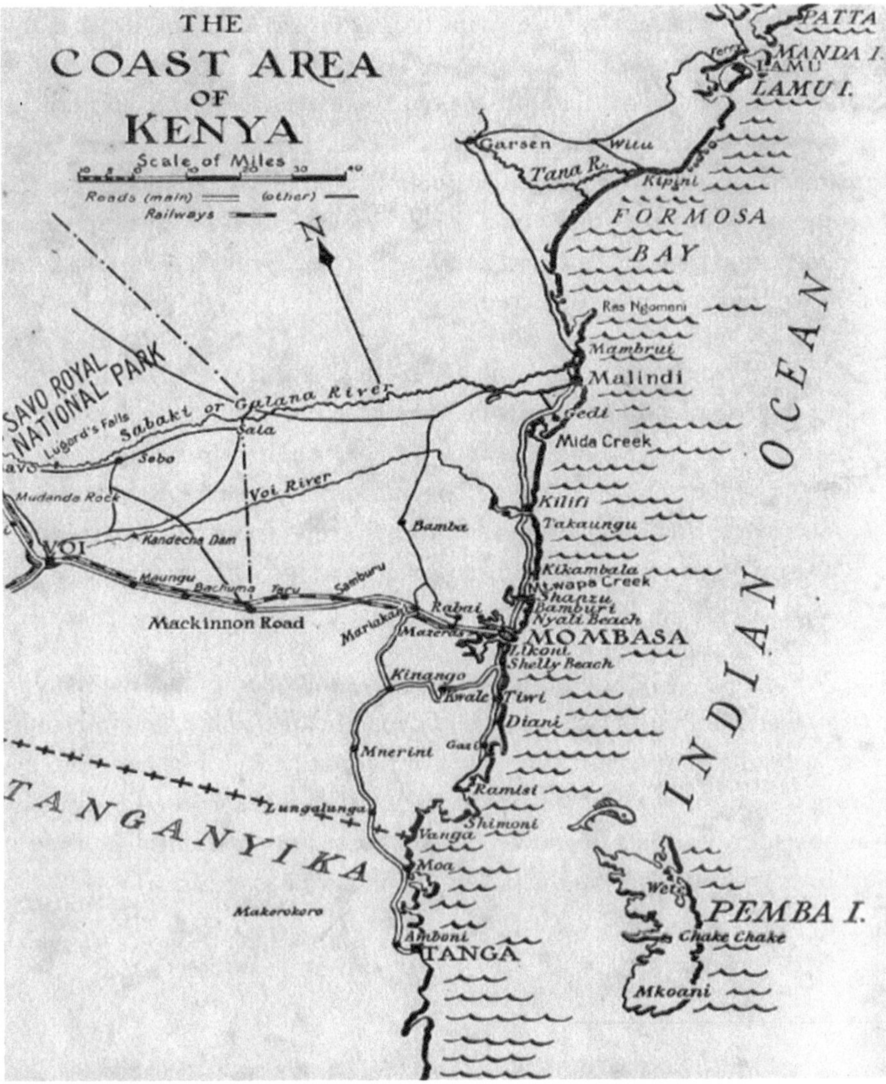

Figure 3: *The Kenyan coastline along which the Muslims (Arabs and Indians) settled*

Source: Strandes, J, *The Portuguese Period in East Africa*, tr. Jean F Wallwork; Edited with Topographical Notes by JS Kirkman (East African Literature Bureau, Nairobi, 1961).

The settlement of the Arabs and few Indians along Kenya's coast preceded Portuguese colonisation. Before the arrival of the Portuguese in the early

15th century, neither the Arabs nor the coastal Indian Muslims[9] created any formal political institutions. An expert interviewee discussing Muslim history remarked that 'the Muslims remained as insular communities whose only objective was to trade'.[10] Their trade routes were later threatened by the arrival and occupation of the coastal region by the Portuguese. Between 1505 and 1698, the Portuguese set up their administration base in Mombasa and Malindi and controlled the coast and its trading route.[11] The expert continued:

> In 1660 the powerful local Arab clans – the Mazrui and Busaidi who lost their trade and economic hegemony to the Portuguese and the native tribes – the Ribe, Chonyi, Kamba, Kauma and Digo then known as the people of Azania, the name given to the East African coast, were frustrated by the Portuguese rule asked the Sultan of Oman who controlled Zanzibar (an archipelago off the Tanzanian coast) to confront the Portuguese.[12]

The Portuguese – who politically and economically dominated the Kenyan coast – were defeated by the Sultan of Oman in 1698 and driven out from their stronghold in Mombasa. However, sporadic fighting between the Portuguese and the Sultan's army continued until 1828, when the Sultan was able to consolidate his powers in Mombasa after taking full control of Fort Jesus (see Figure 4, on the position of the fort in Mombasa).[13]

---

[9] These were distinct from the Indians who arrived as labourers with the British colonialists in late 18th century to construct the railway and pursue economic opportunities. See P Nowrojee, *A Kenyan Journey* (Manqa Books 2019); Lodhi, (n 12), and Mathews, (n 13).

[10] Interviewee No. 132. Interview date 13.02.2020 Nairobi

[11] FJ Berg, 'The Coast from the Portuguese Invasion to the Rise of the Zanzibar Sultanate', in BA Ogot, (ed.) *Zamani: A Survey of East African History* (Nairobi: East African Publishing House 1974), 115-133.

[12] Interviewee No. 132. Interview date 13.02.2020 Nairobi

[13] For a comprehensive study of the history and influence of the Portuguese on the East Africa coast see N Chittick, 'The Coast before the Arrival of the Portuguese', in Ogot (n 20) and FJ Berg, 'The Coast from the Portuguese Invasion to the Rise of the Zanzibar Sultanate', in Ogot (n 20) 115-133.

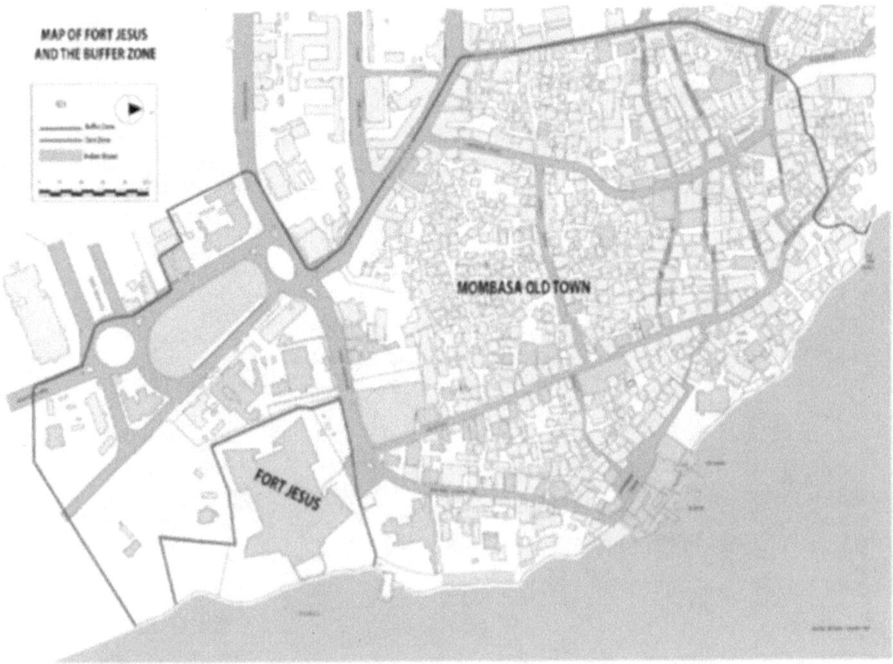

Figure 4: *Fort Jesus in Mombasa*

Source: Kenya Government.

It was not until 1828, when the Sultan of Oman (Said bin Sultan) established his direct rule along the East African coast, that the Arab Muslims organised themselves politically, and began to dominate Kwale, Mombasa, Kilifi, Malindi, and Lamu (see Figure 5 below). These areas are now counties, following the promulgation of the 2010 Constitution of Kenya.

Figure 5: *Modern-day Map of Kenya*

Source: Counties of Kenya, Kenya Institute of Surveying and Mapping, Department of Cartography (2021).

Between 1828 and 1840, the Sultan of Oman appointed *liwalis* (administrators) to rule these coastal areas on his behalf. Muslim politics was influenced externally, and local Arab Muslims implemented the

Omani laws, based on Islamic law. However, the application of Islamic law was limited to contract, family, and succession laws. The application of such Muslim personal law continues to be recognised in the Constitution of Kenya and is enforced by the Kenyan state through the local courts (explained in Chapter 5.)

In 1840, the Sultan moved his court from Oman to Zanzibar, which marked the beginning of Arab Muslim political organisation and domination that was not dependent on Oman.[14] The Sultan's authority extended along the coastal strip of the East African Coast, that stretched from Zanzibar via Mombasa to Mogadishu, in present-day Somalia. Most of the Omanis settled in Zanzibar, while others took up residence along the littoral fringe of the Kenyan coast.[15] The Sultan of Oman exerted his authority along his territories and applied Islamic law. When he died in 1856, his dominions were divided between his two sons.[16] This dual succession marked the permanent separation of Zanzibar from Oman in 1861, following an 'Arrangement for the Settlement of Differences between the Sultan of Oman and the Sultan of Zanzibar, and the Independence of their respective States'.[17]

With Zanzibar becoming autonomous, the Sultan of Zanzibar (Majid bin Said) extended his authority between 1861 and 1895, in all his East African

---

[14] A Lodhi, 'The Arabs in Zanzibar: From Sultanate to People's Republic', (1986) *Journal Institute of Muslim Minority Affairs*, Vol VII, No 2, 404-418; RL Pouwels, *Islam and Islamic Leadership in the Coastal Communities of Eastern Africa, 1700 to 1914* (London: University Microfilms International, 1979); NR Bennett, *A History of the Arab State of Zanzibar* (London, 1978); E Batson, *A Social Survey of Zanzibar*, 1948 (Zanzibar Government Printer, 1962); J Middleton and J Campbell, *Zanzibar: Its Society and Its Politics* (London, 1965); Oliver and Mathews, (n 15).

[15] Harries, (n 8), 15; GS Were, and DA Wilson, *East Africa Through a Thousand Years to the Present Day* (Nairobi, 1968).

[16] N Kaylani, 'Politics and Religion in 'Uman: A Historical Overview', (1979) *International Journal of Middle East Studies*, Vol. 10, No. 4 (Nov), 567-579.

[17] Reports of International Arbitral Awards, Arrangement for the Settlement of Differences between the Sultan of Oman and the Sultan of Zanzibar, and the Independence of their respective States', 2 April 1862, Volume XXVIII, 107-114, http://legal.un.org/riaa/cases/vol_XXVIII/107-114.pdf; NR Bennett, *A History of the Arab State of Zanzibar* (London, 1978); Kaylani, (n 22).

territories – and over their Muslim residents – by appointing a *mudhir* (governor) to govern trade along the coast, and a *kadhi* (judge) to resolve disputes among Muslims and officiate over their marriage ceremonies. During this time, Arabs residing along the Kenyan coast were governed by the socio-economic and political structures and institutions established under the Sultanate.[18]

Salim explains that the Arab Muslims, who were vested with political and economic power, began ordering the coastal society.[19] They built more mosques and *madaris* (plural of *madrassa,* schools for learning religious knowledge) as their society grew, and more migrants came from Yemen and Oman. Having the privilege of power and literacy, the Arabs structured the coastal society based on a social hierarchy, placing themselves at the apex. Through their *madaris*, their missionary activities, and *Kadhis,* they claimed religious superiority and promoted the *Shafi* school of jurisprudence.[20] According to Hashim, they also referred their disputes to the *kadhi,* received executive directives from the *mudhir,* and set up an informal *bait ul maal* (treasury) through which rich Arabs would aid the poor, or dedicate charitable endowments.

While Hashim argues that their political authority, administration, and philanthropy was directed only towards the Muslims,[21] Yahya confirmed that Muslims would also provide charity to the natives during their missionary activities.[22] However, in their literature on the history of

---

[18] Pouwels, (n 23).

[19] Al Salim, 'Native or Non-Native: The Problem of Identity and on Social Stratification of the Arab-Swahili of Kenya', in BA Ogot, (ed.) *Hadith* (Nairobi: East African Publishing House, 1970).

[20] ibid, 78-82.

[21] H Abdulkadir, 'Administration of Waqf Institutions in the Kenyan Coast: Problems and Prospects', (2010) *AWQAF*, no 18, 57-66; SS Yahya, 'The Uses and Abuses of Waqf', in M Bakari and SS Yahya, (eds) *Islam in Kenya: Proceedings of the National Seminar on Contemporary Islam in Kenya* (MEWA Publications, 1995) 214-223.

[22] SS Yahya, 'Compassion and Development: Addressing Social Infrastructure and Poverty Issues in East African Cities Through Waqf Endowments,' (2007) Paper Presented to the International Waqf Conference, Cape Town, South Africa. 17th-19th August.

Muslims in Kenya, neither Hashim nor Yahya discuss whether *zakat* featured as part of these philanthropic activities. Neither does Kenyan Muslim scholarship mention nor discuss the role of *zakat* during this period.

The *bait ul maal* concept reflected the Arabs' perception of a social welfare system, through which efforts were made to raise the real income level of poor Muslims, to ensure that, through charity, a minimum level of living was maintained.[23] Hence, in the society that emerged prior to British colonial rule in 1895, the Arabs placed themselves at the apex of social hierarchy, through their philanthropic nature, political organisation, recognition of the Sultan's authority and economic power. They later used their power to negotiate terms with the British colonial administration in 1895.

At the 1884/85 Berlin Conference, the Western Powers partitioned Africa. The East African region was divided, with the Germans – taking control of Tanzania – and the British – ruling Kenya (then known as the East Africa Protectorate) and Uganda. Both colonial Governments recognised the authority of the Sultan and negotiated treaties with him. Britain wanted the administration of the Kenyan coastline that started at Mombasa and terminated along the southern Somali border. Under the 1895 treaty,[24] administration along this coastline included all the area within ten miles of the Indian Ocean shore.[25] The only conditions imposed by the Sultan was to allow the application of Islamic law among Muslims, and to preserve their freedom of religion.

As a result of the treaty, the coastal province brought under British administration remained a protectorate until independence. The British did not interfere with the Muslim institutions, save for writing legislation and

---

23 Bennett (n 23), Batson (n 23); Middleton, and Campbell J, (n 23); Oliver and Mathews, (n 15); Were and Wilson (n 24); Trimingham (n 15).

24 The text of the 1895 treaty is in *The Kenya Coastal Strip: Report of the Commissioner, Cmnd. 1585* (London: HMSO, 1961).

25 An 1886 Anglo-German agreement delineated the Sultan's sovereignty from the coastline to ten miles into the interior.

ordinances recognising the limited civil jurisdiction of the *Kadhis*. The 1895 treaty enabled the British Government to take over administration and protection of the ten-mile strip from the Imperial British East Africa Company (IBEAC), to whom the Sultan had leased this territory in 1888.[26] The political and legal interactions between the Muslims and the British are also discussed in Chapter 5.

With the colonisation of East Africa by the British, more Indians of various religions came to Kenya and settled in the hinterland.[27] The *sunni* Indian Muslims formed their own Islamic community characterised by the *Hanafi* school and their *'pirs'* (spiritual guides).[28] A historian told me that 'the Indians kept separate from the Arabs'.[29] The Indian Muslims were largely labourers, who had come with the British to construct the railway. They lived together in shared quarters, had a common culture, and spoke Gujrati, Hindi, and Punjabi. They also had class divisions among themselves.[30] Very few understood Arabic, save for reciting the *Qur'an* and chanting supplications in Arabic. They also constructed their own *masjids*, selected their own spiritual guides, and set up a religious sanctuary of their revered spiritual guide at McKinnon Road between Nairobi and Mombasa.[31] Their sanctuary was criticised by the Arab Muslims as being of a heretical nature.[32] Other Indian Muslims were merchants trading in spices, clothing, and household items.[33] They remain concentrated in

---

[26] (n 33).

[27] Were and Wilson (n 24); MHY Kaniki, 'The Colonial Economy: the Former British Zones', in Boahen A. (ed) *General History of Africa: Africa under Colonial Domination 1880-1935* (France: UNESCO Publishing, 1985), 404.

[28] Interviewee No. 131. Interview date 13.02.2020 Nairobi

[29] Interviewee No. 146. Interview date 22.02.2020 Mombasa See also M Adam, 'Panorama of Socio-Religious Communities' in *Indian Africa: Minorities of Indian-Pakistani Origin in Eastern Africa* (Nairobi: Africae, 2015) 24

[30] A Bharati, 'Ideology and Content of Caste among the Indians in East Africa', in Barton Schwartz (ed) *Caste in Overseas Indian Communities* (San Francisco: Chandler, 1967).

[31] A Bharati, *The Asians in East Africa, Jayhind and Uhuru* (Chicago: Nelson Hall, 1972).

[32] H Amiji, 'Some Notes on Religious Dissent in Nineteenth Century East Africa', (1971) *African Historical Studies*, 4, 603-616.

[33] J Ainsworth, 'The Commercial Possibilities of Kenya Colony', (1921) *Journal of the Manchester Geographical Society*, 37, 51-60.

Nairobi and Kisumu, while the Arabs occupied the coastal region. This reinforces my supposition that Muslim communities have historically been insular, based on their race, class, or ethnicity. Whether such racial or class division and selective adherence to a school of jurisprudence played a role in how Kenyan Muslims made decisions around *zakat* became an important question to investigate during fieldwork.

Moving to the present

As a result of this history, two predominant versions of *sunni* Islam took root in Kenya. The *Shafi* school, represented by the Arabs, and the *Hanafi* school, followed by the Indians. The native non-Muslim population, that later reverted to Islam through Arab missionary activities also adhered to the *Shafi* school.[34] The *shia* in Kenya are a minority. While they are also divided into different sects, the *Ismailis* (*Khojas and Bohras*) are predominant.[35] This study focuses only on *sunni* Muslims. While this history is reflective of the Muslims and their schools of jurisprudence today, there have been new developments. The Muslim community makes up 11 per cent of the Kenyan population.[36] A majority of this 11 per cent are *sunni* Muslims subscribing to the *Shafi* school of jurisprudence.[37] However, there are also Muslims who practice Islam guided by the *Maliki* and *Hanbali* schools. Others do not strictly adhere to one school; they accept any school that provides them with a liberal and flexible interpretation of Islam.[38] Some Muslims also practice Islam based on *Sufism*. Others are of the

---

34 Interviewee No. 146. Interview date 22.02.2020 Mombasa

35 AM Sheikh, 'Kenya Shiite Community: A Socio-Historical Perspective' (2014) *IOSR Journal of Humanities and Social Sciences*, Volume 19, Issue 5.

36 The current Kenyan population is approximately 53,771,296, of which 5,914,843 are Muslims. Kenya National Bureau of Statistics, *2019 Kenya Population and Housing Census Volume IV: Distribution of Population by Socio-Economic Characteristics* (Nairobi: Government Printers, 2020) 12 available at: https://www.knbs.or.ke/?wpdmpro=2019-kenya-population-and-housing-census-volume-iv-distribution-of-population-by-socio-economic-characteristics

37 Interviewee No. 131 (13.02.2020, Nairobi), confirmed by interviewee no. 132 (13.02.2020, Nairobi), and interviewee no. 146 (22.02.2020, Mombasa).

38 Interviewee No. 131. Interview date 13.02.2020

Naqshbandi, Salafi or *Tablighi Jamaat* Islamic movements.[39] These sects, while *sunni* in nature and *Shafi* in character, differ in ritual practices.

Sunni Islam has been given a preferential treatment by the Government of Kenya through the establishment of the *Kadhis'* courts, presided over by *Kadhis* who are *sunni* Muslims, enforcing the *Shafi* school – unless the litigating parties ask for the application of another school of Islamic thought.[40] Furthermore, most of the mosques in Kenya are also characterised by the *Shafi* school.[41] Having grown since the arrival of the Arabs, the Muslim community in Kenya are largely *sunni,* but also represent diversity in understanding and interpreting Islam and Islamic law.[42] They foster a spirit of religious pluralism among themselves, and remain divided along their racial and ethnic lines. The Indian/Pakistani Muslims (comprising *Memons, Badalas, Gujrati, Cutchi* and *Punjabi* Muslims of south Asian origins) have formed insular communities. They each have their own social halls at which they hold events, carry out philanthropic activities, and base their *imams,* and they go to specific mosques.[43] For example, in Nairobi, they often go to Imtiaz Masjid in the city centre,

---

[39] The Naqshbandi sect developed in the 16th century as part of Sufism. It claims legitimacy as a school of thought, by tracing its doctrine to the laws and rules established by the first caliph Abu Bakr. Wahhabism is an Islamic movement that seeks to purify Islam of any innovations and practices that deviate from the 7th century teachings of the Prophet and his companions. Because the usage of the term carries negative and derogatory connotations, follows of Wahhabism, refer to themselves as Salafis – those who follow the Prophet and his companions, and shun innovation in religious practices. The Tablighi Jamaat is a missionary movement focused on proselytisation.

[40] E Stilles, *Experience of Muslims in East Africa: Handbook of Contemporary Islam and Muslim Lives* (Springer, 2020); also confirmed by Interviewee, 131, male PB.

[41] Interviewee Nos. 108, 109, 110, 111. Interview date 09.01.2020 Mombasa. Interviewee No. 112. Interview date 13.01.2020Nairobi. Interviewee Nos. 113, 114. Interview date 14.01.2020 Nairobi. Interviewee No. 115. Interview date 17.01.2020 Nairobi..

[42] Lodhi, (n 12); Nordic Journal of African Studies 3(1):88-98; B Funderburk, *Between the Lines of Hegemony and Subordination: The Mombasa Kadhi's Court in Contemporary Kenya* (SIT Kenya, 2010).

[43] A Michel, (ed) *Indian Africa: Minorities of Indian-Pakistani Origin in Eastern Africa* (Nairobi: Africae, 2015); C Salvadori, SM Fisher, B Mauladad et al, *Settling in a Strange Land: Stories of Punjabi Muslim pioneers in Kenya* (Nairobi: Park Road Mosque Trust, 2010); I also make these claims based on observation and my experience living in Nairobi and Mombasa.

Pangani Masjid and the Park Road Mosque.[44] These mosques, therefore, were part of the study sample. They strictly adhere to the *Hanafi* school and their ethnic customs. The Arabs, Somalis (native to the northern part of Kenya which they considered to be part of Somalia before Kenya's borders were demarcated by British colonial rule), Swahilis (Afro-Arabs), and African revertees[45] to Islam usually hold mixed social gatherings, pray at the same mosques, debate legal rulings to arrive at a consensus, and consider themselves the orthodox community.[46]

Having introduced Islam to what became Kenya, the Arabs positioned themselves as the only authorities on Islam with the privilege and status to preach Islamic law, explain the Islamic legal practice, and announce Islamic events. All *imams* and *madrassa* teachers in Kenya have been trained in Saudi Arabia, or by a local teacher who was himself trained in Arabia.[47] Even the Indian/Pakistani *imams* and *madrassa* teachers have been trained through an Arab medium. The Arab hegemony is now challenged by the Somali community, who are increasing in number and political strength.[48] The Arabs and Swahilis continue to dominate the coast, while the Indians/Pakistanis and Somalis represent the Muslim majority in Nairobi.

An interviewee observed that 'Muslims during the general elections also back Muslim candidates based on their race, ethnicity, and geographical

---

[44] ibid.

[45] Islamic law states that everyone is born as a Muslim – that is, one who submits to God and God's law. It is then the parents of the child who convert the child to follow another belief. Thus, when a non-Muslim chooses to accept Islam, it is considered as reverting back to the original faith. Hence the term revertee (reverted) and not convertee (converted).

[46] Interviewee No. 146 (22.01.2020 Mombasa), confirmed by Interviewee No. 131 (13.02.2020 Nairobi).

[47] A Mazrui, 'Religion and Political Culture in Africa,' (1985) *Journal of the American Academy of Religion*, Vol 53, No 4, 817-839, at 830.

[48] N Carrier, and H Elliot, 'Entrust We Must: The Role of Trust in Somali Economic Life', (2018) DIIS Working Paper 2; E Lochery, 'Rendering Difference Visible: The Kenyan State and its Somali Citizens', (2012) *African Affairs*, Volume III, Issue 445, 615-639; also discussed during interview with Interviewee No. 146 (22.01.2020 Mombasa).

location'.[49] The coast is politically represented by Arabs and Swahilis, while Muslim political representation in Nairobi is centred around Somalis.[50] Each Muslim group strives for its own political recognition to secure their social and economic interests. Does such Muslim diversity impact their decisions on *zakat*? The answer to this question is discussed in detail later, when analysing the data. The next subsection addresses the relationship between the Muslims and the state, to explain certain political tensions between the two that could influence Muslim thinking on offering *zakat* to the state. The Kenyan scholarship on *zakat* is then addressed.

Political Tensions with the Kenyan State

Following the increasing demands for independence from British colonial rule, the Muslims at the coast politically organised themselves as Mwambao[51] United Front (MUF) in 1962 to ensure that in gaining independence the 10-mile coastal strip which was granted to the British by the Sultan of Oman to administer under the 1895 treaty would not be annexed to mainland Kenya.[52] These coastal Arab and Swahili Muslims had hoped that the coast would either be recognised as the territory of Oman or Zanzibar. Among their fears was that the independence and successive Christian majority governments would reject Islamic law in governing the personal affairs of the Muslims and would undermine their political significance. They also feared that their properties would not be protected by the state. The problem with leaving out the 10-mile coastal strip from mainland Kenya was that there had been an increase in migration from the hinterland towards the coast and the native residents of the coast objected

[49] Interviewee No. 146 (13.02.2020 Mombasa). This is also confirmed in Ndzovu, H, 'Muslim Relations in the Politics of Nationalism and Secession in Kenya' (2019) *Northwestern University PAS Working Papers*, No 18.

[50] T Scharrer, 'Ambiguous Citizens: Kenyan Somalis and the Question of Belonging', (2018) *Journal of East African Studies*, Volume 12, Issue 3. Also discussed during interview with Interviewee 146, male AL.

[51] Mwambao is a Swahili word meaning the coast, coastal area or coastline.

[52] JR Brennan, 'Lowering the Sultan's Flag: Sovereignty and Decolonization in Coastal Kenya', (2008) *Comparative Studies in Society and History*, 50(4): 831–861.

to the Arab and Swahili position on the 10-mile coastal strip. Later, Swahili Muslims also supported the integration of the coast with mainland Kenya.[53]

The founding president: Jomo Kenyatta, in a bid to unite with the objecting Arab Muslims promised them that, after independence, the Government would legally recognise Islamic law and ensure that Muslim personal law continues to regulate Islamic marriages, divorces, child custody and inheritance.[54] On 5th October 1963, in a letter signed by Kenyatta to the Prime Minister of Zanzibar, the former guaranteed the following safeguards for the Sultan's subjects in the coastal strip: the free exercise and preservation of Islamic worship, the retention of *Kadhis'* jurisdiction over Muslim personal status matters, the appointment of Muslim administrators in predominantly Muslim areas, Arabic instruction for Muslim children, and the protection and continued registration of freehold land.[55]

Somali Muslims also proposed that the Northern Frontier Districts (the region lying north of Kenya and bordering Somalia)[56] should not be integrated as part of independent Kenya. This is because most of the population living within the NFD were Somalis and they preferred to be integrated as part of Greater Somalia.[57] To subdue these secession claims, the Independence Government proposed a Constitution that recognised regional autonomy; a type of decentralised governance structure which allowed regions with political power to make local decisions and raise local

---

53 HJ Ndzovu, *Muslims in Kenyan Politics: Political Involvement, Marginalisation, and Minority Status* (Northwestern University Press, 2014).

54 ibid, 49.

55 See T Wolf, 'Contemporary Politics', in Jan Hoorweg et al. (eds), *Kenya Coast Handbook* (Hamburg: Lit Verlag, 2000), 129–55; and L Misol, *Playing with Fire: Weapons Proliferation, Political Violence, and Human Rights in Kenya* (New York: Human Rights Watch, 2002). Two of the five safeguards—provisions for Muslim Administrative Officers and Arabic education—have largely not been met since independence; the remaining three largely have.

56 The NFD comprised of: Isiolo, Garissa, Mandera, Marsabit, Moyale and Wajir.

57 H Whittaker, *Insurgency and Counterinsurgency in Kenya: A Social History of the Shifta Conflict, c. 1963-1968* (Brill, 2015) 24-49.

revenue with which to finance local development needs.[58] Problems with the NFD peaked after independence resulting in multiple insurgencies between 1963 and 1967. This period was referred to as the Shifta War.[59] As a result, Government oppression of Somali Muslims began and the NFD was economically marginalised.

After independence, there were major changes in the political structure of Kenya. Governance was centralised and multiparty politics was banned in favour of only one political party: the ruling Kenya African National Union (KANU). Several political assassinations took place.[60] Kenya became an autocratic state.[61] The Muslims felt politically marginalised, discriminated, and oppressed within a multiracial state reflecting African dominance. There was a tense relationship between Indians and Africans based on racial difference. The racial consciousness among the Africans resulted out of the presumed Indian control of the economy as most of the small shopkeepers throughout the country, importers of textiles and household items were Indians.[62] This fuelled a claim by the Africans that 'Kenya was a land of and for Africans'.[63] The refusal by President Jomo Kenyatta to allow Indians to retain dual citizenship, both in India and Kenya, reinforced this African claim and forced almost a third of the Indians to migrate to Britain in 1970. Those Indians who remained formed their social

---

[58] D Anderson, 'Yours in Struggle for Majimbo: Nationalism and the Party Politics of Decolonisation in Kneya, 1955-64,' (2005) *Journal of Contemporary History*, Vol 40, No. 3, 547-564; JB Ojwang, *Constitutional Development in Kenya: Institutional Adaptation and Social Change* (Acts Press, African Centre for Technology Studies, 1990).

[59] J Makokha, 'The Islamic Factor in Somali Irredentism: Towards Rationalising the Kenya Government's Stand Against Islamic Political Association', in Mohamed Bakari and Saad S Yahya (ed) *Islam in Kenya* (Nairobi: Signal Press Ltd, 1995).

[60] A Angelo, *Power and the Presidency in Kenya: The Jomo Kenyatta Years* (Cambridge University Press, 2020) 179-200.

[61] J Widner, *The Rise of a Party-State in Kenya: From Harambee! to Nyayo!* (University of California Press, 1992).

[62] S Aiyar, *Indians in Kenya: The Politics of Diaspora* (Cambridge Mass., Harvard University Press, 2015) 261.

[63] ibid 129.

and economic groups through which they lobbied Government and donated funds in return for economic security.[64]

At the coast, the Muslims and the Christians complained of multiple grievances: 'poor education access, the domination of Up-country people in public sector jobs, the grabbing of huge chunks of Coastal land by Kenyatta and others.'[65] They complained of Government neglect of the coastal region and diversion of tourism revenue towards the capital in Nairobi. In 1980, the Government attempted to abolish the *Kadhis'* courts. Against this, the Muslims united to remind the government of the 1895 treaty and pre-independence commitments made by Jomo Kenyatta. In 1991, when multiparty politics was reinstated, the coastal Muslims formed the Islamic Party of Kenya (IPK) to unite politically and demand equal political representation and economic opportunities from the Government. The Government refused to register IPK, citing that the Constitution proscribed religiously affiliated political parties.[66] This move by the Government upset the Muslims and incited secessionist feelings on the Kenyan coast. This history explains the political tensions between Muslims and the state.

The tension between the two has been further aggravated by violence inflicted by the state on Muslims. In 1984, during Daniel Arap Moi's presidency, the Kenyan army carried out a counter insurgency operation in Wajir, a district within the NFD, targeting the Degodia clan (Somali Muslims) whom they accused of being hostile to the interests of the state. The army deployed 'older colonial tactics of villagisation and collective punishment as a means of undermining the support of local communities for the insurgents'.[67] The Kenyan army has been accused of massacre, rape,

---

[64] D Himbara, *Kenyan Capitalists, the State and Development* (East African Educational Publishers, 1994) 65.

[65] J Willis, and G Gona, 'Pwani C Kenya? Memory, Documents and Secessionist Politics in Coastal Kenya', (2013) *African Affairs*, 112 (446), 62.

[66] A Moroff, 'Party Bans in Africa – an Empirical Overview', (2010) *Democratization*, 17:4, 618-641, 630.

[67] D Anderson, 'Remembering Wagalla: state violence in northern Kenya, 1962-1991' (2014) Journal of Eastern African Studies, Vol 8, Issue 4, 658-676, 659.

burning homes and looting property during the operation.[68] Muslims have also been accused of terrorist related attacks and bombings in Kenya. In 1998, the US embassy in Nairobi was bombed. In 2002, an attack was launched at the Paradise hotel in Mombasa. In 2013, Westgate shopping mall in Nairobi was bombed. In 2015, Garissa University was stormed by gunmen leading to the killing of 148 students. In 2019, there was a terrorist attack on DusitD2 a hotel in Nairobi. All these terrorist attacks and bombings were associated with Al Qaeda, and Al Shabab militants.

This led the Government to pass the Prevention of Terrorism Act[69] which the Muslims opposed. They argued that the Act specifically targeted Muslims, and was therefore, discriminatory and violated their human rights. The Act authorised police to raid *masjids, madrassas* and to detain suspected Muslims for days without charging them before courts or releasing them on police bail. The Act elicited a lot of Muslim hostility against the Government. The Government was criticised for deliberately discriminating against Muslims, exacerbating marginalisation and creating a tense relationship forcing Muslims to choose between rebellion or loyalty to the state.[70]

It was the Arab, Swahili and Somali Muslims who felt specifically targeted. As a result, the coastal Muslims began to take secession of the coast seriously, with the emergence of the Mombasa Republic Council (MRC) in 2010, under the political slogan *'Pwani Si Kenya'* (the Coast is not part of Kenya).[71] The Government declared MRC as illegal, citing it an extremist Islamic organisation with ties to external terrorist groups. This led to the assassination of two MRC leaders and waves of arrests of MRC members since 2010. The Muslims perceive the state as a threat to their civil and political rights; the tension around the *Kadhis'* courts also continues to date. This was amplified during the discussion on drafting a new Constitution

---

[68] SA Sheik, Blood on the Runway (Northern Publishing House, 2007).

[69] Government of Kenya, 'Prevention of Terrorism Act, No. 3 of 2012' (Nairobi: National Council of Law Reporting, 2012).

[70] MUHURI, *''We are Tired of taking You to the Court': Human Rights Abuses by Kenya's Anti-Terrorism Police Unit'* (Open Society Foundations, 2013).

[71] (n 74) 48-71.

for Kenya between 2004 and 2009. A court case was filed by a group of Christians, arguing that it is discriminatory to include the establishment of the *Kadhis'* courts in the Constitution and that the state violated the Constitution when it funded the *Kadhis'* courts as part of its judiciary. Christians argued that the establishment of *Kadhis'* courts went against the separation of the state from religion (discussed in Chapter 5). The Muslims continuously have to defend their political, social and religious interests in Kenya, suggesting a tense relationship with the state. It remains to be seen whether their political, social and religious tensions with the state will influence their decision and views on giving *zakat* to the state. This is discussed in Chapter 7. I return to focus on whether scholarship on Islam in Kenya has addressed questions around *zakat*.

Scholarship on *Zakat* in Kenya

There is sparse scholarship specifically focused on *zakat* in Kenya. Male-dominated Muslim scholarship on Islam in Kenya, led by Mazrui,[72] Yahya,[73] Bakari,[74] Lonsdale,[75] Matthews,[76] Kahumbi,[77] Glassman,[78]

---

[72] Mazrui (n 56).

[73] S Yahya, 'Financing social infrastructure and addressing poverty through waqf endowments: experience from Kenya and Tanzania', (1994) *International Institute for Environment and Development* (IIED), Vol 20(2): 427-444; Yahya, 'The Uses and Abuses of (n 30); Yahya, Compassion and Development (n 31).

[74] M Bakari, 'A Place at the Table: The Political Integration of Kenyan Muslims, 1992-2003' (2004) Paper presented at the International Conference, St. Anthony's College, Oxford, 14.

[75] J Lonsdale, and B Berman, 'Coping with the Contradictions: The Development of the Coastal State in Kenya, 1895-1914', (1979) *The Journal of African History*, Vol. 20, No.4, White Presence and Power in Africa, p 487-505.

[76] N Matthews, 'Imagining Arab Communities: Colonialism, Islamic Reform, and Arab Identity in Mombasa, Kenya, 1897-1933', (2013) *Islamic Africa*, Vol. 4, No. 2.

[77] M Kahumbi, 'Continuity and Change in the Legal Regulations of Waqf in Kenya: Oortunities and Challenges' (2008) Available from: http://saadabadi.persiangig.com/Arshive/Kahumbi_Maina.doc/download?490f.

[78] J Glassman, *Feasts and Riots: Revelry, Rebellion, and Popular Consciousness on the Swahili Coast, 1856 – 1888* (Heinemann: James Currey Ltd, 1995) 150.

Brennan,[79] Kindy,[80] Ndzovu[81] and Hashim,[82] is divided into two phases. The first phase – reflected in the writings of Mazrui, Glassman, Brennan, Lonsdale, and Kindy – is centred on an understanding of Islam under British colonial rule and discussing the Islamic response to the changing socio-economic reality. The second phase – reflected in the literature by Ndzovu, Hashim, Bakari, and Yahya – examines preserving Islam under the Kenyan state, ensuring political representation of Muslims, securing the establishment of the *Kadhis'* court in the Constitution, and protecting the application of Muslim personal law (detailed discussion in Chapter 5).

Each of these phases focused on explaining the position of Islamic law amid political, social, and economic changes, brought about by the political order of the day.[83] Mazrui, writing during and after the colonial period, briefly mentions *zakat* – but only as a type of Islamic tax in the context of discussing Islam generally.[84] Waris also refers to *zakat* as a source of tax that was available to the Sultan of Zanzibar, but she does not provide a reference that can be traced for further insight. [85] Latif proposes *zakat* as a potential source of revenue for the Kenyan state,[86] but does not contextualise her discussion on *zakat* based on its history and scholarship from a Kenyan perspective. Thus, scholarship on *zakat* in Kenya is scant. The history of *zakat* and its development should, therefore, be understood in the context of the history of Islam in Kenya discussed earlier. However, what is missing

---

[79] Brennan, (n 61).

[80] H Kindy, *Life and Politics of Mombasa* (Nairobi: East Africa Publishing House, 1972) 27.

[81] Ndzovu, *Muslims in Kenyan Politics* (n 59); H Ndzovu, 'The Politicisation of Muslim Organisations and the Future of Islamic – Oriented Politics in Kenya', (2012) *Islamic Africa*, Vol. 3, No. 1.

[82] Hashim, (n 30), 57-66.

[83] Ndzovu, *Muslims in Kenyan Politics* (n 62), see Chapter 2, on post-colonial Kenyan attitudes towards religion and the predicament of Muslims.

[84] Mazrui, (n 56).

[85] A Waris, 'Taxation without Principles: A Historical Analysis of the Kenyan Taxation System', (2007) *Kenya Law Review*, Vol 1: 272, 280.

[86] LA Latif, 'Framing the Argument to Broaden Kenya's Limited Fiscal Space for Health Financing by Introducing *Zakat*', (2018) *Biomedical Journal of Scientific and Technical Research* 5 (5); LA Latif, 'An Explication on Broadening the Definition and Scope of Maximum Available Resources Under General Comment 14 of the ICESCR to Include Islamic Taxation in Financing the Right to Health' (2017) *Biomed J Sci & Tech Res* 1 (3).

from the studied historical accounts are references to *zakat* on the Kenyan coast. I was unable to find any historical information related to *zakat* within the Nairobi archives.

Scholarship on *zakat* in Kenya has therefore, received little interest. Consequently, I am unable to explain how our Kenyan Muslim predecessors understood and applied the norms on *zakat*, the purpose towards which *zakat* was spent, or to whom it was given. If *zakat* from the Kenyan coast was available to the Sultan of Zanzibar, as assumed by Waris,[87] then surely its administration would have been preserved as a precondition to the 1895 treaty between the British colonial government with the Sultan of Zanzibar, allowing the latter to administer 'His Highness's possessions on the mainland of Africa and the adjacent islands, exclusive of Zanzibar and Pemba'?[88] Faced with the challenge of limited scholarship and official records on *zakat* at the Kenyan coast, I hoped that documents at the Zanzibar National Archives recording official information during the sultanate period might provide some guidance on the subject. However, I was unable to travel to Zanzibar, due to the COVID-19 lockdown restrictions. The full impact of COVID-19 on my research is explained in Chapter 7.

I then turned my attention toward a historical analysis of the Sultanate of Oman (previously administered the Kenyan coast and Arab Muslims living along the coast), and whether it could provide some indication as to whether the sultanate recorded any information on *zakat*. If the Sultan of Oman recorded information on *zakat* in Muscat, then his administration in Zanzibar should similarly keep such records. The interviewee from the University of Nairobi, whose doctorate[89] studied the legal and political system of Oman and pre-independent Zanzibar helped me arrive at the

---

[87] Waris, (n 94).

[88] *Report of the Kenya Coastal Strip Conference, 1962.* Presented to the Parliament by the Secretary of the State for the Colonies by command of Her Majesty, April 1962, (London: Her Majesty's Stationery Office, 1962), 5.

[89] H Abdulkadir, 'Reforming and Retreating: British Policies on Transforming the Administration of Islamic Law and its Institutions in the Busa'idi Sultanate 1890-1963' (PhD, University of Western Cape, 2010).

following conclusions.[90] Between the periods 1828 and 1856, when Zanzibar was brought under the control of the Sultan of Oman, there is no document referencing *zakat* in Zanzibar. However, there is information on *zakat* in Omani literature. The scholar pointed out that 'Al-Salimi's writings have documented that the Sultan collected *zakat* in Oman.'[91] I was able to find references to Al Salimi's work[92] in Ahmed Hamoud Maamiry's *Omani Sultans in Zanzibar, 1832-1964,*[93] and in Calvin Allen's *Oman: The Modernisation of the Sultanate,*[94] from which I was able to piece together the following accounts.

The Sultan appointed *zakat* clerks, who were permanent employees of the Omani state, receiving a fixed share from the *zakat* they collected. These clerks were picked out from villages, of which they had a thorough knowledge of both inhabitants and their properties. The Sultan also had special *zakat* clerks, who collected the *zakat* after it had been levied from the rich, and then deposited it in the *bait ul maal* (public treasury). Other than these accounts on *zakat,* no further phenomenological accounts are given. I asked the scholar whether Al-Salimi discussed *zakat* beyond Oman, and as part of the Sultan's dominions. The scholar responded, 'he does not indicate whether *zakat* was also collected from those territories'.[95]

Between 1856 and 1861, the Sultans of Oman and Zanzibar were embroiled in a succession dispute; during this period there is no record indicative of *zakat* from Zanzibar. From 1862 to 1895, detailed information is available on the administration and governance practices in Zanzibar, but none on *zakat.* After 1895, the administration of the Kenyan coast shifted to the British, who ruled the coast as a protectorate until independence in 1963. The British records and literature on its Kenya colony neither indicate nor note any reference on *zakat.* In the absence of empirical accounts on *zakat,*

---

[90] Interviewee No. 132. Interview date 13.02.2020 Nairobi.

[91] Interviewee No. 132. Interview date 13.02.2020 Nairobi.

[92] Nur al Din Abd Allah bun Humayd Al Salimi, *Tuhfat al-Ayan bi-sirat ahl Uman,* 2 volumes (Cairo: Matba'at al sufliyya, 1928).

[93] A Maamiry, *Omani Sultans in Zanzibar, 1832-1964* (Lancer Book, 1988).

[94] CH Allen, *Oman: The Modernisation of the Sultanate* (Routledge, 1987).

[95] Interviewee No. 132. Interview date 13.02.2020 Nairobi .

and qualitative data explaining how Muslims spent their *zakat*, the history of *zakat* in Kenya can only be described through either the *Shafi* or *Hanafi* madhabs. It is entirely normative, and doctrine based.

Conclusion

Ethnographic accounts of Kenyan Muslim perspectives on their understanding of *zakat* norms and doctrine exist but no one has looked at them. There is also a need for understanding the local views on including *zakat* as part of *maximum available resources* under human rights law on financing health, and its constitutional permissibility. Further research, to generate more knowledge on the understanding of how Islamic norms on *zakat* are understood, interpreted and given meaning by Kenyan Muslims and non-Muslims – in answering the question on whether *zakat* can be given to, and accepted by, the Kenyan Government to finance health – will contribute to relating dynamic interpretive approaches to norm construction and doctrinal analysis. The next chapter produces this original data on *zakat* in Kenya.

Chapter 7
Phenomenological accounts from fieldwork in Mombasa and Nairobi

Introduction

Chapters 4 and 5 argued that Kenya's Constitution and its Islamic law can allow the state to use *zakat* to finance healthcare. This argument, as seen from Chapter 6, cannot be made through a normative or doctrinal inquiry alone. Initially, the argument was investigated through the human rights obligation of *maximum available resources*, and the three principles of Islamic jurisprudence: *ijtihad*, *ijma* and *shura*. Its investigation was based on its context, interpretation, and subjectivity, framed around the positivist tradition, and historicity of interpretation of Islamic law from a *sunni* perspective. These approaches produced a comprehensive understanding on the use of *zakat* to finance health. These approaches were largely doctrinal. The doctrinal method of legal research has been confirmed by Hutchinson and Duncan as the 'core legal research method',[1] and by Posner as the 'core of legal scholarship'.[2]

Despite this, the doctrinal method has been the subject of sustained criticism.[3] Since doctrinal analysis works on the premise that law can only be understood from a close, objective reading of authoritative texts, this approach is characterised as insular, and limited to its own self-referential

---

[1] T Hutchinson, and N Duncan, 'Defining and Describing What We Do: Doctrinal Legal Research' (2012) 17 *Deakin Law Review*, 83, 98-101.

[2] R Posner, 'The Present Situation in Legal Scholarship' (1982) *Yale Law Journal*, 1113.

[3] T Hutchinson, 'Doctrinal Research: Researching the Jury' in D Watkins and M Burton (eds), *Research Methods in Law* (Abingdon: Routledge, 2013), 15-17; R Banakar, 'Review Essay: 'Having One's Cake and Eating It: The Paradox of Contextualisation in Socio-Legal Research' (2011) *International Journal of Law in Context*, 487-489; S Egan, 'The Doctrinal Approach in International Human Rights Law Scholarship' in L McConnell and R Smith, *Research Methods in Human Rights* (Routledge, 2018) 28-30.

nature.[4] 'The legal system itself', according to Westerman, 'is not only the subject of inquiry, but its categories and concepts form the framework and conceptual tools for the research'.[5] This chapter recognises that a narrow epistemological perspective can be inadequate and unconvincing, as it has the potential to shut out external views and empirical methods of investigation to understand how law and rules operate in wider society. Chapter 5 exposed this deficiency, in relying on doctrinal analysis to explain the legal status of Islam in Kenya's Constitution. Generalisations about using *zakat* to finance health in Kenya pervade the doctrinal method, when it comes to considering how the Muslim actors understand and implement the law on *zakat*, and whether they would spend their *zakat* to finance health. While the doctrinal method alone is a sufficient test of validity of Islamic law, the book argues that it does not draw attention to the socially constructed approaches of *zakat* by Muslim actors.

The doctrinal method alone cannot suffice to confirm the findings so far made. Instead, the book considers it as an initial step towards the use of experiential methodologies to enrich the analysis of doctrine and norms. Consequently, other legal methods are needed, to add robustness to the findings. This chapter recognises that a collection of qualitative data – through interviews, focus groups and through quantitative analysis of questionnaires – should be used to cross-check and add depth to qualitative findings. Schwarz,[6] Bradney,[7] McCrudden,[8] and Smits[9] encourage the use of such extra-legal methods in advancing human rights scholarship, recognising their reciprocal value in unpacking the meaning, function, and

---

[4] P Westerman, 'Open or Autonomous: The Debate on Legal Methodology as a Reflection of the Debate on Law' in M Van Hoecke (ed), *Methodologies of Legal Research* (Oxford: Hart, 2013) 86.

[5] ibid, 86.

[6] R Schwarz, 'Internal and External Method in the Study of Law' (1992) 11 *Law and Philosophy*, 179, 194.

[7] A Bradney, 'Law as a Parasitic Discipline' (1998) 25 *Journal of Law and Society*, 71-84.

[8] C McCrudden, 'Legal Research and the Social Sciences' (2006) 33 *Law Quarterly Review* 635.

[9] J Smits, 'Redefining Normative Legal Science: Towards an Argumentative Discipline' in F Coomans, F Gruenfeld and MT Kamminga, *Methods of Human Rights Research* (Cambridge: Intersentia, 2009) 46.

operation of law. Since this book also addresses Islamic scholarship, its legal methods also form part of the research design. This provides the chapter with an opportunity to develop the mixed methods research design, by drawing from the interaction of Western and Islamic research methods in gathering empirical data. The normative account cannot be completed without empirical research into the interpretations, perceptions and attitudes of key actors in Kenya, especially members of relevant Muslim communities.

The Methodology

Islamic researchers have argued that, when researching questions based on Islamic law, the selection of methods requires a balance of several factors.[10] The research question is the starting point. If the question has been previously addressed, its previous ruling will be applied. This is the doctrine of *taqlid* (following precedent). If the question has not been previously addressed, then, given the question, a decision on research strategy follows. Some questions indicate the methods required to answer the question; other questions may be answered by different methods. The first port of call is always the reference to the primary sources of Islamic law: the *Qur'an* and the *sunna.* Reference can be made to an authentically documented explanation, given by a companion of the Prophet (صلى الله عليه وسلم) on the question, or to a school of Islamic thought for a deeper understanding on how to address the question. Different insights can also be obtained from consulting several scholars, who would give their opinion based on their interpretation of the primary sources and historical precedent. Seeking a *fatwa* (ruling) or *nasiha* (advice) would be the appropriate strategy in such instances.

---

[10] AK Langha, 'Understanding Research Methodology for Islamic Studies' (2009) *Al Qalam* 1-27; MS Alias and MS Hanapi, 'Ibn al Haytham's Philosophy on Scientific Research Applied in Islamic Research Methodology: Analysis from Tasawwur, Epistemology and Ontology Perspectives' (2015) *International Journal of Business, Humanities and Technology*, Vol 5, No 1, 83-93.

If the primary sources do not expressly address an issue, reference is made to medieval scholarship, to ascertain whether any authentically documented accounts have been provided of a similar issue and how it was addressed.[11] If no such accounts are available, the use of *ijtihad*, *ijma* or *shura* is then utilised. These discussions have been extensively engaged upon in Chapter 4. However, where the intention of the researcher is to understand the impact on the ground on real people, that may be better understood with the collection of qualitative data, through interviews and *halaqas*.[12] *Halaqa* – as observed in the overview to Part III of the book – is a religious meeting between Muslims for the study and understanding of Islam, and to debate questions from an Islamic perspective.[13] It is a religious gathering, because it begins and ends with praising Allah, followed by *dua* (supplications) and asking Allah to bless Prophet Muhammed (صلى الله عليه وسلم), his family and companions.[14] A religious scholar, teacher or a knowledgeable Muslim must be present at the *halaqa* to guide the discussion, provide reliable reference sources on information being addressed, and to correct errors.[15]

Halaqa needs to be distinguished from socio-legal methods, such as focus group discussions (FGD), precisely because of its religious nature and sense of community. As a result, it is focused on reinforcing existing norms and developing a collective sense of religious identity. While *halaqa* may draw comparisons with FGD, the distinction lies in *halaqa's* requirement that all discussions conform to the *Qur'an* and *sunna* and that the *halaqa* follow a specific procedure. The group sits in a circle on the floor, and usually a religious scholar, teacher or a more knowledgeable Muslim will guide the

---

11 W Hallaq, *A History of Islamic Legal Theories* (Cambridge: Cambridge University Press, 1997) 59.

12 RJ McCarthy (trans.) *Deliverance from Error: An Annotated Translation of al Munkidh min al dalal and Other Related Works of al Ghazali* (Louisville, Kentucky: Fons Vitae, 2004).

13 W Hallaq, *Shari'a. Theory, Practice, Transformations* (Cambridge: Cambridge University Press, 2009) 136.

14 K El FAdl, *The Search for Beauty in Islam. A Conference of the Books* (London: Rowman & Littlefield Publishers, 2005) 257.

15 C Mallat, *The Renewal of Islamic Law* (Cambridge: Cambridge University Press, 1993) 42.

meeting.[16] A 'more knowledgeable Muslim' is anyone who has memorised more verses of the *Qur'an* than the others, knows *hadith*, understands the Arabic language, is more prominent than the others in religious circles, or has been nominated by the others based on their good opinion of the nominee.[17] *Halaqas* are gender segregated. Ahmed has advanced the view that the *halaqa* method is most conducive in conducting research with Muslim participants, because it allows participants to express their views within their own epistemological and ontological context.[18]

According to Islamic scholars, there are specific qualities required and conditions to be met by the persons considered for interview, when addressing an Islamic legal question.[19] Such conditions are not a strict requirement for the use of socio-legal methods. The first condition is knowledge of classical Arabic, which enables the interviewee to understand the *Qur'an* and *sunna* correctly and particularly the verses and *hadith* that contain rulings.[20] Other scholars are of the view that knowledge of the Arabic language is not a mandatory condition when interviewing persons who are not scholars and can refer to translations of the Arabic sources for explanations.[21] Progress has been made in authenticating *hadith,* and there is now easier access to translated reference works, that can be obtained through the aid of the internet. The second condition is a thorough

---

[16] G Hardaker, and AH Sabki, *Pedagogy in Islamic Education* (Bingley: Emerald Publishing Limited, 2019); R Seeseman, 'Changes in Islamic Knowledge Practices in Twentieth Century Kenya, in R Launay (ed) *Islamic Education in Kenya* (Indiana: Indiana University Press, 2016) 216.

[17] T Ramadhan, *Western Muslims and the Future of Islam.* (Oxford: Oxford University Press, 2004), 47.

[18] F Ahmed, 'Exploring *halaqah* as research method: a tentative approach to developing Islamic research principles within a critical 'indigenous framework', (2014) *International Journal of Qualitative Studies in Education*, 27:5, 561-583.

[19] S Shabbar, *Ijtihad and Renewal* (Surrey: The International Institute of Islamic Thought, 2017); AI Al Beirawi, *Essays on Ijtihad in the 21st Century* (Pakistan: Maktaba Islamia, 2016); and Ramadhan, (n 17), Hallaq, (n 11).

[20] Ramadhan, (n 17).

[21] Shabbar, (n 19).

knowledge of the *maqasid* of *shari'ah* (objectives of Islamic law),[22] their classification and the priorities they imply. The third condition is knowledge of the principles of *qiyas* (analogical reasoning) and its methodology. The fourth condition is knowledge of the historical, social, and political context against which the question has been asked and the final condition is the interviewee's own competence, honesty, reliability, and uprightness. This recognition must also come from other scholars and from the Muslim community.

These conditions are so demanding that not all research participants will be able to meet them; in fact, they can only be met by the *ulama* (Muslim scholars). Consequently, my research sample would then exclude ordinary Muslims. To mitigate against a limited sample biased towards the clerics, the *halaqa* method provides a leeway. *Halaqa* provides an opportunity for *ijma* to emerge, based on reflective conversations between the participants who cross-check against each other's Islamic view and understanding. *Halaqa* also makes it possible to have diverse participants who can each satisfy at least one of the conditions set out. *Halaqa* has the potential to offer reliable data, which can be mapped onto the other socio-legal methods, such as FGD and interviews utilised during fieldwork. The use of structured interview questions (to complement the doctrinal work already done) also provide an opportunity to collect views on Islamic and human rights, and constitution-related questions based on personal experiences and practice – which do not require the foregoing conditions to be met. Taken together, interviews with Muslims, their scholars and the *halaqa* method will assure the validity of the research and be used to relate such primary data to extend empirical insight to the general body of laws and doctrine of Islamic law.

To complement the doctrinal research of the previous chapters, an interpretative phenomenological research design supported by the *halaqa*

---

22 These are the five fundamental principles for the protection of which *shari'ah* was instated: the preservation of life, property, progeny, mind, and religion. See Chapter 4, for discussion.

method has been conceptualised. According to Bourne et al,[23] Alase,[24] Paley,[25] and Marshall and Rossman,[26] phenomenological research design helps to fully understand the research questions under inquiry. This is done by conducting intensive individual interviews, in which interviewees describe and interpret their experiences, perspectives, interpretations and understanding of the issues under investigation. Phenomenology focuses on the consciousness of human experiences and understanding. Data is usually obtained by conducting personal, face-to-face, semi-structured or unstructured interviews. Several interview sessions are also carried out with the interviewees, to allow the researcher to fully understand their views and integrate them with those of other participants, to establish common themes. Interpretative phenomenological research design allows the researcher to create codes and concepts that form the basis for accurately describing the participants' experiences, perspectives, interpretations and understanding of the issues under query (this is discussed later in this Chapter). According to Neubauer et al,[27] research on topics that are not easily quantifiable are best based around phenomenology.

Key interview questions

Therefore, six key questions are framed, based on the use of interviews, *halaqa* and FGD, to understand the willingness of Muslim and non-Muslim actors to implement the ideas presented in this book. The findings that

---

[23] V Bourne, A James, K Smith et al, *Understanding Quantitative and Qualitative Research in Psychology: A Practical Guide to Methods, Statistics and Analysis* (OUP, 2021) 425, 515, 514, 634, 646.

[24] A Alase, 'The Interpretative Phenomenological Analysis (IPA): A Guide to a Good Qualitative Research Approach', (2017) *International Journal of Education & Literacy Studies*, vol 5, no 2.

[25] J Paley, *Phenomenology as Qualitative Research: A Critical Analysis of Meaning Attribution* (Routledge, 2016).

[26] C Marshall. and GB Rossman, *Designing Qualitative Research* (Newbury Park, Calif.: Sage 1989).

[27] B Neubauer, C Witkop, and L Varpio, 'How Phenomenology Can Help Us Learn from the Experiences of Others', (2019) *Perspectives on Medical Education* 8, 90-97.

follow later present a phenomenological account based on these six questions:

1. How is *zakat* collected and paid out in Kenya?
2. Which schools of Islamic thought influence Muslim perspectives on *zakat* in Kenya, and how do they implement their understanding of norms and doctrine on *zakat*?
3. What are the perspectives of Muslim decision-makers (*zakat* payers, *ulama,* Muslim leaders) and institutions (Muslim faith-based organisations and informal social welfare groups) on giving *zakat* to the Kenyan state to use for health finance?
4. What are the perspectives of Muslim decision-makers and institutions on giving *zakat* to non-Muslims?
5. What are the perspectives of government officials and healthcare workers on accepting the use of *zakat,* together with its Islamic conditions, to finance health under the Kenyan legal system?
6. What are the local academic insights and non-Muslim views on extending the definition of *maximum available resources* to include *zakat,* and the domestic legal nuances around *zakat's* acceptance?

The answers to these questions clarify the overarching aim of this chapter – that investigates whether Kenyan Muslims and non-Muslim actors consider it feasible to use *zakat* to finance health. The findings are discussed as follows: the next section explains and justifies the research design highlighting how the COVID-19 pandemic restricted the study; this is followed by a presentation of the findings and a discussion of the data, and the final section comments on how the empirical work discussed here contributes to the development of scholarship on *zakat,* human rights law on financing health, and dynamic interpretations around the constitutional separation of state and religion in Kenya.

Getting Started: Research Design

The phenomenon of *zakat* in Kenya, the Muslim approach to understanding the norms regulating *zakat,* and inquiring into its feasibility as a source of revenue to finance health is addressed, using the discursive approach based on an interpretative phenomenological research design, contingent primarily on interviewing and dialogic *halaqa* for gathering data. Bilmes proposed a discursive approach to understand how decisions are made.[28] The use of *halaqa* allows for a discursive approach based on debating questions to generate dialogue. Bilmes argues that internal states (such as intention, motivation, and emotions) explain how people understand the meaning of concepts and rules. Following this, Wood and Kroger developed a systematic methodological strategy, that assisted researchers in understanding the internal states of their respondents,[29] which can also be discovered through *halaqa*. These strategies enable a researcher to comprehend how respondents make their decisions. According to Wood and Kroger, understanding the meaning behind a respondent's answer can be made by identifying analytic codes and categories from their words.[30] The use of codes and placing them into categories enable researchers to develop knowledge and understanding as active participants in their study when engaged in analysing raw data.[31] This approach resonates with phenomenological research, which also relies on the use of codes to generate interpretations based on the interviews.

Interpretative phenomenology and the discursive approach continue to spark growing interest in mixed-method research practice.[32] Studies based

---

[28] J Bilmes, *The Discursive Approach. In: Discourse and Behaviour* (Springer, Boston, MA, 1986) 187-206 at 187-8.

[29] LA Wood, and RO Kroger, *Doing Discourse Analysis: Methods for Studying Action in Talk and Text* (Sage Publications Inc. 2000).

[30] ibid, 69-116.

[31] J Saldana, *The Coding Manual for Qualitative Researchers* (London: SAGE Third edition; 2016); I Dey, *Qualitative Data Analysis: A User-Friendly Guide for Social Scientists* (London: Routledge, 1993).

[32] ibid; K Murakami, *Culture in Action: A Discursive Approach* (The Oxford Handbook of Culture and Psychology, 2012); A Hepburn, and S Wiggins, *Discursive Research in Practice* (Cambridge: Cambridge University Press, 2007); T Basit, 'Manual or Electronic? The Role of Coding in Qualitative Data Analysis', (2003) *Educational Research* Vol 45, No. 2, 143-154; S Taylor, 'Locating and Conducting Discourse Analytic Research' in M Wetherell, S Taylor, and S Yates, (eds) *Discourse as Data: A Guide for Analysis* (SAGE 2001); K Murakami, 'Talk About Rice: A Discursive Approach to Studying Culture', (2001). *Forum Qualitative Sozialforschung / Forum: Qualitative Social Research [On-line Journal]*, 2(3), 48–59. M Billig, (1997). 'Discursive, Rhetorical and Ideological Messages' in C McGarty, SA

on Islamic scholarship,[33] human rights law,[34] and legal systems[35] have utilised this method. Both these approaches describe how scholarship is considered and given meaning by society and individuals, based on their understanding, interpretations, and experiences. Such methods justify a socio-legal approach to the creation and understanding of knowledge, and offers the research participant as the primary, independent measure of testing the reliability of norms and laws. The role that individuals play in giving meaning to Islamic law, human rights law, and interpreting the Constitution can be deduced from their narrative analysis – which helps the researcher to understand in detail their lived experiences with these norms and laws. Applying these approaches to gather the data presented here complements and strengthens the doctrinal and theoretical examination carried out in the previous chapters, by relating the scholarship with empirical evaluations.

Fieldwork: COVID-19 impacts and limitations

To conduct fieldwork, this study received ethical approval from Cardiff School of Law and Politics Ethics Committee under reference number SREC/180619/15. The study was also licensed by the Kenyan National Commission for Science, Technology and Innovation (NACOSTI) under Research Licence Reference Number 358511. All interviewees consented to

---

Haslam, (ed.), *The Message of Social Psychology: Perspectives on Mind in Society* (Cambridge, MA: Blackwell, 1997) 37–53.

33 F Mansouri, 'On the Discursive and Methodological Categorisation of Islam and Muslims in the West: Ontological and Epistemological Considerations' (2020) *Religions* 11; 501; M Ahmad, 'An empirical study of the challenges facing *zakat* and waqf institutions in Northern Nigeria', (2019) *ISRA International Journal of Islamic Finance*, vol 11, no 2, 338-356; M Sharifi, N Ansari, and M Asadollahzadeh, (2016) *A Critical Discourse Analytic Approach to Discursive Construction of Islam in Western Talk Shows: The Case of CNN Talk Shows* (SAGE, 2016).

34 L McConell, and R Smith, *Research Methods in Human Rights* (New York: Routledge, 2018) 1.

35 Ehrlich, S, Eades D and Ainsworth J, 'Discursive Constructions of Consent in the Legal Process', (2016) *The International Journal of Speech, Language and the Law*, Vol 23, No 2, 301-306; D Roth-Isigkeit, 'Promises and Perils of Legal Argument – A Discursive Approach to Normative Conflict between Legal Order', (2014) *Revue Belge de Droit International* 2.

the research and dissemination of their views. I had the opportunity to conduct in-person interviews and *halaqas*. The remaining interviews and focus groups were delayed due to travel restrictions and lockdown measures imposed by Kenya and the United Kingdom, following the COVID-19 pandemic. Some of these interviews were later conducted asynchronously, according to the preferred option of some interviewees, while others were done online in real time.

Key decision-makers in the administration and financing of the health sector were identified for in-person interviews. However, due to the physical distancing requirements and work-from-home directives, it was impossible to interview the legal officer from the Ministry of Health, an officer from the National Hospital Insurance Fund (NHIF), and an officer from the office of the Governor of Mombasa. They also stopped responding to emails during this period; this could have been due to the social and economic difficulties Kenya was experiencing due to the lockdown. In ordinary circumstances it would have been possible to have an in-person meeting with them.

The pandemic-imposed restrictions thus precluded the study from gathering first-hand data from these key public officers, on their understanding of the constitutional parameters to introducing Islamic norms as part of construing the implementation of the right to health under article 43(1)(a) of the Constitution in Kenya. These officers were substituted by interviews with Members of Parliament. Moving focus groups online, meant facing challenges of delay in receiving replies to emails and text messages, poor internet coverage, audio difficulties during online meetings, request for funds by interviewees for mobile data during telephone interviews, and difficulties in observing demeanour and body language of the interviews. It also limited opportunities for follow-up questions and clarifications. These realities were factors presented as limitations to the study.

In designing the methodology for fieldwork, careful attention was given to address the gender gap in Islamic scholarship in Kenya. Male monopoly (discussed in the overview and Chapter 6) in addressing Islamic questions was countered by interviewing 54 Muslim women, so that their views would add to and enrich the contribution to Islamic scholarship on *zakat* in Kenya. Careful attention was also given to respect Islamic and cultural norms when addressing Muslim male and female participants. For example, one *imam* requested that I cover my face when attending the meeting with him, and another *imam* asked that I bring a *mahram*[36] to the meeting with him; I missed out on some face-to-face interviews at different mosques because of not having a *mahram* to accompany me. This did not limit my research as I was able to interview the *imams* through WhatsApp texting.

An overview follows of participant sampling, data collection tools and data organisation round analytic codes and categories.

Participant selection

In designing the study, the use of purposive sampling was selected to conduct the research. Purposive sampling is very common in qualitative research and to generate data for phenomenological analysis.[37] Purposive sampling aids researchers in reducing the risk of bias, by permitting them to use their subjective judgement to select samples which they believe to be 'representative' of the population.[38] Purposive sampling depends on two assumptions: firstly, the researcher's ability to identify in advance the characteristics which collectively capture all variation in the population of interests, and secondly, that the chosen sample will correctly reflect the distributions of these characteristics.[39]

Accordingly, purposive sampling allowed the study to select research participants based on the following predefined criteria: that the Muslim

---

[36] A *mahram* represents a male relative whom the Muslim woman is not permitted to marry under Islamic law. For example, her father, brother, uncle, grandfather.

[37] A Moser, and I Korstjens, 'Series: Practical Guidance to Qualitative Research. Part 3: Sampling, Data Collection and Analysis' (2018) *Eur J Gen Pract.* 24(1):9-18; Ograjensek, I, 'Theory and Practice of Qualitative Research', in T Greenfield and S Greener, *Research Methods for Postgraduates* (UK: John Wiley & Sons Ltd, 2016) 216.

[38] P Lynn, 'Principles of Sampling', in Greenfield and Greener (n 37) 248.

[39] ibid.

male and female interviewees either be drawn from a pool of *zakat* payers; be widely recognised as Islamic authorities in Kenya; have expert Islamic knowledge; be part of Islamic faith-based organisations; or be employed by the Government. Purposive sampling was also applied to identify non-Muslim male and female interviewees, in order to include a non-Muslim perspective within the research. These were Members of Parliament known to the researcher; human rights experts with whom the researcher had previously worked; healthcare workers introduced to the researcher through an activist advocating for the right to health through KELIN; a Nairobi-based NGO; and, people of different faiths selected during an online religion-focused webinar, hosted by Caritas Internationalis (a Catholic-funded charitable organisation). Based on these predefined criteria, participants were categorised into three sample groups.

The first sample group (Group 1) comprised Muslim male and female *zakat* payers, randomly approached for interview, to discover their understanding of the norms regulating *zakat*. Consequently, 107 consenting Muslim male and female *zakat* payers were interviewed in Mombasa and Nairobi.[40] They were asked ten structured questions and their responses were collated as quantitative data.[41] The questions focused on whether the Muslims would be receptive to the use of *zakat* to finance health, whether non-Muslims could also benefit from *zakat*-funded health care, how much *zakat* they paid, on what and to whom, and about their views on paying *zakat* to the Government. These questions helped to relate empirical research on *zakat* to its Islamic norms and doctrine. The answers provided a systematic understanding on how local actors interpret Islamic law to make an informed decision on the use of *zakat,* and whether to make it available to the Kenyan government to finance health. These Muslims were approached before and after prayer hours at the selected mosques in Mombasa and Nairobi. The selection of mosques was based on an

---

40 A list with details of the *zakat* payers interviewed disaggregated by their ethnicity and race across the study sites, is on file with the author. Generally, 59 zakat payers were interviewed in Mombasa, and 48 in Nairobi. Participants interviewed were Swahili, Arab, Somali, Indian, Pakistani, Goan, Luo, Kikuyu and Afghan.

41 The questions asked and the responses gathered are stored on file with the author.

understanding of how Muslim society is structured along their schools of thought and ethnic representation. The mosques represented these Muslim preferences, judging from the description given by most of the interviewees, and therefore were ideal sites to capture this diverse Muslim representation of thought.

Imams (Muslim males who lead prayers in mosques and offer religious advice), *ustadhas* (Muslim females certified to teach Islamic studies by a recognised Islamic training institution[42]) Muslim scholars, Muslim faith-based organisations (FBOs) and informal social welfare groupings among the Kenyan Muslim communities are very influential in guiding action and regulating behaviour. Their role is critical towards moulding Muslim views on *zakat*. It was therefore considered necessary to include them as part of the study sample. The second sample group (Group 2), therefore, comprised selected Muslim male and female participants recognised as Islamic law and human rights experts, authority figures, and prominent organisations involved in decision-making around *zakat*.

Two nationwide FBOs (Mahad Dawah Organisation (MDO) and *Zakat* Kenya) were selected for interview. MDO is a Nairobi-based inclusive Muslim institution, with members from diverse backgrounds. It advances the socio-economic interests of Muslims nationally, teaching and training on Islamic education and offering vocational courses. It does not take part in the country's politics, neither does it represent Muslim political interests.[43] *Zakat* Kenya is another Nairobi-based institution, formed by Swahilis, Somalis, and Arabs. It is an unregistered entity based within Masjid Al Salaam in South C, within Kenya's Langata constituency. Its primary objective is to use *zakat* towards economic empowerment. *Zakat* Kenya provides *zakat* to poor households, supporting household heads to start small informal business enterprises.

These participants represented key figures, whose views are very important in answering the specific research questions outlined on page

---

[42] In Kenya, the Pangani Girls Training Institute trains and certifies *ustadhas*.

[43] Interviewee No. 125. Interview date 02.02.2020 Nairobi.

245. *Zakat* payers, *imams*, Muslim FBOs, and Islamic scholars formed part of the sample, because each is an important part of the *zakat* governance system. The *zakat* governance system comprises formal and informal intermediaries, identified as groups or organisations who take up the responsibility to collect *zakat*, and identify the beneficiaries or projects towards which the *zakat* is remitted. Usually, *zakat* is collected by mosques, FBOs, or community-based organisations. Some households also prefer to pay *zakat* directly to the poor, without referring to intermediaries.

Zakat payers are usually guided by their *imams* and scholars. Most of the *zakat* in Kenya is remitted through institutions. This study sought to understand whether the participants influence one another or work together to decide on the goals toward which *zakat* is to be utilised. The study identified the following two aims: firstly, the need to understand whether *imams* influence who should receive *zakat*, and where it should be paid; secondly, to understand how decisions on the spending of *zakat* are made by the organisations collecting it. The answers to these questions would generate empirical data on *zakat* in Kenya, to understand how Kenyan Muslims regulate and manage their *zakat*. Whether *zakat* distribution is done strategically or haphazardly, it would be helpful to understand whether there is a consistent, systematic way of administering it in Kenya, and whether there is room to reconsider how *zakat* is managed, to make it more effective.

Having identified the dearth in Islamic scholarship on *zakat* from a female Muslim perspective, the study also identified women-led organisations for interview, to understand what role Muslim women play in the *zakat* system. Muslim women from different ethnic groups have formed informal social groups to collect and distribute *zakat*. Documenting their views allows this study to feature their interpretations on Islamic law and *zakat*, and to use those views to provide further understanding of the Islamic norms on *zakat*. In response to reducing male dominance of Islamic law scholarship in Kenya, the study specifically chose to use *halaqa* to allow for the creation and interpretation of Islamic norms on *zakat* from female Muslim perspectives. This technique can help a researcher to understand whether Muslim women have autonomy and agency to decide how their *zakat* is spent; whether they paid *zakat* themselves, or influenced their husbands, fathers, or brothers on where and to whom to remit *zakat*. It would also reveal whether Muslim women are decision-makers in *zakat*, as this would be important to help answer the broader research question, on whether decisions around *zakat* are open for debate, and whether directing *zakat* to financing health (including the health of non-Muslims) would be a matter that Muslim men and women would be open to discuss.

To increase the credibility and validity of the views on *zakat* in Kenya beyond Muslims, a third sample group (Group 3) was chosen, comprising non-Muslim participants from government, an NGO, people of different faiths, academics, and healthcare workers. Non-Muslim participants were selected for interview, to gain in-depth understanding of their views around *zakat* as a source of revenue to fund health in Kenya – from a human rights perspective, and as part of the Kenyan constitutional legal system. Such diverse interviews focusing on Muslim and non-Muslim views on financing health using *zakat* provided the study with a systematic understanding of how the non-Muslim interviewees cast light on Muslim belief and practice. This would contribute to new knowledge on the interpretation of Islamic law on *zakat*, and on human rights law on financing health using *zakat*, from non-Muslim perspectives. Presently, there is no literature on this, or on the practicability of non-Islamic states taking and using *zakat* to finance health. This study, therefore, explains whether the non-Muslim Kenyan interviewees from the government and academia see *zakat* as part of Kenya's legal system, and reveals the kind of debates they engage in when commenting on the position of *zakat* as a source of revenue for the Kenyan Government.

Participants were engaged using three methods of inquiry: interviews, a focus group discussion, and *huluqus*. The *zakat* payers were interviewed using a mix of open- and close-ended interview questions, and all other participants were asked open-ended interview questions, and individually interviewed. Interviews were held in mosques and offices of the interviewees. Two *halaqas* were held for female Muslims. The first *halaqa* was with *ustadhas*; the second *halaqa* was held with a Muslim woman who is an Islamic authority figure in Kenya, and three Muslim women from government. The *halaqas* were organised at Masjid Al Salam in Nairobi. The persons of different faiths were interviewed online as a focus group.

Two separate study sites were chosen. Mombasa was chosen because of its historical significance in Islam (discussed in Chapter 6). Most of its resident population are Muslims of Arab, Swahili, and African ancestry. By focusing on Mombasa, the study was able to understand whether the power asymmetries resulting from the historic social stratification of Muslims continues today; whether Arab dominance in guiding Islamic thought remains the status quo among Muslims on the coast; and whether the political strength of Muslims on the coast has the potential to decide collectively on behalf of all Kenyan Muslims on their approach to *zakat*. By choosing Nairobi as the other study site, the research balances the representation of Indian/Pakistani Muslims who are clustered in Nairobi. The Nairobi study sites provided access to interview Muslims ascribing to the *Hanafi* school, as opposed to the *Shafi* school (which are predominant in Mombasa). These study sites together offer a representative view of *sunni* Muslims in Kenya.

Data organisation

The data gathered from the interviews, *halaqas* and focus group were taken down verbatim, and later transcribed using analytic codes. Data was organised around participants' views referring to the six research questions listed on page 245. The questionnaire-based interviews with *zakat* payers were analysed on Microsoft Excel, to generate bar graphs and percentages. The rest of the data (gathered from the interviews, *halaqas* and the focus group discussion) were analysed by summarising the transcripts and identifying answers to questions, in order to identify (through the use of analytic codes) common statements, words and phrases used by respondents, which in turn would identify emerging data themes, and link the data to the six research questions, and also to select quotations, generate explanations grounded in the data, and write it up.

Coding raw data was crucial to analysing data gathered during the study. Dey explains that the use of codes are important to allocate meaning to the descriptive or inferential information compiled during fieldwork.[44] Seidel and Kelle explain that through coding, the researcher can notice relevant phenomena, and analyse it in the context of finding commonalities, differences, patterns and structures.[45] Coding 'triggers the construction of a conceptual scheme that suits the data'.[46] Coding is an organisational tool helping to manage data in the analysis process.[47] According to Coffey and Atkinson, codes are heuristic devices that help link between locations in the data and sets of concepts and ideas.[48] Codes provide a constant comparative method of analysis, and thus are favourable when using the discursive approach and phenomenological research. Thus, in organising the data gathered during the interviews and *halaqa,* code names were developed from words and phrases used by the respondents themselves. The use of codes across data gathered from different respondents provided triangulation across the findings, illuminating the same issues corroborated by different respondents.

Going into the field

Fieldwork was based around three phases. The first phase involved interviewing *zakat* payers. Nairobi-based *zakat* payers were interviewed by me. Mombasa-based *zakat* payers were interviewed by a male and female research assistant, who interviewed respondents of their respective gender. The second phase involved interviewing male and female Muslim stakeholders. These interviews were also conducted in person. All Nairobi-based respondents were interviewed at their offices – except the *ustadhas,* who were interviewed in a conference room at Masjid Al Salam in Nairobi.

---

44 Dey, (n 31).

45 J Seidel, and U Kelle, 'Different functions of coding in the analysis of textual data', in U Kelle, (ed) *Computer-aided Qualitative Data Analysis: Theory, Methods and Practice* (London: Sage, 1995).

46 Basit, (n 32) 144.

47 R Tesch, *Qualitative Research: Analysis Types and Software Tools* (Basingstoke: Falmer, 1990).

48 A Coffey, and P Atkinson, *Making Sense of Qualitative Data* (London: Sage, 1996).

Mombasa-based respondents were interviewed through WhatsApp (*imams*) and Zoom (all other subgroups).

The final phase involved interviewing non-Muslim leaders and professionals. Nairobi-based healthcare workers were interviewed in their offices. A Mombasa-based healthcare worker was interviewed through WhatsApp. All other interviews with other respondents had to be moved online, following detection of the first COVID-19 case in Kenya in March 2020. As the number of COVID-19 infections continued to rise in Kenya, the Government imposed travel restrictions into and within Kenya between March and August 2020. This made it impossible to physically meet with respondents safely. Online interviews and an online focus group with persons of different faiths were conducted at the respondents' convenience, due to the hardships, mental health concerns and financial and employment distress that resulted from the strict measures put in place to contain the pandemic.

My efforts to reach the Ministry of Health in Nairobi, the Department of Health in Mombasa, and an officer working with the NHIF for online or email-based interviews proved unfruitful. I then improvised, by getting in touch with Members of Parliament for whom I had previously worked during active legal practice. One MP agreed to a WhatsApp call and text-based chat, and three others agreed to asynchronous email interviewing. Of the four MPs interviewed, three were Nairobi-based, and one represented the East Africa Legislative Assembly in Tanzania. I have received no communication from the Ministry of Health and MPs who represent Mombasa. One academic from the University of Nairobi, one from the Catholic University of East Africa, and one from Moi University were also interviewed, using asynchronous email interviewing.

Gibson refers to email interviewing as 'conducting interviews via email'.[49] She explains that there are two ways of conducting email interviews: the

[49] L Gibson, 'Type Me Your Answer: Generating Interview Data via Email', in V Braun, V Clarke and D Gray, *Collecting Qualitative Data: A Practical Guide to Textual, Media and Virtual Techniques* (Cambridge: Cambridge University Press, 2017) 214.

asynchronous and synchronous methods. The former method is used when email interviewing is not conducted in real time, and the latter method is used for email interviewing that happens in real time.[50] The asynchronous method allows research participants the convenience to answer questions sent to them in advance, either all at once, or sequentially, at their own pace and time. The synchronous approach requires that both the researcher and the participant be online at the same time, to ask and answer questions in real time. Given that the COVID-19 pandemic resulted in fundamental disruption to work and family life, I opted for the asynchronous method to collect data, to free participants from the pressure of having to schedule meetings during times of uncertainty and amidst the pressure of working remotely. The asynchronous method mitigated the inconvenience of putting the participants under additional unnecessary stress, by giving them the option to answer at their convenience, or to opt out completely, without the obligation to respond.

The drawback of using this approach is the undefined timeline within which responses from participants may be received. This pitfall was addressed by requesting participants who indicated their desire to respond to do so within two weeks of receiving the interview questions. The advantage of asynchronous interviews lay in the possibility of running multiple interviews simultaneously, and then waiting for responses.[51] The drawback of this is the time spent in receiving and reading responses, and posing further follow up questions, which can take in total more time than a face-to-face interview. In this regard, synchronous interviews would have been better, because they would have elicited faster responses. However, the time spent on asynchronous interviews made up for the additional time that would have been spent transcribing verbal or audio data. Since participants had the flexibility to reflect deeply on the questions asked, prepare their answers, control what they wanted to say, and have the

---

[50] ibid, 214.

[51] H Snee, C Hine, Y Moey, et al, (eds) *Digital Methods for Social Science: An Interdisciplinary Guide to Research Innovation* (Springer, 2016) 147-149; B Golding, *Asynchronous Email Interviewing: A Qualitative Data Collection Method* (SAGE Publications, 2014).

potential to revise and reflect on the content before they emailed it to me, the quality of their data was better. The data gathered through this approach is therefore rich and detailed.[52] Conversely, participants may rush to answer the questions and not provide in-depth detail. [53] Purposively selecting participants, based on their professional background and key involvement with government affairs, served as a good control against the potential for rushed responses lacking detail.

In interviewing persons of different faiths, I took advantage of an online webinar organised by Caritas Internationalis in September 2020, on 'Engaging with faith actors in Kenya in drawing lessons towards sustaining development'. I approached the organisers and asked whether I could use their platform to introduce my research and ask participants if any of them would be comfortable to be interviewed by me; and if so, to share their email addresses so that I could get in touch with them formally. One Catholic person, two Jewish persons and two Hindu persons agreed to be interviewed by me. I separately approached the Sikh Gurdwara in Nairobi and inquired from the caretaker about the possibility of interviewing a Sikh person. A telephone number was shared with me, and in following up with the contact, she agreed to be interviewed by me. These persons of different faiths were interviewed online as a focus group. These interviewees would contribute to new knowledge on the interpretation of Islamic law on *zakat,* and human rights law on financing health using *zakat,* from their own perspectives; their views would generate knowledge on the practicability and constitutional permissibility of the Kenyan state taking and using *zakat* to finance health.

All 166 participants were provided with an information sheet in advance of the interviews, detailing the purpose of the study, and explaining how their data would be handled. Ethical considerations were central to this study. In-person, email and text-based interviewing carefully followed Cardiff University's Research Integrity procedures around informed

---

[52] T Clark, L Foster, L Sloan, et al, *Bryman's Social Research Methods* (Sixth edition OUP, 2021) 467-71

[53] P Leavy, *Popularising Scholarly Research: Research Methods and Practices* (OUP, 2021) 328

consent, the right to withdraw, accuracy of portrayal, and confidentiality, approved by the University Research Integrity and Ethics Committee. Data from all respondents provided in-depth phenomenological perspectives on *zakat,* which were both subjective and objective.

Data Presentation and Analysis

The study approached data analysis with the objective of understanding the underlying assumptions, conceptualisation, doctrinal and even theoretical considerations that informed how the respondents' understood and answered the interview questions. Two approaches to analysing data were utilised: quantitative analysis and coding.

Quantitative data

Quantitative data was generated through analysing the *zakat* payers' answers to questions about their general attitudes towards supporting the Government to meet its health budget using *zakat*. These responses were first decoded on Microsoft Excel, using bar graphs to reveal the frequency of similar responses, and presented in a percentage format to reveal the trend or majority view on the question asked. These responses were encoded based on answers derived from reading the transcripts. The majority view of the *zakat* payers was then compared with the views of Muslim scholars, *imams, ustadhas,* leaders and FBO officers.

Coding

Coding also had an important organisational role in analysing the data. The six research questions listed on page 245 helped to trigger the construction of a conceptual scheme that suited the data. These questions helped me to pick out related data that answered a specific question. This process made data analysis manageable. It also served two purposes: descriptive reporting and generating knowledge of the respondent's worldview outside the law. Coding helped create the links between data and the development of themes. The analysis was a lengthy and complex process. I made several analyses during the fieldwork and after its completion.

Saldana's 'The Coding Manual for Qualitative Researchers'[54] guided my approach to coding data.

I used descriptive codes about everything the respondents talked about what they shared of their personal perceptions, attitudes and belief system about *zakat*, Islam, the right to health, human rights, and the Kenyan state. I also used *in vivo*[55] coding of metaphors, phrases and words used by all respondents, when they seemed very enthusiastic, incensed, curious or encouraging – based on their behaviour, actions, and words. I put these *in vivo* codes in quotation marks. That was the first phase of analysis. In the second phase of decoding data, the aim was to put together all data accompanying similar codes. This helped me to identify emerging common themes that I could link to the six research questions. I was able to group data under 25 codes that had been used repeatedly..

Themes emerging

These repeatedly used codes directed me towards searching for patterns in the coded data, which then helped me place the codes as part of emerging themes, or as part of the bigger picture. The patterns were characterised by how similar, different, and frequent the respondents' views were. These patterns helped manifest the themes that reflected the underlying assumptions, conceptualisation, doctrinal and theoretical considerations that informed the respondents' views. Consequently, the codes were clustered under the following eight major themes, to make sense of phenomena that informed the respondents views:

1. **Authority** (this related to those perceived as decision makers and their views, that is the state and Muslim scholars)
2. **Consent** (this concerned permission given by Muslims, their scholars, leaders, or groups)

---

[54] J Saldana, *The Coding Manual for Qualitative Researchers* (London: SAGE Third edition, 2016) 3-5.

[55] ibid. Saldana describes *in vivo* coding as codes taken directly from what the participants say, placed in quotation marks, (3). This is different from NVivo, which is a coding software program.

3. **Control** (this was about the importance of Muslim groups retaining decision making powers on the use of *zakat*, collecting it and distributing it as per a Muslim group's goals)
4. **Development** (this related to the intended objective of *zakat*)
5. **Identity** (this related to a Muslim identifying with a particular group (Arab) and their group's cause: using *zakat* to support widows etc)
6. **Impact** (this concerned specific evidence resulting from the use of *zakat*)
7. **Legality** (this related to the lawfulness of giving and taking of *zakat* under Islamic law, human rights and the Constitution of Kenya)
8. **Trust** (this related to how Muslims perceived the state)

The codes that produced the eight major themes are listed in the Table 1 below.

Code Numbers	Code Identification
CODE 1	Class differentiation
CODE 2	Collaboration
CODE 3	Colourism
CODE 4	Community building
CODE 5	Conflict
CODE 6	Discretion
CODE 7	Discontent
CODE 8	Distrust
CODE 9	Diversity
CODE 10	Financial protection
CODE 11	Gender

CODE 12	History
CODE 13	Inclusiveness
CODE 14	Interpretation
CODE 15	Law
CODE 16	Leverage
CODE 17	Location
CODE 18	Objective of *zakat*
CODE 19	Permission
CODE 20	Philanthropy
CODE 21	Power
CODE 22	Reform
CODE 23	Schools of thought
CODE 24	Solidarity
CODE 25	Tradition

Table 1: *Codes*

These themes were found to relate to either one or several of the 6 research questions. Several quotations were chosen to test the connection of the research questions to the themes. For example, references to **authority** and **legality** by the respondents primarily determined their decision making around *zakat* – this helped provide insight to the first research question: *'how is zakat collected and paid out in Kenya?'* The importance of creating an **impact,** and sustaining **development** were critical towards giving of *zakat* – this helped answer the third research question: *'what are the perspectives of Muslim decision-makers (zakat payers,* ulama, *Muslim leaders) and institutions (Muslim faith-based organisations and informal social welfare groups) on giving zakat to the Kenyan state to use for health finance?'* The need to preserve their Muslim **identity** and **control** the *zakat* funds at community level were important considerations overruling Government involvement – this helped answer the fourth research question: *'what are the perspectives of Muslim decision makers and institutions on giving zakat to non-Muslims?'* Such theme-based analyses helped answer the research questions.

Responses from *zakat* payers (Group 1)

Amount paid in zakat

The Muslim male and female *zakat* payers who were interviewed followed the *Shafi* and *Hanafi* schools of thought, that have historically been present in Kenya. In Mombasa, most respondents ascribed to the *Shafi* school of thought. In Nairobi, the respondents interviewed were affiliated either with the *Shafi* or the *Hanafi* schools. This sample is reflective of the Muslims in Kenya. As such, the data can be generalised beyond the respondents to represent the general Muslim view on *zakat*. The data does not indicate the percentage of Muslims who pay *zakat* in Kenya. Getting such data was beyond the scope of the study. The study's findings indicate the amount in *zakat* paid by the 107 respondents interviewed. It gives an indication of how much *zakat* was paid by the respondents in 2019.

From the data provided, the total *zakat* paid by the 42 male respondents from Mombasa was KES 1.2 million (GBP 8,425), while KES 428,000 (GBP 2,962) was paid by the 17 female respondents. The Nairobi-based 29 male respondents, in total, paid KES 588,680 (GBP 4,074) in *zakat,* and the 19 women paid KES 410,267 (GBP 2,777). In total the 107 respondents paid KES 2.6 million (GBP 18,238) in *zakat* in 2019. The amount paid in *zakat* was calculated based either on annual savings of KES 260,000 (GBP 1,761) and above or a combination of savings along with the value of gold in possession exceeding 80g.

According to the Kenya Population and Housing Census Report of 2019, the population of Kenya is 47.5 million, out of which Muslims make up 11 per cent (5.2 million). Further research is required to filter *zakat* payers out of the 5.2 million Muslims. If, for example, we assume that 100,000 Muslims pay a minimum of KES 6500 (GBP 45) calculated based on 2.5 per cent *zakat* on savings of KES 260,000 (GBP 1,761), a total of KES 650 million (GBP 4.5 million) in *zakat* can be mobilised. This is a substantial amount. Nine level

3 health facilities in Kenya, each costing KES 70 million (GBP 484,855)[56] can be constructed and equipped with this amount.

Beneficiaries of zakat

The study limited itself to questions on the individual practice of *zakat*, and opinion on using *zakat* to finance health in Kenya by the Government and including non-Muslims as beneficiaries. All respondents from the two study sites indicated that all questions they have concerning *zakat* in Kenya are directed to their *imams* and scholars, who give them guidance based on their schools of Islamic thought. Muslim respondents of Arab, Swahili and Somali ethnicity indicated their preference for the *Shafi* school, while the respondents of Indian/Pakistani heritage confirmed the *Hanafi* school of thought as their preferred approach to understanding Islamic law. These respondents were influenced by reference to **authority** and **legality** in making their decisions on *zakat*.

All the respondents from both the study sites indicated that *zakat* must be prioritised for Muslims. The respondents from Nairobi were open to consider giving *zakat* to non-Muslims if they met the eligibility criteria set out in the *Qur'an* (either as one of the eight beneficiaries mentioned in Chapter 4). The respondents from Mombasa were not sure whether *zakat* could be given to non-Muslims but were agreeable to it. One Mombasa-based female respondent explained that: 'If there are no Muslims to whom I can give *zakat*, then I can give it to a non-Muslim. I can even think about giving the *zakat* to a poor widow who is not Muslim and has nothing to eat.'[57] Another Mombasa-based male respondent said that: 'If there was an emergency, where for example a non-Muslim faced a jail sentence over default on the principal debt and not interest, and I have *zakat* to give, I can give it to him.'[58] During an interview in Nairobi, a female respondent remarked that: 'If *zakat* has been used to finance human rights, and whether

---

[56] Parliamentary Service Commission, *Budget Options for 2022/2023 and the Medium Term* (Parliamentary Budget Office, 2022), 54.

[57] Interviewee No. 50. Interview date 11.12.2019 Mombasa.

[58] Interviewee No. 103. Interview date 17.12.2019 Mombasa.

it is paid to non-Muslims we do not know for sure, but maybe there are Muslims out there who give *zakat* to non-Muslim to pay their medical bills – that is health related, isn't it?'[59] These views are reflective of *zakat* decisions being based on its **impact**.

Zakat to finance health

Many respondents from Mombasa and Nairobi agreed that *zakat* could be used to finance health. When asked whether non-Muslims in their opinion could also access *zakat*-based health care, their general response was that *zakat* is intended for the specific beneficiaries mentioned in the *Qur'an*. A non-Muslim would have to meet the eligibility criteria if they wanted to access healthcare financed using *zakat*. These views also resonate with **authority** and **legality** as contributing factors in decision-making on the use of *zakat*. A Nairobi-based male respondent explained that:

> It is the Government's duty to provide healthcare. If at all, zakat is used to say build a hospital, the hospital or services should be exclusively for the poor Muslims. Others can come for free treatment, but they will have to pay unless they are poor then they can be considered as zakat beneficiaries, I think. There has to be strict control otherwise it can become a habit for others to go to Muslim hospitals because it is free.[60]

Another Nairobi-based male respondent asked me:

> Are you abnormal? Zakat is to help people financially. It is to offer income support. Why should zakat be given to fund healthcare when it's the Government's bloody job? Don't ask ridiculous questions! This is a big no-no-no for me.[61]

A Nairobi-based male respondent suggested that:

[59] Interviewee No. 117. Interview date 19.01.2020 Nairobi.
[60] Interviewee No. 27. Interview date 07.12.2019 Nairobi.
[61] Interviewee No. 14. Interview date 04.12.2019 Nairobi

> Let's tackle the Muslims first, and should there be extra revenues to spare, then we can support non-Muslims. Alternatively, if they are permitted under shari'ah to access our zakat-financed healthcare, then we should have a different scheme for them – an affordable premium.[62]

Offering zakat to the Kenyan Government to support health finance

When asked if the respondents would consider giving their *zakat* to the Government, all the Mombasa-based respondents refused. Their responses reflected issues around **trust** and **control**. One female respondent narrated that, 'Government officials openly steal taxpayers' money, they steal money that is donated in good faith for building schools and hospitals. Ah, I can never trust Government with my *zakat*'.[63] Other Mombasa-based respondents were of the view that 'Government is highly corrupt',[64] 'Government will misuse and steal the *zakat*, they will definitely delay utilising the *zakat* money where needed',[65] 'We are better off doing it ourselves'.[66] A few Nairobi-based respondents said that it would depend on whether this would be permissible under Islamic law. One respondent explained that:

> Only if the Muslims would think of setting up a partnership fund with the Ministry of Health, or set up ourselves a single Muslim-run institution nationally to collect zakat and work with the Ministry to identify poor areas in need of extra healthcare financial help, so that we can give the zakat there, and provided only a Muslim would administer the zakat money, then I think it's okay to give to Government.[67]

---

[62] Interviewee No. 20. Interview date 05.12.2019 Nairobi
[63] Interviewee No. 71. Interview date 12.12.2019 Mombasa
[64] Interviewee No. 91. Interview date 13.12.2019 Mombasa.
[65] Interviewee No. 101. Interview date 17.12.2019 Mombasa.
[66] Interviewee No. 54. Interview date 11.12.2019 Mombasa.
[67] Interviewee No. 24. Interview date 05.12.2019 Nairobi.

I asked the respondents whether there were any conditions they could think of that would allow the Government of Kenya to administer their *zakat,* and that if the Government was to apply the Islamic rules on *zakat,* whether the respondents would then consider giving *zakat* to the Government. Many respondents from both study sites were unanimous in their opinion that under no conditions could Muslims give their *zakat* to a non-Islamic Government. One Nairobi-based female respondent, whose view reflected the general perception of the respondents, said:

> We should ask the maalim (Islamic teacher) about this, he would be best to give this answer. I think zakat cannot be administered by a non-Muslim – unless the Government sets up a national zakat fund and appoints Muslims to oversee it and make decisions on who gets the zakat – then I think we can send them our zakat. Zakat is sacred, and only a Muslim can properly govern zakat. I can trust a Muslim whom I don't know with my zakat, but I can't trust this Government – we would be reading about zakat scandal in the papers.[68]

This data shows that, while the respondents agree that *zakat* can be used to finance health, and even under specific instances, allow non-Muslims to access *zakat*-financed healthcare under specific conditions, many of them are averse to *zakat* being given to non-Muslims and to the Government. Their views were influenced by reference to **authority** and **legality,** based on their understanding of the *Qur'an* and *sunna,* and their views on using *zakat* for health were guided by their commitment to ensuring that their *zakat* created a social **impact**. Finally, their lack of **trust** in the Government and their concern over the **control** of their religious funds formed the basis of their refusal to remit their *zakat* to the Government, or even consider Government involvement.

---

[68] Interviewee No. 11. Interview date 04.12.2019 Nairobi.

Responses from *imams, ustadhas,* Islamic experts, FBOs, and authority figures (Group 2)

Making decisions on zakat: FBOs and women-led social welfare groups

Two approaches to giving *zakat* in Kenya were identified by a female interviewee of a women led Community Based Organisation. According to her 'the *zakat* payer either gives it out directly to the poor or to a Muslim organisation'.[69] The importance that is attached to the giving of *zakat* is on its intended social **impact**. To understand this better, 42 respondents were interviewed in this group. As this section will show, while they agreed to the importance of *zakat* in making an **impact**, they all emphasised that references to **authority** and **legality** must be made as the defining parameters within which Muslims made their decisions. The importance of Islamic rules, perspectives from a school of Islamic thought, and advice from the *ulema* represent the standard of **authority** and **legality** for the Muslims in Kenya. **Legality** is also construed through the processes of *shura* (consultation) and *ijma* (consensus) at either the institutional, community or household levels. *Shura* and *ijma* have been discussed earlier in Chapter 4.

Interviewees from the Nairobi-based FBOs – MDO and *Zakat* Kenya – explained that binding decisions on the use of *zakat* are made at board level.[70] At the institutional level, *shura* is conducted at board level, and then board decisions are presented to the members for *ijma*. This provides the requisite **legality** needed to make decisions on the use of *zakat*. An example of decisions made on how to use the *zakat* funds for social **impact**, an interviewee[71] explained that *Zakat* Kenya has helped several Muslim women start catering businesses (such as selling *mahambri na baazi, ndegu*

[69] Interviewee No. 117. Interview date 19.01.2020 Nairobi .

[70] Interviewee No. 125. Interview date 02.02.2020 Nairobi; Interviewee No. 126. Interview date 05.02.2020 Nairobi

[71] Interviewee No. 126. Interview date 05.02.2020 Nairobi

na chapati [local dishes]), and small roadside kiosks to sell vegetables, milk, oil, and bread.[72]

Decisions around *zakat* at the institutional level are therefore guided by the **impact** to be achieved, and contribution to social **development,** alongside references to **authority** and **legality** derived from the *Shafi* school of Islamic thought by consulting *imams* and scholars. Respondents from these two organisations also explained that their school of thought did not oppose giving *sadaqa* (charity) to non-Muslims, but their *zakat* is reserved for poor Muslims. According to them, their objective in paying out *zakat* was to support the gradual economic empowerment of Muslims. They gave examples from Northern Kenya and the coastal region where Muslims live in poverty.

During interviews[73] with informal social welfare groups led by Muslim women, it was explained that these groups were set up to support poor and destitute women using *zakat* collected from households of similar ethnic groups. For example, Humble Hands collected *zakat* from Arabs and gave the *zakat* to poor Arabs, Pangani Masjid in Nairobi collected *zakat* from Indian/Pakistani Muslims and distributed it to poor Indian/Pakistani Muslim women. Different ethnic groups set up their own informal groups, within which they practiced *shura* and arrived at *ijma*. Several informal women-led social welfare groups had been set up to cater exclusively for the poor from their own ethnic groups.[74] These women set the agenda for which they would collect *zakat* from their groups. *Shura* and *ijma* is therefore conducted by these women, who are neither authority figures nor Islamic scholars. They are a group of women from middle-class families who plan social events and the annual collection of *zakat*. Decisions around *zakat* are made by these women and are dependent on the **development** of

---

72 Interviewee No. 126. Interview date 05.02.2020 Nairobi.

73 Interviewee No. 116. Interview date 18.01.2020 Nairobi; Interviewee No. 117. Interview date 19.01.2020 Nairobi; Interviewee No. 119. Interview date 20.01.2020 Nairobi; Interviewee No. 141. Interview date 18.02.2020 Mombasa (Telephone); Interviewee No. 142. Interview date 18.02.2020 Mombasa (Telephone)

74 For example, the Punjabi *Khidmat Foundation*, the Swahili *Humble Hands*, the Arab *Share What You Can Spare.*

the poor from their groups. The giving of *zakat* to these women-led informal groups is based on **trust,** and the importance of group **control** of their funds.

Two respondents who were interviewed from the informal women-led social welfare groups confirmed that all of their recipients of *zakat* had been Muslims.[75] They explained that, under the *Hanafi* school that informed their understanding of Islamic rules, *zakat* could only be paid to Muslims. They also explained that among the beneficiaries of *zakat* are those whose 'hearts are to be reconciled'. To them, non-Muslims could be placed within this category, but they argued that this could only be determined by the *dawah* givers (Islamic missionaries) who were active in preaching Islam to non-Muslims.

Making decisions on zakat: Imams and mosques

Imams of the mosques selected as study sites engaged in decision making around *zakat*. The *imams* of Landhies and Pangani Mosques in Nairobi guided by the *Hanafi* school of Islamic thought were looked to for guidance on *zakat* by Indian/Pakistani Muslims.[76] The *imams* of Eastleigh and Hurlingham Mosques, also in Nairobi, applied the *Shafi* school of thought and were looked upon by Somali Muslims for guidance on giving *zakat*.[77] Jaamia Mosque was seen as inclusive and representative of different ethnic groups such as the Swahilis, Arabs, Somalis, Africans, and Indians/Pakistanis, who also sought guidance from the *imam* based on the *Shafi* school on the Islamic law on *zakat*.[78] The Westlands Mosque was cited as an outlier principally because it was funded by Saudi Arabia and was subordinate to the *shura* and *ijma* of foreign *ulemas*.[79] *Imams*, therefore are

[75] Interviewee Nos. 116. Interview date 18.01.2020 Nairobi; Interviewee Nos. 119. Interview date 20.01.2020.

[76] Interviewee No. 144. Interview date 20.02.2020 Nairobi.

[77] Interviewee No. 145. Interview date 21.02.2020 Nairobi.

[78] Interviewee No. 120. Interview date 24.01.2020 Nairobi.

[79] Interviewee No. 118. Interview date 19.01.2020 Nairobi.

taken as **authority** figures by the different Muslim ethnic groups when making decisions on the use of *zakat*.

Clearly, the boundaries between the Muslim ethnic groups are socially constructed. One respondent also revealed that Muslim fragmentation is:

> ...[so] deeply engrained, that the Indians will never agree with the Somalis and the Somalis will never agree with the Arabs. It's as if they are each possessed to claiming superiority over the other. They can't even agree on when Ramadhan begins. The Somalis will defy the Kadhi, the Arabs will look towards Saudi and the Indians will keep to their bubble because to them everything an Arab Muslim will say is 'Wahabbi!' This imagined group supremacy has really disunited the Muslims.[80]

Seemingly, the Muslim social reality is multiple, processual, and constructed. This has resulted in class differentiation, conflict, disunity, mistrust, and exclusion. In turn, this has resulted into the fragmentation of *zakat*, with multiple outlets through which *zakat* is collected, matched with ethnic group beneficiaries, and distributed internally.

Making decisions on zakat: household level

Those Muslims who pay *zakat* directly to the poor base their decisions on **impact**. *Shura* and *ijma* are not usually performed. The individual *zakat* payers usually give out their *zakat* directly to the poor Muslims who come to 'beg at the mosques',[81] 'those family members who ask me to give them my *zakat*',[82] 'when I know my neighbour is in need',[83] and 'sometimes I don't know who to give my *zakat*, so normally I just give to the *imam*; you know their salaries are not enough and they really live poor lives'.[84] Some households consult each other on whom to support with their *zakat*. Other

---

80 Interviewee No. 123. Interview date 26.01.2020 Mombasa.

81 Interviewee No. 94. Interview date 13.12.2019 Mombasa.

82 Interviewee No. 67. Interview date 11.12.2019 Mombasa .

83 Interviewee No. 28. Interview date 07.12.2019 Nairobi .

84 Interviewee No. 4. Interview date 04.12.2019 Nairobi.

households either give their *zakat* to their informal groups, or to finance social projects such as digging wells, paying for the education of orphans, or buying bulk ration for poor families.[85]

The governance of *zakat* in Kenya: An adaptive system based around routine solidarity

Maintaining group identity and control of zakat

The analyses made thus far reveal that decisions around the understanding and use of *zakat* are made as part of a system that is adapted around *imams*, mosques, organisations, and scholars interpreting and giving meaning to Islamic law. Such an adaptive system has resulted from the routine practice of Muslims, referring Islamic law to those they consider as **authority** figures. This routine has also emerged out of Muslim group-solidarity, and an *exclusive decision-making pattern* across the institutional, group-based and household levels through which Muslim relationships and consent are negotiated.

The practice of collecting and distributing *zakat* at group level has created invisible boundaries. Stratification has resulted from the need to preserve group **identity** and **control** of agency around the giving and use of *zakat*. Differences in group adherence to a particular school of Islamic thought has also divided collective decision-making by Muslims on common objectives. This will have implications when getting consensus from Muslims on the use of *zakat* by the Kenyan Government to finance health. Arabs and Somalis were criticised 'as bent on pursuing political interests'[86], and Swahilis and Indians/Pakistanis as more focused on 'entertainment, celebrating *maulid* (the Prophet's (صلى الله عليه وسلم) birthday) and asking for donations for this and that; it never stops.'[87] These cleavages of interest currently separate the Muslim community from a collective *shura* (consensus). Whether these boundaries are open to social reconstruction

[85] Interviewee Nos. 133,134,135,136. Interview date 15.02.2020 Nairobi .

[86] Interviewee No. 139. Interview date 15.02.2020 Nairobi.

[87] ibid.

and negotiation was discussed during the *halaqa* with the *ustadhas* from different groups,[88] authority figures from a leading Muslim organisation, and Muslim Government officers.

Consensus on zakat beneficiaries and flexibility as to purpose

The findings emphasised that the rules on *zakat* are historically established. The *Qur'an* is very clear on its use. *Zakat* has come to be resonated with giving to the poor. The poor are also stratified based on their groups. The functional goal of *zakat* is also determined at the group level. This has led to routine based giving of *zakat* between the rich and poor of different Muslim groups. Thus, the motivation to accept *zakat* for financing health, including non-Muslims, and to abide collectively by this decision, will only come from changing this routine. However, despite the differences among the Muslim groups and their schools of thought, the beneficiaries of *zakat* are not disputed. Non-Muslims are not considered as *zakat* beneficiaries.[89] But, the purpose toward which *zakat* is to be used is open for discussion. During the *halaqa*, I asked the respondents to discuss the option of giving *zakat* to the state to finance health and to include non-Muslims as beneficiaries. Two female respondents, one from government and the other, a prominent scholar had the following to say:

> Zakat to finance health is a public issue and if this discussion is to have any legitimacy, it must be considered by the ulema, and not at an individual level. An individual can decide to give his zakat to pay the medical bill of his non-Muslim parent, for example, but when you want to collect zakat at a national level and give it to the Government with which it can support the public healthcare system, we must all **consent** to this.[90]
>
> Our **consent** can only be arrived at after we discuss as the ulema, consult our books, go back to the guidance of Prophet Muhammad, peace be on him, and consider the pros and cons of giving zakat to

---

[88] From the Indian, Swahili and Arab groups.

[89] Interviewee Nos. 133,134,135,136. Interview date 15.02.2020 Nairobi.

[90] Interviewee No. 140. Interview date 15.02.2020 Nairobi.

> the Government for this aim. We must arrive at a decision within this system that we have adapted to, and the Government also, if it wants to benefit from zakat – it must also unconditionally adapt to our system.[91]

The word 'adapt' was mentioned 17 times during the *halaqa*. Islam was referred to as this system to which 'we must adapt'.[92] This adaptive system forms the basis of arriving at a legal decision. Muslims use the adaptive system as a decision-making criterion. The decision will then be binding to all Muslims, and that is an output of the adaptive system of the Muslim society. The different Muslim groups also contribute to the adaptive system, by reinforcing routine solidarity. Group-level contribution to adaptation insofar as *zakat* is concerned, has aided its efficient organisation. Most of the Muslim groups gave out *zakat* based on the **impact** it would create and the **development** it would foster. From my interviews, I could gather that the institutions, groups, and households as part of the adaptive system was conceptualised around *imams*, mosques, organisations, and scholars interpreting and giving meaning to Islamic law. Therefore, these institutions and scholars have much to contribute to the *zakat* system, by way of facilitating the predictions of how *zakat* payers will behave. I find that it is at these institutional, group and household levels that decisions on whether *zakat* can be used to finance health, including the health of non-Muslims, and giving *zakat* to the Government can be debated and negotiated.

One of the most common patterns observed in considering decision-making on *zakat* from an institutional and group level reveals that the decision is concentrated in the hands of a few, and such decisions are almost always considered routine. There is no single locus of decision-making – but rather several loci, each differently structured. Decision makers are free to commit the funds of institutions and groups but must report to the members and explain how the *zakat* was used. These decision makers were able to reach the greatest amount of agreement among their

---

[91] Interviewee No. 137. Interview date 15.02.2020 Nairobi.

[92] ibid.

members on the distribution of *zakat* when routine practice was suggested. Routine maintenance at institutional and group level in giving *zakat* is also systematically built and nurtured by the *imams,* who insist on the congregation helping the poor and needy Muslims during sermons.[93]

Towards unity on zakat

The problem of Muslim fragmentation across institutions and groups has created a conspicuous lack of communication among them, in advancing together in pursuit of a common goal – for example, using *zakat* to finance health, or build a hospital. The problem of separate Muslim groups based on ethnicity– Somalis, Arabs, Indians, and Swahilis means that they look within their own groups to decide on affairs of concern to them. Any success, therefore, in influencing the entire Muslim population will have to be through uniting the leaders of these diverse groups of Muslims.

Successful participation of the Muslims in giving *zakat* to the state is also related to this unity. This unity can be achieved through the creation of a common goal, for example, financing health. All must agree to use *zakat* for this specific purpose. It is certainly not simple. Institutions and groups organised around a particular school of thought adds significance to the sociological problem of fragmentation in the Muslim community. Their routine-based decisions around the distribution of *zakat* reinforces their adaptive system.

Despite these differences, these institutions and groups help fulfil the obligation of the *zakat* payer based on how they interpret the Islamic law on *zakat* using either *Shafi* or *Hanafi* jurisprudence. In this regard, a Muslim male scholar explained that plural approaches to 'regulating the use of *zakat* at institutional level are only based on the schools of Islamic thought from which no derogation is accepted. The *Hanafi* school, for instance requires that *zakat* must be handed to the beneficiary, he must possess the ownership

---

[93] Interviewee Nos. 108,109,110,111. Interview date 09.01.2020 Mombasa (Telephone). Interviewee Nos. 112. Interview date 13.01.2020 Nairobi. Interviewee Nos. 113 and 114. Interview date 14.01.2020 Nairobi. Interviewee No. 115. Interview date 17.01.2020 Nairobi.

of the money, it is his to do as he pleases.'[94] In this regard, the scholar cautioned against giving *zakat* to the state. His view was that 'the purpose of *zakat* is to relieve economic hardship, and this has been the practice of *zakat* for us. Giving it to finance health means cutting off the annual supply chain of money for poor households. *Zakat* creates a direct relationship between the payer and the beneficiary, there should be no intermediary, especially not the Government of Kenya'.[95]

The data from Group 2 Muslim male and female respondents has established the practice of *zakat* in Kenya, and the dominant schools of thought that influence decision-making on *zakat*. It also revealed the mixed Muslim perspectives on whether *zakat* can be used to finance health. Importantly, it confirmed that *zakat* cannot be given to non-Muslims except where necessary, and absolutely rejected giving *zakat* to the Government, or Government involvement.

Responses from members of parliament, healthcare workers, academics, people of different faiths and an NGO (Group 3)

Thus far, diverse interviews focusing on Muslim views on financing health using *zakat* have been discussed. This section provides the study with a systematic understanding of how the non-Muslim interviewees cast light on Muslim belief and practice. This would contribute to new knowledge on the interpretation of Islamic law on *zakat,* and on human rights law on financing health using *zakat,* from non-Muslim perspectives.

I begin by including extracts from my interviews with Members of Parliament, whose views generally reflected the concerns raised by most of the other respondents interviewed as part of Group 3.

A male Christian Member of Parliament explained that:

[94] Interviewee No. 144. Interview date 20.02.2020 Nairobi.

[95] ibid.

> Our [Kenyan] Constitution begins with acknowledging the supremacy of the Almighty God of all creation and confirms pride in Kenya's religious diversity. When you consider Article 8 – this article tells the Government to stay away from religion. You know, the Muslims are a very emotive people and no mheshimiwa [Member of Parliament] will want to be involved in telling them how to practice their religion…[96]

This interviewee reiterated that the Kenyan Constitution separates the state from religion. He argued that if the Kenyan Government was to take and use *zakat* to finance health, it would be a constitutional violation if the Government applied Islamic law to regulate its use. The interviewee recognised the **authority** of Islamic law in guiding Muslim decisions, free from Government interference. In considering the usefulness of *zakat* as an additional source of revenue for the Government, the interviewee explained that:

> …This zakat… I have never thought much of it… of it being considered to support the Government in financing health. But if the Muslim leaders were to come to us and tell us that they want to support us to provide medical equipment for our hospitals, surely, will we refuse to accept? The Government always works on a deficit budget and any financial support is welcomed...[97]

The interviewee's response here indicates that, for the Government to accept to take *zakat*, it must first be offered by the Muslim leaders. *Zakat* is placed by the interviewee as part of 'any financial support' that can be made available to the Government. This resonates with the *maximum available resources* (MAR) obligation under human rights law, as part of the state's duty to finance human rights. This empirical reference to *zakat* as 'financial support' can be seen as echoing the current literature on MAR to recognising *zakat*. This literature was discussed in Chapter 2. Another male Christian Member of Parliament picking up on the acceptance of *zakat* by

96 Interviewee No. 163. Interview dates between 4-9.11.2020 Nairobi (Telephone/Texts).
97 Interviewee No. 163. Interview dates between 4-9.11.2020 Nairobi (Telephone/Texts)

the Government recognised that any such acceptance will have conditions attached to it. He said:

> I understand that the use of zakat will be conditional, and these conditions are listed in the Muslim Holy Books. I do not think if the Minister of Finance when he allocates the zakat to the health budget will be guided by these conditions. I mean in your project summary you explained the purpose of zakat and who its beneficiaries are – now if zakat is donated to us and we buy an MRI machine, are we supposed to police the machine so that only the beneficiaries mentioned are permissible patients?[98]

From this it can be established that any reference to conditions by Muslims in giving *zakat* to the Government will be rejected. Conditions will require the Government to monitor whether Islamic law is being adhered to. I posed a question to another male Christian MP as to whether this would violate Article 8 of the Constitution, which stipulates state separation from religion. The MP explained this, as follows:

> If the zakat is given to us, you know the health budget is a pool of funds nationally drawn, internationally supported with different aid forms and disbursed at county level – how will we separate zakat from the entire budget if we include it as part of the Government's health budget? I think decisions around giving zakat to the Government should not be made with religious conditions in mind. That will complicate the entire process… I do respect the Muslim religion, and I know that Muslims refer to their Holy Book for legitimacy of their actions; and zakat is part of the teachings of Islam, and it cannot be separated from its religious rules. We will not apply these religious conditions. Article 8 cannot accept Islam as part of the legislature's modus operandi. It is for the Muslims to decide by

[98] Interviewee No. 164. Interview dates between 15-21.11.2020 Nairobi (Telephone/Texts).

reference to their books and clergy whether they can donate zakat, and not put across conditions for its use.[99]

Similarly, the other respondents who were interviewed under this group raised **legality** concerns over the application of Islamic law in Kenya in the governance of *zakat*. According to them, 'religious donations to the Government should be devoid of conditions',[100] 'Government does not enforce conditions that are not part of its legislative system',[101] and 'nowhere in the Constitution will you find reference to Government being under an obligation to apply laws that do not originate from the constitution itself'.[102]

Authority was a strong reference point for the MPs. I further interrogated this latter view, by explaining that under Article 2(4), the Constitution recognised the legal validity of any law only if it was not inconsistent with the Constitution. Therefore, I argued that this article had the effect of giving recognition to the Islamic law conditions on *zakat*. An MP explained that my view was correct, to the extent that 'any such law was being applied at a personal or private level and not where the Government is called upon to apply such law'.[103] These views presented here resonate with the themes of **authority** of the state, and **legality** of action – themes that are clearly desiderata of any legal system, in guiding Government on whether to accept *zakat* with its Islamic conditions.

The respondents were recognisant of the impact the *Qur'an* and *sunna* had on the daily lives of Muslims and acknowledged that this presented a significant challenge to a non-Islamic legal system when faced with the option to accept assistance conditional on the application of a divine source

---

[99] Interviewee No. 165. Interview dates between 12-14.11.2020 Nairobi (Telephone/Texts)

[100] Interviewee No. 164. Interview dates between 15-21.11.2020 Nairobi (Telephone/Texts)

[101] Interviewee No. 163. Interview dates 12-14.11.2020 Nairobi (Telephone/Texts)

[102] Interviewee No. 150. Interview date 12.05.2020 Nairobi (Telephone)

[103] Interviewee No. 163. Interview date 12.05.2020 Nairobi (Telephone)

of law. The MP who is a lawyer and was part of the Committee set up to draft the 2010 Constitution of Kenya pointed out that:

> The state is under an obligation to accept international assistance and cooperation and this, in my opinion, also extends to domestic assistance and cooperation. Accepting assistance is important toward the progressive realisation of right to health for instance. Going by this, if zakat is given to assist the Government to partly finance health, it can be given on the condition that the zakat is only to be used for poor cancer patients for example or buying a dialysis machine – there is no harm in imposing conditions on philanthropy. But these conditions cannot be religious; instead, they must reflect the social reality of the health problem in the country that the donations will help mitigate.[104]

Seemingly, the views captured here posit that the decisions around *zakat* should be based on its **impact** on **development,** rather than framing its use under religious conditions.

Respondents interviewed as part of the focus group made up of people of different faiths saw Government as a 'detached observer of religion',[105]

> By offering zakat to the Government, you are asking the Government to interpret scripture. How will Government go about this? Legal interpretation is not the same as scriptural interpretation. Government should not be party to enforce religious terms. It would be better, instead, for the Muslims to organise themselves and offer zakat-funded free medical care.[106]

Their emphasise was in keeping religion separate from the state. It is quite clear, after having considered the respondents' views, that questions around giving *zakat* beyond Islamic institutions or to individual Muslim

---

[104] Interviewee No. 166. Interview date 21.11.2020 Nairobi (Zoom)
[105] Interviewee No. 160. Interview date 23.09.2020 Nairobi (Zoom)
[106] Interviewee No. 157. Interview date 23.09.2020 Nairobi (Zoom)

beneficiaries can only be legally presented by the **consent** of the Muslims. If the Kenyan state is singled out as a recipient of *zakat,* then its government must also give its **consent** to accepting the funds (see discussion in Chapter 5). Since both parties claim **authority**, the former over its funds and the latter over its citizens, when they choose to share their **authority** with another, they do so on their own terms. The Islamic conditions on *zakat* are authoritative, and not open to reform or negotiation. These Islamic conditions, however, do not bind the Kenyan state. The former presents normative authority and the latter political. The key issue that emerges, therefore, is how could **consent** be achieved by both groups in the administration of *zakat*?

One respondent suggested that

> this (consent) problem can be solved by logically thinking of the opportunity presented to the Government. The Government has partnered with the private sector on many climate-mitigation projects for example. Only farmers in ASAL [Arid and Semi-Arid Lands] are supported under these projects. The projects are designed jointly with the Government and stakeholders. This is how the subject of zakat should also be approached. It is a win for Muslims and the Government. Muslims can place their conditions without framing them as religious rules but as aid conditionalities and the Government can accept them as part of meeting you know a target under the health goal.[107]

Perhaps in applying this logic of 'opportunity', Muslims and the Government of Kenya can reach some consensus on using *zakat* to finance health specifically targeted towards supporting access to healthcare for people living in poverty.

Finally, when conceptualising the interpretation of the MAR obligation to potentially consider the inclusion of *zakat,* such interpretative exercise must be conscious of first requiring the **consent** of all parties to be involved.

---

[107] Interviewee No. 155. Interview date 3-5.08.2020 Nairobi (Email)

According to a professor at the University of Nairobi whom I spoke to on phone,

> Human rights are commitments to justice. The underlying objective of zakat, as I understand it, resonates with promoting justice. Supporting the poor is an act of justice. So, I think, framing the achievement of a human right along the idea of promoting justice provides this leeway– to introduce religion-based financing to support provision of healthcare of the poor in a particular area.[108]

Since *zakat* is associated with justice, it should then be considered or used to inform the selection of various meanings we intend to generate from interpreting human rights.

Conclusion

This chapter records expert, political, personal and group intellectual views on the six key questions outlined in the introduction. The pivot upon which the whole of the argument of the chapter turns is of course, the construction of *zakat* within Kenya's socio-legal system, and as part of human rights law. All legal corollaries around the governance of *zakat* were found to be based on the process of interpretation and the influence of **authority**. For the Muslims, the *Qur'an* was their first source of reference. The *imams* and scholars were tasked with the function to draw out its doctrinal meaning. Two schools of jurisprudence aided them with the criteria to do this. However, in the context of the questions asked, the *imams* and scholars have not attempted to grapple with those questions outside the *Hanafi* and *Shafi* schools. For the Government, the Constitution represented the foundation of its authority. The Constitution overrides the application of Islamic conditions, should the Government decide to accept to take *zakat*.

All moral corollaries around the governance of *zakat* were found to be based on the themes of **consent, control, development, identity, impact,**

---

[108] Interviewee No. 150. Interview date 12.05.2020 Nairobi (Telephone)

and **trust**. These themes were divided across the stratified Muslim groups, and their internal objectives based around their schools of thought. The use of *zakat* for health and benefitting non-Muslims were considered as part of their social responsibility toward redistribution of their sources of revenue, in supporting development. This, however, was collectively agreed upon to be in the interests of their fellow poor Muslims only. On the part of the MPs interviewed, the legal barriers to accepting *zakat* with its Islamic conditions seemed to be mitigated by considering the logic of opportunity presented by the *zakat* funds to support its health budget. However, giving *zakat* to the Government for this purpose itself was a contested view, with most Muslim respondents opposing such practice.

The empirical analysis reveals that the Muslim interviewees generally opposed giving *zakat* to the Kenyan Government. This is despite the discussion in the previous chapters that confirm the practicability of *zakat* to finance health under human rights, Islamic law and the Kenyan legal system, albeit under specific conditions. The phenomenological accounts given by interviewees – that explained how they understood, interpreted, and gave meaning to norms and doctrine – revealed that considerations other than law influenced their views on offering *zakat* to the Government to finance health. None of the interviewees mentioned the political tensions with the state (discussed in Chapter 6) when explaining their position on giving *zakat* to the state. These political tensions seemed not to influence Muslim perspectives on the six questions asked but for some the prevalence of corruption in government informed their views against giving *zakat* to the state. For them, what mattered was their understanding of whether Islamic law allowed *zakat* to be used to finance health, and the socio-economic needs towards which *zakat* was best directed.

This chapter, while having presented the first original research on *zakat* in Kenya, and its contemplated usage for financing health at the public level, has shown the phenomenology of beliefs on all sides and whether normative proposals will work in practice. Legal pluralism within Kenya's constitutional legal system is receptive to the application of Islamic law when confined to the private sphere. The Government cannot enforce Islamic law beyond what it has constitutionally accepted to include as part of its judicial system. If it were to do this, then the Islamic law to be applied must be presented as principles or conditions from the point of view of justice. All reference to Islamic law must be removed if it is to have the force of law outside the private sphere or personal status law.

The chapter's findings can be situated within the larger law and politics of doctrine versus practice. On the one hand, doctrinal and legal analyses of Islamic law, human rights law, and the Kenyan Constitution support the use of *zakat* to finance health. These analyses suggest that the use of *zakat* is not only legally permissible but also socially desirable, given the health challenges facing many low-income and poor individuals in Kenya. On the other hand, fieldwork has revealed that local stakeholders, including Muslim leaders and faith-based organisations, were averse to the use of *zakat* as a source of revenue for health financing. This suggests a disjuncture between doctrinal analyses and the actual practices and beliefs of those who are meant to implement such policies.

The tension between doctrine and practice raises important questions about the feasibility and desirability of using religious sources of revenue for public purposes. The reluctance of local stakeholders to endorse the use of *zakat* as a source of revenue may be seen as an expression of their own legal norms and values, which may be in tension with the legal norms and values of the wider society. This tension raises important questions about how to balance competing legal claims and interests, and how to ensure accountability and transparency in the administration of public funds. The findings highlight the complexities of using religious sources of revenue for public purposes, and the need to engage with the views and perspectives of local stakeholders in the design and implementation of such policies as part of socio-legal work. The findings also underscore the importance of understanding the law and politics of doctrine versus practice, and the need to reconcile competing legal claims and interests in a pluralistic and diverse society.

Chapter 8
Conclusion

Overview

This book has provided a comprehensive and interdisciplinary analysis of the legal relationship between *zakat* and financing public health in Kenya, examining the convergence of human rights law, Islamic law, and constitutional law. By incorporating both doctrinal and empirical aspects, the study has shed light on the complex interplay between these legal frameworks and the practical realities on the ground. The doctrinal aspect of the book serves as a theoretical foundation, examining the legal permissibility of recognising and including *zakat* as part of the maximum available resources' obligation under human rights law. It also analyses Islamic doctrinal perspectives on using *zakat* for financing health and the constitutional concerns surrounding the Kenyan state's acceptance of *zakat* with its Islamic conditions for financing public health. This analysis provides a solid foundation for understanding the legal complexities and nuances involved in this interdisciplinary study.

The empirical aspect of the book, on the other hand, enriches the analysis by providing valuable insights into the practical realities and challenges that may impact the implementation of the proposed solutions. It contextualises the doctrinal findings within the socio-political landscape of Kenya, highlights potential implementation challenges arising from the influence of politics and social factors on people's interpretation and understanding of the doctrine, and emphasises the importance of adopting a holistic approach to socio-legal scholarship. The relationship between the doctrinal and empirical aspects of the book is complementary and symbiotic, demonstrating the importance of incorporating both theoretical and practical perspectives in socio-legal scholarship. The interdisciplinary analysis presented in the book underscores the complexity and fluidity of legal systems, especially when different legal frameworks interact, and highlights the need for scholars to consider the role of politics, power dynamics, and cultural beliefs in shaping the application and interpretation of legal principles.

Having presented this overview, I now turn to the key contributions to scholarship made in the book.

Contributions to Scholarship

This book has highlighted a significant challenge in implementing the findings from the doctrinal analysis of Islamic law, human rights law, and the Kenyan Constitution that supports the use of *zakat* to finance health. Local stakeholders, including Muslim leaders and faith-based organisations, have expressed reluctance and distrust towards the implementation of these findings. Fieldwork provided phenomenological accounts that explained why local stakeholders are averse to implementing these findings. There is a lack of trust in the state, as it has historically failed to deliver on its promises, and there is a sense of marginalisation and disempowerment among the Muslim population in Kenya. Additionally, the research found that the Muslim community is divided along ethnic lines, with a tendency to insulate themselves in their own mosques and adhere to traditional Islamic schools that have not addressed the issues raised in the research. This highlights an important aspect of the law and politics of doctrine versus practice, where the theoretical framework and legal analysis may provide a solid foundation for policy and decision-making, but its effectiveness in practice is often determined by the attitudes and beliefs of local stakeholders.

While the doctrinal analysis and legal theory provide a solid framework for understanding the permissibility of using *zakat* to finance health, the reality on the ground may not always match up to these ideals. Fieldwork uncovered the issues surrounding the reluctance of local stakeholders to endorse the use of *zakat* as a source of revenue. This is because the real-world application of *zakat* is complex and requires an understanding of the social, cultural, and political context in which it is being implemented. Fieldwork allowed for the collection of rich and nuanced data that could not be obtained through doctrinal analysis alone, thereby revealing the realities of implementing *zakat* in the Kenyan context.

By understanding the concerns of local stakeholders, the book offers a deep understanding of how the implementation of Islamic law intersects with the politics of healthcare financing in Kenya. By undertaking phenomenological accounts from local stakeholders, including Muslim leaders and faith-based organisations, the book unveils the mistrust of the state and the insularity of Muslim groups that hinder the implementation of *zakat* for healthcare financing. This original contribution sheds light on how the practice of Islamic law is embedded in the socio-political realities of Kenya, which is often neglected in the doctrinal and legal analysis.

Socio legal scholarship

The book makes significant contributions to socio-legal scholarship. Firstly, it highlights the importance of understanding the boundaries of claims around religious groups contributing to the state's financing of public services. By exploring the potential use of *zakat* as a source of revenue for public health in Kenya, the book demonstrates how an existing religious obligation can be leveraged to support the poor and those in need without imposing a new burden on the community. This exploration of how religious communities can contribute to public service financing is particularly relevant in pluralistic societies where diverse communities have varying levels of access to public services. Secondly, the book advances socio-legal scholarship by demonstrating the complexity of legal systems and the need for interdisciplinary approaches. The proposition that the convergence of human rights law, Islamic law, and constitutional law in the context of using *zakat* to finance public health in Kenya provides new interpretations and understandings of legal obligations to ensure maximum available resources for health is an important contribution. The findings from fieldwork reveal the complex relationship between law and politics and the need to consider the social and political dynamics that shape the implementation and interpretation of legal frameworks. This highlights the importance of phenomenological accounts in socio-legal scholarship to provide a more comprehensive understanding of the realities of legal frameworks in practice.

The research also significantly advances human rights, Islamic law, and constitutional law scholarship and contributes to their literature in several ways.

Key takeaways

Firstly, by examining the relationship between human rights law, Islamic law, and constitutional law, the study offers new insights into how legal frameworks can interact and influence each other in the context of public health financing. This highlights the complexity and fluidity of legal systems and the need for an interdisciplinary approach to analyse legal issues.

Secondly, the research advances human rights law scholarship by exploring the potential for convergence and innovation between different legal frameworks in addressing complex legal problems. By arguing that non-state funds such as *zakat* can be included in the maximum available resources' obligation under human rights law, the research broadens the scope of the obligation and highlights the potential for innovative solutions to complex legal problems. This argument also underscores the importance of understanding the political and social dynamics that shape the implementation and interpretation of human rights obligations. It also highlights the potential constitutional and political concerns associated with the inclusion of faith-based funds, such as zakat, in the fulfilment of MAR obligations. Moreover, the book shows that the MAR obligation under human rights law is still evolving, and there is a need for a comprehensive financial MAR scope.

Thirdly, the research contributes to Islamic law scholarship by demonstrating the plasticity of the *Qur'an* and the legitimacy of its interpretation. The book highlights the importance of considering the social, cultural, and political context in which Islamic law is applied and underscores the need for a nuanced understanding of the relationship between law and religion. The book's analysis of *zakat* and its potential use as a source of revenue for public health financing in Kenya underscores the importance of considering the plurality and inbuilt transformative processes of Islamic law. Its examination of the potential use of zakat as a domestic resource for supporting the obligations of the Kenyan state under the right to health raises important questions about the relationship between the state and religious communities, as the use of religious non-state actors to support state budgets may be complex and raise concerns about religious bias or exclusion of non-members of the particular faith. The book acknowledges the importance of constitutional law in determining whether *zakat* can be legally recognized as a source of revenue for public health in Kenya.

Fourthly, the research contributes to constitutional law scholarship by highlighting the importance of considering the specific legal and political context in which constitutional principles are applied. The book's analysis of the Kenyan Constitution's relevance to the potential use of zakat as a source of revenue for public health financing underscores the need for a comprehensive understanding of the legal and political factors that shape constitutional interpretation and implementation. It highlights the tension between religious obligations and state power raising important questions about how to balance competing legal claims and interests and accommodate religious diversity within a secular state. The book's interdisciplinary approach to examining legal issues, consideration of social and political context, and recognition of the complexity and fluidity of legal systems contribute to these fields' scholarship and literature. The research underscores the importance of engaging with the pluralism and diversity of legal systems and the need for an interdisciplinary approach to address complex legal problems.

Specific contributions on the various themes under human rights, Islamic law, constitutional law and *zakat* are discussed next.

Human rights

I have explained that in meeting its financing responsibilities under article 43(1)(a) of the Constitution of Kenya, and article 12(1) of the International Covenant on Economic, Social and Cultural Rights (ICESCR) the government is obliged to utilise to their maximum all locally available resources and to seek international assistance and cooperation to finance health. In so doing, human rights law acknowledges the problem of resource limitations. Therefore, the practicability of linking *zakat* to finance health is justified based on the recurring revenue shortages that have prevented the Government of Kenya from adequately financing health in the country. This allows for further scrutiny into the human rights principle of *maximum available resources* to determine the validity of introducing *zakat,* as part of the available resources recognised under human rights law and scholarship.

The recognition by An Naim[1], Donnelly[2], Brown[3], and Goodhart[4] of socio-cultural influences in understanding and giving meaning to the content of human rights was extended by the book, to introduce and question whether Islamic law and its conditions on the use of *zakat* could suggest new meanings to the content of human rights law. This inquiry contributed towards critiquing the universality aspect of human rights, to allow for new interpretations or broadening the meaning of human rights law from an Islamic perspective. In this regard, an evolutive interpretation was applied, to broaden the meaning of *maximum available resources,* and to extend it to include *zakat*. The book adds a focus on *zakat* to literature on *maximum*

---

1 A An-Naim and F Deng (eds), *Human Rights in Africa. Cross Cultural Perspectives* (The Brookings Institution, 1990).

2 J Donnelly, 'The Relative Universality of Human Rights' (2007) *Human Rights Quarterly* Vol 29, No 2 281-306.

3 C Brown, 'Universal human rights: A critique' (2007) *The International Journal of Human Rights,* Volume 1, Issue 2, 41-65.

4 M Goodhart, 'Neither Relative nor Universal: A Response to Donnelly' (2008) *Human Rights Quarterly,* Vol 30, No1, 183-193.

available resources by Waris[5], Balakrishnan[6], Elson[7], Mcintyre[8], and Robertson[9]. Identifying within human rights how to legally place *zakat* as part of seeking domestic assistance and cooperation to finance health is the significant contribution made to the literature. The book recommends that the phrase *'to the maximum of its available resources'* needs to be interpreted broadly by the Kenyan Government and the Committee on Economic Social and Cultural Rights (CESCR), since the phrase carries with it an implicit justification of the use of *zakat*.

Islamic law

Legal permissibility under human rights law to exact *zakat* as part of the pool of funds that can be made available to a state to finance health does not extend to Islamic law. Thus, a separate examination of Islamic law and scholarship on *zakat* was conducted, to identify the existence of legal criteria that permits including *zakat* as part of the financing framework on the right to health. This additional contribution under Islamic law provided for specific scrutiny in analysing linkages between Islamic law and human rights law. Previously, Ramadhan signalled the use of *zakat* to contribute to the wellbeing of Muslims living in the west.[10] He recommends to those Muslims to pool their *zakat* to support the economic wellbeing of the poor amongst them. The focus of his argument was to influence those Muslims to think about how they can support the achievement of their own

---

[5] A Waris, *Financing Africa* (Cameroon: Langaa, 2019).

[6] R Balakrishnan, D Elson, J Heintz, and N Lusiani. *Maximum Available Resources and Human Rights: Analytical Report* (New Brunswick, NJ: Rutgers, 2011).

[7] D Elson, R Balakrishnan and J Heintz, 'Public Finance, Maximum Available Resources and Human Rights', In: Nolan, A., O'Connell, R., and Harvey C. *Human Rights and Public Finance. Budgets and the Promotion of Economic and Social Rights* (Oxford: Hart Publishing Ltd, 2013)

[8] Di Mcintyre, M Filip, and J A Røttingen, 'What Level of Domestic Government Health Expenditure Should We Aspire to for Universal Health Coverage?' *Health Economics, Policy, and Law* 12, No 2 (April 2017): 125–37.

[9] RE Robertson, 'Measuring State Compliance with the Obligation to Devote the Maximum Available Resources to Realising Economic, Social, and Cultural Rights', (1994): *Human Rights Quarterly* 16:693–714.

[10] T Ramadhan, *Western Muslims and the Future of Islam* (Oxford: Oxford University Press, 2004).

wellbeing in western countries. The persuasiveness of Ramadhan's argument was considered in the book, by extending it to consider the role of *zakat* in Kenya towards financing health, without limiting it to Muslims as the beneficiaries of *zakat and* giving it to the Kenyan state for such use.

The inquiry pushed the book to assess the correct interpretation of the Islamic law on *zakat*, and whether this was different from the scholastic views that disputed the giving of *zakat* to non-Muslims and to a non-Islamic state. Finding a link between the right to health with the *maqasid al shari'ah* (objectives of Islamic law)[11] presented a novel approach, through which the research confirmed that a conditional permissibility existed in using *zakat* to finance health, and giving it to a non-Islamic state. This finding was built on a recognition of health as a norm within the *maqasid al shari'ah,* and was referred to, in justifying the link between *zakat* and financing health. This finding challenged the established views within Islamic scholarship against giving *zakat* to non-Muslims.

It went further, to create new knowledge on the Islamic position on giving *zakat* to a non-Islamic state to use for supporting healthcare. It established that *zakat* can be offered to non-Islamic states, but only if their governments agree to apply Islamic norms governing its use. This finding relates with Tibi's scholarship, which argues that Islamic law should not be confined to Islamic nations;[12] instead, it can be recognised as a source of law for Muslims and implemented by a non-Islamic state. The book resonates with Tibi's approach, to regard Islamic law as a source of law that can be applied by any state – despite the opposing views given by Qutb, that Islamic law provides no authority to a non-Islamic state to apply or exercise any aspect of its law.[13] Qutb's views have been challenged by the Kenyan state, that

---

[11] Discussed in Chapter 4. The *maqasid al shari'ah* is predicated on certain benefits to the individual and the community (protecting life, property). Islamic law is designed to protect these benefits and to facilitate the improvement and perfection of the conditions of human life on earth. One such maqasid is the protection of life through which the health and wellbeing of an individual is given priority.

[12] B Tibi, *The Challenge of Fundamentalism: Political Islam and the New World Disorder* (Berkeley and Los Angeles: University of California Press, 1998).

[13] S Qutb, Milestones (SIME Journal, 2005).

recognises, applies and through its judiciary enforces Muslim personal law as part of its Constitution. Overall, the findings under human rights and Islamic law establish the positions of the two laws towards partly solving revenue limitations in financing health. Addressing whether this suffices to permit the Kenyan Government to accept *zakat* poses constitutional challenges which were addressed by critically examining the Constitution of Kenya against scant literature.

The Constitution of Kenya

Two pertinent constitutional issues were clarified in considering the legal validity and practicability of the use of *zakat* to finance health under the Kenyan legal system. First, the constitutional implications of favouring an evolutive approach to justify reading the ICESCR as a living instrument, capable of absorbing religious norms and accordingly interpreting article 43(1)(a) of the Constitution on the right to health. Second, the legal validity in applying Islamic norms on regulating the use of *zakat* under a constitutional state committed to separating law from religion. Legal pluralism was taken as the methodology to answer these two questions. Rachuonyo claims that positivist theory underpinned the Constitution of Kenya.[14] The Constitution also permits the existence of multiple normative systems, on condition that their norms remain consistent with the Constitution. The problem identified here is that the legal-centric view that the Constitution seemingly established was challenged by the constitutional recognition that was given to those aspects of Muslim personal law that were inconsistent with the Constitution. This exposed a constitutional controversy that required clarification on the parameters within which article 8 of the Constitution: separating the state from religion, operates.

Furthermore, the placing of the historic *kadhis'* courts in the Constitution and recognising Muslim personal law as part of the sources of law in Kenya portrayed a legal system that challenged article 8. The study, therefore,

---

[14] J O Rachuonyo, 'Kelsen's Grundnorm in modern Constitution Making: The Kenya Case,' (1987) *Law and Politics in Africa, Asia and Latin America*, Vol 20, No 4.

disputes the acceptance of legal positivism as the theory defining the Kenyan legal system. It offers Tamanaha's[15] socio-legal positivism to characterise Kenya's legal system, and through it, gives clarity on the legal validity relating to the two constitutional issues. This is the first application of Tamanaha's theory to characterise the Kenyan legal system. It shows that the Kenyan legal system can accept Islamic norms regulating *zakat*. This argument is then further developed, using An-Naim's approach to consider Islamic law in a non-Islamic state as part of its civic reasoning process.[16] An-Naim's argument on referring to Islamic law as law – and not religious law – is sufficient to allow non-Islamic states to use its content for the common good. This book advances this innovative approach to implementing the Islamic law on *zakat* by a non-Islamic state.

Consequently, the study joins the process of civic reasoning to socio-legal positivism. to show how the Kenyan legal system produces its own ways by which it can lend the Islamic law on *zakat* a normative quality, capable of being accepted as part of the Constitution. This contribution to scholarship demonstrates the possibility of the creation of new legal norms and changes to Kenya's positive law, based around *zakat*.

Zakat

The doctrinal, normative, and theoretical considerations made under human rights law, Islamic law and the Kenyan legal system are sufficient to prove the proposition that:

> The convergence of human rights law, Islamic law, and constitutional law in the context of using zakat to finance public health in Kenya provides new interpretations and understandings of legal obligations to ensure maximum available resources for health.

---

[15] B Tamanaha, 'Socio-Legal Positivism and a General Jurisprudence', (2001) *Oxford Journal of Legal Studies*, Vol 21, No 1, 1-32.

[16] A An-Naim, 'The Compatibility Dialectic: Mediating the Legitimate Coexistence of Islamic Law and State Law', (2010) *The Modern Law Review*, Vol 73, No 1, 1-29.

However, neither the doctrinal, normative nor theoretical analyses made offer empirical insight on how the norms and doctrine around the use of *zakat* and its feasibility in financing health would be interpreted, given context and content, and implemented by stakeholders in Kenya. An understanding of the process by which these norms and doctrine acquire meaning in the Kenyan socio-political setting was discovered during fieldwork, presenting fresh insights on the phenomenological accounts on *zakat* by local stakeholders. Such empirical work was necessary to fill the gap in ascertaining the relationship between those norms, doctrine, and theory on one hand, and on the other, on how they guided the interviewees to make decisions on consenting to or opposing the use of *zakat* as a potential source of revenue with which to finance health in Kenya.

This fieldwork has looked to Islamic law, studied its methodology, absorbed it, and then made a move to interpret and reconstruct it from the perspective of Muslims in Kenya. This was done to make some contribution to the development of Islamic legal thought on *zakat* and how it could relate to the right to health. *Zakat* was examined within its historic doctrinal content and properly placed as part of Kenya's sociological context when discussing the findings from fieldwork. The relationship between the structure of the Muslim society and its *zakat* system gave insight on how specific Muslim groups understand, interpret, and make their decisions on how to apply the Islamic law on *zakat*.

The empirical analysis reveals that the interviewees generally opposed giving *zakat* to the Kenyan Government. This is despite the positive conclusions made in the previous chapters that confirm the practicability of *zakat* to finance health under human rights, Islamic law, and the Kenyan legal system, albeit under specific conditions. The phenomenological accounts given by interviewees – that explained how they understood, interpreted, and gave meaning to norms and doctrine – reveal that interpretations, perceptions and attitudes also influenced their views on offering *zakat* to the government to finance health. Stakeholders' views matter most in testing the research proposition. While the law creates avenues through which *zakat* enters the discourse around financing health, in practice, what matters is the consent of the stakeholders, without which the permissibility criteria established under human rights, Islamic law and the Kenyan legal system would remain academic insights and ideas.

Relationship between law and politics

The book also contributes to thinking about the relationship between law and politics. It demonstrates that legal frameworks are not static but rather fluid and complex, shaped by social, cultural, and political factors. This was demonstrated through the investigation of the study's proposition which led to the conclusion that while the convergence of legal frameworks may provide new interpretations and understandings of legal obligations, the actual implementation of such obligations may be hindered by social and political dynamics on the ground. Therefore, the proposition should be understood as an invitation to consider the potential of legal frameworks to address complex legal problems, but not as a guarantee of effective implementation in all circumstances.

By examining the implementation and interpretation of legal principles in practice, the book reveals that power dynamics, cultural and religious beliefs, and political structures shape the application and interpretation of legal frameworks. This underscores the importance of engaging with the perspectives of local stakeholders in the design and implementation of policies and contribute to broader debates within socio-legal scholarship about the role of non-state actors in the implementation of human rights and the potential for religious communities to play a meaningful role in shaping public policy. It also highlights the importance of socio-legal scholarship, which recognises the importance of interdisciplinary approaches to understand the interplay of legal frameworks and the implications for public health financing. The book contributes to highlighting the need to consider the social and political dynamics that shape the implementation and interpretation of legal frameworks, and the potential for convergence and innovation between different legal frameworks to address complex legal problems. In so doing, this original contribution sheds light on how the practice of Islamic law is embedded in the socio-political realities of Kenya, which is often neglected in the doctrinal and legal analysis.

Therefore, combining doctrinal analysis with empirical work provided a more nuanced understanding of how Islamic law is practiced and how it intersects with politics, contributing to the scholarship and literature on Islamic law, constitutional law, and human rights law. The book does not seek to advocate for a change in Islamic legal doctrine but rather to explore the potential for convergence and innovation between different legal frameworks in addressing complex legal problems. The fieldwork findings reveal that local stakeholders, including Muslim leaders and faith-based organisations, were not in favour of using *zakat* to finance public health in Kenya, which highlights the need to consider the complexity of legal systems and the potential disjuncture between doctrinal analysis and actual practices. The book emphasises the importance of engaging with local stakeholders and balancing competing legal claims and interests in a pluralistic and diverse society since the voluntary nature of *zakat* is a crucial aspect of its religious significance, and the state's collection of *zakat* on behalf of the Muslim community could potentially compromise religious freedom. This underscores the need for careful consideration and dialogue around the use of religious obligations to support public health financing.

Hence, in looking forward, a question arises: in practice, where would the findings of the book lead?

Looking Forward

A national model on *zakat* and policy considerations

The fieldwork on *zakat* presents a significant opportunity to understand how *zakat* is governed in Kenya, how much of *zakat* was paid by both male and female *zakat*-paying Muslims and received by FBOs, the formal and informal institutions involved in mobilising *zakat* and making decisions on its use, and the different views on giving *zakat* to the government to finance health, including the health of non-Muslims. The findings portrayed a mixed result. For some interviewees, *zakat* could be used for the benefit of non-Muslims once Muslim needs had been attended to. For others, *zakat* was needed to support Muslims, as many languish in poverty and hardship. Almost all interviewees objected to giving *zakat* to the Kenyan government, and almost all were persuaded to offer *zakat* to finance health. The question on how *zakat* can be used to achieve this purpose is what requires further in-depth investigation.

As potential directions for future research, three exploratory policy suggestions, enabled by this study's findings, are presented. These recommendations are offered as tentative and preliminary ideas.

1. The first option involves Kenyan Muslims establishing a centralized *zakat* fund, into which all Muslims would contribute their annual *zakat*, regardless of their ethnic groups or institutional affiliations. Managed by appointed Muslim officials, this independent fund would be free from government interference. The collected *zakat* could be used to finance healthcare initiatives in low-income counties, such as constructing dispensaries or clinics, or supporting government efforts by purchasing essential medical equipment and medicines for public hospitals. Challenges may arise from disagreements among Muslim groups on the fund's priorities, potential rejection of the fund by some groups, or deciding the fate of existing *zakat* collecting institutions. Further research is needed to develop a practicable *zakat* model for Kenya.

2. Similar to the establishment of *Kadhis'* courts and the *Wakf* Commission, the government could create a national *zakat* fund governed by appointed Muslim scholars. In collaboration with the government, fund managers would mobilise and distribute *zakat* funds to areas in dire need of healthcare services. To encourage participation, the government could allow Muslims to deduct *zakat* contributions from their overall income tax. This approach, however, may discriminate against other Muslim sects, such as Shia Muslims, who have separate *zakat* governance systems. The limitation of this study is that it did not include Shia Muslims in the research sample, as the focus was on the dominant views and legal rulings related to *zakat* within the Sunni tradition. The implications of not examining Shia scholarship is that the analysis

of Islamic law and *zakat* in the book are not fully representative of Islamic legal thought. This limits the applicability and relevance of the findings to the wider Muslim community, particularly the Shia. But it also presents an opportunity for further comprehensive research on *zakat* in Kenya that considers both Sunni and Shia perspectives. Achieving a government-backed national *zakat* fund would require drafting a legislative bill in collaboration with Muslim leadership and seeking public feedback before debating it in Parliament.

3. A county *zakat* fund could be established in Muslim-majority counties, with the Governor working in consultation with local Muslim leadership under Article 209(3)(c) of the Kenyan Constitution. This option appears more feasible, as Muslims could closely monitor and hold fund managers accountable for *zakat* distribution. This approach could be piloted in counties like Mombasa to test its feasibility and garner Muslim support.

Before considering these options, comprehensive research must be conducted to determine the number of Muslims paying *zakat* and the amounts contributed. This data is crucial for making informed policy decisions. A Muslim leadership forum, inclusive of all Islamic schools of thought and Muslim ethnic groups, should be organized to discuss the collective social action, establish a *zakat* strategy, and propose a realistic *zakat*-based fiscal relationship with the government.

However, these policy proposals present challenges, such as the potential blurring of state and religion lines and the risk of marginalizing non-Muslim communities. Future research should explore the experiences of other countries with religious diversity and investigate policy designs that respect religious beliefs while maintaining secular principles. Additionally, research could examine the broader social and political implications of these policies to ensure they are equitable and inclusive. Delving into these issues is beyond the scope of the current study, which focuses on the legal and doctrinal aspects of *zakat* and public health financing within the Kenyan context.

Further insights

Human rights law

The separation of state and religion has precluded *zakat* from the human rights discourse when considering fiscal approaches to financing the right to health. Existing fiscal approaches primarily focus on taxes, while community-based financing remains underexplored. Introducing *zakat* as a potential resource warrants the attention of human rights scholars. If *zakat* could partially support health financing in Kenya, as this book suggests, its consideration by the UN Committee on Economic, Social and Cultural Rights (CESCR) is both necessary and appropriate. This book initiates the exploration of *zakat's* normative expression within the Maximum Available Resources (MAR) principle and the use of state discretion under the International Covenant on Economic, Social and Cultural Rights (ICESCR) and its General Comments (GCs) 3 and 14. The CESCR should further examine the legality and utility of including *zakat* in the MAR definition. However, incorporating *zakat* into human rights law might face resistance due to concerns about the intersection of religion and state policy. This may also give rise to demands from other religious groups for similar considerations, potentially complicating the human rights framework.

Islamic law and wealth taxation

This book inquires whether Islamic law allows a non-Islamic state to use *zakat* for financing healthcare that benefits both Muslims and non-Muslims. Although *zakat* has not been extensively studied in relation to state fiscal practices, it can offer significant benefits to specific citizen groups, promoting economic empowerment. Strengthening the link between *zakat* and redistribution could provide Islamic scholars with new insights on *zakat's* role within both Islamic and non-Islamic states. This study focuses on the *sunni* tradition, and further research should consider other Islamic schools of thought, such as *shia* Islam, as they also warrant independent analysis. However, the adoption of *zakat* as a policy tool in non-Islamic states may face challenges due to differing interpretations of Islamic law and potential opposition from certain religious or political factions. This could hinder the successful implementation of *zakat* as a financing mechanism for healthcare.

Further, the discourse on wealth taxation can be significantly enriched by incorporating the Islamic concept of *zakat,* as it emphasises a moral and social dimension grounded in religious principles. The Islamic wealth taxation approach posits that wealth is a trust from God, and individuals have a responsibility to use it for societal betterment. This perspective cultivates collective responsibility and social justice, contributing to a more equitable wealth taxation system.

A key aspect of *zakat* that bolsters its fairness is its progressive nature. As the contribution is proportionate to an individual's wealth, those with greater financial resources are required to give more, fostering a more equitable distribution of wealth. This characteristic aligns with the principle of vertical equity in taxation, whereby taxpayers with a higher ability to pay contribute a larger share of their income or wealth. Moreover, *zakat* specifically targets the most vulnerable segments of society, such as the poor, the needy, and those in debt. By mandating wealth redistribution to these groups, the Islamic approach addresses both income and wealth inequality, facilitating a more balanced and equitable society. Furthermore, this approach highlights transparency and accountability in the collection and distribution of *zakat,* fostering trust between taxpayers and the institutions responsible for its administration, a crucial element for the success and perceived fairness of any taxation system.

Incorporating the concept of *zakat* into the wealth taxation discourse that predominantly focuses on taxing millionaires and billionaires acknowledges the significance of non-Western legal ideologies and recognises the potential for sustainable and continuous annual funding for social welfare programs. As an annual wealth tax, *zakat* provides a consistent and predictable revenue source, ensuring a more stable funding stream for social programs, facilitating better long-term planning, and enabling more effective resource allocation.

The alignment of *zakat's* focus on addressing wealth inequality and promoting social welfare with the objectives of progressive wealth taxation allows for a more comprehensive approach, encompassing not only wealth redistribution but also the moral and social responsibilities of wealthy individuals. This broader perspective can result in more effective and just wealth taxation policies, promoting the well-being of all members of society. Furthermore, *zakat's* established practice in many Muslim-majority countries offers a foundation for international dialogue and collaboration, fostering a more inclusive and globally relevant approach to wealth taxation. This can help bridge gaps in understanding between different legal systems and cultures and contribute to the development of more equitable and just taxation policies worldwide.

Finally, the current wealth taxation discourse, which emphasises taxing millionaires and billionaires, is incomplete without considering *zakat's* contributions. By acknowledging the annual nature of *zakat*, its focus on social welfare, and its potential for fostering international cooperation, the wealth taxation discourse can be enriched, paving the way for more comprehensive, just, and effective policies that address wealth inequality and promote social cohesion around financing public health for example.

Constitutional law

The right to health in Kenya, anchored in Article 43(1)(a) of the Constitution, emerged from social struggles demanding government action to address healthcare deficiencies.[17] The Health Act, No. 21 of 2017, further elucidates the government's commitment to implementing the right to health. However, the current focus on financing health primarily revolves around taxes, insurance schemes, and cost-sharing, neglecting other potential resources like *zakat*. Amending the Health Act to recognize *zakat* could spur further research and empirical work to identify the most suitable *zakat*-based financing option for Kenya. However, the incorporation of *zakat* into constitutional law may face legal and practical challenges, such as balancing religious considerations with secular

[17] W Mutunga, 'Human Rights States and Societies: A Reflection from Kenya' (2015) The Transnational Human Rights Review 2, 63-102.

principles, ensuring equity and inclusivity, and avoiding the marginalisation of non-Muslim communities. Successfully addressing these concerns requires careful policy design and communication, which might prove difficult in practice.

In conclusion, this book provides a foundation for further research and scholarship on the potential of *zakat* as a locally available resource for financing health in Kenya. Embracing *zakat* within the legal framework and in society's quest for better healthcare may help develop *zakat* as a distinctive legal concept rooted in the struggle for healthcare and the desire to achieve the right to health through people's participation. However, the adoption and policy impact of these suggestions may face challenges related to the interplay of religion and state policy, differing interpretations of Islamic law, and potential opposition from various stakeholders.

Final Remarks: *Zakat* - The Islamic Wealth Tax

The findings in the book aim to encourage further thinking on why and how *zakat* can be used to finance health in Kenya. More research is needed on *zakat* to explore its maximum potential. *Zakat* offers a possible opening for human rights and Islamic scholars to relate religious norms to state fiscal policies. It leads human rights scholarship along an evolutionary track, by aligning social dynamics, where community-pooled finance is already available for redistribution, towards the achievement of rights. Beyond Kenya, *zakat* offers Muslim-majority and -minority countries with a preferential domestic revenue mobilisation system, which has the potential for long-term sustainability. The empirical findings on *zakat* reveal the role of social structures in supporting socio-economic needs. This book concludes with a question: if included in a government's fiscal policy, what kind of effect might *zakat* have? This remains to be seen.

Bibliography

Books

Abduh, Muhammad. *Al Islam Wa'l Nasraniya Ma'al Ilm Wa'l Madaniya: Islam and Christianity in Relationship to Science and Civilisation*. (ed) Muhammad Rashid Rida (Cairo: al Manar, 1924)

Abi Shaibah, Abu Bakr Abdullah bin Muhammad. *Al-Musannaf*. Translated by Hamad Al Jum'a and Muhammad Al Lahidan (2nd ed. 16 vols. Riyadh: Maktabat al Rushd, 2006)

Abiad, Nisrine. *Sharia, Muslim States and International Human Rights Treaty Obligations: A Comparative Study* (18th ed. London: British Institute of International and Comparative Law, 2008)

Adam, M. 'Panorama of Socio-Religious Communities' in *Indian Africa: Minorities of Indian-Pakistani Origin in Eastern Africa* (Nairobi: Africae, 2015)

Aghnides, Nicolas Prodromou. *Mohammedan Theories of Finance* (Columbia University, 1916)

Ahmad, Ilyas. *Sovereignty in Islam* (Allies Book Corp, 1963)

Aiyar, S. *Indians in Kenya: The Politics of Diaspora* (Cambridge Mass., Harvard University Press, 2015)

Akech, Migai. *Administrative Law* (Nairobi: Strathmore University Press, 2016)

Al Baladhuri, Ahmed ibn Yahya. *Futuh Al-Buldan* (Beirut, Lebanon: Dar Al Kotob Ilmiyah, 1981)

Al Banna, Gamal. *Islamic Approaches to Human Rights* (Cairo: Dar al-fikr al-Islami, 1999)

Al Banna, Hasan. *Memoirs of Hasan Al Banna Shaheed* (Karachi: International Islamic Publishers, 1981)

Al Durayni, Muhammad Fathi. *Al-Ijtihad Wa Al-Tajdid Fi Al-Fikr Al-Islami* (Valetta, Malta: Islamic World Studies Center, 1991)

Al Farabi, Abu Nasr. *Al-Madina Al-Fadila* (Beirut: Al-Maktaba al-Sharqiyya, 1980)

Al Ghazali, Abu Hamid. *Moderation in Belief (Al-Iqtisad Fi Al-I'tiqad)*. Translated by Aladdin M Yaqub (University of Chicago Press, 2013)

– – –, *The Mishkat Al-Anwar: The Niche for Lights*. Translated by W. H. T. Gairdner (Cosimo Classics, 2010)

– – –, *The Mysteries of Almsgiving*. Translated by Nabih Amin Faris (London: Folios Limited, 2001)

______. *Al-Iqtisad fi al-Itiqad* (Cairo: Al-Matba'a al-Mahmudiyya, n.d.)

________. *Mishkat al-Anwar* (Aleppo: Al-Dar al Ilmiyya, 6 vols, 1927). 6:310, 511. [*The Niche for Lights* (trans.) WHT Gairdner (1998)]

______. *Ihya Ulum al-Din*, (trans.) K Honerkamp, 'Revival of Religion's Sciences, Volume 1 (Fons Vitae, 2016)

Al Ghofeeli, Ahmed. *Nawazel Al Zakat* (Al Maiman and Bank Al Bilad, 2008)

Al Hilli, Allamah. *Foundations of Jurisprudence - An Introduction to Imami Shi'i Legal Theory* (Leiden: Brill, 2016)

Al Jabiri, Muhammad Abid. *Al-Khitab Al-Arabi Al-Mu'asir: On Contemporary Arab Discourse* (Beirut: Al Tali'a, 1982)

Al Jassas, Abu Bakr. *Al-Ijma: Dirasa Fi Fikratihi: Bab Al-Ijtihad* (Beirut: Dar al-Muntakhab, 1993). https://kitaabun.com/shopping3/usul-jassas-musamma-fusul-usul-imam-bakr-jasas-p-7028.html

Al Jawhari, Abi Nasr Ismail. *Kitab Taj Al-Lughah Wa-Sihah Al- Arabiyah.* 2 vols (Cairo: Al Matba'a al Kubra, 1865)

Al Jaziri, Abd al-Rahman. *Islamic Jurisprudence According to the Four Sunni Schools: Al-Fiqh 'Ala Al Madhahib Al Arba'ah Volume I Acts of Worship*. Translated by Nancy Roberts (Louisville, Ky: Fons Vitae, 2009)

Al Kasaani, Ala al Din Abu Bakr ibn Masud. *Badaa'ie Al Sanaa'ie* (Beirut: Dar Al Kotob Ilmiyah, 2003)

Al Khalidi, Mahmoud. *Ma'alim Al Khilafa Fil Fikr Al Siyasi Al-Islami: Features of Succession in Islamic Political Thought* (Beirut: Dar al Jil, 1984)

Al Khalil, Ahmed. *Kitab Al Ayn* (Baghdad, 1982)

Al Khattab, Nasruddin. *English Translation of Musnad Imam Ahmad Ibn Hanbal. Vol* 1 (Riyadh: Darussalam Publishers, 2012)

Al Khayat, Muhammad Haytham. *Health as a Human Right in Islam*. Health Education through Religion (Cairo, Egypt: World Health Organization, Regional Office for the Eastern Mediterranean, 2004). https://catalog.hathitrust.org/Record/010573771

Al Nabulusi, Sayyid Abd Al Ghani Ibn Ismail. *Al-Hadiqa Al Nadiya Sharh A Tariqa Al Muhammadiya* (Turkey, 1994)

Al Qaddumi, Marwan. *Al Siyasa Al Umawiyya Tuja Ahl Al Dhimma* (Majallat al Dawa al Islamiyya, 1988)

Al Qaradawi, Yusuf. *Fiqh Al Zakat* (Beirut: Mo'asasat Al Risalah, 2002)

———, *Ghayr Al-Muslimin* (2nd ed. Beirut: Mo'asasat Al Risalah, 1983)

Al Qarafi, Shihab. *Al Thaakeerah* (Beirut: Dar algharb al-islami, 1994)

Al Qurtubi, Ibn Abd al Barr. *Kitab Al-Kafi Fi Fiqh Ahl Al-Madina Al-Maliki* (Saudi Arabia: Maktabat al-Riyāḍ al-Ḥadīthah, 1980)

Al Shabani, Muhammad Abd Allah. *Nizam Al-Hukm Wa Al-Idara Fi Al-Dawla Al-Islamiyya* (Cairo: Alam al Kutub, n.d)

Al Shatibi, Ibrahim Ibn Musa Abu Ishaq Al. *The Reconciliation Of The Fundamentals Of Islamic Law - Volume 1 - Al Muwafaqat Fi Usul Al Shari'a*. Translated by Imran Ahsan Khan Nyazee (Garnet Publishing, 2019)

Al Tabari, Al-Imam Abi Ja'far. *Tarikh* (trans.) E Yarshater (Cairo: Al Maktaba al-Husayniyy, 1999)

_______. *Tafsir*, (trans.) W F Madelung and A Jones (Beirut: Dar al Ma'rifa, 1989)

Al Tabari, Muhammad Ibn Garir. *The History of Al Tabari, Vol. 16: The Community Divided: The Caliphate of Ali A.D. 656-657/A.H. 35-35* (Suny Press, 1997)

Al Tahtawi, Rifat. *Takhlis Al Ibriz Fi Talkhis Bariz: The Extraction of Gold or an Overview of Paris* (Bulaq Printing Press, n.d). https://biblio.co.uk/book/takhlis-al-ibriz-fi-talkhis-bariz/d/906714654

Al Tanukhi, Abd al Salam bin Habib. *Al-Mudawwana Al Kubra*. 6 vols (Beirut, Lebanon: Dar Al Ḳotob Ilmiyah, 1905)

Al Turabi, Hasan. *Al Haraka Al Islamiyya Fil Sudan: Al Tatawur Wal Kasb Wal Minhaj* (Khartoum: Unknown, 1989)

———, *Tajdid Al-Fikr Al-Islami* (Rabat: Dar al-Qarafi li'l Nashr wa'l Tawzi, 1993)

Al-Azami, Muhammad Mustafa. *The History of the Quranic Text, from Revelation to Compilation: A Comparative Study with the Old and New Testaments* (Leicester: UK Islamic Academy, 2003)

Al-Baihaḳī, Ibrāhīm ibn Muḥammad. *Kitāb al-māhasin val-masāvī* (Baghdad: Al-Muthanna Library, 1960)

Ali, Abd al Raziq. *Islam and the Principles of Government* (Cairo: Matbaat Misr, 1925)

Ali, Karamat. *A Study of Islamic History* (Lahore: Aziz Publishers, 1978)

Ali, Muhammad, and Mitch Creekmore. *The Early Caliphate* (Lahore: Ahmadiyya Anjuman Ishaat Islam, 2011)

Ali, Shaheen S. *Modern Challenges to Islamic Law* (Cambridge: Cambridge University Press, 2016)

_________. *Gender and Human Rights in Islam and International Law: Equal Before Allah, Unequal Before Man?* (The Hague: Boston: Kluwer Law International, 2000)

Alkhateeb, Firas. *Lost Islamic History: Reclaiming Muslim Civilisation from the Past* (London: C Hurst & Co, 2014)

Allen, C H. *Oman: The Modernisation of the Sultanate* (Routledge, 1987)

Allot, Anthony. *Essays in African Law* (London: Butterworths, 1960)

Al Beirawi, *Essays on Ijtihad in the 21st Century* (Pakistan: Maktaba Islamia, 2016)

Al-Qaradawi, Yusuf. *Fiqh Az Zakat: A Comparative Study: The Rules, Regulations and Philosophy of Zakat in the Light of the Quran and Sunna*. Translated by Kahf Monzer (London: Dar Al Taqwa Ltd, 1999)

Al Salimi, N *Tuhfat al-Ayan bi-sirat ahl Uman*, 2 volumes (Cairo: Matba'at al sufliyya, 1928)

Alston, Philip, and Ryan Goodman. *International Human Rights in Context: Law, Politics, Morals*. (ed) *Henry* J. Steiner. (3rd edition. New York: Oxford University Press, 2007)

Alston, P, and N Reisch, *Tax, Inequality and Human Rights* (OUP, 2019)

Al-Uthaymeen, M.S. *Fiqh of Worship: Purification, Doctrines, Salat, Zakat, Siyam, Hajj*. (trans.) Abdallah Alaceri (London: Al-Firdous Ltd, 2011)

Amari, Rafat. *Islam: In Light of History* (1st edition. Prospect Heights, IL: Religion Research Inst, 2004)

Ameta, Deepti. 'Social Protection and Safety Nets in Palestine' (Institute of Development Studies, 2015)

Angelo, A. *Power and the Presidency in Kenya: The Jomo Kenyatta Years* (Cambridge University Press, 2020)

An Naim, Abdullahi. *Islam and the Secular State. Negotiating the Future of Shari'a* (Cambridge, Mass: Harvard University Press, 2008)

——— and F Deng (eds), *Human Rights in Africa. Cross Cultural Perspectives* (The Brookings Institution, 1990)

———, *Toward an Islamic Reformation: Civil Liberties, Human Rights and International Law* (New York: Syracuse University Press, 1990)

Ansary, Tamim. *Destiny Disrupted: A History of the World Through Islamic Eyes* (New York, NY: Public Affairs, 2010)

As Sallabi, Ali Muhammad. *Biography of Umar Bin Abdul Aziz* (Darussalam Publishers, 2011)

As Sayyad, Sabiq. *Fiqh Us Sunnah: Alms Tax and Fasting* (Washington: American Trust Publications, 1986)

Atkinson, Paul, and Amanda Jane Coffey. *Making Sense of Qualitative Data: Complementary Research Strategies* (SAGE Publications, Inc, 1996)

Averroës. *Kitab al-muqaddimat al-mumahhidat li-bayan ma iqtadathu rusum al-mudawwanah min al-ahkam al-shar`iyat wa-al-tahsilat al-mahkamat al-shar`iyat li-ummahat masa'iliha al-mushkilat* (Iraq: Dar Sadir, 1970)

Baderin, Mashood A. *International Human Rights and Islamic Law* (Oxford Monographs in International Law. Oxford, New York: Oxford University Press, 2003)

Bahn, P. *Great Sites of the Ancient World* (Frances Lincoln, 2020)

Bakhtiar, Laleh, and Kevin A Reinhart. *Encyclopedia of Islamic Law: A Compendium of the Views of the Major Schools* (Kazi Publications, 1996)

Bantekas, I and C Lumina (eds), *Sovereign Debt and Human Rights* (OUP, 2018)

Barelvi, Ahmad Raza Khan. *Al-Ataya Al-Nabawiyah Fi Al-Fatawa Al-Radawiyah* (n.p. 1917)

Batson, E. *A Social Survey of Zanzibar, 1948* (Zanzibar Government Printer, 1962)

Bayhaqi, *Al-Mahasin wa'l-masawi*, (ed.) Friedrich Schwally (Giessen 1902)

Baxi, Upendra. *Development as a Human Right or as Political Largesse? Does It Make Any Difference?* (Chennai: Madras Institute of Development Studies, 2006)

———, *The Development of the Right to Development* (Routledge, 2019) https://doi.org/10.4324/9780429398629-4.

Beck, Ann. *A History of the British Medical Administration of East Africa, 1900-1950* (Cambridge, Mass: Harvard University Press, 1970)

Bell, Richard. *Introduction to the Qur'ān* (Edinburgh University Publications. Language & Literature; No 6. Edinburgh: University Press, 1953)

Belshaw, Deryke, Chris Sugden, and Robert Calderisi, eds. *Faith in Development: Partnership between the World Bank and the Churches of Africa* (Washington, DC: Oxford, England: World Bank; Regnum Books, 2001)

Bennett, N. R. *A History of the Arab State of Zanzibar* (London, 1978)

Bennett, G. *Kenya: A Political History: The Colonial Period* (Oxford University Press, 1964)

Bentzon, A. W., A Hellum, J Stewart, W Ncube, and T Agersnap. *Pursuing Grounded Theory in Law* (Norway: Tano Aschehoug AS, 1998)

Bernheimer, Teresa, and Andrew Rippin. *Muslims: Their Religious Beliefs and Practices*. (Abingdon, Oxon; New York, NY: Routledge, 2011)

Beuving, Joost, and Geert de Vries. *Doing Qualitative Research. Theorizing Society: Grounded Theory in Naturalistic Inquiry* (Amsterdam: Amsterdam University Press, 2015)

Bilmes, J. *The Discursive Approach. In: Discourse and Behaviour* (Springer, Boston, MA, 1986)

Bharati, A. *The Asians in East Africa, Jayhind and Uhuru* (Chicago: Nelson Hall, 1972)

Boahen, A. Adu. *General History of Africa: Africa under Colonial Domination 1880-1935*. (London; Berkeley, Calif., U.S.A.: Heinemann; University of California Press, 1985)

———, ed. *General History of Africa: Africa Under Colonial Domination, 1880-1935 v. 7*. (U.S.A: Heinemann International Literature & Textbooks, 1985)

Bourne, V, James, A, Smith, K, et al, *Understanding Quantitative and Qualitative Research in Psychology: A Practical Guide to Methods, Statistics and Analysis* (OUP, 2021)

Boyle, Kevin, and Juliet Sheen. *Freedom of Religion and Belief: A World Report* (Routledge, 1997) https://doi.org/10.4324/9780203411025

Braun, Virginia, Victoria Clarke, and Debra Gray, eds. *Collecting Qualitative Data: A Practical Guide to Textual, Media and Virtual Techniques* (Cambridge: Cambridge University Press, 2017). https://doi.org/10.1017/9781107295094

Brems, E *Human Rights: Universality and Diversity* (Kluwer Law International, 2001)

Brockopp, J. (ed), *Islamic Ethics of Life. Abortion, War and Euthanasia* (University of California Press, 2003)

Bsoul, Labeeb Ahmed. *Islamic History and Law: From the 4th to the 11th Century and Beyond* (Palgrave Macmillan US, 2016). https://doi.org/10.1057/978-1-137-57867-9

Buchanan, A, *The Heart of Human Rights* (OUP, 2013)

Buhooti, lghofee. *Khashaf Al Keenaa' Fi Matn AlIqnaa*. (Riyadh: Dar Aa'lam AlKutub, 2003)

Cane, Peter, and Kritzer, Herbert. *The Oxford Handbook of Practical Legal Research* (Oxford: Oxford University Press, 2010)

Casanova, Jose. *Public Religions in the Modern World* (University of Chicago Press, 1994). https://press.uchicago.edu/ucp/books/book/chicago/P/bo3683997.html

Charmaz, Kathy. *Constructing Grounded Theory* (SAGE Publications Ltd, 2013)

Clark, TL Foster, Sloan, L, et al, *Bryman's Social Research Methods* (Sixth edition OUP, 2021)

Clough, Marshall. *Mau Mau Memoirs: History, Memory, Politics* (Lynne Rienner Publishers, 1998) https://www.rienner.com/title/Mau_Mau_Memoirs_History_Memory_Politics

Cohen, David William, and E.S. Atieno Odhiambo. *The Risks of Knowledge: Investigations into the Death of the Hon. Minister John Robert Ouko in Kenya, 1990* (Athens, OH: Ohio University, 2004)

Comstock, A L, *Committed to Rights: UN Human Rights Treaties and Legal Paths for Commitment and Compliance* (Cambridge University Press, 2021)

Constantine, Stephen. *The Making of British Colonial Development Policy, 1914-1940* (London: Frank Cass, 1984)

Cotterrell, Roger. *Law, Culture and Society: Legal Ideas in the Mirror of Social Theory* (Routledge, 2006). https://www.routledge.com/Law-Culture-and-Society-Legal-Ideas-in-the-Mirror-of-Social-Theory/Cotterrell/p/book/9780754625117

Crozier, A. *Practising Colonial Medicine: The Colonial Medical Service in British East Africa* (I. B. Taurius, 2007)

Daftary, Farhad. *The Isma'ilis: Their History and Doctrines* (Cambridge: Cambridge University Press, 2007). https://doi.org/10.1017/CBO9780511497551

Damiri, M, (1906), *Hayat al-hayawan al-kubra,* (trans.) A S G Jayakar (Bombay, 1937)

Dey, Ian. *Qualitative Data Analysis: A User-Friendly Guide for Social Scientists* (London: Routledge, 1993)

Diesfeld, HJ, and Hecklau, HK, *Kenya: A Geomedical Monograph*. (Berlin Heidelberg: Springer-Verlag, 1978). https://doi.org/10.1007/978-3-642-66935-4

Dunn, Shannon. *Islamic Law and Human Rights* (The Oxford Handbook of Islamic Law, 2018). https://doi.org/10.1093/oxfordhb/9780199679010.013.26

Ead, Hamed. *Alchemy in Ibn Khaldun's Muqaddimah* (Heidelberg University, 1998)

El-Fadl, K. *The Search for Beauty in Islam. A Conference of the Books* (London: Rowman & Littlefield Publishers, 2005)

El-Hibri, Tayeb. *Parable and Politics in Early Islamic History: The Rashidun Caliphs* (Columbia University Press, 2010)

Elliesie, Hatem, ed. *Beiträge Zum Islamischen Recht VII: Islam Und Menschenrechte / Islam and Human Rights*. Bilingual edition. Frankfurt, M; (New York: Peter Lang GmbH, Internationaler Verlag der Wissenschaften, 2010)

Emon, Anver M., Mark Ellis, and Benjamin Glahn. *Islamic Law and International Human Rights Law* (Oxford, New York: Oxford University Press, 2012)

Esposito, John. *Future of Islam* (New York: Oxford University Press, 2010)

———, *Islam and Development: Religion and Sociopolitical Change* (Syracuse: Syracuse University Press, 1980)

———, *Islam and Politics*. (3rd ed. Syracuse: Syracuse University Press, 1991)

———, *The Oxford Encyclopaedia of the Modern Islamic World*. (New York: Oxford University Press, 1995)

Faruqi, Muhammad Yusuf. *Development of Usul Al Fiqh: An Early Historical Perspective* (Adam Publishers, 2007)

Flathman, Richard E. *The Practice of Political Authority: Authority and the Authoritative* (University of Chicago Press, 1980)

Fraenkel, Jack R., and Norman E. Wallen. *How To Design and Evaluate Research in Education* (New York: McGraw Hill Publishing Co, 1990)

Furedi, Frank. *The Mau Mau War in Perspective* (London: James Currey, 1989)

Funderburk, B. *Between the Lines of Hegemony and Subordination: The Mombasa Kadhi's Court in Contemporary Kenya* (SIT Kenya, 2010)

Gann, L. H. *The Rulers of British Africa, 1870-1914* (London: Croom Helm, 1978)

Garlake, P. *The Early Islamic Architecture of the East African Coast* (British Institute of History and Archaeology in East Africa, 1966)

Gerring, John, and Dino Christenson. *Applied Social Science Methodology: An Introductory Guide* (Cambridge: Cambridge University Press, 2017)

Ghai, Yash Pal, and John Patrick William Buchanan McAuslan. *Public Law and Political Change in Kenya: A Study of the Legal Framework of Government from Colonial Times to the Present* (Oxford: Oxford University Press, 1970)

Ghazali, Imam Mohammad Al, and Dar Ul Thaqafah. *Al Mustasfa Min Ilm Al Usul: On Legal Theory of Muslim Jurisprudence*. Translated by Ahmad Zaki Mansur Hammad (CreateSpace Independent Publishing Platform, 2018)

Gibb, H. A. R. (Hamilton Alexander Rosskeen). *Modern Trends in Islam* (University of Chicago Press, 1947)

Glaser, Barney G., and Anselm L. Strauss. *The Discovery of Grounded Theory: Strategies for Qualitative Research* (Chicago: Aldine de Gruyter, 1967)

Glassman, Jonathon P. *Feasts and Riot: Revelry, Rebellion and Popular Consciousness on the Swahili Coast, 1856-1888* (Heinemann: James Currey Ltd, 1995).

Goldberg, Elizabeth Swanson, and Schultheis Moore, Alexandra. *Theoretical Perspectives on Human Rights and Literature* (Routledge, 2012)

Golding, B. *Asynchronous Email Interviewing: A Qualitative Data Collection Method* (SAGE Publications, 2014)

Goldsworthy, Jeffrey. *Interpreting Constitutions: A Comparative Study* (Oxford: Oxford University Press, 2007)

Goldziher, Ignác. *Introduction to Islamic Theology and Law*. Translated by Andras Hamori and Ruth Hamori (Princeton, New Jersey: Princeton University Press, 1981)

Gostin, Larry, Meier, Benjamin, and Huffstetler, Hanna. *Human Rights in Global Health Governance* (Georgetown Law, 2018)

Green, Leslie. *The Authority of the State* (Oxford: Oxford University Press, 1990)

Hallaq, Wael B. *A History of Islamic Legal Theories: An Introduction to Sunni Usul Al Fiqh* (Cambridge: Cambridge University Press, 1997)

———, *Sharia: Theory, Practice, Transformations* (1st edition. Cambridge, UK; New York: Cambridge University Press, 2009)

Hamidullah, Muhammad. *The Emergence of Islam*. Translated by Afzal Iqbal (Islamabad: Islamic Research Institute, 1993)

Hanbal, Imam Ahmed. *Musnad*. Translated by Nasruddin Al Khattab (Darussalam Publishers, 2012)

Hannigan, A. *What Is Local Government? A Study of Local Government in Kenya and England* (Nairobi: Eagle Press of the East African Literature Bureau, 1958)

Hannun, H. *Rescuing Human Rights. A Radically Moderate Approach* (Cambridge University Press, 2019)

Hardaker, G and Sabki, AH, *Pedagogy in Islamic Education* (Bingley: Emerald Publishing Limited, 2019)

Harrington, J. *Traditional Medicine and the Law in Kenya* (Routledge Handbook of Complementary and Alternative Medicine, 2015)

_______. *Health*, in *Oxford Handbook on International Law and Development* (2022)

_______ and Stuttaford, M, *Global Health and Human Rights: Legal and Philosophical Perspectives* (Routledge, 2010)

Hart, HLA. *The Concept of Law* (Oxford: Oxford University Press, 1961)

Hasan, S. *Muslim Philanthropy and Social Security: Prospects, Practices, and Pitfalls* (Bangkok, 2006)

Harries, LP, *Islam in East Africa* (London: Universities' Mission to Central Africa, 1954)

Helfont, S. *Yusuf Al-Qaradawi: Islam and Modernity* (Tel Aviv University Press, 2009)

Hellerstein J R and Hellerstein, W, *State Taxation* (Warren Gorham Lamont, 1998)

Herbert, David. *Religion and Civil Society: Rethinking Public Religion in the Contemporary World* (Ashgate, 2003)

Hepburn, A and Wiggins, S, *Discursive Research in Practice* (Cambridge: Cambridge University Press, 2007)

Hidayatullah, AA. Feminist Edges of the Quran (Oxford University Press, 2014)

Higgins, Rosalyn. *Problems and Process: International Law and How We Use It* (Oxford, New York: Oxford University Press, 1995)

Himbara, D. *Kenyan Capitalists, the State and Development* (East African Educational Publishers, 1994)

Hirst, Paul Q. *From Statism to Pluralism: Democracy, Civil Society, and Global Politics* (London; Bristol, Penn: UCL Press, 1997)

Hoecke, Mark Van. *Methodologies of Legal Research* (Oxford: Hart Publishing, 2013). https://doi.org/10.5040/9781472560896

Hooker, M. B. *Legal Pluralism: An Introduction to Colonial and Neo-Colonial Laws* (Oxford: Clarendon Press, 1975)

———, *Legal Pluralism: An Introduction to Colonial and Neo-Colonial Laws* (Oxford: Clarendon Press, 1975)

Hornsby, C. Kenya: A History Since Independence (Bloomsbury Academics, 2013).

Horovitz, J., and Ch Pellat. *Al-Kumayt b. Zayd Al-Asadī* (Encyclopaedia of Islam, Second Edition, 2012)

Horton, Mark, and Middleton, John. *The Swahili: The Social Landscape of a Mercantile Society* (Oxford: Blackwell, 2000)

Hourani, George F. *Averroes on the Harmony of Religion and Philosophy: A Translation with Introduction and Notes of Ibn Rushd's Kitab Fasl Al-Maqal with Its Appendix* (Gibb Memorial Trust, 1961)

Hughes, Anthony J. *East Africa, the Search for Unity: Kenya, Tanganyika, Uganda and Zanzibar* (Penguin Africa Library. Harmondsworth: Penguin Books, 1963)

_____, *Muslim Identities* (New York: Columbia University Press, 2013)

———, *Researching and Writing in Law* (Sydney: Thomson Reuters, 2010)

Ibn Abi Shaybah, *Al-Musannaf,* Volume 3 (trans.) M Awwamah (Dar ul Islam Publishers, n.d)

Ibn Abd Al Barr, *Jami bayan al-ilm wa fadlihi* (trans.) M Al Misri, *Knowledge and its Virtue* (Darul Imam Bukhari, 2010)

Ibn Ashur, *Treaties on Maqasid al Shari'ah,* (trans.) Mohamed El Tahir El Mesawi (The International Institute of Islamic Thought, 2006)

Ibn Durayd, Abu Bakr Muhammad. *Kitab Jamharat Al Lugha* (Hyderabad, 1926)

Ibn Kathir, Ismail ibn Umar. *From The Beginning to the End: Al-Bidayah Wa'an-Nihayah* (Dar-ul-Ishaat, 2014)

Ibn Khaldun, *The Muqaddimah: An Introduction to History,* (trans.) F Rosenthal (Princeton University Press, 2015)

Ibn Mundhir, Muhammad bin Ibrahim. *Consensus of The Islamic Jurists: Al-Ijma.* Translated by S Abd al Hamid (USA: The Islamic Literary Foundation, 2014)

_______. *Al Ijma,* (trans.) S Abd al Hamid (The Islamic Literary Foundation 2014)

Ibn Qutayba, Abd Allah ibn Muslim. *Kitab 'Uyun Al-Akhbar* (Cairo: Dar al Kitab al Misar, 1930)

Ibn Sa'd, Abu Abdalla Muhammad. *Kitab Al-Tabaqat Al-Kabir*. Translated by Eduard Sachau (Leiden: Brill, 1904)

Ibn Taymiyyah, Taqi ad Din Ahmed. *Al-Ḥisbah Fī Al-Islām*. Translated by Abd al Aziz Rabah (Damascus: Maktabah Dar al Bayan, 1967)

———, *Majmu Al-Fatawa Shaikh Al Islam Ibn Taymiyyah* (Beirut: Dar al Kutub, 1987)

———, *Maqaasid Ash-Shari'ah* (Cork: Sifatu Safwa Publications, n.d)

Ibn Qutayba, *Uyun al-Akhbar* (trans.) L Kopf, *[Book of Choice Narratives]* (Cairo: Al-Mu'assa al-Misriyya, 1963)

Idris, FM, Seraj, M and Ozdeser, H, 'Assessing the possibility of financing social health insurance from *zakat*, case of Sudan: ARDL bounds approach', (2022) *Journal of Islamic Accounting and Business Research*, Vol 13 No 2, 264-276

Iliffe, John. *East African Doctors: A History of the Modern Profession* (Cambridge: Cambridge University Press, 1998)

Iqbal, Muhammad. *The Reconstruction of Religious Thought in Islam* (Stanford University Press, 2013). http://www.sup.org/books/title/?id=21804

Ishmawi, Muhammad Said. *Al-Khilafa Al-Islamiyya* (Cairo: Sina li al-Nashr, 1992)

Jackson, Sherman A. *Islamic Law and the State: The Constitutional Jurisprudence of Shihab Al-Din Al-Qarafi* (Leiden: New York: Brill, 1997)

Jacobsohn, Gary J. *The Wheel of Law. India's Secularism in Comparative Constitutional Context* (Princeton: Princeton University Press, 2005)

Jagjeet, Lally. *The Pattern of Trade in Seventeenth Century Mughal India: Towards an Economic Explanation* (London School of Economics, 2009)

Jayyusi, Salma K, Lucy Gent, and Nigel Llewellyn. *Human Rights in Arab Thought: A Reader* (New York: IB Tauris, 2005)

Juynboll, Gautier Hendrik Albert. *The Authenticity of the Tradition Literature: Discussions in Modern Egypt* (Leiden: E.J. Brill, 1969)

Kahf, Monzer. *The Performance of the Institution of Zakah in Theory and Practice* (Kuala Lumpur, 1999)

Kamali, Muhamad Hashim. *Principles of Islamic Jurisprudence* (Cambridge: Islamic Texts Society, 1991)

Kangu, John Mutakha. *Constitutional Law of Kenya on Devolution* (Nairobi: Strathmore University Press, 2015)

Kanogo, Tabitha. *Squatters and the Roots of Mau Mau, 1905–1963* (Athens: Ohio University Press, 1987)

Kawtharani, Farah. *Political Thought in Contemporary Shi'a Islam: Muhammad Mahdi Shams Al-Din* (Middle East Today. Palgrave Macmillan, 2020). https://doi.org/10.1007/978-3-030-28057-4

Kawtharani, Wajih. *Mashru Al-Nuhud Al-Arabi* (Cairo: Dar al Tali'a, 1995)

Kerr, Malcolm H. *Islamic Reform: The Political and Legal Theories of Muhammad 'Abduh and Rashid Rida* (1st edition. University of California Press, 1966)

Kesner, Richard. *Economic Control and Colonial Development: Crown Colony Financial Management in the Age of Joseph Chamberlain* (Oxford, 1981)

Khadduri, Majid. *The Islamic Law of Nations* (Baltimore: JHUP, 2001)

Khan, Muhammad M. *The Translation of the Meanings of Summarized Sahih Al-Bukhari: Arabic-English* (Lahore, Pakistan: Darussalam Publishers, 1995)

Khan, Qamar-ud-Din. *The Political Thought of IBN Taymiyah* (Adam Publishers & Distributors, 2007)

Khumayni, Ayatollah. *Al Hukummah Al Islamiyya* (Kuwait, n.d)

Kindy, Hyder. *Life and Politics in Mombasa* (Nairobi: East African Pub. House, 1972)

Kuru, Ahmet T. *Secularism and State Policies toward Religion: The United States, France, and Turkey*. (Cambridge Studies in Social Theory, Religion and Politics: Cambridge University Press, 2009). https://doi.org/10.1017/CBO9780511815096

Kvale, Steiner, and Svend Brinkman. *Interviews: Learning the Craft of Qualitative Research Interviewing* (2nd ed. London: SAGE Publications Ltd, 2009)

Kyle, K. *The Politics of the Independence of Kenya. Contemporary History in Context* (Palgrave Macmillan UK, 1999). https://doi.org/10.1057/9780230377707

Leavy, P. *Popularising Scholarly Research: Research Methods and Practices* (OUP, 2021)

Leckie s and A Gallagher, *Economic, Social and Cultural Rights: A Legal Resource Guide* (University of Pennsylvania Press, 2006)

Louer, L. *Sunni and Shi'a. A Political History of Discord,* (trans.) Ethan Rundell (Princeton: Princeton University Press, 2017)

Lucas, Scott. *Constructive Critics, Hadith Literature, and the Articulation of Sunni Islam: The Legacy of the Generation of Ibn Sa'd,Ibn Ma'in and Ibn Hanbal* (Leiden: Brill, 2004)

Luhmann, Niklas. *Introduction to Systems Theory*. Translated by Peter Gilgen (1st edition. Cambridge, UK: Polity, 2012)

Lynch, Ryan J. *Arab Conquests and Early Islamic Historiography. The Futuh Al Buldan of Al Baladhuri* (I.B. Tauris, 2019). https://www.bloomsbury.com/us/arab-conquests-and-early-islamic-historiography-9781838604400/

Mahmoudi, Abdelrashid. *Taha Husain's Education: From Al Azhar to the Sorbonne* (Routledge, 1998)

Makokha, Joseph. *The District Focus: Conceptual and Management Problems* (Nairobi: Africa Press Research Bureau, 1985)

Malik, Anas. *Polycentricity, Islam, and Development: Potentials and Challenges in Pakistan* (USA: Lexington Books, 2018)

Malik, Imam. *Al-Muwatta of Imam Malik Ibn Anas: The First Formulation of Islamic Law*. Translated by Aisha Abdurrahman Bewley (Revised edition. Inverness: Bookwork, 2001)

Mallat, C. *The Renewal of Islamic Law* (Cambridge: Cambridge University Press, 1993)

Maamiry, A. *Omani Sultans in Zanzibar, 1832-1964* (Lancer Book, 1988)

Manie, Abdullah Ibn. *Bohoth fi Al Ektisad Al Islami* (Mecca: Al Maktab Al Islami, 1996)

Marshall, Catherine, and Gretchen B Rossman. *Designing Qualitative Research* (Newbury Park: Sage Publications, Inc, 1989)

Marshall, Katherine, and Lucy Keough. *Mind, Heart and Soul in the Fight Against Poverty* (The World Bank, 2004). https://ideas.repec.org/b/wbk/wbpubs/14927.html

__________, and Richard Marsh. *Millennium Challenges for Development and Faith Institutions* (The World Bank, 2003). https://doi.org/10.1596/0-8213-5590-2

Martin, David. *A General Theory of Secularization* (New edition. Bristol: Western Printing Services Limited, 1978)

Marx, Karl, and Daniel De Leon. *The Eighteenth Brumaire of Louis Bonaparte* (New York: International Pub. Co, 1898)

Massoud, MF. *SHARI'A, INSHAALLAH: Finding God in Somali Legal Politics* (Cambridge University Press, 2021)

Masud, Muhammad Khalid. *Islamic Legal Philosophy: A Study of Abu Ishaq Al-Shatibi's Life and Thought* (Islamabad: Islamic Research Institute, 1977)

Maududi, Sayyid Asad Gilana. *Thought and Movement* (Lahore: Islamic Publications, 1984)

Mawdudi, Sayyid Abu A'ala. *Economic Problems of Man and Its Islamic Solution* (Chicago: Kazi Publications Inc, 1987)

Maxon, Robert M. *Struggle for Kenya: The Loss and Reassertion of Imperial Initiative, 1912-13* (London: Associated University Presses, 1993)

Mayer, Ann Elizabeth. *Islam and Human Rights: Tradition and Politics* (2nd ed. London: Westview Press, 1995). http://capitadiscovery.co.uk/brighton-ac/items/291142

McCarthy, R J, (trans.) *Deliverance from Error: An Annotated Translation of al Munkidh min al dalal and Other Related Works of al Ghazali* (Louisville, Kentucky: Fons Vitae, 2004)

McConnell, Lee, and Rhona Smith. *Research Methods in Human Rights* (Routledge, 2018). https://doi.org/10.4324/9781315672632

McGoldrick, D. *The Human Rights Committee – Its Role in the Development of the International Covenant on Civil and Political Rights* (Clarendon Press, Oxford 1991)

McGowan, Bruce, and Bruce William McGowan. *Economic Life in Ottoman Europe: Taxation, Trade and the Struggle for Land, 1600-1800* (Cambridge University Press, 1981)

McHugo, J. *A Concise History of Sunnis and Shi'is* (Washington DC: Georgetown University Press, 2017)

McNair, Lord. *The Law of Treaties* (Oxford, New York: Oxford University Press, 1986)

Melchert, Christopher. *The Formation of the Sunni Schools of Law, 9th – 10th Centuries CE* (Leiden: Brill, 1997)

Menski, Werner. *Comparative Law in a Global Context: The Legal Systems of Asia and Africa* (Platinum Publishing Limited, 2000)

Mervyn, F. *Constituting Human Rights: Global Civil Society and the Society of Democratic States* (London: Routledge, 2002)

Michel, A (ed) *Indian Africa: Minorities of Indian-Pakistani Origin in Eastern Africa* (Nairobi: Africae, 2015)

Middleton J and J Campbell, *Zanzibar: Its Society and Its Politics* (London, 1965)

Miller, Gale, and Robert Dingwall. *Context and Method in Qualitative Research* (London: SAGE Publications Ltd, 1997)

Milner, Sir Alfred. *Questions of the Hour* (London, 1923)

Misol, Lisa. *Playing with Fire: Weapons Proliferation, Political Violence, and Human Rights in Kenya* (New York: Human Rights Watch, 2002). https://www.hrw.org/reports/2002/kenya/

Moghissi, H. *Feminism and Islamic Fundamentalism: The Limits of Postmodern Analysis* (Zed Books, 1999)

Mohammed, Abdi Shakur, and Salina Kassim. *The Lost Treasure Trove of Waqf in Kenya* (Malaysia: International Islamic University Malaysia, 2016)

Mohiddin, *African Socialism in Two Countries* (Croom Helm, 1981)

Morris, Stephen, Nancy Devlin, David Parkin, and Anne Spencer. *Economic Analysis in Healthcare* (2nd ed. Chichester: John Wiley & Sons Limited, 2007)

Morse, Geoffrey K, and David Williams. *Davies: Principles of Tax Law* (6th ed. London: Sweet & Maxwell, 2008)

Moussa, Mohammed. *Politics of the Islamic Tradition: The Thought of Muhammad Al-Ghazali* (Routledge, 2015)

Moussalli, Ahmad S. *The Islamic Quest for Democracy, Pluralism, and Human Rights* (University of Florida Press, 2001)

MUHURI, *''We are Tired of taking You to the Court': Human Rights Abuses by Kenya's Anti-Terrorism Police Unit'* (Open Society Foundations, 2013)

Muir, Sir William. *The Caliphate. Its Rise, Decline, and Fall* (Edinburg, 1915)

Murakami, K. *Culture in Action: A Discursive Approach* (The Oxford Handbook of Culture and Psychology, 2012)

Musgrave, RA and PB Musgrave, *Public Finance in Theory and Practice* (New York: McGraw-Hill, 1989).

Musharraf, M.N. *A Roadmap for Studying Fiqh: An Introduction to the Key of the Four Madhabs* (Australian Islamic Library, 2020)

Mutua, Makau. *Kenya's Quest for Democracy: Taming Leviathan* (Lynne Rienner Publishers, 2008)

Mwakimako, M. *Mosques in Kenya: Muslim Opinions on Religion, Politics and Development* (De Gruyter, 2021)

Nasr, Vali. *The Shia Revival: How Conflicts within Islam Will Shape the Future* (Reprint edition. New York: W. W. Norton & Company, 2007)

Ndege, George Oduor. *Health, State and Society in Kenya: Faces of Contact and Change* (Boydell & Brewer, 2001). https://www.jstor.org/stable/10.7722/j.ctt1bh2msr

Ndzovu, Hassan Juma. *Muslims in Kenyan Politics: Political Involvement, Marginalisation, and Minority Status* (Northwestern University Press, 2014). https://nupress.northwestern.edu/content/muslims-kenyan-politics

Nolan, Aoife, ed. *Economic and Social Rights after the Global Financial Crisis* (Cambridge: Cambridge University Press, 2014). https://doi.org/10.1017/CBO9781107337954

Norris, Pippa. *Sacred and Secular: Religion and Politics Worldwide* (2nd edition. Cambridge: Cambridge University Press, 2012)

Nowrojee, P. *A Kenyan Journey* (Manqa Books 2019)

Obiechina, Emmanuel N. *Culture, Tradition and Society in the West African Novel.* African Studies Series 14 (Cambridge: Cambridge University Press, 1975)

OECD, *OECD Development Co-operation Peer Reviews: Germany* (OECD Publishing, 2015)

O'Dair, Richard, and Andrew Lewis, eds. *Law and Religion: Current Legal Issues 2001 Volume 4.* (Oxford: Oxford University Press, 2001)

Ojwang, J B. *Constitutional Development in Kenya: Institutional Adaptation and Social Change* (Acts Press, African Centre for Technology Studies, 1990)

Okia, O. *Communal Labor in Colonial Kenya: The Legitimization of Coercion,* 1912-1930 (Palgrave MacMillan, 2012)

Oliver, Roland, and J. D Fage. *A Short History of Africa* (Middlesex: Harmondsworth, 1970)

Paley, J. *Phenomenology as Qualitative Research: A Critical Analysis of Meaning Attribution* (Routledge, 2016)

Philips, Abu Ameenah Bilal. *The Evolution of Fiqh* (Riyadh: International Islamic Publishing House, 2006)

Pickthall, Muhammad Marmaduke. *The Meaning of the Glorious Qur'an* (Birmingham: Islamic Dawah Centre International, 2013)

Porta, Donatella Della, and Michael Keating. *Approaches and Methodologies in the Social Sciences: A Pluralist Perspective* (Cambridge: Cambridge University Press, 2008)

Pospisil, Leopold J. *Anthropology of Law: A Comparative Theory* (New York: Harper and Row, 1971)

Pouwels, Randall Lee. *Islam and Islamic Leadership in the Coastal Communities of Eastern Africa, 1700 to 1914* (London: University Microfilms International, 1979)

Prihatna, Andy Agung. *Muslim Philanthropy: Potential and Reality of Zakat in Indonesia: Survey Results in Ten Cities* (Kurniawati, 2005)

Qinawi, Abd al Razziq Muhammad. *Fatawa Al-Sawm* (1st ed. Dar al Amin, 1998)

Qutb, Sayyid. *Al Salam Al Alami Wa Al Islam* (Beirut: Dar al Shuruq, 1983)

———, *Milestones*. (ed) A. B. al-Mehri (CreateSpace Independent Publishing Platform, 2017)

Qutb, Sayyid, and Hamid Algar. *Social Justice in Islam*. Translated by John B. Hardie (Revised edition. Oneonta, NY: Islamic Publications International, 2000)

Rahman, Abdur. *Non-Muslims under Shari'ah* (Brentwood, MD.: International Graphics, 1979)

Rahman, Habib Ur. *A Chronology of Islamic History, 570-1000 CE* (G.K. Hall, 1989).

Rahnema, Ali. *Pioneers of Islamic Revival - Studies in Islamic Society* (2nd Revised edition. New York: Zed Books Ltd, 2005)

Ramadan, Tariq. *Western Muslims and the Future of Islam* (Reprint edition. Oxford: Oxford University Press, 2005)Redding, J.A. *A Secular Need: Islamic Law and State Governance in Contemporary India* (University of Washington Press, 2020).

Ricardo, David. *On the Principles of Political Economy and Taxation* (London: John Murray, 1821)

Robertson, Bridget M. *Angels in Africa: Memoir of Nursing with the Colonial Service* (London: Radcliffe Press, 1993)

Robson, Colin, and Kieren McCartan. *Real World Research. A Resource for Users of Social Research Methods in Applied Settings* (4th ed. Wiley, 2016)

Rotberg, Robert, and Ali Al Amin Mazrui. *Protest and Power in Black Africa* (New York: OUP, 1970)

Sachedina, Abdulaziz. *The Islamic Roots of Democratic Pluralism* (Oxford University Press, 2001)

Saeed, Abdulla. *Islam and Human Rights. Vol. 1, Key Issues in the Debates* (Human Rights Law Series. Cheltenham: Elgar, 2012)

———, *Islamic Political Thought and Governance: Critical Concepts in Political Science* (Routledge, 2010)

Saldana, Johnny. *The Coding Manual for Qualitative Researchers* (Los Angeles, Calif: Sage Publications Ltd, 2009)

Salim, Ahmed I. *The Swahili-Speaking Peoples of Kenya's Coast, 1895-1965* (East African Publishing House, 1973)

Salomon, Margot E. *Global Responsibility for Human Rights: World Poverty and the Development of International Law* (Oxford University Press, 2008)

Salvadori, C, SM Fisher, B Mauladad et al, *Settling in a Strange Land: Stories of Punjabi Muslim pioneers in Kenya* (Nairobi: Park Road Mosque Trust, 2010)

Sandberg, Russell, ed. *Religion and Legal Pluralism* (1st edition. USA: Routledge, 2015)

Schacht, Joseph. *An Introduction to Islamic Law* (New Ed edition. Oxford; Oxford University Press, 2002)

Schumpeter, Joseph Alois. *The Crisis of the Tax State. Contemporary Issues from the Field of Sociology* (Reprint 1976. Hickel, 1918)

S Shabbar, *Ijtihad and Renewal* (Surrey: The International Institute of Islamic Thought, 2017)

Shafi, Abu Abdillah Muhamed ibn Idris, and Majid Khadduri. *Risala: Treatise on the Foundation of Islamic Jurisprudence* (Islamic Text Society, 1997)

Shafi, Mohamed. *The Quran- How It Was Revealed and Compiled* (Dar al Islam, n.d). http://www.daralislam.org/portals/0/Publications/TheQURANHowitwasRevealedandCompiled.pdf.

Sharifi, M, N Ansari, and M Asadollahzadeh. *A Critical Discourse Analytic Approach to Discursive Construction of Islam in Western Talk Shows: The Case of CNN Talk Shows* (SAGE, 2016)

Sheik, SA. Blood on the Runway (Northern Publishing House, 2007).

Shemesh, Ben, trans. *Abu Yusuf's Kitab Al-Kharaj* (Leiden: E.J. Brill, 1970)

Sherbeeni, K. *Mughni Al Muhtaaj* (Beirut: Dar al Maferah, 1997)

Shivji, I, *The Concept of Human Rights in Africa* (CODESRIA, 1989)

Shue, Henry. *Basic Rights* (New Jersey: Princeton University Press, 1980)

Siddqui, M. *My Way. A Muslim Woman's Journey* (I.B. Tauris, 2014)

___________, *How To Read The Quran* (Granta Books, 2007)

Siddiqui, Sajidur Rahman. *Studies in Islamic Jurisprudence; Zakat and Tax* (Beirut: Dar Al Kotob Ilmiyah, 2006)

Siddiqi, A.H. *The Origins and Development of Muslim Institutions* (Jamiyat Ul Fallah Publications, 1962)

Sijistānī, Abū Dā'ūd Sulaymān ibn al-Ash'ath al-. *Sunan Abu Dawud*. 2 vols (Cairo: Dar al-Yusr & Dar al-Minhaj, 1980)

Silverman, David. *Qualitative Research* (London: SAGE Publications Ltd, 2016)

Sionaidh, Douglas-Scott. *Law after Modernity* (Hart Publishing Limited, 2013)

Siraj, Sait, and Hilary Lim. *Land, Law & Islam: Property and Human Rights in the Muslim World* (London: Zed Books Ltd, 2006)

Smith, Adam. *An Inquiry into the Nature and Causes of the Wealth of Nations* (London: Methuen and Co, 1904)

Smith, Charles D. *Muhammad Husayn Haykal: An Intellectual and Political Biography* (University of Michigan Press, 1968)

Smith, Jonathan, Paul Flowers, and Michael Larkin. *Interpretative Phenomenological Analysis: Theory, Method and Research* (London: SAGE Publications Ltd, 2009)

Snee, H, C Hine, Y Moey, et al, (eds) *Digital Methods for Social Science: An Interdisciplinary Guide to Research Innovation* (Springer, 2016)

Snowdon, Christopher. *The Wages of Sin Taxes* (London: Adam Smith Institute, 2012)

Stichter, Sharon. *Migrant Labour in Kenya: Capitalism and African Response 1895–1975* (London: Longman, 1982)

Stiglitz, JE. *Economics of Public Sector* (New York: WW. Norton & Company, 2000).

Stilles, E. *Experience of Muslims in East Africa: Handbook of Contemporary Islam and Muslim Lives* (Springer, 2020)

Strauss, Anselm, and Juliet M. Corbin. *Basics of Qualitative Research: Grounded Theory Procedures and Techniques* (Sage Publications, Inc, 1990)

Stigand, C.H. *The Land of Zinj: Being an Account of British East Africa, its Ancient History and Present Inhabitants* (London, 1966)

Taha, Mahmoud Mohamed. *The Second Message of Islam* (Syracuse: Syracuse University Press, 1987)

Taylor, Steven, and Robert Bogdan. *Introduction to Qualitative Research Methods: A Guidebook and Resource* (New York: John Wiley & Sons Limited, 1998)

Tesch, R. *Qualitative Research: Analysis Types and Software Tools* (Basingstoke: Falmer, 1990)

Teubner, Gunther. *How the Law Thinks: Toward a Constructivist Epistemology of Law* (Routledge, 2017). https://doi.org/10.4324/9781315091891-8

Throup, David. *Economic & Social Origins of Mau Mau, 1945–1953* (Athens: Ohio University Press, 1990)

Tibi, Bassam. *The Challenge of Fundamentalism: Political Islam and the New World Disorder* (Berkeley: University of California Press, 1998)

Tobin, John. *The Right to Health in International Law* (Oxford: Oxford University Press, 2012)

Toth, James. *Sayyid Qutb: The Life and Legacy of a Radical Islamic Intellectual* (Oxford University Press, 2021)

Toynbee, Arnold J. *Civilization on Trial* (Oxford University Press, 1949)

Trakman, Leon, and Sean Gatien. *Rights and Responsibilities* (Toronto: University of Toronto Press, 1999)

Trimingham, Spencer J. *Islam in East Africa* (Oxford: Clarendon Press, 1964)

Tschalaer, M H. *Muslim Women's Quest for Justice. Gender, Law and Activism in India* (Cambridge University Press, 2017)

Vaughan, M. *Curing Their Ills: Colonial Power and African Illness* (Palo Alto, Stanford University Press, 1991)

Vishanoff, David. *The Formation of Islamic Hermeneutics: How Sunni Legal Theorists Imagined a Revealed Law* (Ann Arbor: American Oriental Society, 2010)

Wagstaff, Adam, and Eddy van Doorslaer. *Equity in Health Care Finance and Delivery* (Elsevier, 2000). https://doi.org/10.1016/S1574-0064(00)80047-5

Walters, P. E. 'NFD Annual Report 1960' (Kenya National Archives, n.d)

Wansharisi, Ahmad b. Yahya l-. *Al-Mi'yar Al-Mu'Rib,*. (ed) Muhammad Hajji. 5 vols (Beirut: Dar algharb al-islami, 1990)

Waris, Attitya. *Financing Africa* (Cameroon: Langaa, 2019)

Watts, Swanson G. E. *Religion and Regime* (Ann Arbour: University of Michigan Press, 1970)

Wellhausen, Julius. *The Arab Kingdom and Its Fall* (Calcutta, 1927)

Westerman, Pauline. *Open or Autonomous: The Debate on Legal Methodology as a Reflection of the Debate on Law* (Oxford: Hart Publishing Limited, 2013)

Whittaker, H. *Insurgency and Counterinsurgency in Kenya: A Social History of the Shifta Conflict, c. 1963-1968* (Brill, 2015)

Widner, J. *The Rise of a Party-State in Kenya: From Harambee! to Nyayo!* (University of California Press, 1992)

Wiedner, D. L. *A History of Africa South of the Sahara* (New York: Vintage Books, 1964)

Wilson, Bryan R. *Religion in Secular Society* (London: Oxford University Press, 1996)

———, *Religion in Sociological Perspective* (Oxford: Oxford University Press, 1992)

Winter, Michael, and Amalia Levanoni. *The Mamluks in Egyptian and Syrian Politics and Society* (Leiden: BRILL, 2004)

Witte J and C Green (eds), *Religion and Human Rights: An Introduction* (OUP, 2012)

Wood, LA and RO Kroger, *Doing Discourse Analysis: Methods for Studying Action in Talk and Text* (Sage Publications Inc. 2000)

Yilmaz, V. *Private Healthcare Provider Organisations as New Actors in the Politics of Healthcare* (Springer, 2017) 195-239

Young, K (eds) *The Future of Economic and Social Rights* (Cambridge University Press, 2019)

Yourow, Howard Charles. *The Margin of Appreciation Doctrine in the Dynamics of European Human Rights Jurisprudence* (Kluwer Law International, 1996)

Zallum, A. *Funds in the Khilafa State* (Milli Publications, 2002)

Zarkashī, Muḥammad ibn Bahādur. *al Burhan fi ulum al Qur'an* (Beirut, Lebanon: Dar ul Fikr, 1988)

Zeghal, Malika, and Marilyn R. Waldman. 'Islamic World, Prehistory and History of the Islamic Community' (BRITANNICA, n.d)

Ziebertz, H G and F Zaccaria (eds), *The Ambivalent Impact of Religion on Human Rights. Empirical Studies in Europe, Africa and Asia* (Springer, 2021)

Zulfiqar, Muhammad. *Zakat According to the Qur'an and Sunna* (Riyadh: Darussalam Publishers, 2011)

Chapters in Books

Al Salim, 'Native or Non-Native: The Problem of Identity and on Social Stratification of the Arab-Swahili of Kenya', in BA Ogot, (ed.) *Hadith* (Nairobi: East African Publishing House, 1970)

Al Turabi, Hasan, 'The Islamic State.' In *Voices of Resurgent Islam,* (ed) JL Esposito, 241–51. (New York: Oxford University Press, 1983)

Berg, FJ 'The Coast from the Portuguese Invasion to the Rise of the Zanzibar Sultanate', in BA Ogot, (ed.) *Zamani: A Survey of East African History* (Nairobi: East African Publishing House 1974), 115-133

Bharati, A. 'Ideology and Content of Caste among the Indians in East Africa', in Barton Schwartz (ed) Caste *in Overseas Indian Communities* (San Francisco: Chandler, 1967)

Billig, M, 'Discursive, Rhetorical and Ideological Messages' in C McGarty, SA Haslam, (ed.), *The Message of Social Psychology: Perspectives on Mind in Society* (Cambridge, MA: Blackwell, 1997)

Chatterjee, Meera. 'Health for Too Many: India's Experiments with Truth.' In *Reaching Health for All,* (ed) Jon Rohde, Meera Chatterjee, and David Morley (Oxford University Press, 1993)

Chynoweth, Paul. 'Legal Research.' In *Advanced Research Methods in the Built Environment,* (ed)Andrew Knight and Les Ruddock (Hoboken: Wiley-Blackwell, 2008)

Djermakoye, Fournier. 'Village Health Teams in Niger (Maradi Department).' In *Health by the People,* (ed) KW Newell, 128–206 (Geneva: World Health Organization, 1975)

Doe, Norman, and Anthony Jeremy. 'Justifications for Religious Autonomy.' In *Law and Religion,* (ed) Richard O'Dair and Andrew Lewis, 421–42. Current Legal Issues (Oxford University Press, 2001)

Egan, Suzanne. 'The Doctrinal Approach in International Human Rights Law Scholarship.' In *Research Methods in Human Rights,* (ed) Lee McConnell and Rhona Smith (Routledge, 2018)

Eide, Asbjørn. 'Economic, Social and Cultural Rights as Human Rights.' In *Economic, Social and Cultural Rights: A Textbook,* (ed) Catarina Krause, Allan Rosas, and Asbjørn Eide (Leiden: Brill Nijhoff, 2001). https://brill.com/view/title/9432

El Shamsy, Ahmed. 'The Wisdom of God's Law: Two Theories.' In *Islamic Law in Theory: Studies on Jurisprudence in Honor of Bernard Weiss,* (ed) Kevin Reinhart and Robert Gleave (BRILL, 2014)

Elson, Diane, Radhika Balakrishnan, and James Heintz. 'Public Finance, Maximum Available Resources and Human Rights.' In *Human Rights and Public Finance. Budgets and the Promotion of Economic and Social Rights,* (ed) Aoife Nolan, R O'Connell, and C Harvey. (Oxford: Hart Publishing Limited, 2013)

Fauzia, A. 'A History of Islamic Philanthropy in Indonesia', in M Ricklefs and B Lockhart (eds) *Faith and the State* (Leiden: Brill, 2013)

Gibson, Lucy. 'Type Me Your Answer: Generating Interview Data via Email.' In *Collecting Qualitative Data: A Practical Guide to Textual, Media and Virtual Techniques,* (ed) Virginia Braun, Victoria Clarke, and Debra Gray (Cambridge: Cambridge University Press, 2017)

Gleave, RM 'Interpreting Scriptures in Judaism, Christianity and Islam' in M Z Cohen and A Berlin (eds) *Overlapping Inquiries* (Cambridge University Press, 2016)

Harrington J and M Stuttaford, 'Introduction; in J Harrington and M Stuttaford (eds), *Global health and human rights: Legal and philosophical perspectives* (London: Routledge 2010)

Henkin, L. 'The International Bill of Rights: The Universal Declaration and the Covenants' in R Bernhardt and JA Jolowics (eds) *International Enforcement of Human Rights* (1985)

Herskovits, M 'Statement on Human Rights' (1947) *American Anthropologist,* 539-543, reprinted in Morton E Winston (ed), *The Philosophy of Human Rights* (Belmont, Wadsworth, 1989)

Hood, Jane. 'Orthodoxy versus Power: The Defining Traits of Grounded Theory.' In *Handbook of Grounded Theory,* (ed) A Bryant and K Charmaz, (London: Sage Publications, Inc, 2007)

Hughes, Mark. 'Interviewing.' In *Research Methods for Postgraduates*, (ed) Tony Greenfield and Sue Greener, (3rd ed., Wiley, 2016)

Hutchinson, Terry. 'Doctrinal Research: Researching the Jury.' In *Research Methods in Law*, (ed) M. Burton and D. Watkins, (United Kingdom: Routledge, 2013). http://www.routledge.com/books/details/9780415672146/

Kahf, Monzer. 'Applied Institutional Models for Zakah Collection and Distribution in Islamic Countries and Communities.' In *Institutional Framework of Zakah: Dimensions and Implications*, (ed) Ahmad Abdulfattha El Asker and Muhammad Sirajul-Haq (Jeddah: Islamic Research and Training Institute, 1994

Karimova, Takhmina. 'The Nature and Meaning of 'International Assistance and Cooperation' under the International Covenant on Economic, Social and Cultural Rights.' In *Economic, Social, and Cultural Rights in International Law: Contemporary Issues and Challenges*, (ed) Eibe Riedel, Gilles Giacca, and Christophe Golay (Oxford University Press, 2016)

Keller H and L Grover (eds), 'General Comments of the Human Rights Committee and their Legitimacy', in: *UN Human Rights Treaty Bodies: Law and Legitimacy* (Cambridge University Press, 2012)

Kaniki, MHY. 'The Colonial Economy: The Former British Zones', in Boahen A. (ed) General *History of Africa: Africa under Colonial Domination 1880-1935* (France: UNESCO Publishing, 1985)

Khadduri, Majid. (trans.) (n.d.), 'The *Zakat* (Legal Alms)', in al Shafi'i's Risala, *Treatise on the Foundation of Islamic Jurisprudence* (Islamic Text Society, n.d)

Khaled, Abou El Fadl. 'The Human Rights Commitment in Modern Islam.' In *Human Rights and Responsibilities in the World Religions*, (ed) Joseph Runzo, Nancy Martin, and Arvind Sharma (Oxford: Oneworld Publications, 2002)

Makokha, Joseph. The Islamic Factor in Somali Irredentism: Towards Rationalising the Kenya Government's Stand Against Islamic Political Association.' In *Islam in Kenya*, (ed) Yahya S Saad and Mohamed Bakari. Nairobi: Signal Press Ltd, 1995

Mathews, G. 'The East African Coast until the Coming of the Portuguese', in R Oliver, and G Mathew (eds) *History of East Africa Vol* 1, (Oxford, 1963)

Mburu, F.M. 'The Impact of Colonial Rule on Health Development: The Case of Kenya.' In *The Political Economy of Health in Africa*, (ed) Toyin Falola and Dennis Ityavyar (Athens: Ohio University Center for International Studies, 1992)

Mirpuri, Ahmed M. '*Zakat*- Islamic Obligatory Charity.' In *Fatawa Sirat-e-Mustaqeem*, translated by Mohammed Abdul Hadi (Riyadh: Darussalam Publishers, 1998)

Morrow, R. H. 'A Primary Health Care Strategy for Ghana.' In *Practising Health for All*, (ed) David Morley, Jon Rohde, and G. Williams (Oxford: Oxford University Press, 1983)

Mwanzi, H. A. 'African Initiatives and Resistance in East Africa, 1880-1914.' In *General History of Africa: Africa under Colonial Domination, 1880-1935*, (ed) A. Adu Boahen (U.S.A.: Heinemann; University of California Press, 1985)

Newell, Peter. 'Taking Accountability into Account: The Debate So Far.' In *Rights Resources and the Politics of Accountability*, (ed) Peter Newell and Joanna Wheeler (London: Zed Books, 2006)

Odhiambo, E.S. Atieno. 'Economic Mobilization and Political Leadership: Oginga Odinga and the Luo Thrift and Trading Corporation to 1956.' In *Politics and Leadership in Africa*, (ed) A Ajuko and W Ochieng (East African Literature Bureau, 1975)

Ograjensek, I, 'Theory and Practice of Qualitative Research', in T Greenfield and S Greener, *Research Methods for Postgraduates* (UK: John Wiley & Sons Ltd, 2016)

Seeseman, R 'Changes in Islamic Knowledge Practices in Twentieth Century Kenya, in R Launay (ed) Islamic *Education in Kenya* (Indiana: Indiana University Press, 2016)

Seidel, J, and U Kelle. 'Different Functions of Coding in the Analysis of Textual Data.' In *Computer-Aided Qualitative Data Analysis: Theory, Methods and Practice*, (ed) U Kelle (London: SAGE Publications, Inc, 1995)

Shanguhyia M and MM Koster, 'Land and Conflict in Kenya's Rift Valley: Historical and Contemporary Perspectives', in T Falola and M M Heaton (eds) *Contemporary Africa: Challenges and Opportunities* (Palgrave MacMillan, 2014)

Shestack, J. 'The Philosophical Foundations of Human Rights', in: Janusz Symonides, *Human Rights: Concepts and Standards* (Vermont, USA: UNESCO Publishing, 2000)

Smith, R, and L Smith. 'Qualitative Methods.' In *Research Methods in Human Rights*, (ed) Lee McConnell and Rhona Smith (New York: Routledge, 2018)

Smits, Jan M. 'Redefining Normative Legal Science: Towards an Argumentative Discipline.' In *Methods of Human Rights Research*, (ed) Fons Coomans, Fred Gruenfeld, and Menno Kamminga. (Cambridge: Intersentia, 2009)

Snape, Dawn, and Liz Spencer. 'The Foundations of Qualitative Research.' In *Qualitative Research Practice: A Guide for Social Science Students and Researchers,* (ed) Jane Ritchie and Jane Lewis (London: SAGE Publications Ltd, 2003)

Steiner, H. 'Individual Claims in a World of Massive Violations: What Role for the Human Rights Committee', in P Alston and J Crawford (eds) *The Future of UN Human Rights Treaty Monitoring* (Cambridge: Cambridge University Press, 2000)

Sutphen, Mary Preston. 'Rumoured Power: Hong Kong, 1894 and Cape Town, 1901.' In *Western Medicine as Contested Knowledge,* (ed) Andrew Cunningham and Andrews Bridie (Manchester University Press, 1997)

Taylor, S 'Locating and Conducting Discourse Analytic Research' in M Wetherell, S Taylor, and S Yates, (eds) *Discourse as Data: A Guide for Analysis* (SAGE 2001)

Van Ho, T 'Obligations of International Assistance and Cooperation in the Context of Investment Law', In: Erdem Turkelli, Gamze and Gibney, Mark and Krajewski, Markus and Vandenhole, Wouter (eds) *Routledge Handbook on Extraterritorial Human rights Obligations* (Routledge, 2021)

Vandemoortele, Jan. 'The Limits of the MDGs' Design. Six Caveats for Human Rights.' In *The Millennium Development Goals and Human Rights, Past, Present and Future.,* (ed) Malcolm Langford, Andy Sumner, and Alicia Ely Yamin (Cambridge University Press, 2013)

Watt, Montgomery W. 'The Closing of the Door of Ijtihad.' In *Orientalia Hispanica,* (ed) J. M. Barral, *Vol* 1 (Leiden: Brill, 1974)

Webley, Lisa. 'Qualitative Approaches to Empirical Legal Research.' In *The Oxford Handbook of Practical Legal Research,* (ed) Peter Cane and Herbert Kritzer (Oxford: Oxford University Press, 2010)

Wilkinson, Sue. 'Analysing Focus Group Data.' In *Qualitative Research,* (ed) David Silverman (London: SAGE Publications Ltd, 2016)

Williams, A., and R. Cookson. 'Equity in Health.' In *Handbook of Health Economics,* (ed) Culyer A. Newhouse, 1863–1910 (Netherlands: Elsevier Science BV, 2000)

Wolf, Thomas. 'Contemporary Politics.' In *Kenya Coast Handbook,* (ed) Jan Hoorweg (Hamburg: Lit Verlag, 2000)

Wolfrum, R 'Obligation of Result Versus Obligation of Conduct: Some Thoughts About the Implementation of International Obligations' in M H Arsanjani, J Cogan, R Sloane and S Wiessner (eds) *Looking to the Future: Essays on International Law in Honor of W Michael Reisman* (Brill | Nijhoff, 2010)

Journal Articles

Aboul-Enein, Basil H. 'Health-Promoting Verses as Mentioned in the Holy Quran' *Journal of Religion and Health* 55, no. 3 (June 2016): 821–29. https://doi.org/10.1007/s10943-014-9857-8

Ahlberg, B 'Integrated Health Care Systems and Indigenous Medicine: Reflections from the Sub-Sahara African Region' (2017) *Front. Sociol*

Ahmad, Mahadi. 'An Empirical Study of the Challenges Facing *Zakat* and Waqf Institutions in Northern Nigeria.' (2019) *ISRA International Journal of Islamic Finance* 11, no. 2 (January): 338–56. https://doi.org/10.1108/IJIF-04-2018-0044

Ahmed, Farah. 'Exploring Halaqah as Research Method: A Tentative Approach to Developing Islamic Research Principles within a Critical 'Indigenous' Framework.' (2014) *International Journal of Qualitative Studies in Education* 27, no 5 (May): 561–83. https://doi.org/10.1080/09518398.2013.805852

Aiman, Wan Khairul, and Wan Mokhtar. 'Thematic Concept Research for Al-Hadith (Al-Hadith Al-Mawdu'Iy)' (2017) *International Journal of Academic Research in Business and Social Sciences* 7, no. 2: 591–99

Ainsworth, J. 'The Commercial Possibilities of Kenya Colony', (1921) *Journal of the Manchester Geographical Society*, 37, 51-60

Alase, A. 'The Interpretative Phenomenological Analysis (IPA): A Guide to a Good Qualitative Research Approach', (2017) *International Journal of Education & Literacy Studies*, vol 5, no 2

Al Sayyid, Ridwan. 'Contemporary Muslim Thought and Human Rights.' (1995) *Islamochristiana* 21

Alazzam, Isa Mahmoud. 'The Economic and Social Life in Egypt during the Reign of Ayyubid Sultan Saladin (567 AH -1171 AD) -589 AH/1193AD) a Vision through the Journey (Rihlat) of Ibn Jubayr.' (2014) *Asian Culture and History* 6, no. 1

Ali, Shaheen S. 'The Conceptual Foundations of Human Rights: A Comparative Perspective.' *European Public Law* 3, no. 2 (1997): 261–82

Alias, Mohd Syahmir, and Mohd Shukri Hanapi. 'Ibn Al Haytham's Philosophy on Scientific Research Applied in Islamic Research Methodology: Analysis from Tasawwur, Epistemology and Ontology Perspectives.' (2005) *International Journal of Business, Humanities and Technology* 5, no. 1: 83–93

Alpers, E. 'Gujarat and the Trade of East Africa, c.1500-1800' (1967) *International Journal of African Historical Studies*, 9, 22-44

Alston, P and G Quinn, The Nature and Scope of State Party Obligations under the International Covenant on Economic, Social and Cultural Rights (1987) *Human Rights Quarterly*, Vol 9, No 2, 156-229, 166

Altman, Drew E., and Douglas H. Morgan. 'The Role of State and Local Government in Health' (1983) *Health Affairs* 2, no. 4 (January 1): 7–31. https://doi.org/10.1377/hlthaff.2.4.7

Amico, Peter, Christian Aran, and Carlos Avila. 'HIV Spending as a Share of Total Health Expenditure: An Analysis of Regional Variation in a Multi-Country Study.' (2010) *PLoS ONE* 5, no. 9 (September). https://doi.org/10.1371/journal.pone.0012997

Amiji, H. 'Some Notes on Religious Dissent in Nineteenth Century East Africa', (1971) *African Historical Studies*, 4, 603-616

Anderson, D. 'Remembering Wagalla: state violence in northern Kenya, 1962-1991' (2014) Journal of Eastern African Studies, Vol 8, Issue 4, 658-676, 659.

__________. 'Yours in Struggle for Majimbo: Nationalism and the Party Politics of Decolonisation in Kenya, 1955-64,' (2005) *Journal of Contemporary History*, Vol 40, No. 3, 547-564

An Naim, A 'The Compatibility Dialectic: Mediating the Legitimate Coexistence of Islamic Law and State Law' (2010) *The Modern Law Review* 73, no. 1 1–29

Anderson, David. 'Yours in the Struggle for Majimbo: Nationalism and the Party Politics of Decolonisation in Kenya, 1955 to 1964' (2005) *Journal of Contemporary History* 39: 547–64

Anderson, GVW. 'Medical Practice after the War', (1942) *East African Medical Journal*, Vol 19, No7, 208

As Salafiya, ASR. 'A Scientometric Analysis of *Zakat* Literature Published in times of COVID-19 Pandemic', (2021) *International Journal of Zakat*, Vol 6, No.2, 1-14

Atighetchi, D. 'The Position of Islamic Tradition on Contraception' (1994) *Med Law* 13(7-8):717-25

Bagheri, Pezhman, Mohammad Reza Mohammadi, and Nematollah Shafiei. 'Thematic Analysis of Persian Documents in the Field of Quran Study and Medicine in National Scientific-Research Journals from 1992 to 2013: An Opportunity for Evidence Based Decision Making' (2017) *J Relig Health* 56): 755–75

Baig, Mustafa. 'Operating Islamic Jurisprudence in Non-Muslim Jurisdictions: Traditional Islamic Precepts and Contemporary Controversies in the United States' (2015) *Chi.-Kent. L. Rev.* 90, No. 1

Banakar, Reza. 'Having One's Cake and Eating It: The Paradox of Contextualisation in Socio-Legal Research' (2011) *International Journal of Law in Context* 7, no. 4 (December): 487–503. https://doi.org/10.1017/S1744552311000267

Barasa, FO. 'The Church and the Healthcare Sector in Kenya: A Functional Analysis of its Development through Evangelisation' (2020) *International Journal of Innovative Science and Research Technology*, Vol 5, Issue 9, 1058-1064, 1061

Barber, Nick. 'The Rechtsstaat and the Rule of Law.' (2003) *University of Toronto Law Journal* 53, no. 4: 443–54

Barkan, Joel D., and Michael Chege. 'Decentralising the State: District Focus and the Politics of Reallocation in Kenya' (1989) *The Journal of Modern African Studies* 27, No 3: 431–53

Bashear, Suliman. 'On the Origins and Development of the Meaning of Zakāt in Early Islam.' (1993) *Arabica* 40, no. 1 (January): 84–113. https://doi.org/10.1163/157005893X00273

Basit, Tehmina. 'Manual or Electronic? The Role of Coding in Qualitative Data Analysis.' (2003) *Educational Research* 45, No. 2 (June): 143–54. https://doi.org/10.1080/0013188032000133548

Bennett, Karen, Danna Ingleton, Alice M. Nah, and James Savage. 'Critical Perspectives on the Security and Protection of Human Rights Defenders.' (2015) *The International Journal of Human Rights* 19, No. 7 (October): 883–95. https://doi.org/10.1080/13642987.2015.1075301

Berman BJ and JM Lonsdale, 'Crises of Accumulation, Coercion and the Colonial State: The Development of the Labour Control System in Kenya, 1919-1929' (1980) *Canadian Journal of African Studies* Vol 14, No 1, 55-81

Benthall, Jonathan. "Financial Worship: The Quranic Injunction to Almsgiving.' *Journal of the Royal Anthropological Institute* 5, no. 1 (n.d.): 27–42

Benvenisti, Eyal. 'Margin of Appreciation, Consensus, and Universal Standards' (1999) *International Law and Politics* 31, no. 843

Berg, F. J. 'The Swahili Community of Mombasa, 1500–19001' (1968) *The Journal of African History* 9, no. 1 (January): 35–56. https://doi.org/10.1017/S0021853700008343

Bielefeldt, Heiner. 'Muslim Voices in the Human Rights Debate' (1995) *Human Rights Quarterly* 17: 518–617

Bijsterveld, Sophie C. van. 'Freedom of Religion: Legal Perspectives' (2001) *Law and Religion*, 4:299–309.

Birsh S and A Gafni, 'Economists' Dream or Nightmare? Maximising Health Gains from Available Resources Using the NICE Guidelines', (2007) *Health Economics, Policy and Law*, Vol 2: 193-202

Bird, RM 'The Taxation of Personal Wealth in International Perspective' (1991) *Can. Pub. Pol'y – Analyse De Politique* 17

Bos, Maarten. 'Theory and Practice of Treaty Interpretation' (1980) *NILR* 27: 364–70

Bowen, Glenn A. 'Document Analysis as a Qualitative Research Method.' (2009) *Qualitative Research Journal* 9, no. 2: 27–40

Bradney, Anthony. 'Law as a Parasitic Discipline.' (1998) *Journal of Law and Society* 25, no. 1: 71–84. https://doi.org/10.1111/1467-6478.00080

Brennan, James R. 'Lowering the Sultan's Flag: Sovereignty and Decolonization in Coastal Kenya' (2008) *Comparative Studies in Society and History* 50, no. 4 (October): 831–61. https://doi.org/10.1017/S0010417508000364

Brown, C. 'Universal human rights: A critique' (2007) *The International Journal of Human Rights*, Volume 1, Issue 2, 41-65

Browne, RC. 'Social Medicine in England and East Africa', (1950) *East African Medical Journal*, Vol 27, No 2, 70

Chaiken, Miriam S. 'Primary Health Care Initiatives in Colonial Kenya' (1998) *World Development* 26, no. 9 (September 1,): 1701–17. https://doi.org/10.1016/S0305-750X(98)00067-9

Chenwi, Lillian, 'Unpacking 'Progressive Realisation', Its Relation to Resources, Minimum Core and Reasonableness, and Some Methodological Considerations for Assessing Compliance' (2013) *De Jure Law Journal* 46, no. 3 (March): 742–69

Chuma, Jane, Janet Musimbi, Vincent Okungu, Catherine Goodman, and Catherine Molyneux. 'Reducing User Fees for Primary Health Care in Kenya:

Policy on Paper or Policy in Practice?' (2009) *International Journal for Equity in Health* 8 (May 8): 15. https://doi.org/10.1186/1475-9276-8-15

Clark, Dana. 'The World Bank and Human Rights: The Need for Greater Accountability' (2002) *Harvard Human Rights Journal* 15: 205–26

Clarke, Gerard. 'Agents of Transformation? Donors, Faith-Based Organisations and International Development' (2007) *Third World Quarterly* 28, no. 1 (January): 77–96. https://doi.org/10.1080/01436590601081880

Clarke, S 'The Research Council System and the Politics of Medical and Agricultural Research for the British Colonial Empire, 1940-51', (2013) *Medical History*, Vol 57, Issue 3, 338-358

Conn, HM 'Islam in East Africa: An Overview', (1978) *Islamic Studies*, Vol17, No 2, 75-91

Cooper, Frederick. 'Mau Mau and the Discourses of Decolonization' (1988) *The Journal of African History* 29, no. 2: 313–20. https://doi.org/10.1017/S0021853700023707

Crowe, Jonathan. 'The Limits of Legal Pluralism' (2015) *Griffith Law Review* 24, no. 2: 314–31. https://doi.org/10.1080/10383441.2015.1048584

Cufino Svitone, E., R. Garfield, M. I. Vasconcelos, and V. Araujo Craveiro. 'Primary Health Care Lessons from the Northeast of Brazil: The Agentes de Saúde Program' (2000) *Revista Panamericana De Salud Publica Pan American Journal of Public Health* 7, no. 5 (May): 293–302. https://doi.org/10.1590/s1020-49892000000500002

Cussac, Ann. 'Muslims and Politics in Kenya: The Issue of the Kadhis Courts in the Constitution Review Process' (2008) *Journal of Muslim Minority Affairs* 28, no. 2: 289–302

Dalhat, Yusuf. 'The Concept of Aql (Reason) in Islam' (2015) *International Journal of Humanities and Social Science* 5, No. 9

Davies, Margaret. 'The Ethos of Pluralism' (2005) *Sydney Law Review* 27, No. 1

Dean, H, and Khan, Z. 'Muslim Perspectives on Welfare' (1997) *Journal of Social Policy* 26: 193–209. https://doi.org/10.1017/S0047279497004972

Donnelly, Jack. 'The Relative Universality of Human Rights' (2007) *Human Rights Quarterly* 29, no. 2: 281–306

Dowell-Jones, Mary, and David Kinley. 'Minding the Gap: Global Finance and Human Rights' (2011) *Ethics & International Affairs* 25, no. 2: 183–210. https://doi.org/10.1017/S0892679411000062

Ehrlich, S, Eades D and Ainsworth J, 'Discursive Constructions of Consent in the Legal Process', (2016) *The International Journal of Speech, Language and the Law,* Vol 23, No 2, 301-306

Eide, Asbjørn 'Making Human Rights Universal: Achievements and Prospects' (1999) *Human Rights in Development Online* 6, no. 1 (January): xiii–50. https://doi.org/10.1163/221160800X00028

El-Affendi, AA 'The Long March from Lahore to Khartoum: Beyond the Muslim Reformation' (1990) *British Society for Middle Eastern Studies Bulletin* 17, No. 2

Esbeck, Carl H. 'A Typology of Church-State Relations in American Thought' (1988) *Religion & Public Education* 15, No. 1 (January): 43–50. https://doi.org/10.1080/10567224.1988.11488009

Esposito, John. 'Political Islam: Beyond the Green Menace' (1994) *Current History* 93

Evans, David, and Carissa Etienne. 'Health Systems Financing and the Path to Universal Coverage' (2010) *Bulletin of the World Health Organization* 88: 402–402

Faridi, FR '*Zakat* and Fiscal Policy' (1980) *Studies in Islamic Economics,* 119–30

Faridy, Nahida, and Tapan Sarker. 'Who Really Pays Value Added Tax (VAT) in Developing Countries? Empirical Evidence from Bangladesh' (2011) *International Journal of Modelling and Optimization* 11

Forman, Lisa, Claudia Beiersmann, Claire E. Brolan, Martin Mckee, Rachel Hammonds, and Gorik Ooms. 'What Do Core Obligations under the Right to Health Bring to Universal Health Coverage?' (2016) *Health and Human Rights* 18, no. 2 (December): 23–34

Forman, Lisa, Gorik Ooms, and Claire E. Brolan. 'Rights Language in the Sustainable Development Agenda: Has Right to Health Discourse and Norms Shaped Health Goals?' (2015) *International Journal of Health Policy and Management* 4, no. 12 (December): 799–804. https://doi.org/10.15171/ijhpm.2015.171

Fox, Jonathan. 'Separation of Religion and State and Secularism in Theory and in Practice' (2011) *Religion, State and Society* 39, no. 4 (December): 384–401. https://doi.org/10.1080/09637494.2011.621675

Gebeye, Berihun A. 'Decoding Legal Pluralism in Africa' (2017) *The Journal of Legal Pluralism and Unofficial Law* 49, No. 2 (May): 228–49. https://doi.org/10.1080/07329113.2017.1351746

Gertzel, Cherry. 'The Provincial Administration in Kenya' (1966) *Journal of Commonwealth Political Studies* 4, no. 3: 201–15

Giacomazzi, Mia. 'Human Rights and Human Responsibilities: A Necessary Balance?' (2005) *Santa Clara Journal of International Law* 3, no 2 (January): 164

Glenngard A H and Maina TM, 'Reversing the Trend of Weak Policy Implementation in Kenya Health Sector? A Study of Budget Allocation and Spending of Health Resources Versus Set Priorities' (2007) *Health Research Policy Systems*, Vol 5, No 3

Gokmen, G, Vermeulen WN, and Vezina PL, 'The Imperial Roots of Global Trade', (2020) *Journal of Economic Growth*, 25, 87-145

Golay, Christophe, Claire Mahon, and Ioana Cismas. 'The Impact of the UN Special Procedures on the Development and Implementation of Economic, Social and Cultural Rights' (2011) *The International Journal of Human Rights* 15, no. 2 (February): 299–318. https://doi.org/10.1080/13642987.2011.537472

Goodhart, M. 'Neither Relative nor Universal: A Response to Donnelly' (2008) *Human Rights Quarterly*, Vol 30, No1, 183-193

Gostin, Larry, Klock K, Clark H et al., Financing the Future of WHO (2022) *The Lancet*, Vol 399, Issue 10334, 1445-1447

Greer, S 'The Margin of Appreciation: Interpretation and Discretion under the European Convention on Human Rights', (2000) *Human Rights Files* No 17, Council of Europe

Griffiths, John. 'What Is Legal Pluralism?' (1986) *The Journal of Legal Pluralism and Unofficial Law* 18, no. 24 (January): 1–55. https://doi.org/10.1080/07329113.1986.10756387

Grover, A, and Irwin, A, 'The Power of Community in Advancing the Right to Health: A Conversation with Anand Grover', (2009) *Health and Human Rights*, Vol. 11, No. 1, 1-3.

Gunther, Klaus. 'Legal Pluralism or Uniform Concept of Law?' (2008) *No Foundations*

Hallaq, Wael B. 'On The Authoritativeness of Sunni Consensus' (1986) *International Journal of Middle East Studies* 18, No. 4: 427–54

———, 'Was the Gate of Ijtihad Closed?' (1984) *International Journal of Middle East Studies* 16, No. 1: 3–41

Halmai, Gábor. 'Varieties of State-Church Relations and Religious Freedom Through Three Case Studies' (2017) *Michigan State Law Review* 2017, no. 2 (January): 175

Hammonds, R, Ooms, G, and Vanderhole W, 'Under the (Legal) Radar Screen: Global Health Initiatives and International Human Rights Obligations' (2012) *BMC International Health and Human Rights* 12

Harrington, J 'Governing traditional medicine in Kenya: Problematization and the role of the Constitution', (2017) *African Studies* Volume 77, Issue 2

______________, 'Framing the National Interest: Debating Intellectual Property and Access to Essential Medicines in Kenya' (2014) The Journal of World Intellectual Property, Vol 17, Issue 1-2, 16-33.

Hasan, A. 'The Principle of Qiyas in Islamic Law – An Historical Perspective', (1976*) Islamic Studies,* Vol 15, No 3 201-210

Hashim, Abdulkadir. 'Administration of Waqf Institutions in the Kenyan Coast: Problems and Prospects' (2010) *Awqaf Journal* 10, No. 18: 57–66

Hirsch, Susan F. 'Religion and Pluralism in the Constitution,' (2018) *Katiba Institute.* https://katibainstitute.org/religion-and-pluralism-in-the-constitution-susan-f-hirsch-professor/

Hoque, Nazamul, Mohammad Aktaruzzaman Khan, and Kazi Deen Mohammad. 'Poverty Alleviation by Zakah in a Transitional Economy: A Small Business Entrepreneurial Framework' (2015) *Journal of Global Entrepreneurship Research* 5, No. 1 (May): 7. https://doi.org/10.1186/s40497-015-0025-8

Hossein, Esmaeili. 'The Role of Islamic Law and Integration of Muslims into Australian Society' (2015) *FLJ* 17, No. 69

Howland, O. 'Fakes and chemicals: indigenous medicine in contemporary Kenya and implications for health equity' (2020) *International Journal for Equity in Health* 19:199

Hunt, Paul. 'Interpreting the International Right to Health in a Human Rights-Based Approach to Health' (2016) *Health and Human Rights* 18, no. 2 (December): 109–30

Hutchinson, Terry, and Duncan, Nigel. 'Defining and Describing What We Do: Doctrinal Legal Research' (2012) *Deakin Law Review* 17: 98–101

Ibrahim, Khalil Mohamed. 'Islam and the Challenges of Modernity' (2004) *Georgetown Journal of International Affairs* 5, No. 1

Illinca, S, Di Giorgio, L, Salari, P, et al., 'Socio-economic inequality and inequity in use of health care services in Kenya: evidence from the fourth Kenya household health expenditure and utilisation survey', (2019) *International Journal for Equity in Health* 18, No: 196

Iqbal, Khurshid. 'Re-Conceptualising the Right to Development in Islamic Law' (2010) *The International Journal of Human Rights* 14, No. 7 (December): 1013–41. https://doi.org/10.1080/13642980902933597

Iqbal, Muhammad. 'Challenges to Islam and Muslims: What is to be Done?', (2003) *Islamic Studies,* Vol 42, No 4, 595-637

Jackson, Sherman. 'Legal Pluralism Between Islam and the Nation-State: Romantic Medievalism or Pragmatic Modernity?' (2006) *Fordham International Law Journal* 30, no. 1 (January): 158

Jaffer, A. 'Conversion to Shi'ism in East Africa', (2013) *Journal of Shi'a Islamic Studies* 6, 131-154

Johari, F, AFM. Ali, and MRA Aziz. 'A Review of Literatures on Current *Zakat* Issues: An Analysis between 2003-2013' (2015) *International Review of Research in Emerging Markets and the Global Economy* 1, no. 2: 336–633

Johnston, David L. 'Maqāṣid Al-Sharī'a: Epistemology and Hermeneutics of Muslim Theologies of Human Rights' (2007) *Die Welt Des Islams. New Series* 47, No. 2: 149–87

Juma, Thomas Otieno, Jacob Kipkemboi Rotich, and Leonard Simiyu Mulongo. 'Devolution and Governance Conflicts in Africa: Kenyan Scenario' (2014) *Public Policy and Administration Research* 4, No. 6: 1–10

Kabia, E, R Mbau, R Oyando et al, 'We are called the et cetera: experiences of the poor with health financing reforms that target them in Kenya', (2019) *International Journal for Equity in Health* 18, No: 98

Kahf, Monzer. 'Potential Effects of *Zakat* on Government Budget.' *IIUM Journal of Economics and Management* 5, No. 1 (1997): 67–85

———, '*Zakat*: Unresolved Issues in Contemporary Fiqh.' *IIUM Journal of Economics and Management* 2, No. 1 (1989): 1–22

Kamali, Muhamad Hashim. 'Maqāṣid Al-Sharī'ah: The Objectives of Islamic Law' (1999) *Islamic Studies Islamabad* 38, No. 2

Karner, Christian, and Alan Aldridge. 'Theorizing Religion in a Globalizing World' (2004) *International Journal of Politics, Culture, and Society* 18, no. 1 (December): 5–32. https://doi.org/10.1023/B:IJPS.0000048105.59395.d0

Kasilo, OMJ, C Wambebe, JB Nikema et al, 'Towards universal health coverage: advancing the development and use of traditional medicines in Africa', (2019) BMJ Global Health, Vol 4, Issue 9, 1-11

Kasri, Rahmatina. 'Maqasid Al Shariah and Performance of Zakah Institutions' (2016) *Kyoto Bulletin of Islamic Area Studies* 9: 19–41

Katz, Alison. 'The Sachs Report: Investing in Health for Economic Development-- or Increasing the Size of the Crumbs from the Rich Man's Table? Part I' (2004) *International Journal of Health Services: Planning, Administration, Evaluation* 34, No. 4: 751–73. https://doi.org/10.2190/6BVE-W9G4-GWBN-LNVK

Kawabata, Kei, Ke Xu, and Guy Carrin. 'Preventing Impoverishment through Protection against Catastrophic Health Expenditure' (2002) *Bulletin of the World Health Organization* 80, No. 8: 612

Keen, Michael. 'What Do (and Don't) We Know about the Value Added Tax? A Review of Richard M. Bird and Pierre-Pascal Gendron's The VAT in Developing and Transitional Countries' (2009) *Journal of Economic Literature* 47, No. 1 (March): 159–70. https://doi.org/10.1257/jel.47.1.159

Kendrick, Abby. 'Measuring Compliance: Social Rights and the Maximum Available Resources Dilemma' (2017) *Human Rights Quarterly* 39, No. 3 (August): 657–79. https://doi.org/10.1353/hrq.2017.0036

Kaylani, N. 'Politics and Religion in 'Uman: A Historical Overview', (1979) *International Journal of Middle East Studies, Vol* 10, *No* 4 (Nov), 567-579

Kesgin, Salih. 'A Critical Analysis of the Schacht's Argument and Contemporary Debates on Legal Reasoning throughout the History of Islamic Jurisprudence' (2011) *Journal of International Social Research* 4, No. 9

Khadduri, Majid. 'The Juridical Theory of the Islamic State' (1951) *The Muslim World* 41, No. 3: 181–85

Khaunya, Mukabi Fredrich, Barasa Peter Wawire, and Viola Chepng'eno. 'Devolved Governance in Kenya; Is It a False Start in Democratic Decentralization for Development?' (2015) *International Journal of Economics, Finance and Management* 4, No. 1 (January). http://erepository.kibu.ac.ke/handle/123456789/1106

Kimambo, I. N. 'The Economic History of the Kamba' (1970) *Hadith* II: 79–103

Kimathi, Leah. 'Challenges of the Devolved Health Sector in Kenya: Teething Problems or Systemic Contradictions?' (2017) *Africa Development* 42, No. 1: 55–77. https://doi.org/10.4314/ad.v42i1

Kreps SE and AC Arend, 'Why States Follow The Rules: Toward A Positional Theory of Adherence To International Legal Regimes', (2006) *Duke Journal of Comparative & International Law*, Vol. 16, 331-414.

Kresse, K (ed), 'Guidance (Uwongozi) by Sheikh al-Amin Mazrui: Selections from the First Swahili Islamic Newspaper', (2017), *African Sources for African History*, Volume 14

Labuschagne, Adri. 'Qualitative Research – Airy Fairy or Fundamental?' (2003) *The Qualitative Report* 8, No. 1

Langha, Abdul Karim. 'Understanding Research Methodology for Islamic Studies' (2009) *Al Qalam*, 1–27

Lapidus, Ira M. 'The Separation of State and Religion in the Development of Early Islamic Society' (1975) *International Journal of Middle East Studies* 6, No. 4 (October): 363–85. https://doi.org/10.1017/S0020743800025344

Latif, LA, 'An Explication on Broadening the Definition and Scope of Maximum Available Resources Under General Comment 14 of the ICESCR to Include Islamic Taxation in Financing the Right to Health' (2017) *Biomed J Sci & Tech Res* 1, No. 3

———, 'Framing the Argument to Broaden Kenya's Limited Fiscal Space for Health Financing by Introducing *Zakat*', (2018) *Biomedical Journal of Scientific and Technical Research* 5 (5).

———, Simiyu, Faith, and Waris, Attiya. 'A Case Study on the Application of Human Rights Principles in Health Policy Making and Programming in Cherang'any Sub County in Kenya' (2017) *Integrative Journal of Global Health* 1, No. 1 (January)

Lee S and Adam A, 'Designing a Logic Model for Mobile Maternal Health e-Voucher Programmes in Low- and Middle-Income Countries: An Interpretive Review', (2022) *Int. J. Environ Res. Public Health*, 19:295

Lewin, Julius. 'The Recognition of Native Law and Custom in British Africa' (1938) *Comp. Legis & Int'l L* 20, No. 16

Lochery, E. 'Rendering Difference Visible: The Kenyan State and its Somali Citizens', (2012) *African Affairs*, Volume III, Issue 445, 615-639

Lodhi, A. 'The Arabs in Zanzibar: From Sultanate to People's Republic', (1986) *Journal Institute of Muslim Minority Affairs,* Vol VII, No 2, 404-418

________. 'Muslims in Eastern Africa – Their Past and Present', (1994) *Nordic Journal of African Studies* 3(1): 89-98, 89

Lonsdale, John. 'Mau Maus of the Mind: Making Mau Mau and Remaking Kenya' (1990) *The Journal of African History* 31: 393–421

Lonsdale, John, and Berman, Bruce. 'Coping with the Contradictions: The Development of the Coastal State in Kenya, 1895-1914' (1979) *The Journal of African History* 20, No. 4: 487–505

Lumina C and Tamale N, 'Sovereign Debt and Human Rights: A Focus on Sub-Saharan Africa' (2021) *African Sovereign Debt Justice Paper Series*

Lyons, D. 'Human Rights Derogations: Souring and Analysing the Concluding Observations of the International Human Rights Treaty Bodies', (2021) *Irish Studies in International Affairs,* Vol 32, No 1, 153-169

MacDonald, Duncan Black. 'Moral Education of the Young among Muslims' (1905) *International Journals of Ethics* XV: 286–304 (Chicago University Press)

Madan, T. N. 'Secularism in Its Place' (1987) *The Journal of Asian Studies* 46, No. 4 (November): 747–59. https://doi.org/10.2307/2057100

Madeley, John. 'European Liberal Democracy and the Principle of State Religious Neutrality' (2003) *West European Politics* 26, No. 1 (January): 1–22. https://doi.org/10.1080/01402380412331300177

Maggs, Peter B. 'Islamic Banking in Kazakhstan Law' (2011) *Review of Central and East European Law* 36: 369–96

Magnarella, P 'Questioning the Universality of Human Rights', (2003) *Human Rights and Human Welfare,* Volume 3, Issue 1, Article 6

Mahajneh, M.A, I Greenspan and MM Haj-Yahia, '*Zakat* Giving to Non-Muslims: Mufti's attitudes in Arab and Non-Arab Countries (2021) *Journal of Muslim Philanthropy & Civil Society,* Vol V, No II, 66-86

Mahmud, Mek Wok, and Sayed Sikandar Shah Haneef. 'Debatable Issues in Fiqh Al-*Zakat*: A Jurisprudential Appraisal' (2008) *Journal Fiqh* 5 (December): 117–41

Mahmud M.W and SS Shah, 'The Use of *Zakat* Revenue in Islamic Financing: Jurisprudential Debate and Practical Feasibility', (2009) *Journal on Studies in Islam and the Middle East,* Vol 6, No 1

Malik, Bilal Ahmad. 'Philanthropy in Practice: Role of *Zakat* in the Realization of Justice and Economic Growth' (2016) *International Journal of Zakat* 1, No. 1 (November): 64–77. https://doi.org/10.37706/ijaz.v1i1.7

Makau wa Mutua, 'Looking Past the Human Rights Committee: An Argument for De-Marginalizing Enforcement', (1998) 4 *Buffalo Human Rights Law Review* 211, 231

Mansouri, F. 'On the Discursive and Methodological Categorisation of Islam and Muslims in the West: Ontological and Epistemological Considerations' (2020) *Religions* 11

Mathews, Nathaniel. 'Imagining Arab Communities: Colonialism, Islamic Reform, and Arab Identity in Mombasa, Kenya, 1897-1933' (2013) *Islamic Africa* 4, No. 2: 135–63

Mazrui, A. 'Religion and Political Culture in Africa' (1985) *Journal of the American Academy of Religion,* Vol 53, No 4, 817-839

Mbate, Michael. 'Decentralization, Governance and Accountability: Theory and Evidence' (2017) *Journal of African Democracy and Development* 1, No. 2

McCrudden, Christopher. 'Legal Research and the Social Sciences' (2006) *Law Quarterly Review* 122: 632–50

Mechlem, K. 'Treaty Bodies and the Interpretation of Human Rights', (2009) 42 *Vanderbilt Law Review* 905

Meier BM, J B de Mesquita, and C Williams, 'Global Obligations to Ensure the Right to Health', (2022) *Yearbook of International Disaster Law Online, 3*(1), 3-34

Mcintyre, Di, Filip Meheus, and John-Arne Røttingen. 'What Level of Domestic Government Health Expenditure Should We Aspire to for Universal Health Coverage?' (2017) *Health Economics, Policy, and Law* 12, No. 2 (April): 125–37. https://doi.org/10.1017/S1744133116000414

Meheus, Filip, and Di McIntyre. 'Fiscal Space for Domestic Funding of Health and Other Social Services' (2017) *Health Economics, Policy, and Law* 12, no. 2 (April): 159–77. https://doi.org/10.1017/S1744133116000438

Merry, Sally Engle. 'Legal Pluralism' (1988) *Law & Society Review* 22, No. 5: 869–96. https://doi.org/10.2307/3053638

_________. 'Review: Law and Colonialism', (1991) *Law and Society Review,* Vol 25, No 4, 889-922

Mitchell, Richard C. 'Grounded Theory and Autopoietic Social Systems: Are They Methodologically Compatible?' (2007) *Qualitative Sociology Review* 3, No. 2

Moroff, A. 'Party Bans in Africa – an Empirical Overview', (2010) *Democratization*, 17:4, 618-641, 630

Moser, A and I Korstjens, 'Series: Practical Guidance to Qualitative Research. Part 3: Sampling, Data Collection and Analysis' (2018) *Eur J Gen Pract.* 24(1):9-18

Moussalli, Ahmad S. 'Hasan Al-Turabi's Islamist Discourse on Democracy and Shura' (1994) *Middle Eastern Studies* 30, No. 1: 52–63

Moyana, H V 'Underdevelopment in Kenya and Southern Rhodesia, 1890-1923: A Comparative Study' (1976) *Journal of Eastern African Research & Development*, Vol 6, No 2, 269-293

Munge, Kenneth, and Andrew Harvey Briggs. 'The Progressivity of Health-Care Financing in Kenya' (2014) *Health Policy and Planning* 29: 912–20

Murakami, K. 'Talk About Rice: A Discursive Approach to Studying Culture', (2001) *Forum Qualitative Sozialforschung / Forum: Qualitative Social Research [On-line Journal]*, 2(3), 48–59

Musgrave, Richard. 'Schumpeter's Crisis of the Tax State: An Essay in Fiscal Sociology' (1992) *Journal of Evolutionary Economics* 2, No. 2: 89–113

W Mutunga, 'Human Rights States and Societies: A Reflection from Kenya' (2015) The Transnational Human Rights Review 2, 63-102.

__________. 'The 2010 Constitution of Kenya and Its Interpretation: Reflections from the Supreme Court's Decisions' (2015) *Speculum Juris* 19, No. 1. http://www.saflii.org/za/journals/SPECJU/2015/6.html

Mwabu, Germano. 'Health Care Reform in Kenya: A Review of the Process' (1995) *Health Policy (Amsterdam, Netherlands)* 32, No. 1–3 (June): 245–55. https://doi.org/10.1016/0168-8510(95)00738-e

Mwabu, Germano, J Mwanzia, and W Liambila. 'User Charges in Government Health Facilities in Kenya: Effect on Attendance and Revenue' (1995) *Health Policy and Planning* 10, No. 2 (June): 164–70. https://doi.org/10.1093/heapol/10.2.164

Mwabu, Germano, and J Wang'ombe. 'Financing Rural Health Services in Kenya' (1998) *Springer* 17, No. 1: 55–70

Mwenda, N, R Nduati, M Kosgei et al., 'What Drives Outpatient Care Costs in Kenya? An Analysis with Generalised Estimating Equations', (2021) *Front. Public Health*

Ndzovu, Hassan Juma. 'The Politicization of Muslim Organizations and the Future of Islamic-Oriented Politics in Kenya' (2012) *Islamic Africa* 3, No. 1: 25–53

Neubauer, B, C Witkop, and L Varpio, 'How Phenomenology Can Help Us Learn from the Experiences of Others', (2019) *Perspectives on Medical Education* 8, 90-97

Neumark T and R J Prince, 'Digital Health in East Africa: Innovation, Experimentation and the Market' (2021) *Global Policy,* Vol 12, Issue S6, 65-74

Nott, J. 'No One May Starve in the British Empire: Kwashiorkor, Protein and the Politics of Nutrition Between Britain and Africa', (2021) *Soc His Med* 34(2):553-576

O'Flaherty, M. 'Concluding Observations of United Nations Human Rights Treaty Bodies', (2006) *Human Rights Law Review* 6(1) 27-52

O'Hare, BAM. 'Tax and the Right to Health,' (2018) Health Hum Rights, 20(2): 57-63

Okoth-Ogendo, H. W. O. 'The Politics of Constitutional Change in Kenya since Independence, 1963-69' (1972) *African Affairs* 71, No. 282

Oomen, Barbara M. 'The Application of Socio-Legal Theories of Legal Pluralism to Understanding the Implementation and Integration of Human Rights Law' (2014) *European Journal of IIuman Rights* 4: 471–95

Ooms, Gorik, Claire Brolan, Natalie Eggermont, Asbjørn Eide, Walter Flores, Lisa Forman, Eric A. Friedman, et al. 'Universal Health Coverage Anchored in the Right to Health' (2013) *Bulletin of the World Health Organization* 91, No. 1 (January): 2-2A. https://doi.org/10.2471/BLT.12.115808

Ooms, Gorik, L. A. Latif, Attiya Waris, Claire E. Brolan, Rachel Hammonds, Eric A. Friedman, Moses Mulumba, and Lisa Forman. 'Is Universal Health Coverage the Practical Expression of the Right to Health Care?' (2014) *BMC International Health and Human Rights* 14, No. 1 (February): 3. https://doi.org/10.1186/1472-698X-14-3

Oran, Ahmed, and Salim Rashid. 'Fiscal Policy in Early Islam' (1989) *Public Finance* 44, No. 1: 75–101

Ouma, PN, AN Masai and IN Nyadera, 'Health coverage and what Kenya can learn from the COVID-19 pandemic' (2020) *J Glob Health* 10(2):020362

Oyaya, Charles O., and Susan B. Rifkin. 'Health Sector Reforms in Kenya: An Examination of District Level Planning' (2003) *Health Policy (Amsterdam, Netherlands)* 64, No. 1 (April): 113–27. https://doi.org/10.1016/s0168-8510(02)00164-1

Padela, Asif. 'A Grounded Theory Study of the Prophet Muhammad's Leadership Behaviors: A Model for Islamic School Principals' (2015) *Education Doctoral.* https://fisherpub.sjfc.edu/education_etd/243

Pemberton, J. 'Origins and Early History of the Society for Social Medicine in the UK and Ireland' (2002) *Journal of Epidemiology & Community Health* 56:342-346

Pellissier, A. 'A Defence of the Human Right to Health' (2021) *Studies in Philosophy, Politics and Economics* 3(1), 27-31

Peters, Ruud. 'Islamic Law and Human Rights: A Contribution to an Ongoing Debate' (1999) *Islam and Christian–Muslim Relations* 10, No. 1 (March): 5–14. https://doi.org/10.1080/09596419908721166

Pimentel, David. 'Legal Pluralism in Post-Colonial Africa: Linking Statutory and Customary Adjudication in Mozambique' (2014) *Yale Human Rights and Development Law Journal* 14, No. 1 (February). https://digitalcommons.law.yale.edu/yhrdlj/vol14/iss1/2

Powell, Russell. '*Zakat*: Drawing Insights for Legal Theory and Economic Policy from Islamic Jurisprudence' (2010) *PITT. Tax Review* 7, No. 43 (January). https://digitalcommons.law.seattleu.edu/faculty/90

Posner, Richard. 'The Present Situation in Legal Scholarship' (1980) *Yale Law Journal* 90 (January): 1113

Pulla, Venkat. 'An Introduction to the Grounded Theory Approach in Social Research' (2016) *International Journal of Social Work and Human Services Practice* 4, No. 4 (September): 75–81. https://doi.org/10.13189/ijrh.2016.040401

Rachuonyo, J O 'Kelsen's Grundnorm in modern Constitution Making: The Kenya Case,' (1987) *Law and Politics in Africa, Asia and Latin America,* Vol 20, No 4

Rahman, Faridi. 'Islam and the Problem of Economic Justice' (1974) *Pakistan Economist*, 14–39

Reeves, A, Y Gourtsoyannis, S Basu, Sanjay et al, 'Financing Universal Health Coverage – Effect of Alternative Tax Structures on Public Health Systems', (2015) *The Lancet*

Rini, R. 'A Review of the Literature on Zakah between 2003 and 2019', (2020) *International Journal of Economics and Financial Issues* Vol. 10, No. 2. 156-164

Rishmavi, Mervat. 'The Revised Arab Charter on Human Rights' (2005) *Human Rights Law Review* 5, No. 2: 361–75

Robertson, Robert E. 'Measuring State Compliance with the Obligation to Devote the 'Maximum Available Resources' to Realising Economic, Social, and Cultural Rights' (1994) *Human Rights Quarterly* 16: 693–714

Roth-Isigkeit, D 'Promises and Perils of Legal Argument – A Discursive Approach to Normative Conflict between Legal Order', (2014) *Revue Belge de Droit International* 2

Russel, S, and L Gilson. 'User Fee Policies to Promote Health Service Access for Poor: A Wolf in Sheep's Clothing?' (1997) *International Journal Health Services* 27: 359–79

Sahn D and R Bernier, 'Have Structural Adjustments Led to Health Sector Reform in Africa?' (1995) *Health Policy*, Vol 32, Issues 1-3, 193-214

Salim, Islam Mohamed. 'Expanding the Islamic Financial Services Frontier: Lessons from Islamic Finance Sector in Kenya' (2017) *Journal of Islamic Banking and Finance* 5, No. 1: 1–6

Sandberg, Russell. 'The Failure of Legal Pluralism' (2016) *Ecclesiastical Law Journal* 18, No. 2 (May): 137–57. https://doi.org/10.1017/S0956618X1600003X

———, 'The Sociology of the Law on Religion,' 2007. https://doi.org/10.2139/SSRN.2032647

Scharrer, T. 'Ambiguous Citizens: Kenyan Somalis and the Question of Belonging', (2018) *Journal of East African Studies*, Volume 12, Issue 3

Schwartz, Richard L. 'Internal and External Method in the Study of Law' (1992) *Law and Philosophy* 11, No. 3 (September): 179–99. https://doi.org/10.1007/BF01000641

Sekwati, L, and Brothers W Malema. 'Potential Impact of the Increase in VAT on Poor Households in Botswana' (2011) *International Journal of Economics and Research* 2, No. 1

Sepulveda, Magdalena. 'Obligations of 'International Assistance and Cooperation' in an Optional Protocol to the International Covenant on Economic, Social and Cultural Rights' (2006) *Netherlands Quarterly of Human Rights* 24, No. 2: 271–303

———, 'The Obligations of International Assistance and Cooperation' under the International Covenant on Economic, Social and Cultural Rights. A Possible Entry Point to a Human Rights Based Approach to Millennium Development Goal 8' (2009) *The International Journal of Human Rights* 13, No. 86

Shah, Mustafa. 'Al Ṭabarī and the Dynamics of Tafsīr: Theological Dimensions of a Legacy' (2013) *Journal of Qur'anic Studies* 15, No. 2: 83–139

Shahin, F. 'Islamic Feminism and Hegemonic Discourses on Faith and Gender in Islam', (2020) *International Journal of Islam in Asia,* 1(1), 27-48

Sheikh, AM. 'Kenya Shiite Community: A Socio-Historical Perspective' (2014) *IOSR Journal of Humanities and Social Sciences,* Volume 19, Issue 5

Shirazi, Nasim. 'Providing for the Resource Shortfall for Poverty Elimination through the Institution of *Zakat* in Low Income Muslim Countries' (2006) *IIUM Journal of Economics and Management* 14, No. 1

Shirazi, Nasim Shah, and Md Fouad bin Amin. 'Prospects of Poverty Elimination through Potential *Zakat* Collection in OIC Member Countries: Reappraised' (2010) *Journal of Islamic Economics, Banking and Finance* 6, No. 3

Shuriye, Abdi O. 'Explorations on the Abbasids Political Culture in Pursuit of Sustainable System of Governance in the Muslim World' (2016) *Mediterranean Journal of Social Sciences* 7, No. 4 (July): 228

Siems, Mathias M. 'The Taxonomy of Interdisciplinary Legal Research: Finding the Way Out of the Desert' (2009) *Journal of Commonwealth Law and Legal Education* 7, No. 1: 5–17. https://doi.org/10.1080/14760400903195090

Skogly, Sigrun. 'The Requirement of Using the 'Maximum of Available Resources' for Human Rights Realisation: A Question of Quality as Well as Quantity?' (2012) *Human Rights Law Review* 12, No. 3 (September): 393–420. https://doi.org/10.1093/hrlr/ngs022

Sridhar, Devi, Martin McKee, Gorik Ooms, Claudia Beiersmann, Eric Friedman, Hebe Gouda, Peter Hill, and Albrecht Jahn. 'Universal Health Coverage and the Right to Health: From Legal Principle to Post-2015 Indicators' (2015) *International Journal of Health Services: Planning, Administration, Evaluation* 45, No. 3: 495–506. https://doi.org/10.1177/0020731415584554

Swenson, Geoffrey. 'Legal Pluralism in Theory and Practice' (2018) *International Studies Review* 20, no. 3 (September): 438–62. https://doi.org/10.1093/isr/vix060

Tamanaha, Brian Z. 'Socio-Legal Positivism and a General Jurisprudence' (2001) *Oxford Journal of Legal Studies* 21, No. 1 (January): 1–32. https://doi.org/10.1093/ojls/21.1.1

________. 'The Folly of the 'Social Scientific' Concept of Legal Pluralism' (1993) *Journal of Law and Society* 20, No. 2: 192–217. https://doi.org/10.2307/1410167

Tangcharoensathien, Viroj, Walaiporn Patcharanarumol, Warisa Panichkriangkrai, and Angkana Sommanustweechai. 'Policy Choices for Progressive Realization of Universal Health Coverage; Comment on 'Ethical Perspective: Five Unacceptable Trade-Offs on the Path to Universal Health Coverage' (2017) *International Journal of Health Policy and Management* 6, No. 2 (February): 107–10. https://doi.org/10.15171/ijhpm.2016.99

Tayob, Abdelkader. 'Kadhis Courts in Kenya's Constitutional Review (1998-2010): A Changing Approach to Politics and State Among Kenyan Muslim Leaders' (2013) *Islamic Africa* 4, No. 1: 103–24

Teubner, Gunther. 'How the Law Thinks: Toward a Constructivist Epistemology of Law' (1989) *Law & Society Review*. https://doi.org/10.1007/978-94-017-2975-8_6

Tilley, H 'Medicine, Empires, and Ethics in Colonial Africa' (2016) *AMA Journal of Ethics*, Vol 18, *No* 7:743-753

Tyndale, W. 'Faith and Economics in ''Development': A Bridge across the Chasm?' (2000) *Development in Practice* 10, No. 1

Vageesh, J, 'Harnessing the Power of Health Taxes' (2020) *BMJ* 369

Vanderlinden, Jacques. 'Return to Legal Pluralism' (1989) *The Journal of Legal Pluralism and Unofficial Law* 21, No. 28 (January): 149–57. https://doi.org/10.1080/07329113.1989.10756411

Walt, G., M. Perera, and K. Heggenhougen. 'Are Large-Scale Volunteer Community Health Worker Programmes Feasible? The Case Study of Sri Lanka' (1989) *Social Science & Medicine* 29, No. 5: 599–608

Waris, Attiya. 'A Historical Analysis of the Kenyan Taxation System' (2007) *Kenya Law Review* 1: 272

Waris, Attiya, and L. A. Latif. 'A State's Legal and Financial Responsibility in Promoting Health Equity in Kenya' (2015) *JKUAT Law Journal* 1

– – –, 'Financing the Progressive Realisation of Socio Economic Rights in Kenya' (2015) *UNLJ* 8, No. 1

———, 'Towards Establishing Fiscal Legitimacy Through Settled Fiscal Principles in Global Health Financing' (2015) *Health Care Analysis: HCA: Journal of Health Philosophy and Policy* 23, No. 4 (December): 376–90. https://doi.org/10.1007/s10728-015-0305-z

Weiss, Bernard. 'Interpretation in Islamic Law: The Theory of Ijtihâd' (1978) *American Journal of Comparative Law* 26, No. 2: 199–212

Williams, OD. 'COVID-19 and Private Health: Market and Governance Failure', (2020) *Development* 63, 181-190

Willis, Justin, and George Gona. 'Pwani C Kenya? Memory, Documents and Secessionist Politics in Coastal Kenya' (2013) *African Affairs* 112: 48–71

Willis, Justin. 'Tradition, Tribe, and State in Kenya: The Mijikenda Union, 1945–1980' (2013) *Comparative Studies in Society and History* 55, No. 2 (April): 448–73. https://doi.org/10.1017/S0010417513000091

Woodman, Gordon R. 'Legal Pluralism and the Search for Justice' (1996) *Journal of African Law* 40, No. 2: 152–67. https://doi.org/10.1017/S0021855300007737

———, 'Legal Pluralism in Africa: The Implications of State Recognition of Customary Laws Illustrated from the Field of Land Law' (2011) *Acta Juridica*, 35–58

Wylie, D. 'Confrontation over Kenya: The Colonial Office and its Critics 1918-1940' (1977) *The Journal of African History* Vol 18, No 3, 427-447

Wyon, Rohde J. 'Community-Based Health Care: Lessons from Bangladesh to Boston' (2002) *J. Management Sciences for Health*

Xu, Ke. 'Analysing Health Equity Using Household Survey Data: A Guide to Techniques and Their Implementation' (2008) *Bulletin of the World Health Organization* 86, No. 10 (October): 816. https://doi.org/10.2471/BLT.08.052357

Yahya, Saad, S. 'Financing Social Infrastructure and Addressing Poverty Through Wakf Endowments: Experience from Kenya and Tanzania' (1994) *Environment and Urbanization* 20, No. 2: 427–44

Yamin, Alicia Ely. 'The Right to Health Under International Law and Its Relevance to the United States' (2005) *American Journal of Public Health* 95, No. 7 (July): 1156–61. https://doi.org/10.2105/AJPH.2004.055111

Yildirim, Onur. 'Pious Foundations in the Byzantine and Seljuk States: A Comparative Study of Philanthropy in the Mediterranean World during the Late Medieval Era' (1999) *Rivista Degli Studi Orientali* 73: 27–52

Yuniar, AM, A Natasya, RA Kasri et al, '*Zakat* and Digitalisation: A Systematic Literature Review', (2021) paper presented at the 5th International Conference of *Zakat* Proceedings

Zaaba, NMA and R Hassan. 'A Systematic Literature Review on *Zakat*', (2021) *Journal of Islamic Finance*, Vol 10, No. 2, 101-111

Zainal, H. 'Reputation, Satisfaction of *Zakat* Distribution, and Service Quality as Determinant of Stakeholder Trust in *Zakat* Institutions', (2016) *International Journal of Economics and Financial Issues*, Vol 6, Issue 7, 72-76.

Reports

Balakrishnan, Radhika, Diane Elson, James Heintz, and Nicholas Lusiani. *Maximum Available Resources and Human Rights: Analytical Report* (New Brunswick, NJ: Rutgers, 2011).

Chenwi, Lillian. 'Monitoring the Progressive Realisation of Socio-Economic Rights: Lessons from the United Nations Committee on Economic, Social and Cultural Rights and the South African Constitutional Court.' Studies in Poverty and Inequality Institute, 2010

Committee of Experts on Constitutional Review, 'Final Report of the Committee of Experts on Constitutional Review', 11 October 2010

De Schutter, Olivier. 'Report of the Special Rapporteur on the Right to Food, Mission to Brazil, (A/HRC/13/33/Add.6).' United Nations, 2009

Himes, James R., and International Child Development Centre. 'Implementing the United Nations Convention on the Rights of the Child: Resource Mobilisation and The Obligations of the State Parties.' *Child Rights Series* (Florence, Italy : UNICEF International Child Development Centre, 1992). http://digitallibrary.un.org/record/184811

International Confederation of Free Trade Unions. 'Having Their Cake and Eating It Too: The Big Corporate Tax Break' (Brussels, 2006)

International Service for Human Rights. 'Model Law for the Recognition and Protection of Human Rights Defenders.' ESCR-Net. https://www.escr-net.org/resources/model-law-recognition-and-protection-human-rights-defenders

Isanga, Joseph M. 'Kadhi's Courts and Kenya's Constitution: An International Human Rights Perspective. Rule of Law Report 2009-2010' (Kenya Section of the International Commission of Jurists, 2009)

Jahn, Albrecht, Claudia Beiersmann, and O Mueller. 'The Prescription for Women's Health: The MDGS and Beyond.' Global Development Goals: Leaving No One Behind (UNA-UK, 2013)

Kahumbi, M 'Continuity and Change in the Legal Regulations of Waqf in Kenya: Opportunities and Challenges' (2008) Available from: http://saadabadi.persiangig.com/Arshive/Kahumbi_Maina.doc/download?490f

Kimalu, Paul, Nancy Nafula, and Damiano Kulundu Manda. 'A Review of the Health Sector in Kenya.' (2004) Kenya Institute for Public Policy Research and Analysis

Küng, Hans. 'Don't Be Afraid of Ethics! Why We Need to Talk of Responsibilities as Well as Rights (InterAction Council) https://www.interactioncouncil.org/publications/dont-be-afraid-ethics-why-we-need-talk-responsibilities-well-rights

Mazni Abdullah, (n.d). 'The Role of *Zakat* on Muslims' Tax Compliance Behaviour – From Qualitative Perspectives' https://pdfs.semanticscholar.org/b46b/a63b1ae70135e2daabb12ac8ecf7864455a8.pdf

McGuire, William J. 'Democracy, Social Policy, and Mortality Decline in Brazil.' (Harvard Center for Population and Development Studies, 2002)

Mohammad, Wahida. 'Islamic Banking and Economic Infrastructure Development – Kenya's Prospects' (Kenya Bankers Association, 2015)

Muga, Richard, Paul Kizito, Michael Mbayah, and Terry Gakuruh. 'Overview of the Health System in Kenya' (Kenya service provision assessment survey, 2005)

Murrill, Brandon J. 'Modes of Constitutional Interpretation' (Congressional Research Service Report, 2018)

Mwangi, Oscar Gakuo. 'Religious Fundamentalism, Constitution-Making and Democracy in Kenya: The Kadhis Courts Debate' *The Round Table*, 2012

Narayan, Deepa, Robert Chambers, Meera K. Shah, and Patti Petesch. 'Voices of the Poor: Crying Out for Change' (World Bank Publications, 2000). https://econpapers.repec.org/bookchap/wbkwbpubs/13848.htm

Nauk, Gisela, and Vanessa Steinmayer. *Integrated Social Policy: Rethinking the Role of the State, the Market and Civil Society in the Provision of Social Protection and Social Services. Report V: Towards a New Welfare Mix?* (Beirut, Lebanon: ESCWA, 2014)

Nyakundi, Caroline Kwamboka, Caroline Teti, Howard Akimala, Esther Njoya, Matthias Brucker, Richard Nderitu, and Joshua Changwony. 'Health Financing in Kenya. The Case for Reproductive Health and Family Planning' (German Foundation for World Population, 2011)

O'Donnell, Owen, Eddy van Doorslaer, Adam Wagstaff, and Magnus Lindelow. 'Analysing Health Equity Using Household Survey Data: A Guide to Techniques and Their Implementation' (The International Bank for Reconstruction and Development/The World Bank, 2008)

Othieno, Nyanjom. 'Devolution in Kenya's New Constitution' (Society for International Development (SID), Regional Office for East & Southern Africa, 2011)

Owino, W, and M Were. 'Delivery and Financing of Healthcare Services in Kenya: Critical Issues and Research Gaps' (Institute for Policy Analysis and Research, 1997)

Perales, Nicole, Arin Dutta, and Thomas Maina. 'Resource Needs for the Kenya Health Sector Strategic and Investment Plan: Analysis Using the OneHealth Tool' (Futures Group, Health Policy Project, 2015)

Preston, Augustine Chitere. 'The Provincial Administration in Kenya: A Study of Its Characteristics and Potential for Sustainment under Devolved System of Government'. Proceedings of the Kenya National Academy of Sciences (Heinrich Boll Foundation, 2005)

Razwy, A. A. *A Restatement of the History of Islam & Muslims CE. 570 to 661. Restatement of the History of Islam and Muslims* (Stanmore, Middlesex, U.K.: World Federation of Muslim Communities Islamic Centre, 1997). https://catalog.hathitrust.org/Record/003246487

Reuter, P (eds), *Draining Development? Controlling Flows of Illicit Funds from Developing Countries* (World Bank, 2012)

Salingan, Gülçin. 'Unleashing the Potential of Islamic Finance and Impact Investing for the SDGs.' (UNDP, 2018)

Salomon, Margot E. 'Is There a Legal Duty to Address World Poverty?' (Robert Schuman Centre for Advanced Studies, European University Institute, May 2012)

Sánchez, Oscar Arias. 'Some Contributions to a Universal Declaration of Human Obligations' (Inter Action Council, 1997). https://www.interactioncouncil.org/publications/some-contributions-universal-declaration-human-obligations

Schutter, Oliver De. 'Report of the Special Rapporteur on the Right to Food – Mission to Brazil. UN Doc A/HRC/13/33/Add.6, 2009 (United Nations, 2009)

Sepulveda, Magdalena. *The Nature of Obligations under the International Covenant on Economic Social and Cultural Rights* (Intersentia, 2003)

Shehu Usman Rano, Aliyu. 'A Treatise on Socioeconomic Roles of Zakah.' Munich Personal RePEc Archive, September 1, 2017. https://mpra.ub.uni-muenchen.de/81155/

Siddiqui, Shariq, Rafeel Wasif and Micah Hughes et al., 'Muslim American *Zakat* Report 2022' (*Muslim Philanthropy Initiative at Indiana University Lilly Family School of Philanthropy*, 2022)

Tandon, Ajay, and Cheryl Cashin. 'Assessing Public Expenditure on Health from a Fiscal Space Perspective' (World Bank, Washington DC., 2010)

Tomaseyski, Katarina. 'Background Paper Submitted by Special Rapporteur on the Right to Education, UN Doc E/C.12/1998/18' (United Nations, 1998)

Türk, Danilo. 'Report of the Special Rapporteur to the U.N. Commission on Human Rights, Sub-Commission on Prevention of Discrimination and Protection of Minorities, 44th Sess., Prov. Agenda Item 8, UN Doc. *No* E/CN.4/Sub.2/1992/16' (United Nations, 1992)

________. 'The Realization of Economic, Social and Cultural Rights' (United Nations, 1992). http://digitallibrary.un.org/record/146643

World Bank Group. 'Prospects for Achieving the Sustainable Development Goals and the Role of Islamic Finance' (World Bank Group, 2018)

World Health Organisation. 'Anchoring Universal Health Coverage in the Right to Health: What Difference Would It Make?' (World Health Organization, 2015)

________. 'The World Health Report: Health Systems Financing: The Path to Universal Health Coverage' (World Health Organization, 2010)

________. 'Country Cooperation Strategy, 2008-2013 Kenya' (World Health Organization, 2009)

Yahya, Saad, S. 'Indonesia: Implementation of the Health-for-All Strategy.' In *Achieving Health for All by the Year 2000,* (ed) E. A. C Tarimmo (Geneva: World Health Organization, 1990)

Conference and Working Papers

Abdullah, M. 'The Role of *Zakat* on Muslims' Tax Compliance Behavior – from Qualitative Perspectives', 1–9. Park View Hotel, Jerudong, Negara Brunei Darussalam, 2017. http://eprints.um.edu.my/18582/

Ahmad, H. 'Role of Zakah and Awqaf in Poverty Alleviation', (2004) Islamic Development Bank, *Occasional Paper* No 8

Al-Alwani, T.J. 'Ijtihad' (1991) *Working Paper Series, No 4,* International Institute of Islamic Thought, 6-9

Ali, Khalifa Mohamed, and Abdelrahman Elzahi. 'Zakah for Poverty Alleviation: Evidence from Sudan.' Working Papers. The Islamic Research and Teaching Institute (IRTI), May 1, 2016. https://ideas.repec.org/p/ris/irtiwp/2016_011.html

Alston, P. 'The Historical Origins of the Concept of 'General Comments' in Human Rights Law' in L Boisson de Chazournes and V Gowlabd Debbas (eds), *The International Legal System in Quest of Equity and Universality: Liber Amicorum Georges Abi-Saab* (The Hague: Martinus Nijhoff, 2001)

Anderson, Edward. 'A New Approach to Assessing State Compliance with the Obligation to Devote Maximum Available Resources to Realise Economic, Social and Cultural Rights' (The School of International Development, University of East Anglia, 2010)

Anyangu-Amu, S. 'Kenya: Proposed Constitutional Amendment Sets Back Women's Rights', Inter Press Service, 11 March 2010, available at www.globalissues.org/news/2010/03/11/4821

Asare, Opoku K. 'Religion in Africa during the Colonial Era.' In *General History of Africa: Africa under Colonial Domination 1880-1935,* (ed) A. Adu Boahen. (London: Berkeley, Calif., U.S.A: Heinemann; University of California Press, 1985)

Bakari, Mohamed. 'A Place at the Table: The Political Integration of Kenyan Muslims, 1992-2003.' (Oxford: St Anthony's College, 2004)

Bellows, N 'Vouchers for Reproductive Health Care Services in Kenya and Uganda', (2012) KFW Discussion Paper

Carrier, N and H Elliot, 'Entrust We Must: The Role of Trust in Somali Economic Life', (2018) DIIS Working Paper 2

Chesworth, John. 'Kadhi's Courts in Kenya: Reactions and Responses,' 3–17. Cape Town, South Africa: National Research Foundation, 2010

Glied, Sherry A. 'Health Care Financing, Efficiency, and Equity.' NBER Working Papers. National Bureau of Economic Research, Inc, March 2008. https://ideas.repec.org/p/nbr/nberwo/13881.html

Mohamed Ali, Khalifa. 'Integrating Zakah, Awqaf and Islamic Microfinance for Poverty Alleviation: Three Models of Islamic Micro Finance.' Working Papers. The Islamic Research and Teaching Institute (IRTI), January 19, 2014. https://ideas.repec.org/p/ris/irtiwp/1435_019.html

Ndzovu, Hassan. 'Is the Inclusion of the Kadhi Courts in the Kenyan Constitution Against the Principle of a Secular State?' Rochester, NY: Social Science Research Network, September 18, 2013

Waldron, Jeremy. 'No Barking: Legal Pluralism and the Contrast between Hart's Jurisprudence and Fuller's' Australian National University College of Law, 2008

Yahya, Saad S. 'Compassion and Development: Addressing Social Infrastructure and Poverty Issues in East African Cities Through Waqf Endowments.' Cape Town, South Africa, 2007

_________. 'The Uses and Abuses of Waqf. In Islam in Kenya.' In *Proceedings of the National Seminar on Contemporary Islam in Kenya* (MEWA Publications, 1995)

Unpublished Dissertations

Craven, MCR. 'The International Covenant on Economic, Social and Cultural Rights—A Perspective on its Development', (PhD thesis, University of Nottingham 1995)

Hashim, Abdulkadir. 'Reforming and Retreating: British Policies on Transforming the Administration of Islamic Law and its Institutions in the Busa'idi Sultanate 1890-1963' (PhD, University of Western Cape, 2010)

Mwangi Wa-Githumo, 'Land and Nationalism in East Africa: The Impact of Land Expropriation and Land Grievances Upon the Rise and Development of

Nationalist Movements in Kenya 1884-1939' 200-04 (1974) (PhD. Dissertation, Faculty of Education, New York University)

Omusule, Monone. 'Political and Constitutional Aspects of the Origins and Development of Local Government in Kenya, 1895-1963' (PhD Dissertation, Syracuse University, 1975)

Newspaper Articles

Gachuhi, Roy. 'The Steady Growth of Islamic Banking in Kenya.' *Daily Nation,* June 2, 2016. www.nation.co.ke/business/The-steady-growth-of-Islamic-banking-in-Kenya/996-3064236-p9h3fy/index.html

Hilali, A. 'It was presented by Al-Nahda Movement. Why did the Tunisian parliament drop the '*Zakat* Fund'?' Teller Report, 12 December 2019

Kakah, Maureen. 'Kenya: Parents Sue Over Ban on Islamic Prayers at School.' *AllAfrica,* November 3, 2019. https://allafrica.com/stories/201903110212.html

Leftie, P. 'Uhuru's Madaraka Gifts.' *Saturday Nation,* February 6, 2013

Maina, B. 'Medics Raise Alarm over Maternity Care.' *Daily Nation,* April 6, 2013. https://nation.africa/kenya/news/medics-raise-alarm-over-maternity-care--867002

Ngugi, Mumbi, and Singanga Ngugi. 'Kadhi Courts Exceed Limits of the Law.' *Africa News Service, Opposing Viewpoints in Context,* 2009

Njora, Geoffrey. 'African Finance Ministers Dismiss Development Declarations | Pambazuka News,' 2010. https://www.pambazuka.org/governance/african-finance-ministers-dismiss-development-declarations

Wachira M et al, 'Human Rights Group Protests Clause Exclusion', Daily Nation, 22 January 2010, available at www.nation.co.ke/News/politics/-/1064/847716 /-/wsc3i5z/-/index.html

African and International Instruments

Abuja Declaration On HIV/Aids, Tuberculosis and Other Related Infectious Diseases, Abuja, Nigeria, 26-27 April 2001 | Commit4Africa,' January 13, 2021. http://www.commit4africa.org/declarations/17/Abuja/0/0

Addis Ababa Declaration on Community Health in the African Region, 20-22 November 2006. http://www.afro.who.int/publications/addis-abeba-declaration-community-health-african-region-20-22-november-2006

African Union Commission. 'Agenda 2063: A Shared Strategic Framework for Inclusive Growth and Sustainable Development'. (2013)

Africa Union Commission, 'A Shared Strategic Framework for Inclusive Growth and Sustainable Development, First Ten-Year Implementation Plan 2014-2023' (2015). Available at: https://www.un.org/en/africa/osaa/pdf/au/agenda2063-first10yearimplementation.pdf

OHCHR, United Nations Human Rights Treaty Bodies: UN Treaty Body Database, Available: https://tbinternet.ohchr.org/_layouts/15/treatybodyexternal/TBSearch.aspx?Lang=en&TreatyID=9&DocTypeID=5

Organisation of African Unity. 'Abuja Declaration On HIV/Aids, Tuberculosis and Other Related Infectious Diseases, Abuja, Nigeria, 26-27 April 2001 OAU/SPS/ABUJA/3. Declaration.PDF (safaids.net)

Regional Committee for Africa, 'Adoption of the Ouagadougou Declaration on primary health care and health systems in Africa: achieving better health for Africa in the new millennium' (World Health Organization. Regional Office for Africa, 2008). http://www.who.int/iris/handle/10665/19989

United Nations General Assembly, Universal *Declaration of Human Rights*, 10 December 1948, 217 A (III)

_________, General Assembly Official Records, Document A/2929 Annotations on the text of the draft International Covenants on Human Rights, Agenda item 28 (Part II) Annexes, Tenth Session, UN Doc A/2929 (1/7/1955). para. 19

_________, Committee on Economic and Social Council. 'International Covenant on Civil and Political Rights, 16 December 1966.' United Nations, Treaty Series, December 16, 1966

_________, 'Declaration on the Right to Development: Resolution, A/RES/41/128.' United Nations, Treaty Series, 1986. http://www.un.org/documents/ga/res/41/a41r128.htm

_________, Commission on Human Rights. 'Note Verbale Dated 5 December 1986 from the Permanent Mission of the Netherlands to the United Nations Office at Geneva Addressed to the Centre for Human Rights ('Limburg Principles'), E/CN.4/1987/17.' United Nations, August 1, 1987. http://www.refworld.org/docid/48abd5790.html

________, Committee on Economic, Social and Cultural Rights (CESCR), General Comment No 3: The Nature of States Parties' Obligations (Art. 2, Para. 1 of the Covenant), 14 December 1990, E/1991/23

________, General Assembly. 'Declaration on the Right and Responsibility of Individuals, Groups and Organs of Society to Promote and Protect Universally Recognized Human Rights and Fundamental Freedoms, Resolution A/RES/53/144.' United Nations, 1999

________, Committee on Economic and Social Council. 'General Comment No 14: The Right to the Highest Attainable Standard of Health (Art. 12 of the Covenant), E/C.12/2000/4.' United Nations, November 8, 2000

________, Committee on the Rights of the Child. 'Concluding Observations of the Committee on the Rights of the Child, Georgia, U.N. Doc. CRC/C/15/Add.124 (2000).' United Nations, 2000. http://hrlibrary.umn.edu/crc/georgia2000.html

________, Committee of Economic, Social and Cultural Rights, An Evaluation of the Obligation to Take Steps to the Maximum of Available Resources under an Optional Protocol to the Covenant, 38th session (30 April-18 May 2007) E/C12/2007/1

________, Office of the High Commissioner for Human Rights (OHCHR), *Commentary to the Declaration on the Right and Responsibility of Individuals, Groups and Organs of Society to Promote and Protect Universally Recognized Human Rights and Fundamental Freedoms*, July 2011. Available at: https://www.refworld.org/docid/4e2fc3f02.html

________, Committee of Economic, Social and Cultural Rights, Concluding Observations on the Combined Second to Fifth Periodic Reports of Kenya, adopted by the Committee at its 57th session (22 February-4 March, 2016) E/C.12/KEN/CO/2-5

________, Committee on the Elimination of Discrimination against Women (CEDAW), General Recommendation No 35 on Gender-Based Violence Against Women, Updating General Recommendation No 19, 2017

Constitutions

Republic of Kenya, Constitution of Kenya, 2010 (Nairobi: National Council for Law Reporting, 2010)

Republic of Zambia. 'The Constitution of Zambia.' Zambia: Government Printer, 1996

Statutes

Bahrain: Decree Law No. 8 of 1979

Bangladesh: Ordinance No. VI of 1982

Egypt: Law No. 66 of 1977

Jordan: *Zakat* Act of 1978

Indonesia: Law of *Zakat* Management No. 38 (1999)

Kuwait: Law No. 5 of 1982

Republic of Kenya, Public Health Act, Chapter 242 LN142/1963 (Nairobi: Government Printers, 1963)

___________, Prevention of Terrorism Act, No. 3 of 2012 (Nairobi: National Council of Law Reporting, 2012)

___________, Wakf Commissioners Act, Chapter 109 (Nairobi: National Council for Law Reporting, 2012)

___________, The Banking Act, Chapter 488 (Nairobi: National Council for Law Reporting, 2012)

___________, The Health Act, No 17 of 2017 (Nairobi: National Council for Law Reporting, 2017)

___________, The Finance Act, Act No 15 of 2017 (Nairobi: National Council for Law Reporting, 2017)

___________, The Central Bank Act, Chapter 491 of the Laws of Kenya' (Nairobi: National Council for Law Reporting, 2019)

___________, Stamp Duty Act, Chapter 480 (Nairobi: National Council for Law Reporting, 2021)

___________, Capital Markets Act, Chapter 485A (Nairobi: National Council for Law Reporting, 2021)

___________, Income Tax Act (Nairobi: National Council for Law Reporting, 2021)

Government Papers, Policies & Plans

Government of Kenya, 'Sessional Paper No 10 of 1965: African Socialism and Its Application to Planning in Kenya' (Nairobi: Government Printed, 1965)

__________, 'Development Plan 1966-1970' (Nairobi, Government Printers, 1965)

__________, 'Development Plan 1970-1974' (Nairobi, Government Printers, 1969)

__________, 'Development Plan 1974-1978' (Nairobi, Government Printers, 1974)

__________, 'Development Plan 1978-1982' (Nairobi, Government Printers, 1977)

__________, Ministry of Health. 'Kenya Expanded Program on Immunization' (Nairobi: Government Printer, 1980)

__________, 'Development Plan 1982-1986' (Nairobi, Government Printers, 1982)

__________, 'District Focus Rural Development' (Nairobi: Government Printers, 1982)

__________, 'Development Plan 1986-1990' (Nairobi, Government Printers, 1986)

__________, 'National Guidelines for the Implementation of Primary Health Care' (Nairobi: Government Printer, 1986)

__________, 'Development Plan 1990-1994' (Nairobi, Government Printers, 1989)

__________, Ministry of Health, 'Kenya's Health Policy Framework' (Nairobi: Government Printer, 1994)

__________, 'Second Participatory Poverty Assessment Study in Kenya, Volume 1' (Nairobi: Government Printer, 1997)

__________, Ministry of Health, 'The First National Health Sector Strategic Plan of Kenya 1994-2004' (Nairobi: Government Printer, 1994)

__________, Ministry of Health, 'Health Management Information System: 1966-1999 Report' (Nairobi: Government Printer, 2001)

__________, 'National Development Plan 2002-2008: Effective Management for Sustainable Economic Growth and Poverty Reduction' (Nairobi: Government Printer, 2002)

__________, 'Sessional Paper on National Social Health Insurance in Kenya' (Nairobi: Government Printer, 2004)

__________, Ministry of Health, 'The Second National Health Sector Strategic Plan of Kenya 2005-2010' (Nairobi: Government Printer, 2005).

__________, 'Public Expenditure Tracking Survey' (Nairobi: Government Printer, 2008)

__________, 'Kenya Household Health Expenditure and Utilisation Survey Report' (Nairobi: Government Printer, 2009)

__________, Ministry of Medical Services and Ministry of Public Health and Sanitation, 'Health Care Financing Policy and Strategy: Systems Change for Universal Coverage' (Nairobi: Government Printer, 2009)

__________, 'Sessional Paper No 7 of 2012 on the Policy on Universal Health Care Coverage in Kenya' (Nairobi: Government Printer, 2012)

__________, 'Sessional Paper No 10 of 2012 on Kenya Vision 2030' (Office of the Prime Minister, Ministry of State for Planning, National Development and Vision 2030, 2012)

__________, Ministry of Health, 'Abolition of User Fees and Provision of Free Maternal Health Care' (Nairobi: Government Printer, 2013)

__________, Ministry of Health, 'Kenya Health Policy 2014-2030: Towards Attaining the Highest Standards of Health' (Nairobi: Government Printer, 2014)

__________, Ministry of Health, 'Kenya Health Sector Strategic Plan 2014-2018' (Nairobi: Government Printer, 2014)

__________, Ministry of Health, 'Kenya Health Sector Strategic Plan 2018-2023' (Nairobi: Government Printer, 2018)

__________, 'Comprehensive Public Expenditure Review: From Evidence to Policy' (National Treasury and Planning State Department for Planning Monitoring and Evaluation Department, 2018)

__________, Kenya National Bureau of Statistics, '2019 Kenya Population and Housing Census Volume IV: Distribution of Population by Socio-Economic Characteristics.' (Nairobi: Government Printer, 2020).

__________, Ministry of Health Kenya, 'Health Sector Strategic Plan 2018-2023: Mid Term Review Synthesis Report' (Nairobi: Government Printer, 2021)

__________, Parliamentary Service Commission, 'Budget Options for 2022/2023 and the Medium Term' (Parliamentary Budget Office, 2022)

Cases

Government of the Republic of South Africa & Others v Grootboom, 2000 (11) BCLR 1169 (CC), 94

Joseph Kimani & 2 others v Attorney General & 2 others (2010) eKLR, full decision available at: http://kenyalaw.org/caselaw/cases/view/70143/

Methodist Church in Kenya v Mohamed Fugicha & 3 Others (2019) eKLR. Available at: http://kenyalaw.org/caselaw/cases/view/165289/

Minister of Health & Others v Treatment Action Campaign & Others, 2002 (10) BCLR 1033 (CC), 35 (South Africa)

Wemhoff v Federal Republic of Germany, 1 Eur Ct HR (ser A) 55, 75 (1968

Internet Sources

Dial Daktari, available: https://www.dial-daktari.com/

KEMSA, Legal Mandate available at: https://www.kemsa.co.ke/legal-mandate/

Mutunga, Willy. 'Developing Progressive African Jurisprudence: Reflections from Kenya's 2010 Transformative Constitution.' *The Mast*, October 9, 2017. https://www.themastonline.com/2017/09/10/developing-progressive-african-jurisprudence-reflections-from-kenyas-2010-transformative-constitution/.

Wamai, R. G. 'Healthcare Policy Administration and Reforms in Post-Colonial Kenya and Challenges for the Future,' (2009). https://www.sylff.org/wp-content/uploads/2009/03/wamai.pdf.

WHO. Analyzing Health Equity Using Household Survey Data Analyzing: A Guide to Techniques and Their Implementation. https://www.who.int/pmnch/knowledge/topics/r_economics20080506/en/.

WHO. Ministerial Conference on Value for Money, Sustainability and Accountability in the Health Sector. https://www.who.int/workforcealliance/media/news/2012/hhaconf2012story/en/.

www.ingramcontent.com/pod-product-compliance
Lightning Source LLC
La Vergne TN
LVHW102009210926
848483LV00010B/236